Thinking Developmentally from Constructivism to Neuroconstructivism

In the *World Library of Psychologists* series, international experts present career-long collections of what they judge to be their finest pieces – extracts from books, key articles, salient research findings, and their major practical theoretical contributions.

This influential volume of papers, chosen by Professor Annette Karmiloff-Smith before she passed away, recognises her major contribution to the field of developmental psychology. Published over a 40-year period, the papers included here address the major themes that permeate through Annette's work: from typical to atypical development, genetics and computation modelling approaches, and neuroimaging of the developing brain. A newly written introduction by Michael S. C. Thomas and Mark H. Johnson gives an overview of her research journey and contextualises her selection of papers in relation to changes in the field over time.

Thinking Developmentally from Constructivism to Neuroconstructivism: Selected Works of Annette Karmiloff-Smith is of great interest to researchers and postgraduates in child development specialising in atypical development, developmental disorders, and developmental neuroscience. It also has appeal to clinical neuropsychologists and rehabilitation professionals.

Annette Karmiloff-Smith was a world leading researcher in the field of developmental neuroscience. She worked with Jean Piaget, and held positions at the Max Planck Institute for Psycholinguistics in Nijmegen, followed by the MRC Cognitive Development Unit in London, the UCL Institute of Child Health, and the Centre for Brain & Cognitive Development, at Birkbeck, University of London.

Michael S. C. Thomas, Developmental Neurocognition Lab, Centre for Brain and Cognitive Development, Department of Psychological Sciences, Birkbeck, University of London.

Mark H. Johnson, Department of Psychology, University of Cambridge, and Centre for Brain and Cognitive Development, Birkbeck, University of London.

World Library of Psychologists

The *World Library of Psychologists* series celebrates the important contributions to psychology made by leading experts in their individual fields of study. Each scholar has compiled a career-long collection of what they consider to be their finest pieces: extracts from books, journals, articles, major theoretical and practical contributions, and salient research findings.

For the first time ever the work of each contributor is presented in a single volume so readers can follow the themes and progress of their work and identify the contributions made to, and the development of, the fields themselves.

Each book in the series features a specially written introduction by the contributor giving an overview of their career, contextualizing their selection within the development of the field, and showing how their thinking developed over time.

From Obscurity to Clarity in Psychometric Testing
Selected Works of Professor Peter Saville
Professor Peter Saville, with Tom Hopton

Discovering the Social Mind
Selected Works of Christopher D. Frith
Christopher D. Frith

Towards a Deeper Understanding of Consciousness
Selected Works of Max Velmans
Max Velmans

Thinking Developmentally from Constructivism to Neuroconstructivism
Selected Works of Annette Karmiloff-Smith
Edited by Annette Karmiloff-Smith, Michael S. C. Thomas, Mark H. Johnson

Acquired Language Disorders in Adulthood and Childhood
Selected Works of Elaine Funnell
Edited by Nicola Pitchford, Andrew W Ellis

Exploring Working Memory
Selected Works of Alan Baddeley
Alan Baddeley

Thinking Developmentally from Constructivism to Neuroconstructivism

Selected Works of Annette Karmiloff-Smith

Edited by Annette Karmiloff-Smith, Michael S. C. Thomas and Mark H. Johnson

Routledge
Taylor & Francis Group
LONDON AND NEW YORK

First published 2018
by Routledge
4 Park Square, Milton Park, Abingdon, Oxon OX14 4RN

and by Routledge
605 Third Avenue, New York, NY 10017

First issued in paperback 2022

Routledge is an imprint of the Taylor & Francis Group, an informa business

Publisher's Note
The publisher has gone to great lengths to ensure the quality of this reprint but points out that some imperfections in the original copies may be apparent.

British Library Cataloguing in Publication Data
A catalogue record for this book is available from the British Library

Library of Congress Cataloging in Publication Data
A catalog record for this book has been requested

ISBN: 978-1-03-247613-1 (pbk)
ISBN: 978-1-138-69947-2 (hbk)
ISBN: 978-1-315-51669-1 (ebk)

DOI: 10.4324/9781315516691

Typeset in Times New Roman
by Swales & Willis Ltd, Exeter, Devon, UK

Contents

Acknowledgements viii

Introduction: Karmiloff-Smith from Piaget to neuroconstructivism – a history of ideas 1
MICHAEL S. C. THOMAS AND MARK H. JOHNSON

PART I
From implicit to explicit knowledge: typical development 21

1 **"If you want to get ahead, get a theory" (1975)** 23
ANNETTE KARMILOFF-SMITH AND BÄRBEL INHELDER

2 **Constraints on representational change: evidence from children's drawing (1990)** 40
ANNETTE KARMILOFF-SMITH

3 **Précis of *Beyond modularity: A developmental perspective on cognitive science* (1994)** 64
ANNETTE KARMILOFF-SMITH

PART II
From typical to atypical development 95

4 **Development itself is the key to understanding developmental disorders (1998)** 97
ANNETTE KARMILOFF-SMITH

5 **Dethroning the myth: cognitive dissociations and innate modularity in Williams syndrome (2003)** 118
ANNETTE KARMILOFF-SMITH, JANICE H. BROWN, SARAH GRICE, AND SARAH PATERSON

6 **Exploring the Williams syndrome face-processing debate: the importance of building developmental trajectories (2004)** 132
ANNETTE KARMILOFF-SMITH, MICHAEL THOMAS, DAGMARA ANNAZ, KATE HUMPHREYS, SANDRA EWING, NICOLA BRACE, MIKE VAN DUUREN, GRAHAM PIKE, SARAH GRICE, AND RUTH CAMPBELL

PART III
Genetics and computational modelling approaches 161

7 **Different approaches to relating genotype to phenotype in developmental disorders (2002)** 163
ANNETTE KARMILOFF-SMITH, GAIA SCERIF, AND MICHAEL THOMAS

8 **Using case study comparisons to explore genotype-phenotype correlations in Williams-Beuren syndrome (2003)** 182
ANNETTE KARMILOFF-SMITH, JULIA GRANT, SANDRA EWING, MARTIN J. CARETTE, KAY METCALFE, DIAN DONNAI, ANDREW P. READ, AND MAY TASSABEHJI

9 **Mechanisms of developmental regression in autism and the broader phenotype: a neural network modeling approach (2011)** 192
MICHAEL S. C. THOMAS, VICTORIA C. P. KNOWLAND, AND ANNETTE KARMILOFF-SMITH

PART IV
Taking the brain seriously 229

10 **Neuroimaging of the developing brain: taking "developing" seriously (2010)** 231
ANNETTE KARMILOFF-SMITH

PART V
Taking the environment seriously 245

11 **Genetic and environmental vulnerabilities in children with neurodevelopmental disorders (2012)** 247
ANNETTE KARMILOFF-SMITH, DEAN D'SOUZA, TESSA M. DEKKER, JO VAN HERWEGEN, FEI XU, MAJA RODIC, AND DANIEL ANSARI

PART VI
And, always, taking development seriously 259

12 **Ontogeny, genetics, and evolution: a perspective from developmental cognitive neuroscience (2006)** 261
ANNETTE KARMILOFF-SMITH

13 **Nativism versus neuroconstructivism: rethinking the study of developmental disorders (2009)** 273
ANNETTE KARMILOFF-SMITH

14 **An alternative to domain-general or domain-specific frameworks for theorizing about human evolution and ontogenesis (2015)** 289
ANNETTE KARMILOFF-SMITH

Index 305

Acknowledgements

Chapter 1, "If you want to get ahead, get a theory" by Karmiloff-Smith, A. & Inhelder, B. in *Cognition*, 3(3), 195–212 (1975), reprinted by permission of Elsevier.

Chapter 2, "Constraints on representational change: evidence from children's drawing" by Karmiloff-Smith, A. in *Cognition*, 34, 1–27 (1990), reprinted by permission of Elsevier.

Chapter 3, "Précis of *Beyond modularity: A developmental perspective on cognitive science*" by Karmiloff-Smith, A. in *Behavioral and Brain Sciences*, 17(4), 693–706 (1994), reprinted by permission of Cambridge University Press.

Chapter 4, "Development itself is the key to understanding developmental disorders" by Karmiloff-Smith, A. in *Trends in Cognitive Sciences*, 2(10), 389–398 (1998), reprinted by permission of Elsevier.

Chapter 5, "Dethroning the myth: cognitive dissociations and innate modularity in Williams syndrome" by Karmiloff-Smith, A., Brown, J. H., Grice, S., & Paterson, S. in *Developmental Neuropsychology*, 23(1&2), 229–244 (2003), reprinted by permission of Taylor and Francis.

Chapter 6, "Exploring the Williams syndrome face-processing debate: the importance of building developmental trajectories" by Karmiloff-Smith, A., Thomas, M., Annaz, D., Humphreys, K., Ewing, S., Brace, N., van Duuren, M., Pike, G., Grice, S., & Campbell, R. in *Journal of Child Psychology and Psychiatry*, 45(7), 1258–1274 (2004), reprinted by permission of Wiley.

Chapter 7, "Different approaches to relating genotype to phenotype in developmental disorders" by Karmiloff-Smith, A., Scerif, G., & Thomas, M. S. C. in *Developmental Psychobiology*, 40, 311–322 (2002), reprinted by permission of Wiley.

Chapter 8, "Using case study comparisons to explore genotype-phenotype correlations in Williams-Beuren syndrome" by Karmiloff-Smith, A., Grant, J., Ewing, S., Carette, M. J., Metcalfe, K., Donnai, D., Read, A. P., & Tassabehji, M. *Journal of Medical Genetics*, 40(2), 136–140 (2003), reprinted by permission of BMJ Journals.

Chapter 9, "Mechanisms of developmental regression in autism and the broader phenotype: a neural modeling approach" by Karmiloff-Smith, A., Thomas, M. S. C., & Knowland, V. C. P. in *Psychology Review*, 118(4), 637–654 (2011), reprinted by permission of PsychNet.

Chapter 10, "Neuroimaging of the developing brain: taking 'developing' seriously" by Karmiloff-Smith, A. in *Human Brain Mapping*, 31(6), 934–941 (2010), reprinted by permission of Wiley.

Chapter 11, "Genetic and environmental vulnerabilities in children with neurodevelopmental disorders" by Karmiloff-Smith, A., D'Souza, D., Dekker, T. M., Van Herwegen, J., Xu, F., Rodic, M., & Ansari, D. in *PNAS*, 109(2), 17261–17265 (2012), reprinted by permission of the authors.

Chapter 12, "Ontogeny, genetics and evolution: a perspective from developmental cognitive neuroscience" by Karmiloff-Smith, A. in *Biological Theory*, 1(1), 44–51 (2006), reprinted by permission of Springer.

Chapter 13, "Nativism versus neuroconstructivism: rethinking the study of developmental disorders" by Karmiloff-Smith, A. in Special Issue on the Interplay of Biology and Environment, *Developmental Psychology*, 45(1), 56–63 (2009), reprinted by permission of PsychNet.

Chapter 14, "An alternative to domain-general or domain-specific frameworks for theorizing about human evolution and ontogenesis" by Karmiloff-Smith, A. in *AIMS Neuroscience*, 2(2), 91–104 (2015), doi:10.3934/Neuroscience.2015.2.91. Originally published Open Access under the Creative Commons Attribution License.

Introduction: Karmiloff-Smith from Piaget to neuroconstructivism

A history of ideas

Michael S. C. Thomas and Mark H. Johnson

Introduction

Annette Karmiloff-Smith was a seminal thinker in the field of child development in a career spanning more than 45 years. She was the recipient of many awards, including the European Science Foundation Latsis Prize for Cognitive Sciences (the first woman to be awarded this prize), Fellowships of the British Academy, the Cognitive Science Society, the Academy of Medical Sciences, and the Royal Society of Arts, as well as honorary doctorates from universities across the world. She was awarded a CBE for services to cognitive development in the 2004 Queen's Birthday Honours list. Annette passed away in December 2016, but she had already selected a set of papers that charted the evolution of her ideas, which are collected in this volume.

At the time of her death, Annette was engaged in an innovative research project studying development and ageing in Down syndrome (DS) as a model to study the causes of Alzheimer's disease. This multidisciplinary project, advanced by the LonDownS consortium, brought together experts in cognitive development, psychiatry, brain imaging, genetics, cellular biology, and mouse modelling. Annette's focus in this project was to explore early development in infants and toddlers with DS. How could this inform Alzheimer's disease? The logic is a mark of Annette's brilliant theoretical insight. One of the genes implicated in Alzheimer's disease (the amyloid precursor protein or APP gene) is on chromosome 21. DS is caused by a genetic mutation where there is an extra copy of chromosome 21, and therefore of the APP gene. With extra APP production, the incidence of dementia in DS is much elevated. By age 40, nearly all adults with DS show evidence of protein build-up in their brains, the so-called plaques and tangles associated with Alzheimer's. Yet, notably, not all adults with DS go on to show the cognitive decline associated with dementia. This suggests that there are resilience factors in some individuals with DS which mean their cognitive functioning is resistant to the protein build-up. Annette speculated that these resilience factors should be visible in the early developmental profiles of infants and toddlers with DS, both in the emergence of their memory abilities and in functional brain activations. To understand dementia in DS, therefore, Annette argued for the importance of taking a developmental perspective.

This multidisciplinary project, rooted in developmental cognitive neuroscience, was far removed from Annette's early work in the laboratory of the renowned developmental psychologist, Jean Piaget. This volume charts Annette's physical journey, from Geneva, to Nijmegen, London, San Diego, and back to London. And it charts the journey of her ideas, from Piaget, to a reconciliation of nativist and constructivist theories of development in her ground-breaking book, *Beyond Modularity*; to her extension from typical to atypical development, her gradual move to a multidisciplinary investigation of the mind; and her continued focus on understanding the process of development, rather than treating it as a set of static snapshots.

Let us start in a bookshop in Geneva in 1969. At that time, Annette was working as a simultaneous interpreter for the United Nations. In her own words:

> I was bored, because I was always repeating other people's thoughts and not allowed, as an interpreter, to have any of my own. So I decided to go back to university. I originally thought of medicine, particularly child psychiatry. I was therefore often in the university bookshop looking at books under "P" for Psychiatry. Naturally, I also noticed those by Piaget on Psychology. Well, one day he walked into the bookshop (I recognized him from photos on his books), picked up a book he had ordered and then crossed to the University building. I followed him and audited his class. I was utterly amazed. *Un cou de foudre!* [A thunderbolt!] Psychology turned out to be much more than measuring reaction times. For Piaget, it included epistemology, logic, philosophy of mind, and philosophy of science. I was hooked, signed up that autumn and did my degree (Licence) in psychology at Geneva University. It was there I developed my absolute passion for research.
>
> (Borovsky, 2005, p. 1)

Jean Piaget was a founding figure of developmental psychology, and his theories dominated the field during most of the 20th century. Throughout her career, Annette's work was deeply influenced by Piagetian thinking in several ways. Like Piaget, she believed that the key to development was to understand the mechanisms that underlie the trajectory of changes across developmental time and which give rise to increasing complexity in behaviour. As we will see, she modernised this view by helping to establish the 'neuroconstructivist' approach to human development. Also, like Piaget, Annette believed that the study of development is inherently an interdisciplinary topic requiring input from many disciplines including philosophy, linguistics, genetics, and cognitive and developmental neuroscience – all fields to which she contributed. Finally, like Piaget she believed in the scientific value of observation (as a key supplement to experiments); one of her early contributions was to pioneer a radically different research strategy for understanding development, the so-called 'microgenetic' approach.

Part I: From implicit to explicit knowledge: typical development

Annette completed her PhD at Geneva University in Piaget's laboratory, under the supervision of Bärbel Inhelder and Hermine Sinclair De Zwart. Her thesis was published in 1979 under the title "A functional approach to child language". After her thesis defence, Annette was recruited by Bärbel Inhelder to participate in a research program on the cognitive strategies used by children to move from one stage of cognitive development to the next.

At the end of the first paper in this volume, "If you want to get ahead, get a theory", published with Inhelder, there is a list of projects in progress in Piaget's laboratory. It gives an indication of the research emphasis and methods at that time. Among the studies are: building bridges with materials of varying physical properties; balancing blocks of varying physical properties; constructing instruments to move objects; controlling water levels by immersion of combinations of objects with varying properties; spontaneous exploratory activities in observed play with Russian Matriona dolls; and modifying the order of locomotives and carriages in a closed circuit. Development was being studied in terms of gaining an understanding of physical systems, operations, and transformations.

In this first paper, Annette reports research carried out on children of different ages as they work with a balance beam. In the balance beam task, children are given blocks of wood and asked to balance them on a thin metal bar. Some of the blocks are heavier at one end than the other, either because their shapes are asymmetric or because weights are hidden inside. The first intuition is to balance the beams in the middle. But of course, some of them need an offset because of the uneven weight distribution. Annette watched as children figured out the problem, testing children of three different ages: 4–5-year-olds, 6–7-year-olds, and 8–9-year-olds. The key methodological innovation of this paper was not just to focus on macro-development – change across age – but also micro-development, "children's spontaneous organizing activity in goal-oriented tasks with relatively little intervention from the experimenter [where] the focus is not on success or failure per se but on the interplay between action sequences and children's theories-in-action" as they explore and figure out how the balance beam task works (p. 23, this volume).

Four- and five-year-olds could solve the balance beam task using proprioceptive information, that is, by feel. The children move the block over the metal bar, releasing and catching it until eventually when they release it, the beam balances. In other words, 4–5-year-olds could eventually achieve mastery of the task. However, 6–7-year-olds in some respects performed more poorly. These children came to the task with a theory, a belief that objects should balance at their geometric centre. They would continually start by trying to balance beams in the middle, causing them to make more errors than the younger children. By contrast, 8–9-year-olds were more sophisticated, pausing first to weigh up the options (so to speak), and sometimes explicitly verbalising: "you have to be careful, sometimes it's just as heavy on each side, sometimes it's heavier on one side". While these children also had a theory, they could talk about the theory and extend it flexibly.

The key theoretical insight Annette gained from this study was that in development, behavioural mastery of a task is not enough. Children need to move beyond this to form a deeper understanding, and sometimes, in doing so, will get worse at the task. When a sophisticated theory is in place, accuracy will return, and with it, both an ability to extend knowledge to new situations and verbalise it. Annette made links between this pattern of 'U-shaped' learning and a similar pattern observed in children's learning of inflectional morphology in language. For example, when learning the past tense of English verbs, children first learn to produce a small number of high frequency past tenses correctly, including irregular verbs (e.g., *thought*); later, irregular verbs are then sometimes inflected erroneously (e.g., *thinked*); before finally all past tenses are produced accurately. Analogously, children implicitly seek a more general principle that moves beyond initial mastery of a small number of verbs. The principle is the regular past tense rule, which is then inappropriately applied to irregulars. The children finally adjust the scope of the rule to exclude irregular verbs. This parallel between physical systems and language acquisition gave the first hint that Annette was striving for a more general theory of developmental change, as the paper concludes: "leading us closer to the general processes underlying cognitive and linguistic behaviour" (p. 37, this volume).

Annette left Geneva to take up the position of Visiting Scientist at the Max Planck Institute for Psycholinguistics in Nijmegen (1981–1982). Before we consider the next step her research took, we might reflect for a moment on Annette's relationship with Jean Piaget. Piagetian theory was a launching point, and in *Beyond Modularity*, Annette would later seek to identify which parts of the theory should be taken forward and which let go. In Annette's own words:

> I spent some 13 years immersed in Piagetian theory at Geneva University, first as a student and then as a research collaborator. During that time, the home-grown Piagetians always considered me a heretic, both personally and theoretically. I refused to address Piaget as *Patron*, meaning "Boss", as he expected everyone in his department to do; I dared to put in writing that Piaget had underestimated the role of language in cognitive development; and, worse, I argued that sensorimotor development alone could never explain how language acquisition initially got off the ground – that there had to be some innate component, even if more general processes might operate.
>
> (Preface to *Beyond Modularity*)

It is perhaps unfortunate that at the time Annette was in Geneva the Piagetian School was under attack from a number of prominent 'anti-Piagetians', who demonstrated apparently precocious infant and toddler abilities before Piagetian stage theory had predicted. These attacks led to a closing of ranks within Geneva around defending a precise and literal interpretation of Piaget's statements. As a student of Piaget who questioned aspects of the theory, it was inevitable that conflict with her mentors would arise. Her filed correspondence reveals angry exchanges over a mysteriously withdrawn conference abstract on the limits of the Piagetian account of language acquisition, a position that she later articulated in the book based on her PhD thesis – "A functional approach to child language" (Cambridge University Press, 1979). The quote above alludes to these troubled years, and her uncomfortable position straddling between the Piagetian School and its critics. Happily, over more recent years as Piaget's contribution to the field is seen more as foundational, rather than literal gospel, Karmiloff-Smith was welcomed back to Geneva and her visits increased. It is unfortunate that her terminal illness prevented her delivering a lecture at a major tribute conference to Piaget in the summer of 2016. Her correspondence and working notes from the Geneva period are now lodged with the Piaget Archives.

When Annette left Geneva, there was perhaps an opportunity missed. As Jean-Paul Bronckart from the University of Geneva recently wrote:

> During her Geneva period, Annette was distinguished by her intelligence and by a theoretical requirement that sometimes led her to take positions different from those of her thesis director, and even from "le patron" (Piaget) she nevertheless venerated. Appreciated by a few, Annette's liberty was only moderately pleasing to the Piagetian "guardians of the temple" … Annette gradually took her distance from Geneva and, with her departure for Nijmegen, began the long and rich scientific journey that was to make her famous. Had she succeeded Inhelder, she would no doubt have been able to ensure a genuine critical continuity to the Piagetian project, now almost abandoned.
>
> (Bronckart, 2017)

At the Max Planck Institute for Psycholinguistics in Nijmegen, Annette focused on language acquisition, collecting data that were subsequently published in a 1986 paper entitled "From meta-process to conscious access: Evidence from children's metalinguistic and repair data" (Karmiloff-Smith, 1986). This paper gave a much fuller exposition of Annette's theoretical ideas. The research considered French-speaking children's gradual construction of a system of nominal markers, including definite and indefinite articles and possessive adjectives (in English: *the, a, my, her*). In French, these markers must agree with the grammatical gender and number of the noun to which they refer. While focused on language acquisition, the theoretical goals of her work were much wider, and the beginning of the paper lays out a more fully formed model of what happens when children proceed beyond behavioural mastery, including introduction of the key theoretical idea of *representational redescription* (RR).

The empirical data driving these ideas revolved around a developmental asynchrony in three types of behaviour – that is, behaviours that emerged at different ages. Children were presented with situations to elicit language using articles and possessives. Annette would then ask the children why they chose the words they did. The first emerging pattern of behaviour was increasingly levels of accuracy: between 4 and 5 years, children were starting to produce the correct linguistic form. However, later emerging was the phenomenon of self-repair: children would sometimes start to output a certain linguistic form and then stop and correct themselves, as if they were monitoring their own output and had spotted an error. Still later emerging was the demonstration of meta-linguistic awareness, where the child was able to verbalise why they chose the linguistic form they did (e.g., a child of 8 years 4 months says: "I said *the* book because all the other things aren't books, there's just one"; Karmiloff-Smith, 1986, p. 123).

The developmental asynchrony between these three types of behaviour, where behavioural mastery is only the first, led Annette to think in much more detail about what might be happening at a representational level. The paper argues for a "recurrent 3-phase model, which stresses the distinction between implicitly defined representations and progressive representational explicitation at several levels of processing, culminating in the possibility of conscious access" (p. 95). Behavioural mastery could be achieved by implicit representations, but some intrinsic process would continue to recode this knowledge, making it more general and more flexible, taking knowledge that was *in* the system and making it available *to* the system. This was the proposed process of RR. The two types of behaviour Annette observed beyond mastery, self-repair followed by explicit, verbalisable meta-linguistic knowledge, suggested to her that the process was iterative and involved several levels, listing in the paper at least four: Implicit (I), Primary explicitation (E-i), Secondary explicitation (E-ii), and Tertiary explicitation (E-iii), with knowledge in each case more general and more flexible.

As Tomasello and Rochat (1994, p. 38) comment, this proposal marks a divergence from Piagetian theory:

> cognitive changes in terms of redescription occur when a stable state is achieved, this stability being viewed as necessary for the RR process to occur. This position is in sharp contrast to views that emphasize conflicts and contradictions as major sources of progress in development (i.e., Piaget's model of equilibration).

Two points are notable in the 1986 paper. First, Annette appears to endorse Fodor's idea that there might be at least some innate 'modules': specialised, self-contained cognitive processing devices dedicated to specific cognitive domains (Fodor, 1983). But she proposes for the first time that such innate modules might also be complemented by another sort of module, those that arise as product of development.

Second, the terminology of this paper makes it evident that Annette is striving for a notion of mechanism. Here she appeals to the information processing terminology of the time, in terms of symbolic computer programs. There are terms like scanning, recoding, control, closed feedback loops; information is stored, indexed, accessed, restructured; there are procedures and routines. Sometimes this leads to rather painful exposition:

> It thus follows from the model that *unconscious* metaprocedural processes could operate on the representations of *conscious* inter-domain metacognition, thereby defining in E-i form new connections which remained implicitly defined for as long as the representations were in different codes.
>
> (Karmiloff-Smith, 1986, p. 143)

Annette would ultimately give up on the specific model of RR articulated in this paper, with its particular set of phases and levels, and become more interested in computational approaches constrained by the properties of the neural substrate (e.g., connectionism). As we shall see, there was little further discussion of RR in the middle part of her career, until it re-emerges in the final paper included in this volume.

The second paper in the volume is also addressed to RR, but now in the domain of children's drawing: "Constraints on representational change: Evidence from children's drawing". The goal of the study was to hone in further on how representations change during the iterative process of RR. Imagine a child has mastered a motor program for drawing a human, or a house, or an animal (however rudimentary). Under the RR scheme, the initial representation is inflexible and only allows for the sequential execution of the program. Annette asked children in two age groups, 4–6 and 8–10 years, to produce such drawings. But crucially, she then asked them also to draw a human, house, or animal 'that does not exist'. By definition, the pictures should now be novel. She then examined what the children altered to make their pictures novel.

In the 4–6-year-olds, the novel picture was always drawn in the same sequence; merely the size or shape of the elements was altered (e.g., a human might have a larger head, or a square head). In the 8–10-year-olds, however, both the position and orientation of elements could be altered, and children could add elements from other conceptual categories (e.g., they might draw a human with two heads, or a half human half four-legged animal). Construed as RR, 4–6-year-olds had carried out a redescription of 'drawing a human' that gave some flexibility, but the program was still constrained by the list of elements and their order. The further redescription of the older children released those constraints and additionally allowed links across categories, or as the paper describes it, 'inter-representational flexibility'.

Perhaps the young children were simply less inventive? In a fascinating second experiment, Annette recruited another group of 4–6-year-old children, and specifically asked them to draw a human with two heads. If, at this age, their motor program had not been re-represented sufficiently to allow flexibility over the elements of drawing a human, this challenge should have been beyond them. Annette continues:

> As the first young subject began to draw a second head, I was reminded of T. E. Huxley's lament: "the great tragedy of science; the slaying of a beautiful hypothesis by an ugly fact"! However the first subject, and all but one of the seven others tested, then went on laboriously and very slowly to draw two bodies, two arms and legs on each body, etc.; that is, they used a complete man-drawing procedure for each head, and they kept starting again because dissatisfied with the result.
>
> (p. 48, this volume)

Once more, this paper strived for the more general picture, drawing parallels with similar phenomena in other domains where flexibility in sequencing only seems to emerge with developmental time. Examples include seriation, number, phonological knowledge, and learning to play tunes on the piano. Once more, mechanism is discussed in terms of symbolic computation (data structures, data formats, procedural sequences and sub-routines, compiled and automatised programs). Indeed, here Annette makes explicit links to artificial intelligence research, noting that in AI, there is a distinction between procedures that generate outcomes and those that operate on other procedures, thereby changing those procedures (p. 41, this volume). We find Annette once more willing to entertain the possibility of innate modularity alongside her theory of representational change, a possibility she would go on to reject in later years: "My view is that the basic syntactic component of language is innately specified and modular" (p. 56, this volume).

The culmination of this line of theorising came with the publication of Annette's 1992 book, *Beyond Modularity*, which integrated her multiple lines of research to date. This book was largely written during a sabbatical year at Carnegie Mellon University in Pittsburgh during which Annette was more frequently exposed to the emerging field of cognitive neuroscience, and the associated advances in brain-inspired connectionist computational modelling. These fields offered new ways of mechanistic thinking that Annette integrated into her book. The third paper in this volume is a précis of the main arguments, published in 1994. *Beyond Modularity* remains a highly influential book. As Ansari recently commented: "[it] represents, in my view, the most complete post-Piagetian theory of developmental change and is still a must read for anybody studying cognitive development, almost 25 years following its publication" (2017).

The majority of the book comprises a consideration of RR in several domains, summarising empirical findings with the child viewed as a linguist, a physicist, a mathematician, a psychologist, and a notator. Each characterises the initial state of the infant, subsequent domain-specific learning, and then explores empirical data on older children's problem solving and theory building, with particular focus on evolving cognitive flexibility and metacognition. Annette describes it as her "best shot at giving an integrated account of data across a wide variety of domains which in isolation may be better accounted for by a series of different explanations" (Karmiloff-Smith, 1994, p. 740).

However, the book had two more far-reaching aims. The first was to situate development more firmly within cognitive science, encouraging researchers to go beyond characterising the on-line processing of steady state systems and to investigate mechanisms of developmental change at the cognitive/representational level, rather than simply the behavioural level, or as she puts it, to

> treat cognitive development as a serious theoretical science contributing to the discussion of how the human mind/brain develops and is organized internally, and not merely as a cute empirical database addressing the question of the age at which external behaviour can be observed.
>
> (p. 64, this volume)

The second was to attempt a reconciliation of the then dominant and opposing theoretical views of development, those of Fodor and Piaget. In Fodor's nativist theory, the mind/brain is made up of genetically specified, independently functioning, special-purpose modules, with their own dedicated processes and proprietary inputs. Each module then outputs data in a common format suitable for central, domain-general processing. In Piaget's constructivist theory, all data are processed by the same mechanisms, while development involves domain-general changes in representational structures. Annette's solution to the opposing positions was to accept some degree of Fodor's modularity as an endstate in adults, but now to argue that this was always the outcome of a domain-general developmental process of modularisation from a less specialised initial state. "I hypothesize that if the human mind/brain ends up with any modular structure, then this is the result of a process of modularization as development proceeds" (p. 68, this volume). Emergent specialisation would be complemented by RR, with sharing of information proceeding beyond mastery to generate the (perhaps unique degree of) cognitive flexibility observed in humans. With some prescience, Annette argued that the degree of specialisation in the infant would only be established with the emergence of technologies for measuring on-line brain activation with neonates and young infants.

> If Fodor's thesis of pre-specified modules is correct, such studies should show that, from the very outset (or the moment at which the infant shows sensitivity to particular forms of input), specific brain circuits are activated in response to domain-specific inputs.
>
> (p. 68, this volume)

By contrast, her emergentist view would predict less differentiated and specialised brain activation in infants. When these technologies arrived, the results would broadly prove her right (see, e.g., Dehaene-Lambertz, 2017).

The précis of *Beyond Modularity* was published in *Behavioral and Brain Sciences* as a target article, and was accompanied by a range of commentaries, along with Annette's response. It is instructive to consider some of those commentaries, for they ultimately picked up on the direction in which Annette's thinking was already headed. Johnston (1994) argued that a serious theory of development situated in cognitive science could not incorporate any notion of 'innateness'. This is a non-developmental concept that stands in place of an account of how gene activity contributes to cognitive development via brain-cognition relationships at the cellular and molecular level. Similarly, Quartz and Sejnowski (1994) argued that modularity is ultimately a thesis about how information is processed in the brain. The then available data from neurobiology suggested that the nativist position and the related modularity thesis were highly implausible. Shultz (1994) endorsed Annette's growing belief in the importance of formal models, arguing that the latest computational models in the field – connectionist or artificial neural network models – were powerful enough to capture patterns of experience-dependent developmental change. Annette accepted many of these suggestions, but if anything, she was looking for more:

> I have been somewhat disappointed in that, with a few exceptions, many commentators reiterated what I had already stated in Modularity, by simply pointing to the under-specification of my framework rather than suggesting potential solutions from their domain of expertise.
>
> (Karmiloff-Smith, 1994, p. 732)

Nevertheless, the pointers here were clear: the next step was towards an approach that integrated multiple disciplines, embracing developmental cognitive neuroscience, neurocomputation, and genetics.

The theory of RR was not completed in *Beyond Modularity*, but the book represented a monumental effort in attempting to reconcile Fodorian nativism and Piagetian constructivist approaches. A sprinkling of doubts remained: where is the role of culture in Karmiloff-Smith's development theory? Is there no place for domain-general skills such as executive functioning, whose development can constrain the emergence of other skills? What about exogenous environmental drivers of development, rather than just the internal processes of modularisation and RR? What limits the rate of RR, such that it can be differentiated from learning and expertise (if indeed they differ)? Why do there remain in adults areas of well-established behavioural mastery where no explicitation has taken place, such as the notorious complexities of syntax? What are the overarching principles revealing why RR should work in the way it does and not some other way?

However, we should note the magnitude of the challenge RR took on – to explain the emergence of cognitive flexibility. The challenge has still not been met. Even in the field of machine learning, with its recent great advances, cognitive flexibility remains out of reach. Cutting-edge AI methods, such as deep neural networks, have learned behavioural mastery in individual domains such as image recognition, voice recognition, and chess playing. Yet they cannot demonstrate flexibility to draw links across domains. As Aaron Sloman, a philosopher and researcher on artificial intelligence and cognitive science, commented on *Beyond Modularity*:

> The theory in Beyond Modularity is a considerable advance both on Piaget's general ideas on development and also an advance on the presuppositions of many of the people working on machines (including robots) that perceive, act, develop, or learn – because most of those researchers think only about how to get robots to achieve behavioural mastery (e.g. catching a ball, juggling, walking, running, following a human, picking things up, carrying things, going through doorways, avoiding obstacles, obeying instructions, answering simple questions, etc.). Such behavioural mastery can be achieved without giving a machine the ability to think about what it has done, what it has not done, what it might have done, what the consequences would have been, what it could not have done, etc. Those additional competences require something like what Karmiloff-Smith calls Representational Redescription, and we need to find ways to get robots to go through such processes if we wish to give them the kind of intelligence young humans, nest-building birds,

hunting mammals, monkeys, and other primates seem to have. Developing such mechanisms will help us understand the processes that occur in children and other animals in a new, deep way. The book does not provide mechanisms, but Karmiloff-Smith is clearly aware of the need to do so.

(Sloman, 2015)

Part II: From typical to atypical development

Annette completed *Beyond Modularity* while at the MRC Cognitive Development Unit in London. There, several colleagues were working on autism and DS, which began to deepen her thinking about atypical development. Previously, she had referred to developmental disorders as possibly informative about domain specificity and modularity by virtue of the uneven cognitive profiles that could be observed, such as particular developmental weaknesses in social cognition or language; or as offering cases such as savant ability where behavioural mastery was not followed by RR and increasing flexibility. But now she was struck by limitations in theorising of the time, which viewed developmental disorders in a static, profoundly non-developmental way.

Another change in her thinking was crystallised by her collaborative book *Rethinking Innateness*, jointly written with Jeff Elman, Elizabeth Bates, Mark Johnson, Dominic Parisi, and Kim Plunkett (Elman et al., 1996). This was an influential volume that married a constructivist view of human development with connectionist modelling and developmental neuroscience. While previously sceptical that connectionist modelling could address anything other than implicit learning, Annette's enthusiasm for it had been spurred by a study visit to San Diego, working with Jeff Elman and Liz Bates. *Rethinking Innateness* bridges Annette's transition into developmental cognitive neuroscience, representing an attempt to consider development in terms of a complex, multi-level, dynamic process. The period marks her increasing conviction that the study of atypical development was a key avenue to shed light on the nature of the developmental process – and by the same token, that the developmental process itself was the key to understanding atypical development.

The first paper in this section is seminal in the field of developmental disorder research. "Development itself is the key to understanding developmental disorders" was published in 1998, the year that Annette moved to become Head of the Neurocognitive Development Unit at the Institute of Child Health in London. During her eight years at the Institute of Child Health, Annette investigated a number of genetic syndromes, including Williams syndrome (WS), Fragile X, and DS.

Up until this point, the study of cognitive impairments in developmental disorders had proceeded as if they could be viewed as directly analogous to cases of acquired deficits in adults (e.g., Temple, 1997). Selective deficits in adults were viewed as a principal source of evidence for the presence of modules: a selective deficit was explained by damage to a single module. Cognitive deficits in developmental disorders were therefore analogously viewed as damage to an innate module, whereby the relevant ability did not develop typically in the first place.

Annette rejected this view on several grounds. The first was that such an account either takes no account of development at all, or poses a developmental theory that is obviously wrong (that development occurs independently in separate modules). Given that, since *Beyond Modularity*, Annette had rejected modularity as a plausible start state in infancy, the alternative was to view uneven cognitive profiles as the product of an atypical developmental process. The second grounds was that, given the way gene expression tends to have widespread influence on brain development, it was implausible that it would lead to very narrow/specific effects on cognitive outcomes. The alternative was that the effects were widespread, but the changed properties of the brain impacted the development of some abilities more than others.

Beyond Modularity had pitted Fodor's domain specificity against Piaget's domain generality. Here was a new idea, the middle ground of *domain relevance*. In this view, the start state is differentiated to some degree, but processing properties have different degrees of relevance to some abilities than others. Across development, regions and pathways specialise so that domain-relevant properties become domain specific (Box 4.2 of the paper illustrates the idea with respect to a connectionist model of visual cortex). Widespread disruptions to domain-relevant properties would produce greater effects on the development of abilities with greater reliance on those properties, and perhaps more subtle anomalies in other abilities with weaker reliance. The arguments are well captured by Annette's views on WS, a disorder showing a markedly uneven cognitive profile:

> Brain volume, brain anatomy, brain chemistry, hemispheric asymmetry, and the temporal patterns of brain activity are all atypical in people with Williams syndrome. How could the resulting cognitive system be described in terms of a normal brain with parts intact and parts impaired, as the popular view holds? Rather, the brains of infants with WS develop differently from the outset, which has subtle, widespread repercussions at the cognitive level.
>
> (p. 105, this volume)

Several methodological implications stemmed from these insights. First, the investigation of developmental deficits should proceed by studying infants and then tracing the unfolding of atypical trajectories, rather than by characterising cognitive deficits in the endstate of adulthood. Second, researchers should not focus merely on deficits or weaknesses, but should also use sensitive measures to probe for subtle anomalies in areas of strength. Here we see an idea reappearing from Annette's early work on RR. Recall, U-shaped developmental profiles suggested the same levels of accuracy – each side of the U – could be produced by different types of representation, initially implicitly, later re-represented. In the developmental disorder context, Annette now raised the possibility that similar levels of behavioural accuracy, for instance in domains of apparent strength in a disorder, could be produced by qualitatively atypical underlying representations. And this could particularly be the case where a researcher employs coarse standardised tests to establish cognitive profiles, since such tests are insensitive to the nature of underlying processes. The third methodological implication was that the key data to reveal the constraints operating on development are cross-domain: the longitudinal study of multiple domains can separate domain-general changes from domain-specific ones. Cross-sectional data alone cannot address this crucial issue.

The final methodological implication is also a theoretical one, and corresponds to the laying out of a new framework: *neuroconstructivism* (see Box 4.6 of the paper). Annette argued that plausible cognitive theories of developmental deficits have to be constrained by an understanding of – and therefore data from – genetic influences on brain development and function; and must take into account the history of an individual's dynamic interactions with their environment. Future research in developmental disorders would therefore have to be multidisciplinary.

The two further papers in this section exemplify these ideas in the research Annette and her team carried out with infants, children, and adults with WS. WS is a rare genetic disorder caused by the deletion of a small number of genes from one copy of chromosome 7. It leads to a characteristic pattern of physical and cognitive deficits, including an average IQ of 70. Notably, the WS cognitive profile is uneven, with relative strengths in language and face processing, and relative weaknesses in visuospatial processing and problem solving. In addition to its clinical significance, WS was theoretically important since it had been used by nativist researchers to argue that it represented one part of a genetic dissociation between language and general cognition (Pinker, 1994). Juxtaposed with Specific Language Impairment, a heritable language disorder with relative strength in nonverbal cognition but weakness in language, Pinker (1999) argued that the two represented a genetic double dissociation between language and cognition, and were evidence in favour of innate modularity.

In "Dethroning the myth", Annette marshals a range of empirical evidence to argue forcefully that this is a mischaracterisation of WS, and a misconceived explanation of the uneven cognitive profile. For both language and face processing, development is traced back to early childhood, and evidence presented that skills are atypical from early on, sometimes subtly. In support of her criticism of focusing on adult endstates in developmental disorders, Annette describes a study carried out in her lab that contrasted language and number processing skills in WS and DS (Paterson et al., 1999). In adults, language skills were shown to be stronger in individuals with WS than DS, while the opposite was true for number skills. However, when these two domains were assessed in infants with the disorders, infants with DS outscored infants with WS on a number task, while there was no difference in language abilities. The respective uneven cognitive profiles were different at different ages. A snapshot of the adult cognitive profile was therefore actively misleading with respect to developmental origins.

In "Exploring the Williams syndrome face-processing debate", Annette shifts to focus on an area of relative strength in the disorder, face recognition skills. There are three points of interest in this paper. First, sensitive tests showed that where children and adults with WS were scoring at chronological age level expectations in a standardised test of face recognition (i.e., showing no deficit), the underlying cognitive processes nevertheless appeared to be atypical, lacking the expected expertise in processing configurations of facial features. Second, the paper showed how atypical development could be described statistically using cross-sectional trajectory analysis, to show how the level, rate, or shape of development could be different, or to assess atypicalities in the relationship between skills. These trajectory methods were later developed more fully in Thomas et al. (2009). Third, for the first time, Annette integrates brain-imaging evidence to support the proposal that cognitive level skills develop atypically. Here, notably, electrophysiology is used to argue that processes of face recognition are less localised (to the right hemisphere) and less specialised (to faces but not cars or houses) in WS than in typically developing controls. Since localisation and specialisation would both be expected markers of modular functioning, this evidence suggests that emergent modularisation is disrupted in WS.

Part III: Genetics and computational modelling approaches

The next set of three papers considers the multiple methods and data sets that Annette used to link genotype to phenotype. Here we see more biological terminology present in Annette's writing, as she considers the relationship between sources of genetic variation or mutation in an individual (the genotype) and the subsequent cognitive profile (phenotype). In the first paper, "Different approaches to relating genotype to phenotype in developmental disorders", Annette and her colleagues criticise simplistic one-to-one mappings between genes and specific cognitive outcomes. These simplistic mappings can be found when researchers use phrases like "*a gene (or set of genes) for X* where X is a purported higher level cognitive module such as face processing, grammar, number, or so on" (p. 163, this volume), such as those found in the proposals of Pinker (1999) and Marcus (2006). Instead, Annette and colleagues argue that the pathway from genes to cognition is complex and indirect.

The paper then summarises the multiple methods that are required to unpack this pathway. These include quantitative genetics (population level measures of the heritability of phenotypes); molecular genetics (the study of DNA variation correlated with phenotypes); animal models, such as transgenic mice created to have identical or analogous mutations to human disorders; and computational modelling, viewed as an intermediate level at which hypotheses may be generated concerning the link between low-level neurocomputational differences and high-level cognitive outcomes.

In support of the concept of domain-relevance, the example of Fragile X is discussed in some detail. This developmental disorder is caused by the mutation (silencing) of a single gene, FMR1, yet it leads to an uneven cognitive profile with strengths and weaknesses. Notably, FMR1 appears to impact on experience-dependent plasticity, with lack of this protein affecting dendritic spines, structures involved in the signalling between neurons. Research is described where a mouse model of Fragile X was used to investigate the impact of the mutation on these low-level brain structures. Crucially, the effect of the

Fragile X mutation is widespread in the brain yet, through the developmental process, the impact on cognition is uneven.

In line with Piaget, Annette was more inclusive than usual in the different approaches that she took to understand human development. While empirical controlled experiments were a mainstay, individual observations and case studies were also considered important sources of insight. Annette's person-centred approach to atypical development was as rewarding for her science as it was for the children and families that she studied. A particular fascination was why no two children with DS, Fragile X, or WS were the same, and to what extent genetic or environmental differences could influence their later outcomes.

In the next paper, "Using case study comparisons to explore genotype-phenotype correlations in Williams-Beuren syndrome", Annette and her colleagues focus on the specific case of relating the genetic mutation in WS to its characteristic uneven cognitive profile. Recall, WS is caused by the deletion of a small number of genes from one copy of chromosome 7. By the time of publishing this paper, 19 had been characterised within the deleted region of DNA, while that number now stands at 27 (Broadbent et al., 2014). Annette addressed a particular argument present at the time that the mapping between genes and physical and cognitive outcomes might be straightforward. Specifically, deletion of one of the genes, elastin (ELN), is associated with the connective-tissue abnormalities and cardiovascular disease (supravalvular aortic stenosis [SVAS]). Deletion of another gene, LIM kinase-1 (LIMK1), would account for the particular weakness in visuospatial cognition.

This simple mapping was evaluated via two case studies. The first was a 43-year-old adult with WS who was particularly high functioning, recording an overall IQ of 93. She had the typical genetic deletion of WS and correspondingly, exhibited the characteristic visuospatial deficit. The second case was an 11-year-old girl who had a deletion of 60% of the region of DNA normally deleted in WS, including both ELN and LIMK1. While the girl exhibited SVAS, her cognitive profile was in the normal range, and there was no evidence of a deficit in visuospatial cognition. LIMK1 alone could not explain the spatial deficit. Together, the case studies reveal the scale of the challenge in relating uneven cognitive profiles to specific genes. Indeed, a decade later, Annette and her team reported two further case studies of children with partial deletions of the stretch of DNA associated with WS (Broadbent et al., 2014). Here, visuospatial cognition was explored in greater depth, distinguishing between small-scale and large-scale space. Notably, different partial deletions revealed contrasting profiles across these scales, suggesting a "complex, dynamic, and combinatorial role of different genes within the WS critical region on disparate phenotypic expression within the visuospatial domain" (Broadbent et al., 2014). The complexity only increased!

The third paper in this section exemplifies Annette's belief that formal models represent an important tool to link data from multiple levels of description within causal mechanistic accounts. The paper, "Mechanisms of developmental regression in autism and the broader phenotype: a neural network modeling approach" presents a connectionist model of developmental regression in autism. In a minority of children with autism (20%–40%), cognitive skills decline in the second year of life after a period of apparently normal-looking early development. The paper, co-authored with Thomas and Knowland, considers the hypothesis that such regression is caused by the exaggeration of an otherwise normal phase of brain development, synaptic pruning. Computer modelling is first used to establish the mechanistic viability of the idea, linking a low-level neurocomputational property to a high-level deficit in behaviour via an implemented developmental process. Second, it is employed to explore the idea that individual differences in other neurocomputational parameters can add risk or protective factors in determining whether the pathology, atypical synaptic pruning, results in atypical cognitive development, thereby accounting for variation in the atypical phenotype and patterns of family inheritance (see also Thomas et al., 2016). For Annette, this model linked with her ideas of specialisation and localisation of function (generated here by pruning), combined with the crucial importance of timing in development. Should the brain commit too rapidly to specialisation and localisation of function, the result would be less flexibility for processing novel stimuli. Moreover, the pivotal role of the time course of developmental change demonstrated once more the need to progress theory beyond the simple metaphor of static intact and impaired modules (Karmiloff-Smith, 2015).

Part IV: Taking the brain seriously

In 2006, Annette left the Institute of Child Health to join Birkbeck, University of London, as a Professorial Research Fellow. At Birkbeck, she was based in the Developmental Neurocognition Lab in the Centre for Brain and Cognitive Development. The papers in this and the next section exemplify Annette's continued broadening of her multi-level, dynamic approach to development, embracing epigenetics, brain structure/function, network connectivity, cognition, behaviour, and the environment. "Neuroimaging of the developing brain: taking 'developing' seriously" considers the utility of functional brain imaging for studying developmental change. Paradoxically, in this paper she views many current brain imaging studies of infants and children as non-developmental, and as merely portraying snapshots of brain function at different ages, instead of revealing processes of progressive change. In a review of the strengths and weaknesses of the main brain imaging methodologies (functional magnetic resonance imaging, function near-infrared spectroscopy, event-related electrophysiology), her key themes emerge. Imaging must be hypothesis-driven and test mechanistic accounts (or as she says, "as a tool, brain imaging is no better than a pencil or a fishing trip, unless it is hypothesis driven", p. 231, this volume). Neural data can be most informative when they show that similar-looking behaviour is generated by alternative underlying circuitries, as in the case of atypical development, or the case of compensatory changes in healthy ageing. Given limits in spatial or temporal resolution, development is best studied by a multi-method converging approach, combining imaging methods and the study of trajectories of change. In this paper,

Annette also looks to the future: the possibility that brain imaging can test her RR hypothesis through studying emerging hierarchical network structure in 'resting state' brain networks; and the possibility that advances in wireless technology will eventually allow imaging to move beyond a child lying flat in a scanner into the real world, with the child interacting naturally in their environment.

Part V: Taking the environment seriously

Annette's neuroconstructivist framework for explaining developmental disorders stressed the importance of considering the environment as much as the internal causes of the disorders. In the paper in this section, "Genetic and environmental vulnerabilities in children with neurodevelopmental disorders", Annette and her colleagues work through this idea in greater detail. They focus on the methodological approach of tracing cognitive level functions back to their basic level roots in infancy and then probing their ontogenetic progression. The importance of interaction with the environment is considered in three examples. In the first, numeracy skills are contrasted in two disorders, WS and DS. In adults with WS, there are difficulties with large approximate number discrimination, whereas in DS there are difficulties with small exact numbers. The origins of the profiles are traced to a single basic level problem for each syndrome. During infancy, visual attention shifting deficits in WS lead to difficulties in discriminating large approximate quantities, while visual sustained attention deficits produce difficulties in individuating objects in small displays in DS. The low-level deficits alter the history of experience in number processing in each disorder, leading to later diverging patterns of deficit in high-level numeracy skills. In the second example, Annette and colleagues consider the possibility that social deprivation can sometimes produce cognitive impairments that show similarities to those observed in genetics disorders. The authors describe an experimental paradigm designed with the ambition to distinguish syndrome-specific versus general and modality-specific versus general characteristics of deficits originating in genetic versus environmental causes (see also Karmiloff-Smith et al., 2014). In the third example, the authors present evidence to suggest that, when a child has a genetic disorder, aspects of their environment are simultaneously changed. Developmental profiles are a product of the combination and interaction of these effects. Evidence comes from how parents constrain their infant's exploration of the physical environment, and how parents respond to errors in their toddler's productive naming skills. As the authors say, "nothing is static in biology or psychology, and this finding holds equally for the environment" (p. 255, this volume).

Part VI: And, always, taking development seriously

The three papers of the final section represent the fruition of Annette's neuroconstructivist approach, and the multiple lines of research it spawned. In "Ontogeny, genetics, and evolution: a perspective from developmental cognitive neuroscience", Annette demonstrates how the accumulating body of empirical evidence led away from the simple notion of innate modularity to an emergentist account of adult specialisation of function, considered, respectively, in the fields of evolution, genetics, and development. In "Nativism versus neuroconstructivism: rethinking the study of developmental disorders", Annette revisits her seminal 1998 paper some ten years later, reviewing progress in the field of disorder research and validation of its primary methodological lessons. In "An alternative to domain-general or domain-specific frameworks for theorizing about human evolution and ontogenesis", Annette focuses on the notion of domain-relevance, the intermediate position between domain generality and specificity. She grounds the idea more firmly at computational, neural, genetic, and evolutionary levels. She then shows how it synthesises with contemporary accounts, such as Dehaene's *neuronal recycling hypothesis* (Dehaene, 2009). In the neuronal recycling hypothesis, cultural inventions such as reading and writing invade older cortical circuits, thereby inheriting their structural constraints. As Annette says, "the notion that these new functions seek out a 'neuronal niche', i.e., a cortical area in the brain *relevant* to the processing required, is clearly along the same lines as the domain-relevant approach" (p. 293, this volume). Finally, in the context of Dehaene's proposal of a global workspace for flexible use of knowledge (and indeed, conscious access), Annette sees the possibility of a brain basis for her concept of RR (Dehaene et al., 2014). Domain-specific systems enable plasticity and flexibility through a process of cross-domain interactions in a global workspace, where information is available to conscious access.

Conclusion

The history of Annette's ideas also charts the history of the emergence of developmental cognitive neuroscience as a field. What started as observations about the behaviour of children at different ages became the study of mechanisms of change in a multi-level dynamic framework, embracing neuroscience, genetics, and evolution. Rudimentary concepts of modularity were replaced with neurally grounded concepts of increased localisation and specialisation, while clunking metaphors of procedures, data structures, and subroutines were replaced by the language of brain-inspired computation. A research career that began with a chance meeting with Jean Piaget in a bookshop in Geneva, and ended with a sophisticated multidisciplinary investigation of DS as a molecular model for Alzheimer's disease almost half a century later, has set the stage for a future understanding of development that unifies the many disciplines of the cognitive and biological sciences.

Acknowledgements

The writing of this chapter was partially funded by a Wellcome Trust Strategic Award (Grant Number: 098330/Z/12/Z) conferred upon The London Down Syndrome (LonDownS) Consortium.

References

Borovsky, A. (2005). Column: Interview with Annette Karmiloff-Smith. *Cognitive Science Online*, *3*(1). http://cogsci-online.ucsd.edu/column_archive/CSO3-1-interview.pdf. Retrieved 5/12/17.

Broadbent, H., Farran, E. K., Chin, E., Metcalfe, K., Tassabehji, M., Turnpenny, P., Sansbury, F., Meaburn, E., & Karmiloff-Smith, A. (2014). Genetic contributions to visuospatial cognition in Williams syndrome: Insights from two contrasting partial deletion patients. *Journal of Neurodevelopmental Disorders*, *6*: 18.

Bronckart, J.-P. (2017). Remembering Annette Karmiloff-Smith. *Association for Psychological Science Observer*, *30*(9), November, online edition. https://www.psychologicalscience.org/publications/observer/obsonline/remembering-annette-karmiloff-smith.html. Retrieved 5/12/17.

Dehaene, S. (2009). *Reading in the brain: The science and evolution of a human invention*. New York, NY: Penguin Group.

Dehaene, S., Charles, L., King, J. R., & Marti, S. (2014). Toward a computational theory of conscious processing. *Current Opinions in Neurobiology*, *25*, 76–84.

Dehaene-Lambertz, G. (2017). The human infant brain: A neural architecture able to learn language. *Psychonomic Bulletin and Review*, February, *24*(1): 48–55.

Elman, J., Karmiloff-Smith, A., Bates, E., Johnson, M., Parisi, D., & Plunkett, K. (1996). *Rethinking innateness: A connectionist perspective on development*. Cambridge, MA: MIT Press.

Fodor, J. A. (1983). *The modularity of mind*. Cambridge, MA: MIT Press.

Johnston, T. D. (1994). Genes, development, and the "innate" structure of the mind. *Behavioral and Brain Sciences*, *17*(4), 721–722.

Karmiloff-Smith, A. (1986). From meta-processes to conscious access: Evidence from children's metalinguistic and repair data. *Cognition*, *23*, 95–147.

Karmiloff-Smith, A. (1992). *Beyond modularity: A developmental perspective on cognitive science*. Cambridge, MA: MIT Press/Bradford Books.

Karmiloff-Smith, A. (1994). Transforming a partially structured brain into a creative mind. *Behavioral and Brain Sciences*, *17*(4), 732–745.

Karmiloff-Smith, A. (2015). An alternative to domain-general or domain-specific frameworks for theorizing about human evolution and ontogenesis. *AIMS Neuroscience*, 19 June, *2*(2): 91–104.

Karmiloff-Smith, A., Casey, B. J., Massand, E., Tomalski, P., & Thomas, M. S. C. (2014). Environmental and genetic influences on neurocognitive development: The importance of multiple methodologies and time-dependent intervention. *Clinical Psychological Science*, *2*(5), 628–637.

Marcus, G. F. (2006). Cognitive architecture and descent with modification. *Cognition*, September, *101*(2): 443–465.

Paterson, S. J., Brown, J. H., Gsödl, M. K., Johnson, M. H., & Karmiloff-Smith, A. (1999). Cognitive modularity and genetic disorders. *Science*, *286*, 2355–2358.

Pinker, S. (1994). *The language instinct*. London: Penguin.

Pinker, S. (1999). *Words and rules*. London: Weidenfeld & Nicolson.

Quartz, S. R., & Sejnowski, T. J. (1994). Beyond modularity: Neural evidence for constructivist principles in development. *Behavioral and Brain Sciences*, *17*(4), 725–726.

Shultz, T. (1994). The challenge of representational redescription. *Behavioral and Brain Sciences*, *17*(4), 728–729.

Sloman, A. (2015). *Comments on Annette Karmiloff-Smith's (1992) book: Beyond Modularity: A Developmental Perspective on Cognitive Science.* School of Computer Science, University of Birmingham, UK. http://www.cs.bham.ac.uk/research/projects/cogaff/misc/beyond-modularity.html. Retrieved 5/12/17.

Temple, C. M. (1997). Cognitive neuropsychology and its applications to children. *Journal of Child Psychology and Psychiatry, 38*, 27–52.

Thomas, M. S. C., Annaz, D., Ansari, D., Serif, G., Jarrold, C., & Karmiloff-Smith, A. (2009). Using developmental trajectories to understand developmental disorders. *Journal of Speech, Language, and Hearing Research, 52*, 336–358.

Thomas, M. S. C., Davis, R., Karmiloff-Smith, A., Knowland, V. C. P., & Charman, T. (2016). The over-pruning hypothesis of autism. *Developmental Science, 19*(2), 284–305.

Tomasello, M., & Rochat, P. (1994). "Beyond modularity: A developmental perspective on cognitive science" by Annette Karmiloff-Smith. *Philosophical Psychology, 7*(4), 536–539.

Part I

From implicit to explicit knowledge

Typical development

1 "If you want to get ahead, get a theory"

Annette Karmiloff-Smith and Bärbel Inhelder

Introduction

How can we go about understanding children's processes of discovery in action? Do we simply postulate that dynamic processes directly reflect underlying cognitive structures or should we seek the productive aspects of discovery in the interplay between the two? This is not an entirely new concern in the Genevan context since in the preface of *The Growth of Logical Thinking* (Inhelder & Piaget, 1958) it was announced rather prematurely that ". . . the specific problem of experimental induction analyzed from a functional standpoint (as distinguished from the present structural analysis) will be the subject of a special work by the first author". Two decades have elapsed. With hindsight it is realized how much more experimentation and reflection were required to undertake the structural analysis. Operational structures are clearly an important part of the picture. They provide the necessary interpretative framework to infer the lower and upper limits of the concepts a child can bring to bear on a task. But they obviously do not suffice to explain all facets of cognitive behavior.

Our first experiments that focused directly on processes were undertaken as part of some recent work on learning (Inhelder, Sinclair & Bovet, 1974). The results illustrated not only the dynamics of interstage transitions but also the interaction between the child's various subsystems belonging to different developmental levels. Though the learning experiments were process-oriented, they failed to answer all our questions (Cellérier, 1972; Inhelder, 1972). What still seemed to be lacking were experiments on children's spontaneous organizing activity in goal-oriented tasks with relatively little intervention from the experimenter. The focus is not on success or failure per se but on the interplay between action sequences and children's 'theories-in-action', i.e., the implicit ideas or changing modes of representation underlying the sequences. Although what happens in half an hour cannot be considered simply as a miniature version of what takes place developmentally, it is hoped that an analysis of the processes of microformation will later enable us to take a new look at macrodevelopment.

While not very typical of our current studies on goal-oriented behavior[1] where the child needs to devise lengthy and complex action plans, the block-balancing experiment reported here has been selected as a first sample of the current work. Because of the fairly simple nature of this experimental task, a clearer initial picture could be drawn of the interplay between action sequences and theories-in-action.

Experimental procedure

Subjects were requested to 'balance so that they do not fall' a variety of blocks across a narrow bar, i.e., a 1 × 25 cm metal rod fixed to a piece of wood. There were seven types of blocks, with several variants under each type. Some were made of wood, others of metal, some were 15 cm long, others 30 cm. One example of each type is illustrated in Figure 1.1. Type A blocks had their weight evenly distributed; B blocks consisted of two identical overlapping blocks glued together, weight being evenly distributed in each block. In A and B blocks, the center of gravity thus coincided with the geometric center of the length of the solid as a whole. We shall refer to A and B types as 'length blocks' since dividing the length in half gives the point of balance. The child can succeed without being aware that weight is involved. C types consisted of a block glued to a thin piece of plywood; D types were similar, except that the plywood was much thicker and thus the weight of the glued block had less effect. We shall call C and D types 'conspicuous weight blocks' since the asymmetrical distribution of the weight could readily be inferred. E blocks were invisibly weighted with metal inside one end, and F types had a cavity at one end into which small blocks of various weights could be inserted. E and F types will be referred to as 'inconspicuous weight blocks'. An 'impossible' block (G type) was also used which could not be balanced without counterweights.

The experiment took place in two phases. In phase I, subjects were left free to choose the order in which they wished to balance each block separately on the bar. It was hoped in this way to gain insight into the ways in which children spontaneously endeavor to apprehend the various properties of the blocks: whether they group analogous blocks together, how they transfer successful action sequences from one block to another, and how they regulate their actions after success or failure. Once each block had been placed in equilibrium, children were requested to repeat certain items in a new order proposed by the experimenter. As an experimental precaution to make sure that no psychomotor difficulties would affect the results, subjects were first asked to balance two identical cylinders (2 cm diameter) one on top of the other.

When analyzing the results of phase I, it was hypothesized that children interpret the results of their actions on the blocks in two very different ways: either in terms of success or failure to balance the blocks which will be referred to as positive or negative *action-response*, or in terms of confirmation or refutation of a theory-in-action, which will be called positive or negative *theory-response.* A negative theory-response, for instance, implies contradiction of a theory either through failure to balance when the theory would predict success, or through successful balancing when the theory would predict failure. In other words, the same result was interpreted by children either as positive action-response or as negative theory-response and vice versa.

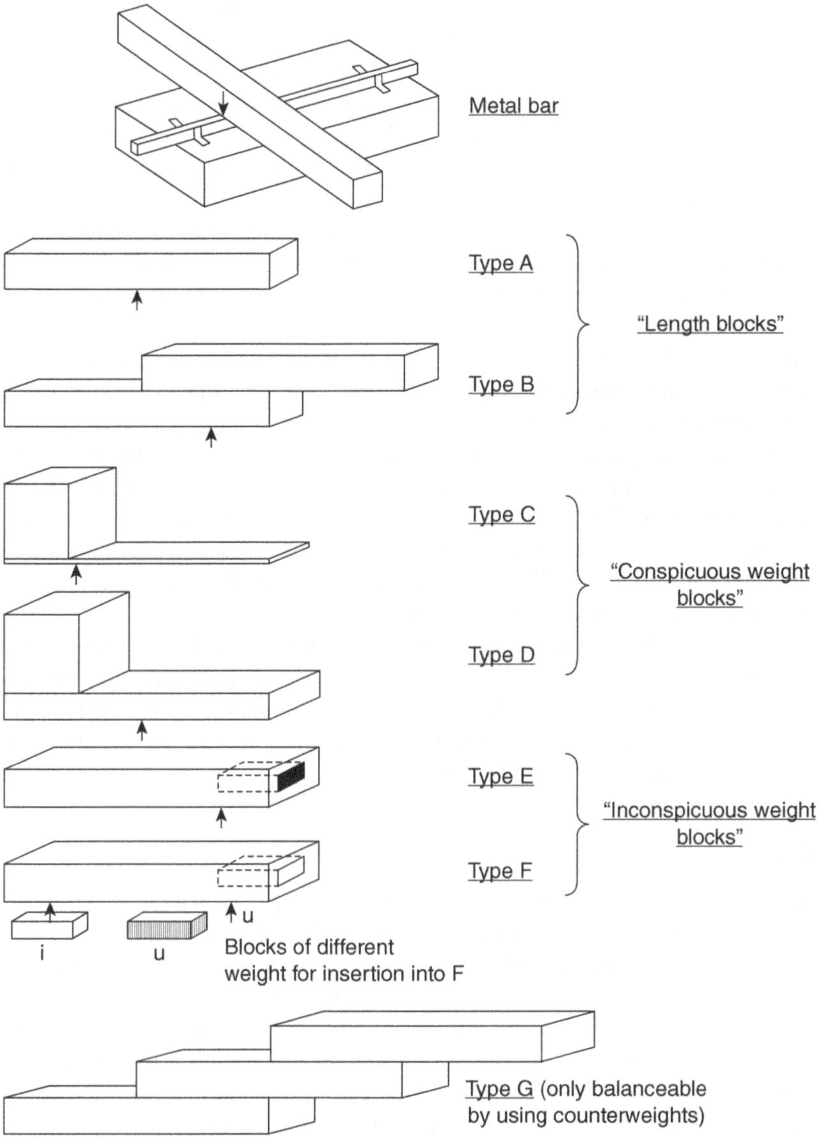

Figure 1.1

Note. Arrow underneath each block indicates the point of contact with the bar when the block is in equilibrium. For Type F blocks, this point is a function of the weight of the blocks to be inserted into the cavity.

Phase II focused on this problem. About half of the phase I subjects in each age group were interviewed again some twelve months later. The purpose was twofold. First, to verify the cross-sectional analysis, the interpretative hypotheses we had made, as well as to determine the progress achieved by each subject. Secondly, since we now had a detailed description of the phase I developmental trends, we wanted to intervene rather more systematically in phase II by providing increased opportunity for positive and negative action- and theory-response, in order to study their interplay during the course of a session. Apart from balancing each of the blocks separately on the bar, subjects were also asked to leave one block in balance and try to balance in front of it on the same bar another block that looked similar but which had a strikingly different center of gravity (e.g., A types with E types), to add to blocks already in balance several small cubes of various size and weight, etc.

In both phases, a written protocol was taken by one observer and a continuous commentary was tape-recorded by a second observer on all the child's actions, corrections, hesitations, long pauses, distractions, gross eye movements and verbal comments.[2]

Unlike many other problem-solving studies, tnis new series of experiments did not strive to keep tasks untainted by conceptual aspects. Indeed, we purposely chose situations in which physical, spatial or logical reasoning was involved but which we had already analyzed from a structural point of view, thus providing additional means for interpreting data. Both for constructing the material and interpreting results of the block-balancing task information was used from previous research (inter alia, Inhelder & Piaget, 1958; Vinh Bang, 1968; Piaget & Garcia, 1971; Piaget et al., 1973) about the underlying intellectual operations and children's modes of interpreting weight and length problems.

The exact order of presentation of items and the types of problems set were not standardized in advance. Indeed, just as the child was constructing a theory-in-action in his endeavor to balance the blocks, so we, too, were making on-the-spot hypotheses about the child's theories and providing opportunities for negative and positive responses in order to verify our own theories!

Population

Sixty-seven children between the ages of 4;6 and 9;5 years from a Geneva middle-class state school were interviewed individually.[3] Phase I covered 44 subjects; 23 of these children were interviewed again in phase II. Five young subjects between 18 and 39 months were observed in provoked play sessions with the blocks.

In the results, some rough indications are given of the ages at which the various action sequences and theories-in-action are encountered, but this should not imply that the processes described are considered to be stage-bound. 22 subjects from this experiment were also asked to perform quite a different task, that of constructing toy railway circuits of varying shapes, and it was quite clear that children interpreting success or failure as theory-responses in one task might be interpreting success or failure as action-responses in the other task. Furthermore, similar action-sequences for block-balancing were encountered not only in many children of the same age but also during the course of a session with children of very different ages. On the basis of children's verbal explanations of the relevant physical laws, the developmental trend falls into neat stages. If the analysis is based on children's goal-oriented actions, this is not so obviously the case.

However, both the nature and the order of action sequences as described in our results were overwhelmingly confirmed by changes during sessions as well as the longitudinal results of phase II.

Observational data

We felt it would be instructive to have an indication of how very small children go about balancing blocks. Accordingly, five subjects between 18 and 39 months were observed in provoked play sessions with our experimental material. This led us to interpret the older subjects' seemingly anomalous behavior in conflict situations as rather clearcut regressions to earlier patterns. None of the five subjects failed in balancing the two cylinders used for checking psychomotor problems. As far as the experimental blocks were concerned, it was possible to coax the children into trying to balance a few blocks, but only for very short periods of time. Nevertheless, what they did was often organized. The following was the basic pattern: Place the block in physical contact with the bar at *any* point (e.g., extremities, center, pointed edge, side, etc.), let go, repeat. Their attention was frequently diverted to the noise made by the falling block; indeed, the two youngest subjects rapidly made their goal that of causing a loud noise. Gradually, with the first chance successes on the 15 cm "length blocks" (easier than the 30 cm ones), the three oldest subjects (32–39 months) lengthened their action sequences in a systematic way, as follows: Place the block at any point of physical contact with the bar, push hard with finger above that point of contact, let go, repeat immediately. However, these subjects did not move the block to another point of contact before letting go, although they had consistently done so when trying to balance the two cylinders or when building towers or houses with wooden cubes. It would appear that in such cases they were simply forming the parallel plane surfaces; in other words the problem of finding the appropriate point of contact between two objects of different shape did not arise. Nonetheless, even though the subjects placed the blocks at random points of contact, further development of action sequences by pushing on the block above the point of contact (i) seemed to denote that the need for spatio-physical contact had become clearer for the child, his finger acting somethat like a nail and thus simplifying the balancing problem and, (ii), provided the child with an indication through diffuse proprioceptive information of the fact that blocks have properties that counteract his actions.

The experimental material was in fact designed to allow for proprioceptive information. In previous research (e.g., Inhelder & Piaget, 1958; Vinh Bang, 1968) on equilibrium with a fixed fulcrum, subjects could only obtain visual information which then had to be expressed via another mode of representation.

Experimental data

Unlike previous Genevan research articles in which extensive quotations were given from what children said, this study's protocols consist mainly of detailed descriptions of children's actions. We shall, however, occasionally refer to children's spontaneous comment when it is particularly illustrative. Here we will describe those action sequences that were encountered among most children of a given age and repeated several times by each child on the various blocks.

Many of the subjects in the experiment proper started the session in a similar way to the young subjects just described in the observational data. However, what seemed to take place developmentally between 18 and 39 months was observed during part of a single session among 4–6 year olds. Thus the initial approach was as follows: Place block at any point of contact, let go; this was immediately followed by a second attempt with the same block: Place at any point of contact, push hard above that point, let go. As the block kept on falling, the children gradually discovered through their act of pushing that the object had properties independent of their actions on it. Negative response sparked off a change from an action plan purely directed at the goal of balancing, to a subgoal of discovering the properties of the object in order to balance it. These children then undertook a very detailed exploration of each block trying one dimension after another, as follows: Place the block lengthwise, widthwise, upended one way, then the other and so forth. Such sequences were repeated several times with each block. Although the order of the dimensions tried out differed from one child to the next, each child's exploration of the various dimensions became more and more systematic. Yet only one point of contact was tried for each dimension—for quite some time the children would never change the point of contact along any one dimension. Frequently, even when children were successful in balancing an item on one dimension (e.g., at the geometric center of length-blocks or along the length of the bar), they went on exploring the other dimensions of each block. It was as if their attention were momentarily diverted from their goal of balancing to what had started out as a subgoal, i.e., the search for means. One could see the children oscillating between seeking the goal and seeking to 'question' the block. Successful balancing was certainly registered since, in the course of their investigation of the blocks, the children returned more and more frequently to the dimension that had yielded the solution. Yet they continued to explore, as if seeking an alternative solution. Although such behavior seems to indicate that the child is beginning to differentiate between his own actions and the properties of the block, this seeking for alternative solutions may be interpreted to mean that the child does not yet understand that a physical law, unalterable by his action, governs the object's behavior. We hypothesize that during his exploration the child is endeavoring to make a sort of 'catalogue' of the different actions he may make on the blocks; once he has set the limits of these actions, he is then in a position to narrow them down to those that appear to be more relevant to his goal.

More advanced subjects did not lose sight of their goal; once they found a solution, they registered the positive response and no longer explored the block in any observable way. As balancing of length-blocks became progressively easier, children attempted to balance all items on their longest, flat dimension, only reverting to 'exploration' and even to 'pushing hard above the contact point' when grappling with the difficult item G.

After opting for the longest dimension and retaining some form of representation of a previously balanced block on that dimension, children began their first real search for the effective point of balance. Here is where spatial symmetry, already so prevalent in young children's behavior in solving other problems, is used by the child as possibly relevant for success. Action sequences were as follows: first place more or less symmetrically on the support bar, i.e., close to the geometric center, correct in the right direction guided by the sensation of falling (adjustments were rarely made in the wrong direction), readjust in the other direction (corrections were frequently excessive), continue correcting back and forth but gradually more carefully until equilibrium is achieved.

It was already suggested that for some time children treat the problem as one not governed by a physical law. By contrast, what was particularly apparent at the next level, either developmentally or later in a session, was that *all* blocks were systematically first tried at their geometric center. Almost all children aged 6–7;5 and also some younger subjects, did this. Here we witness the beginnings of an important theory-in-action (i.e., spatial symmetry or as the children put it "I'll try the middle first", ". . . half-way along"), which was generalized to all blocks and was to pervade behavior at the next level. Action sequences ran as follows: Place at geometric center, release hold very slightly to observe result, correct very slightly, correct a little more, return carefully to geometric center, repeat until balance is achieved. Depending on the block, the further the child had to move away from the geometric center, the more often he returned to it before further adjusting. These frequent returns to the geometric center seem to denote that the child is using a form of spatial notation as a known location from which to orient his corrections and are an obvious prelude to the 'geometric center theory' that develops next.

Another important change took place at this level. The children no longer seemed to be merely registering the fact of balance but beyond that something about the balancing position of the block. The new action sequence, which alternated with the one described previously, was as follows: First place at geometric center, next place at the point of contact corresponding to the previous success (irrespective as yet of the differences between the two blocks and often far removed from possible empirical success—see Figure 1.2), return to geometric center, continue as in previous sequence. At this point, some corrections were made away from the center of gravity, a feature to be discussed later. Notable in the various action sequences of these children was the interplay between the endeavor to use information acquired from previous actions and the gradual introduction of a coherent, analogous approach to *all* items.

Interestingly enough, most of those subjects who had been successful in balancing conspicuous or inconspicuous weight blocks because they had been concentrating on the goal, began later in the session to experience serious difficulties in repeating the successful action as their attention shifted to the means. They now placed the very same blocks more and more systematically at the geometric center, with only very slight corrections around this point. They showed considerable surprise at not being able to balance the blocks a second time ("Heh, what's gone wrong with this one, it worked before"). This was in fact to

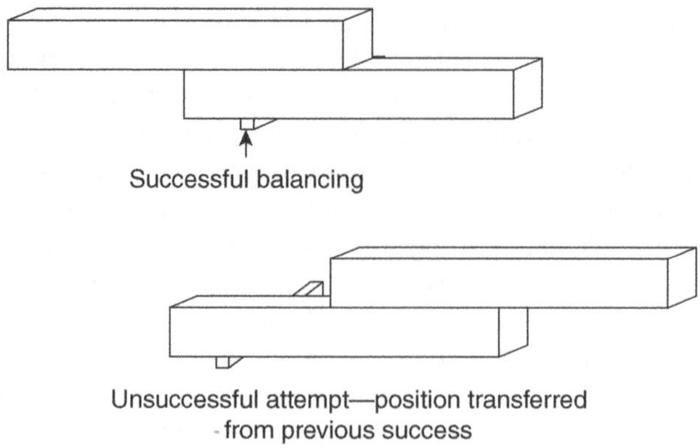

Figure 1.2

be the dominating behavioral pattern for a long period to follow, either during the session or developmentally. Action sequences then became reduced to: Place carefully at geometric center, correct very slightly around this center, abandon all attempts, declaring the object as 'impossible' to balance. It is interesting to note that the child remained unflinchingly at the geometric center and completely ignored the proprioceptive messages that had proved useful earlier. What is striking is that when these very same subjects were asked to close their eyes and attempt to balance inconspicuous weight blocks, success was very rapid. But once they reopened their eyes, they again resolutely tried the geometric center and expressed surprise at their blind success. In fact we observed more failures to balance blocks among 5;6 to 7;5 year olds than among 4;5 to 5;5 year olds. How can this be explained? It would appear that a strong theory-in-action, i.e., that the center of gravity necessarily coincides with the geometric center of an object (or as one child put it "things always balance in the middle" though others did not express verbally what was obvious in their actions), pervaded the actions of the older children. Not only did they place all blocks at their geometric center with substantially no corrections of the position, but when asked to add small blocks of varying shapes and sizes to blocks already in balance, they added up to ten blocks precariously one on top of the other at the geometric center rather than distributing them at the extremities, as did both the younger subjects ("it's like a see-saw, you put a block at each end") and those 8/9 year olds who placed blocks equidistant from the point of contact.

If this 'geometric center theory' is so pervasive and persistent despite negative theory-response (blocks fall when placed at the center or balance at points other than the center), how does the child ever come to change it? We postulate three interacting causes: (1) The ever-increasing regularity of counterexamples, (2) changes taking place in the child's *general* conceptual competence and (3) the integration of the earlier proprioceptive information into a theory-in-action. Let us take up each of these points separately.

Frequent counterexamples do not alone induce a change in the child's behavior. If they did, then progress could be achieved by simply providing a large number of counterexamples. The child must first form a unifying rule based on regular patterns he has observed: In this study, the geometric center theory, which in fact accounts adequately for some blocks and for many situations in his daily life. Only when this theory is really consolidated and generalized, is he ready to recognize some form of unifying principle for the counterexamples which he earlier rejected as mere exceptions ('impossible to balance').

One obvious reason for giving up the geometric center theory would be that the child considers weight and no longer exclusively length as being relevant. From previous studies, it is known that around 7 years children consider weight to be a significant property in problems involving equilibrium, and it is not until even later that the child differentiates between weight as an absolute property and weight as a force. Is this to imply that younger children are unaware that objects can be heavy or light or that imbalance is caused by heaviness? No, but what younger children do not understand is the role of weight in situations of *balance.* As the child attains conservation of weight and recognizes weight as being relevant in other situations, so in recognizing the regularity of counterexamples he looks by way of explanation for some aspect other than length, i.e., weight: ("Oh, it's always just the opposite of what I expect . . . maybe it's this block glued to the end here"). And the first corrections away from the geometric center took place with conspicuous weight blocks (type D) while inconspicuous weight blocks were still resolutely centered.

Though children may not have a conceptual understanding of the role of weight in equilibrium, it should be recalled that the younger children did react to weight communicated proprioceptively. It thus seems plausible that once weight is considered to be relevant, the proprioceptive information is integrated gradually into the child's theory-in-action. Interestingly enough, many corrections at this level were made away from the center of gravity, denoting that the correction did not stem from proprioceptive information but from a conceptualized need for a change of position. Younger subjects relying on proprioceptive information alone rarely if ever made corrections in the wrong direction.

We have seen that three interrelating factors seem to bring about corrections to the weight items as distinct from the length items. Once this happens, do children then easily change their geometric center theory and opt for a new and broader one? It is hypothesized that for some time they tend to hold on to the earlier theory. Among the conspicuous weight blocks, for instance, type D (thick plywood base) were clearly easier for these subjects than type C (thin plywood base on which the weight of the glued block has more effect), because the center of gravity of D blocks is much closer to the geometric center than in C blocks. Correcting a D block from its geometric center to its point of equilibrium is thus less of a challenge to the child's geometric center theory than a C block which balances much nearer its extremity.

Furthermore, even when adjusting all conspicuous weight blocks children continued resolutely to center the inconspicuous weight blocks. It would thus appear that the geometric center theory was not abandoned when the child started taking negative responses and weight into account; it was retained for most situations where the theory could still hold true and a new theory, quite independent of it, was developed to deal with the most obvious exceptions. Length and weight were thus considered independently, which was apparent not only from the child's actions but also from the explanations he gave at the end of a session. For length blocks, weight was considered to play no role and symmetry of length was the sole property invoked; for conspicuous weight items, weight was used in the explanation. (For A blocks: "it's the same length each side, there's no weight"; for C blocks: "it's heavy on one side and long on the other . . . no in this one (D) there's weight all the way along the bar, in that one (C) there's only weight where the block is").

Gradually, and often almost reluctantly, the 7 to 8 year olds began to make corrections also on the inconspicuous weight blocks. It is to be recalled that 4 to 5 year olds did this immediately, but for different reasons. Whereas the young subjects were relying solely on the proprioceptive information, the older subjects (7;5–8;6 years) provided explicit references not only to equal length but simultaneously to equal weight for all items balanced at their geometric center (types A and B). Previously length alone had sufficed to explain equilibrium. At this point, we observed many pauses during action sequences on the inconspicuous weight items: Place at geometric center, correct slightly, pause, lift object, rotate object, pause, place at geometric center, correct position slightly, release hold slightly, readjust carefully, pause longer, glance at a conspicuous weight item, pause, place again slowly at geometric center, shake head, glance again at conspicuous weight item, then suddenly correct continuously and rapidly in the right direction until balance is achieved. Repetition of a success was thereafter immediate, even if the object was rotated. As the children were now really beginning to question the generality of their geometric center theory, a negative response at the geometric center sufficed to have the child rapidly make corrections towards the point of balance. We obviously do not mean to imply that he had a full, explicit understanding of the inverse relationship of weight and distance, but simply that he now implicitly understood the importance of both length and weight.

To give an indication of action sequences at the upper level, by 8;7 years of age children paused *before* each item, roughly assessed the weight distribution of the block by lifting it ("you have to be careful, sometimes it's just as heavy on each side, sometimes it's heavier on one side"), inferred the probable point of balance and then placed the object immediately very close to it, without making any attempts at first balancing at the geometric center. These subjects demonstrated, when adding extra blocks to already balanced items, that the point of balance was for them not a fixed, but a relative point, for they could alter it several times by correcting simultaneously the fulcrum and the position of the added blocks. Both negative and positive responses had immediate effect. Adding two equal blocks to an inconspicuous weight block already in balance was not made at the two extremities, as the otherwise successful 7 to 8 year olds would have done, but at an equal distance from the center of gravity. The principles of the law of moments were at this point apparent in the child's actions.

A number of other apparently minor aspects of behavior seem important. There is for example the manner in which children held the blocks. The very youngest children and many others at the outset of a session tended to hold blocks from above in one hand when trying to balance them and then to push with the same hand on the block above the point of contact. Next children tended to hold the blocks at each extremity with both hands, which is a much more informative method proprioceptively. Thus, the rather diffuse proprioceptive information by pushing with one hand above the point of contact, became a definite feeling of heaviness in one of the child's hands, indicating the side on which the block would fall (see Figure 1.3). However, the child gradually seemed to realize that one of his hands was in fact superfluous. As his attention moved from his own actions on the blocks to the properties of the blocks, the child attempted (not without difficulty) to replace his hand by placing a small cube on top of the block as a counter-weight, or replaced his other hand by a cube underneath the block; thus providing a second support. The latter was not satisfactory for the child since the small cubes were purposely all lower or higher than the vertical distance between the table and the point of support: thus the block remained slanted. This again reinforced the need for either the use of counter-weights (rarely used spontaneously, except by the older subjects) or for corrections of the point of contact along the dimension chosen.

A second aspect was the order in which subjects chose to treat items in phase I where choice of order was left to the child. Many children (including all the youngest but also a certain proportion in the other age groups up to 7 years) chose blocks closest to them on the table in a haphazard order, not bothering to group identical or similar ones together. It was as if each block constituted a separate

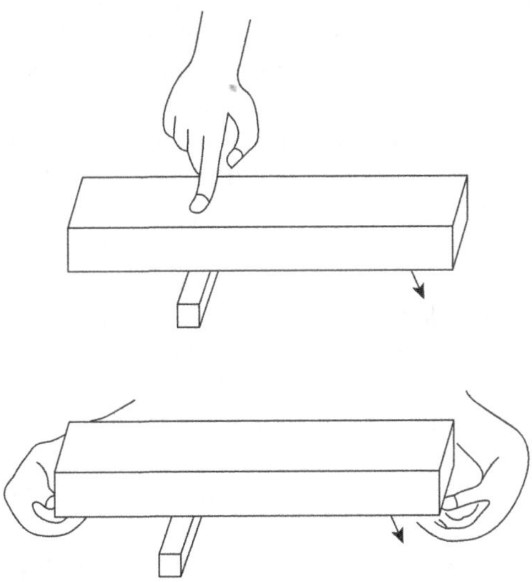

Figure 1.3

problem for them and as if there was no anticipation of the differences in complexity nor any effort to transfer acquired information intentionally during these initial attempts. Furthermore, when, after completing the free choice session, we then imposed a more 'informative' order (e.g., following C by D) children did finally begin to make transfers from one block to another. Only very gradually during a session, or more systematically for older subjects (as of roughly 7 years and including all subjects above 8;7 years) did children from the outset stretch out for blocks so as to group them in an organized fashion. When the children dealt with two seemingly analogous blocks, either spontaneously or because of the experimenter's imposed order, there were many erroneous yet informative transfers from one item to the next.

Discussion

What are the processes of discovery in history, in ontogenesis and during an experimental session? In his interesting book on Darwin's creativity, Gruber (1974) suggests that "there is nothing necessarily creative in being immediately trapped by every original thought one has". Indeed, in our particular field of enquiry, the processes of cognitive discovery involve far more than simply isolating the properties of weight and length. We have seen that action sequences are not merely a reflection of the child's implicit theories. The very organization and reorganization of the actions themselves, the lengthening of their sequences, their repetition and generalized application to new situations give rise to discoveries that will regulate the theories, just as the theories have a regulating effect on the action sequences. What is the role of experience or of the object's 'responses' in generating change?

It may seem surprising that an event as obvious as the falling of a block is not always clearly evaluated as negative theory-response but merely as negative action-response. While the child is solely success-oriented, all balancing—irrespective of which block—will be read as 'positive' information and all falling of blocks as 'negative'. However, if considered from the standpoint of theories-in-action, then the child's interpretation of the object's 'response' will depend on the block. For instance, for a child with the geometric center theory, conspicuous or inconspicuous weight blocks in balance will, when not rejected as mere exceptions, be read as negative theory-response since such balancing indeed counteracts the child's theory-in-action. On the contrary, the balancing of a length block and the falling of any block placed at a point outside the geometric center will be read by the child as positive (positive to his theory, though not immediately to his goal). And the reading of identical events can change from positive to negative or vice versa as the child modifies his theories.

Positive and negative action- and theory-responses seem to have varying roles at different times. While the child is exclusively success-oriented, i.e., concentrating on balancing, positive action-response is all-important. It encourages the child's natural tendency to repeat successful actions. Then gradually negative action-response shifts the child's attention to the means, i.e., 'how to balance'.

At this point we witness experimentation for experimentation's sake; for attending to the means implies seeking knowledge of the approximate range of possible actions on an object. Koslowski and Bruner (1972) found a similar phenomenon when experimenting on young babies' use of a rotating level to obtain a distant object. The authors report a stage when babies continued experimenting with the various movements of the lever, thus becoming 'enmeshed in the means', ignoring the goal which they had meanwhile moved within their reach, whereas previously they had been solely goal-oriented.

As the child gradually begins to construct a theory for interpreting the regularity of positive action-responses, these become positive theory-responses. Negative responses remain action-responses until the child's theory is generalized and consolidated, after which they progressively become negative theory-responses, once the child becomes aware of their regularity. A further important fact is that younger subjects make use of proprioceptive information in an uncontaminated fashion since they have not yet developed a unifying theory. For the more advanced subject the object's 'behavior' is evaluated conceptually, and they are only able to use the proprioceptive information if they close their eyes.

As long as the child is predominantly success-oriented, there are rarely any pauses in his action sequences. As his attention shifts to means, however, pauses become more and more frequent in the course of the sequence. Only when goal and means are considered simultaneously do pauses *precede* action. Such differences in the occurrence of pauses are potentially meaningful for the observer.

Although negative responses are a necessary condition for progress, they are clearly not a sufficient one; in order to be effective, such responses must counteract a powerful theory-in-action, such as the geometric center theory. It should be noted in passing that we purposely chose to speak of 'theories' and not of 'hypotheses' since the latter tend to have the connotation of intentionally seeking to verify. Previous research (Inhelder & Piaget, 1958) showed that the formal operational child was frequently capable of attempting to test hypotheses and verify theories by deliberately seeking counterexamples. In those experiments, however, tasks were often well beyond the capacities of the concrete operational child; his experimental method was therefore defined in terms of what was lacking as compared to the formal operational child. Our present research was aimed at elucidating the *positive* aspects of the younger child's behavior by using simpler situations and looking more closely at how he goes about his task. Our observations indicate that the younger child does not intentionally *seek* counterexamples; rather, children in this research, whatever their theory-in-action (from the elementary need for physical contact to the more sophisticated geometric center theory) constructed and generalized theories, and gradually *recognized* counterexamples. However, the earlier claim (op. cit.) that "at the concrete level, the child does not formulate any hypotheses" needs to be reconsidered in the light of the strong tendency of our children to act under the guidance of a powerful theory-in-action which involves far more than mere observation of immediate empirical reality. Nonetheless, their theories remain implicit, since the younger child clearly cannot reflect on hypothetical situations which might confirm or refute his theory. Indeed, although the child's action sequences bear eloquent witness to a theory-in-action implicit in his behavior, this should not be taken as a capacity to conceptualize explicitly on what he is doing and why. Recent experimental work (Piaget et al., 1974a and 1974b) has confirmed that a developmental gap exists between succeeding in action and being capable of explaining it.

Our present analysis is focused less on particular, explicit notions than on the gradual unification of ideas as observed in action sequences. There is no doubt that the generalized application of a theory will ultimately lead to discoveries which in turn serve to create new or broader theories. However, it seems possible for the child to experience surprise and to question his theory only if the prediction he makes emanates from an already powerful theory expressed in action. Our observations indicate that children hold on to their initial theory for as long as they can. Even when they finally do take counterexamples into consideration, they first prefer to create a new theory, quite independent of the first one, before finally attempting to unify all events under a single, broader theory.

The tendency to explain phenomena by a unified theory, the most general or simplest one possible, appears to be a natural aspect of the creative process, both for the child and the scientist. The construction of false theories or the over-generalization of limited ones are in effect productive processes. Overgeneralization, a sometimes derogatory term, can be looked upon as the *creative simplification* of a problem by ignoring some of the complicating factors (such as weight in our study). This is implicit in the young child's behavior but could be intentional in the scientist's. Overgeneralization is not only a means to simplify but also to unify; it is thus not suprising that the child and the scientist often refuse counter-examples since they complicate the unification process. However, to be capable of unifying positive examples implies that one is equally capable of attempting to find a unifying principle to cover counterexamples.

The history of physics abounds in examples analogous to those we have observed among children. Dugas (1950) recalls that the really creative scientists were those who did not merely study the positive examples of well-known principles but who endeavored to *extend* the principles to other phenomena. It is in this way that scientists, and children, are able to discover new properties which in turn make it possible for new theories to be constructed. And psychology experiments on adults (Claparède, 1934; Miller, Galanter & Pribam, 1960; Wason and Johnson-Laird, 1972) illustrate the general tendency to construct powerful, yet often inappropriate, hypotheses which adults try to verify rather than to falsify. This temporarily blinds the adult to counterexamples which should actually suffice to have them reject their hypothesis immediately. Our present results on young children seem to point to the fact that constructing and extending a powerful theory-in-action is a very general aspect of discovery which has a deeprooted function.

The observations stemming from this study suggest some thought-provoking analogies between the processes of acquiring physical knowledge and language. Ruth Weir's fascinating recordings of language in the crib (1962) show how small children use language not only for symbolic representation and direct communication, but also how they 'explore' language by trying out in presleep monologues series of word combinations, almost as if they were looking for the most appropriate-sounding ones. Children's exploration of each block's dimensions in this study is not an unsimilar process. Furthermore, many authors (e.g., Ervin, 1964; Klima & Bellugi, 1966) have observed that certain morphological markers such as the plural, the past-tense, negation, etc., first enter the child's corpus in an unanalyzed, isolated fashion, rather than as part of a unified system. Young children are able to assimilate irregular forms they hear such as 'feet' and 'went', and first produce them in their *correct* form, alone or in combination with other words. Such utterances seem as yet 'uncontaminated' by rules, or by what might be called implicit 'theories-in-language', and thus very comparable to the way in which our young subjects were able to make use of proprioceptive input, uncontaminated by a theory-in-action. Just as our subjects gradually recognize regular patterns in the objects' responses and construct a theory-in-action, so children progressively recognize patterns in their linguistic environment and construct 'theories-in-language'. The tendency to generalize these implicit theories results in the temporary disappearance of the correct, irregular forms in favor of theory-revealing errors (e.g., 'foots', 'goed', etc.), just as successful balancing of weight blocks ceases temporarily in favor of the geometric center theory. It is clearly not sufficient to provide the child with frequent counterexamples to induce him immediately to drop this theory. A striking example of this phenomenon in language is seen when a child repeatedly produces errors which resist adult corrections until the child is ready spontaneously to recognize that there are exceptions to his implicit theory-in-language. When the correct linguistic forms do reappear, they are no longer unanalyzed entities as in the first phase, but exceptions to a unified system, just as subsequent successful balancing of weight blocks is the result of a broader, implicit theory.

Attempts to compare language and cognition were initially made by authors comparing syntactical structures and concrete operational structures. The more recent trend has been to analyze, both theoretically and experimentally, the sensory-motor foundations of language and thought (e.g., Sinclair, 1971; Inhelder et al., 1972; Brown, 1973; Sinclair, 1973). It may be that a comparison between the experimental results of the Genevan psycholinguistics team and our new data on goal-oriented behavior, will prove to have a heuristic value in leading us closer to the general *processes* underlying cognitive and linguistic behavior.

Acknowledgments

This research was supported by Grant No. 16610.72 of the Fonds National Suisse de la Recherche Scientifique. The authors wish to express thanks to G. Cellérier, R. Garcia and H. Sinclair for useful comments on the research manuscript covering this study. They are particularly grateful to Morris Sinclair for editing the final English version of this paper.

Notes

1 See list of Internal Research Manuscripts, following the list of references. The results of these experiments are to be published later.
2 Having completed this level of experimental analysis, our team is presently making a very detailed analysis from videotapes of two subjects undergoing all the different experimental tasks.
3 Appreciation is extended to the staff and pupils of Pinchat Infants' and Primary School, Geneva. Faculty students M. H. Lavanchy, C. Mainardi, M. Mergulies, C. Mulliez, P. A. Schneider and J. Zürcher are thanked for their assistance in data collection.

References

Brown, R. (1973) *A First Language: The Early Stages*. Harvard University Press, Cambridge, Mass.

Cellérier, Guy (1972) Information processing tendencies in recent experiments in cognitive learning: Theoretical implications. In S. Farnham-Diggory (ed.), *Information Processing in Children*. Academic Press, New York, pp. 115–123.

Claparède, E. (1934) *La genèse de l'hypothèse*. Kundig, Genève, Switzerland.

Dugas, René (1950) *Histoire de la Mécanique*. Editions du Griffon, Neuchâtel, Switzerland.

Ervin, S. (1964) Imitations and structural changes in children's language. In Lenneberg, *New Directions in the Study of Language*. MIT Press, Cambridge, Mass., pp. 163–189.

Gruber, H. E. (1974) *Darwin on Man: A psychological study of scientific creativity*. Dutton & Co., New York.

Inhelder, B. (1972) Information processing tendencies in recent experiments in cognitive learning: Empirical studies. In S. Farnham-Diggory (ed.), *Information Processing in Children*. Academic Press, New York, pp. 103–114.

Inhelder, B., Lézine, I., Sinclair, H. & Stambak, M. (1972) Les débuts de la fonction symbolique, *Arch. Psychol. 41*, pp. 187–243.

Inhelder, B. & Piaget, J. (1958. French edition 1955) *The Growth of Logical Thinking from Childhood to Adolescence*. Basic Books Inc., New York.

Inhelder, B., Sinclair, H. & Bovet, M. (1974) *Learning and the Development of Cognition*. Harvard University Press, Cambridge, Mass. (French edition PUF France, 1974).

Klima, E. S. & Bellugi, U. (1966) Syntactic regularities in the speech of children. In J. Lyons & R. J. Wales (eds.), *Psycholinguistic Papers*. Edinburgh University Press, pp. 183–208.

Koslowski, B. & Bruner, J. S. (1972) Learning to use a lever. *Child Develop.*, *43*, 790–799.

Miller, G., Gallanter, E. & Pribam, K. (1960) *Plans and the Structure of Behaviour*. Holt, New York.

Piaget, J. (1951) Play, dreams and imitation in childhood. Heineman, Melbourne-London, (French edition, 1946).

Piaget, J. (1974a) *La Prise de Conscience*. PUF, Paris.

Piaget, J. (1974b) *Réussir et Comprendre*. PUF, Paris.

Piaget. J. & Garcia, R. (1974) *Understanding Causality*. Norton, New York. (French edition, 1971).

Piaget, J. et al. (1973) *La formation de la notion de force*. EEG XXIX, PUF, Paris.

Sinclair, H. (1971) Sensorimotor action patterns as a condition for the acquisition of syntax. In R. Huxley & L. Ingram (eds.), *Language Acquisition: Models and Methods*. Academic Press, New York, pp. 121–135.

Sinclair, H. (1973) Language acquisition and cognitive development. In T. E. Moore, *Cognitive Development and the Acquisition of Language*. Academic Press, New York, pp. 9–25.
Vinh Bang (1968) Le rapport inversément proportionnel entre le poids *P* et la distance *D* dans l'équilibre de la balance. In J. Piaget, J. B. Grize, A. Szeminska and Vinh Bang *Epistémologie et Psychologie de la Fonction*. PUF, Paris, pp. 151–163.
Wason, P. & Johnson-Laird, P. N. (1972) *Psychology of Reasoning*. Batsford, London.
Weir, R. H. (1962) *Language in the Crib*. Mouton, The Hague.

Internal Research Manuscripts on children's goal-oriented strategies

(Provisional titles, translated into English, indicate sphere of research)

Blanchet, A. (1973/74) Constructing multi-stage mobiles.
Coll, C. (1974) Discovering maximum number of routes for loading lorries.
Karmiloff-Smith, A. (1973) Building closed railway circuits of varying shapes and sizes.
— (1973/74) Balancing of blocks of varying physical properties.
Kilcher, H. (1973) Building bridges with materials of varying physical properties.
— (1974) Constructing instruments to move objects.
de Marcelius, O. (1973) Skittles.
— (1974) Modifying order of locomotives and carriages in a closed circuit.
Montangero, J. (1973/74) Controlling water levels by immersion of combinations of objects with varying properties.
Robert, M. (1973) Spontaneous exploratory activities in observed play with Russian Matriona dolls.
— (1974) Building staircases with various sized blocks.
Valladao-Ackermann, E. (1973) Simplified chess situations.
— (1973/74) Combining serial orders of boxes and ladder rungs.
— (1974) Path puzzle leading to combined destinations.
Wagner, S. (1974) Constructing resisting chains for hauling weights.

2 Constraints on representational change

Evidence from children's drawing

Annette Karmiloff-Smith

Introduction

Why study children's drawing? One reason is to explore the acquisition of drawing skills per se, that is, spatio-geometric relations, part–whole relations, planning strategies, motor execution, cross-cultural influences, artistic talent, etc. (e.g., Bialystok & Olson, 1987; Freeman, 1980; Freeman & Cox, 1985; Gardner, 1980; Goodnow, 1977, 1978; Luquet, 1927; Millar, 1975; Moore, 1986; Pemberton, 1987; Piaget & Inhelder, 1948; Stiles-Davis, 1987; Van Sommers, 1984; Willats, 1977). Research of this type aims primarily at describing the slow developmental progression towards adult-like geometric and pictorial competence.

Another reason to focus on children's drawing is to use it as a source of evidence with respect to more general processes of notational competence and representational change (Bolger, 1988; Bolger & Karmiloff-Smith, 1990; Catan, 1987; Cohen, 1985; Goodnow & Levine, 1973; Karmiloff-Smith, 1979b, c, 1984). The present study is of this second type: children's drawings being used to analyse internal representational[1] change and flexibility, and the constraints thereupon.

There is considerable debate (see Freeman, 1987, for full discussion) about the extent to which children's drawings can be used as data about internal representations (Kosslyn, Heldmeyer, & Locklear, 1977; Laszlo & Broderick, 1985; Olson & Bialystok, 1983). However, these reservations concern the possibility of being able to directly externalize the content of internal representations of spatial relations. This is not my concern. Rather than focusing on the *content* of children's *inadequate* drawings, here I explore the processes that children can call forth for changing their already successful drawing procedures, when they are set new goals.

The present study was designed to test further hypotheses emanating from a model of representational change used to account for certain aspects of the lexico-morphology of language acquisition (Karmiloff-Smith, 1979a, 1986), as well as of children's problem solving (Karmiloff-Smith, 1979b, 1984). While the study of children's drawing tests the plausibility of the model in yet another domain, the present focus is on the identification of the specific constraints on representational change. In previous work on children's spontaneous theories about physical causality and language, it was established that an endogenous process of representational change does indeed take place (Karmiloff-Smith, 1979a, b, 1984, 1986; Karmiloff-Smith & Inhelder, 1974) and may, in some cases, even give rise to a form of cognitive encapsulation that mimics the modular organization of input systems (Karmiloff-Smith, 1985; Karmiloff-Smith, Johnson, Grant, Jones, Karmiloff, Bartrip, & Cuckle, 1993). However, important questions remained unaddressed. Why does representational change take developmental time? What are the constraints on representational change, i.e. on the child's capacity to operate on the knowledge components embedded in earlier, efficiently functioning procedures?

Whilst full details of the model can be found elsewhere (Karmiloff-Smith, 1986, 1992), certain theoretical issues are particularly relevant to the present study and will be reiterated briefly here. How is knowledge acquired? There are, in my view, three ways. One is to have the knowledge innately specified, that is, via evolutionary processes. Another is to add new representations on the basis of interactions with the external physical and socio-cultural environments. However, a third and important way to gain new knowledge is to exploit the knowledge already represented, that is, to engage in an endogenous process of internal representational change. The model hypothesizes a phase of development in which knowledge is represented procedurally, followed by a phase of representational redescription at which point the knowledge embedded in the previously efficiently functioning procedures becomes available as a data structure to other parts of the cognitive system. In other words, elements of the same knowledge are re-represented at different levels of abstraction. The distinction is somewhat similar to that used in artificial intelligence research. As pointed out by Rutkowska (1987), program procedures in artificial intelligence usually have a dual function: (1) they can be activated to generate processes; or (2) they can be manipulated or reorganized by other procedures, in which case they are being treated as part of the program's data. My argument is that part of cognitive development consists in building the second of these two functions for each procedure, by redescribing the procedure at a higher level of abstraction such that the knowledge is then represented at two different levels. The pervasiveness – although not the existence – of this process of representational redescription may well be unique to the human species and account for representational flexibility and creativity (Karmiloff-Smith, 1979b).

It is with these theoretical distinctions in mind that a domain of study was chosen in which it was already known that early in development children develop efficiently functioning procedures. If, as the model maintains, behavioural mastery is a prerequisite for subsequent representational change, then subjects who can already successfully perform a task should be ripe for displaying such change. Four-year-olds' capacity to draw familiar objects with automaticity turned out to be an ideal choice in this regard.

Previous research has demonstrated that once the child has reached behavioural mastery the resulting compiled procedures undergo representational redescription, after which the knowledge embedded in them becomes available to other parts of the system (Karmiloff-Smith, 1979a, b, 1986). Logically there are many formats in which such knowledge could be available. The specific hypothesis to be tested here is that, as the child becomes able to operate on the knowledge embedded in a procedure, the redescribed representation of the knowledge is initially specified in such a way as to restrict both intra- and inter-representational flexibility. What is meant by this? The hypothesis is that at the first level of redescription the internal representation is specified as a sequentially fixed list, embodying a constraint that was inherent at the procedural level. This constraint means that there is relatively little intra-representational flexibility, that is, the child is limited with respect to changes she can introduce into the representation. Inter-representational flexibility is also constrained at this level, that is, the child cannot link the new representation to other representations outside the domain. Later in development, it is hypothesized that via further redescription this sequential constraint is relaxed, yielding an internal representation specified as a structured yet flexibly ordered set of manipulable features. This not only makes possible intra-representational flexibility within a domain, but opens the system to inter-representational flexibility, that is, across different domains. Let us now look at how these hypotheses were tested in the empirical study.

Population

Fifty-four children between the ages of 4 and 11 were tested. There were 22 children in the 4–6-year-old group (mean age: 5;4), 15 children in the 8–9-year-old group (mean age: 8;2), and 17 in the 9–10-year-old age group (mean age: 10;4). Since the results of the 8- and 10-year-olds were to all intents and purposes identical, these have been grouped ($N = 32$) for the purposes of analysis and contrasted with the 4–6-year-olds ($N = 22$).

In keeping with my research strategy for exploring representational change in both language and problem solving (Karmiloff-Smith, 1979a, b, 1984), I have chosen an age group at which children are already successful at producing the particular drawings and also have adequate conceptual knowledge about the objects being drawn. This contrasts with the usual focus of drawing research which traces the errorful, laborious process that ultimately leads to behavioural success (e.g., Freeman & Cox, 1985). All subjects of the present study had already reached behavioural mastery for the chosen drawing procedures, making it possible for the analysis to concentrate on subsequent representational change.

Method

Subjects were first asked to produce copies of drawings of four geometric forms, to ensure that their overall drawing levels were within their age norms and that they had no motor or planning problems. Then each subject was asked to draw a house and, after her or his drawing was removed, to “draw a house that doesn’t exist”. The same procedure was used for drawing a man and an animal. The order of the three categories (man, house, animal) was randomly varied across subjects. To ensure that children understood what was expected of them, several different formulae were used with every child, in random order, such as "an X that doesn't exist", "an X you invent", "a pretend X", "an X we have never seen before", etc. In all, 324 drawings of X's that exist and X's that do not exist were produced and fully analysed.

The rationale behind the experimental design was as follows: over time in early childhood, children spontaneously build procedures for drawing a house, a man, an animal. This often involves a laborious developmental process, but by around 4–5 years of age children can run these procedures efficiently and in an automatized fashion. When children are asked to draw a house, for example, they do so rapidly and well. When they are asked to draw a house that does not exist, they are forced into operating in some way on their internal representation. As long as one focuses on subjects who have no difficulty in the actual planning and execution of the drawing itself, then an analysis of the types of modification that children produce will allow the researcher to capture essential facets of the constraints on representational change.

One of the techniques piloted used the instructions "draw me a different X", but this gave rise to almost no developmental differences. For example, with the instruction "different" children changed from one to several windows, from no chimney to one chimney, from no hat to a hat, etc. However, with the final technique adopted (e.g., "draw me an X that doesn't exist"), children altered fundamental features of househood, manhood or animalhood and, as we shall see, huge developmental differences emerged between the age groups, not in "success" at producing an X that doesn't exist, but in the types of change that children of different ages introduced.

The technique used here of explicitly instructing the child to make changes differs somewhat from those used in previous research in which I analysed *spontaneous* changes in output and their internal representational implications (Karmiloff-Smith, 1979a, b, 1984, 1986). Having established by the earlier work that change does occur spontaneously after behavioural mastery, it was now possible to choose the relevant age and domain to be sure of tapping already compiled procedures ripe for different degrees of internal change. Predictions could therefore be made as to when representational redescription should occur, and subjects were selected accordingly. Let me stress that by my instructions I am inducing the external manifestation of change, not the already existing internal capacity for it.

Results

All 54 subjects tested corresponded to their age norms in copying the four geometric forms and were therefore included in the study. We shall first briefly look at the results as they pertain to children's capacity to produce the requested drawings, and subsequently analyse in detail the precise nature of the changes that children introduced.

To give an example of what would count as "a house that does exist" versus "a house that does not exist", the following criteria were taken into account. For a normal house: rectangular shape, roof, door, window, and optionally: chimney, curtains, various numbers of windows, normal decorative objects such as a doorknob. To draw successfully a house/man/animal that does not exist, subjects must introduce appropriate changes while simultaneously retaining core concepts of household/manhood/animalhood. For example, to count as "a house that doesn't exist", children had to place the roof, door, window, chimney, etc. in the wrong position or orientation, delete some essential feature, change the usual shape of the house to, say, a circle, add some unusual feature such as eyes or wings to a house or, in the case of a "man that doesn't exist", add two heads, etc.

Two analyses were carried out, first with respect to success at drawing an X which did/did not exist, and second with respect to the types of change children introduced. We will start with the first analysis. Two independent judges categorized children's productions as an existing house (man or animal) or as a non-existing house (man or animal). Inter-judge agreement was very high: .94 with respect to the younger age group's productions and .98 with respect to older children. Disagreements were settled with a third person. In fact, the only disagreements concerned the category "animal", which is understandable given the wide range of possible drawings from, say, bird to elephant. From the very high inter-rater agreement levels, it is obvious that no difficulties were encountered in judging whether children's productions successfully met the analytical criteria.

One hundred percent of subjects produced adequate drawings of existent houses, men and animals. Table 2.1 gives the results of children's ability to produce the various drawings of the non-existent categories. Of the total population of 54 subjects, only 2 were unable to draw any non-existent X's. Previous work has shown that behavioural mastery is a prerequisite to the first level of representational redescription (Karmiloff-Smith, 1979b, 1984, 1986), and these two children may not quite have reached behavioural mastery; that is, their normal drawing procedures may not have been entirely compiled and automatized. However, the focus of the present paper is not on whether or not children succeeded in drawing a non-existent house, man or animal. As the results show, most of the children did. Indeed, 91% of the 8- to 10-year-olds and 50% of the 4- to 6-year-olds succeeded on all three categories and, if one adds those subjects who succeed on house and man, but fail on animal,[2] then 94% of the older group and 91% of the younger group were successful. The important question here is, given that the vast majority of children did succeed in introducing appropriate changes, what types of change did they make?

Table 2.1 Percentage success rates for drawings of non-existing houses, men and animals

Age group (years)	*Number of subjects*	*Unsuccessful on all three categories (%)*	*Successful on one category (%)*	*Successful on two categories (%)*	*Successful on all three categories (%)*
4–6	22	9	5	36	50
8–10	32	0	6	3	91

We now turn to the second and more important analysis which concerns the different types of modification children introduced into their drawings and the extent to which developmental constraints obtain in children's capacity to operate on the knowledge components embedded in earlier, efficiently functioning procedures. The following types of change were observed:

- shape and size of elements changed
- shape of whole changed
- deletion of elements
- insertion of new elements
- position/orientation changed
- insertion of elements from other conceptual categories
- other (e.g., dinosaur, mermaid, which are conventionalized forms and could, of course, already exist as independently stored procedures – in fact, this turned out to be irrelevant because it represented such a minute percentage of the results as to be unquantifiable).

Figures 2.1 to 2.6 illustrate the different types of change. Figure 2.1 gives examples of children who changed the shape and/or size of elements but left the contour outline unchanged. Figure 2.2 provides examples of drawings in which children changed the shape of the whole. Figure 2.3 gives illustrations from children who deleted elements from their drawing procedure. Figure 2.4 shows, by contrast, how children inserted new elements into their productions. Drawings from subjects who changed the orientation/position of elements or the whole are given in Figure 2.5. Finally, Figure 2.6 shows examples of productions in which children inserted elements from other conceptual categories.

The histogram in Figure 2.7 gives the breakdown per age group for the different types of change. The figures represent the percentage of children making a particular category of change as a function of the total number of children analysed. The independent judges reached .84 and .91 agreement respectively on this second analysis when categorizing the younger and older age groups' productions with respect to type of change. Differences were settled in consultation with a third person. The categories were not treated as mutually exclusive, since children often introduced several types of change in a drawing (e.g., changed both the contour outline and deleted an element or inserted a cross-category element). However, a second analysis treating the categories as mutually exclusive (scoring only the most advanced type of change) yielded the same overall pattern of developmental differences.

Any drawing which did not meet the judges' criteria for a house/man/animal which does not exist was excluded from the analysis. This involved 21 out of a total of 214 drawings of houses/men/animals which did not exist. These were excluded because when a drawing includes changes, such as adding a hat to a man or a chimney in the correct position on a house, such changes do not constitute modifications to househood/manhood/animalhood. Indeed, as pointed out at the beginning of this section, additions had to violate in some way househood, manhood or animalhood whilst retaining other core aspects of the concept.

Figure 2.1 Shape and/or size of elements changed (ages are in years, months)

Thus, a chimney added to a second house-drawing would not represent a house that does not exist. By contrast, a pair of eyes added to a house would, as would the addition of a chimney upside down on the bottom of the house. Likewise with deletions. Deleting a hat or walking stick in a second man-drawing would not constitute a violation of an aspect of manhood and would therefore not be a successful drawing of a man that does not exist. By contrast, deleting eyes or mouth or adding extra ones would.

The results in Figure 2.7 show that children of all ages made changes that fall under the categories up to and including "deletion of elements"; that is, children of all age groups changed the shape/size of elements, the shape of whole and they deleted essential elements. However, a systematic analysis of deletions shows important differences between the two age groups (see discussion below). With respect to insertions of elements, position/orientation changes, and cross-category insertions, Figure 2.7 shows a dramatic contrast between the two age groups. The differences are highly significant ($\chi^2 = 17.64379$, d.f. = 1, $p < .0001$).

Although children of all ages used deletions, this category turned out to be particularly interesting across the two age groups. It is not possible to make a formal statistical analysis of the differences in the sequence of deletions between the two age groups, because video recordings were not taken. However, written notes were made on the protocols wherever deemed necessary (e.g., "added wings at the end of the drawing", "left leg was last thing drawn"). These notes, together with a

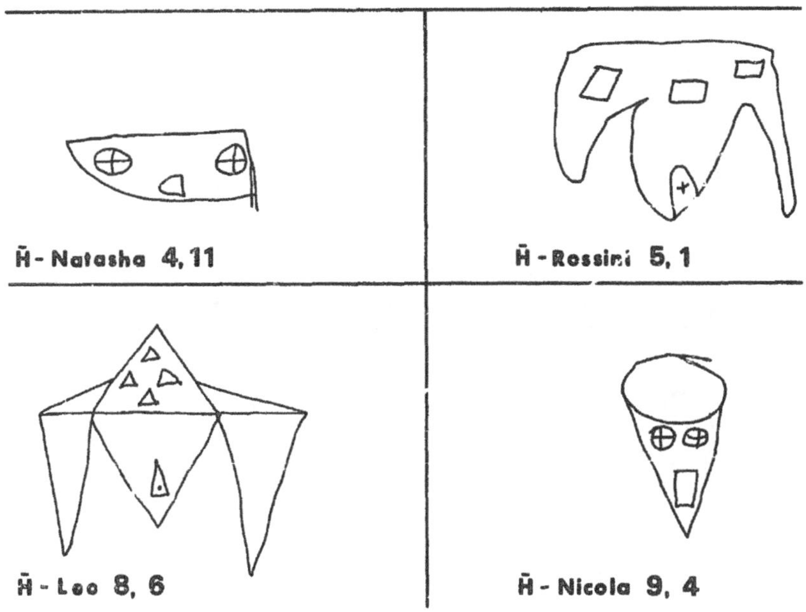

Figure 2.2 Shape of whole changed (ages are in years, months)

systematic analysis of what can be inferred from the product of many of the drawings (see, for example, Figure 2.3), made it possible to assert with some assurance that older children frequently deleted in the middle of their drawing procedure, whereas the younger age group made deletions of elements which are drawn towards the end of a procedure and did not continue drawing after deletions. The subjects in the follow-up study, for which sequence was carefully recorded on a copy drawn by a second experimenter during their productions, confirmed this.

The very few 4- to 6-year-olds who made changes classifiable in the last three categories (insertions of elements, position/orientation changes, cross-category insertions) all added elements after finishing a normal X, for example by adding a chimney emerging horizontally from the side wall of a house, or a smile on a house, and did not make insertions into the middle of their drawing procedure as did older children when drawing, for instance, a man with two heads.

Follow-up experiment

A second experiment was carried out to verify whether the absence of certain changes made by otherwise successful 4- to 6-year-olds was merely due to a lack of inventiveness, that is, that they simply had not thought of making insertions and cross-category changes when drawing X's that did not exist, or whether a deeper reason lay behind this. Ten 5-year-olds (mean age 5;7) were first tested with the above experimental technique. Eight of the subjects were retained

Figure 2.3 Deletion of elements (ages are in years, months)

because they successfully made changes to all three drawings but only changes that involved size, shape and deletion. These children were then asked to "draw a man with two heads" and to "draw a house with wings"; that is, they were explicitly instructed to introduce types of change typical of the spontaneous productions of older subjects.

As the first young subject began to draw a second head, I was reminded of T.E. Huxley's lament: "the great tragedy of science; the slaying of a beautiful hypothesis by an ugly fact"! However the first subject, and all but one of the seven others tested, then went on laboriously and very slowly to draw two bodies,

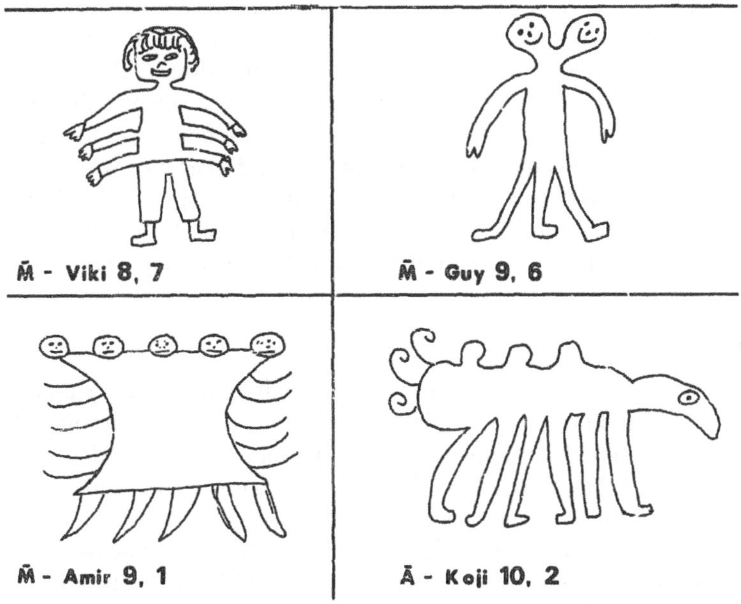

Figure 2.4 Insertion of new elements (ages are in years, months)

Figure 2.5 Position/orientation changed (ages are in years, months)

two arms and legs on each body, etc.; that is, they used a complete man-drawing procedure for each head, and they kept starting again because dissatisfied with the result. They manifested similar difficulties simply copying a model provided by the experimenter and succeeded only very laboriously and slowly. By contrast, when 8- to 10-year-olds interrupted sequential order to insert a new subroutine for drawing a second head, they continued drawing a single body with the speed of their normal drawing procedure. Moreover, when the 5-year-olds were asked to draw "a house with wings" (a spontaneous cross-category response also typical of older subjects' solutions), they all did so rapidly and successfully. The reason for these differences will be discussed in the final section, to which we now turn.

Discussion

In the 1960s and early 1970s, mainstream research in cognitive development focused on early and middle childhood, the neonate and infant being considered a sensori-motor organism with no built-in symbolically represented knowledge. By contrast, the last decade has seen a flourishing of infancy research, mainly within a nativist framework. The infant has been shown to be born with an impressive repertory of domain-specific knowledge and computational capacities (e.g., Anderson, 1988; Baillargeon, 1986; Diamond & Gilbert, 1989; Johnson et al., 1991; Leslie & Keeble, 1987; Handler, 1988; Mehler et al., 1988; Spelke, 1982). It might therefore seem that middle childhood should be relegated to a relatively secondary position in developmental theorizing. However, it is important to bear in mind that the greater the proportion of biologically specified properties of the infant mind, the more constrained its system is likely to be (Chomsky, 1988). In other words, despite the initial adaptive advantage, the consequence of the efficiency and automaticity of the infant's cognitively encapsulated systems is that they are relatively rigid. This means that the more complex a picture ultimately built of the innate capacities of the infant mind, the more important it is for developmentalists to focus on explaining the subsequent flexibility of the mind. Representational change, and constraints thereupon, thus constitute an essential complement to the current focus on infancy.

This paper set out to explore constraints on representational change beyond infancy; that is, how procedures are not only activated and run, but how knowledge embedded in procedures gradually becomes available, after redescription, as part of the system's data structures. Note that the original procedures continue to be available as compiled unit that is, children can still run, say, their normal house-drawing procedure. It is a redescription of the procedures that is operated on to introduce change.

It has been shown that two sequential constraints obtain. One is at the procedural level, a procedure being by definition a set of sequential instructions. The second sequential constraint operates at the first level of representational redescription. The results of the present study show that for younger children redescribed components of the drawing procedure are available as data and can therefore take new variables with respect to size and shape, for instance.

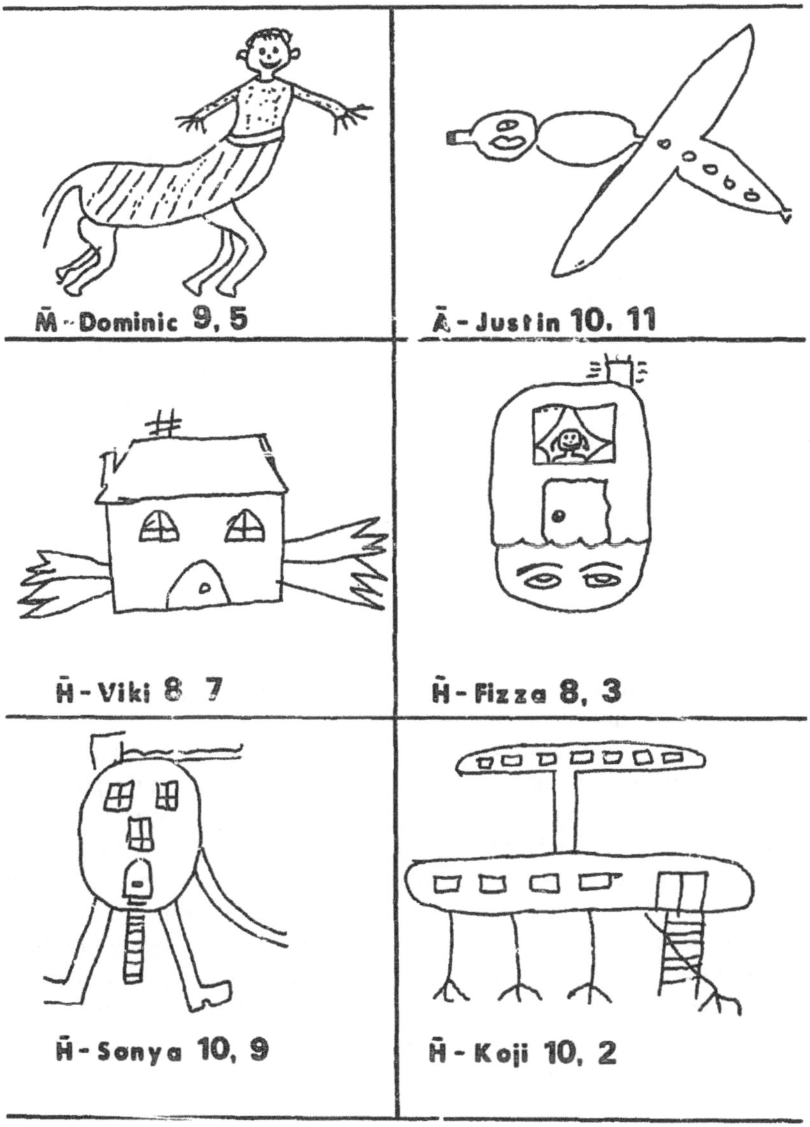

Figure 2.6 Insertion of cross-category elements (ages are in years, months)

However, the order in which components are operated on is constrained by the same sequential specification as at the procedural level. The striking developmental difference brought to light here suggests that children's subsequent redescriptions of representations are not constrained by a sequential specification, thus allowing for intra- and inter-representational flexibility.

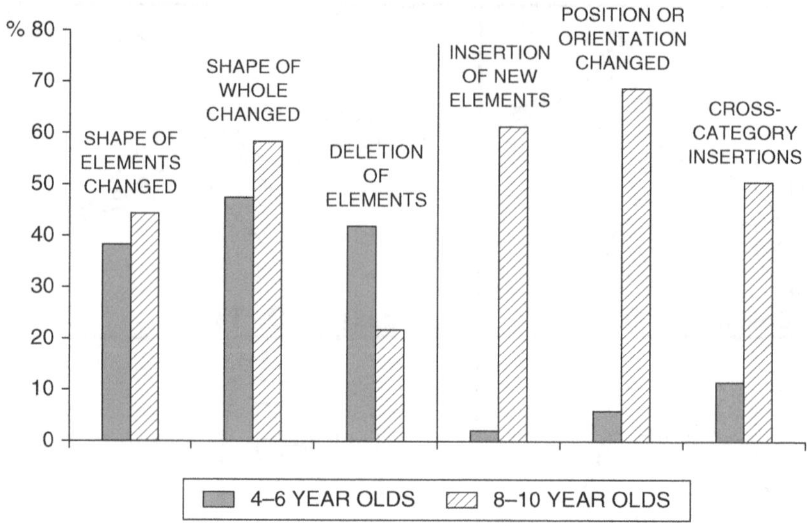

Figure 2.7

The difference between levels of redescription was particularly clear in the case of deletions and insertions. Figure 2.3 gave some typical examples of the difference between younger and older children's capacities. Younger children deleted at the end of procedures, involving no interruption in sequential order (see, for example, Peter, 5;3 years). Older children tended to delete at any point in the procedure and to continue with the rest of the drawing (see, for example, Valerie, 9;0 years). Whilst changes in position and orientation do not necessarily involve interruption of sequence and treating components as separate entities, in many cases of the 8- to 10-year-olds they did (see, for example, Jessie, 9;8 years and Justin, 10;11 years, in Figure 2.5). Very few younger children used within- or cross-category insertions and those who did made their additions at the end of their drawing procedure. By contrast, older children interrupted sequence to add extra heads or arms (see, for example, Viki, 8;7 years and Guy, 9;6 years in Figure 2.4, and Sonya, 10;9, in Figure 2.6). When, as is the case for 8- to 10-year-olds, the sequential constraint is relaxed, this does not mean that sequence is no longer represented, but rather that it does not rigidly constrain output. Obviously we continue to use sequence when it is appropriate, as is the case for some of the changes introduced by older subjects. Moreover, the relaxation of the sequential constraint does not only mean that children become capable of interrupting sequence and introducing sub-routines. It results in much greater intra- and inter-representational flexibility, allowing children to access elements from other conceptual categories and establish inter-representational links – an essential component of human creativity.

Why were the younger subjects in the follow-up experiment able to rapidly draw a house with wings although unable, except very laboriously, to draw a man with two heads? My argument is that it is for the very same reasons of constraint on sequence. In the case of a man with two heads, the sequential order of the normal drawing procedure must be interrupted. However, in the case of a house with wings, the child can add the wings at the end of a house-drawing procedure which, when called, has been run through in its entire sequence. Moreover, it is the experimenter who supplied the cross-category reference for the addition of wings which could be accessed independently of the house-drawing procedure, after it had been run.

One might argue that older subjects who insert something at the beginning of a procedure are also "merely running a procedure in its entirety". This is not so, in my view. To run a procedure, the system must call the procedure and, once called, it must run through in its entirely, if "merely run". By contrast, if, once called, something is then inserted prior to running it, this involves a subroutine interrupting the procedural sequence. The child capable of adding something to the end of a procedure, that is, merely putting a stop function on their procedure, is not yet at this level. Moreover, when young subjects are finally successful at drawing (or copying) a two-headed man, they are not using the flexibility of a redescribed man-drawing procedure that can be pursued rapidly. Rather, they are laboriously and slowly creating de novo a new procedure. This is in contrast to older children who inserted a sub-routine into their rapid drawing procedure. It would be an error of confounding external product and internal representation to think that the same product (e.g., the finished drawing of a two-headed man) is necessarily generated from identical internal representations. The same holds for identical output in language which can stem from very different internal representations (Karmiloff-Smith, 1979a).

That at the procedural level skills are sequentially constrained has been amply discussed and documented (Bruner, 1970; Dean, Scherzer & Chabaud, 1986; Fuson, Richards & Brians, 1982; Goodnow & Levirie, 1973; Greenfield & Schneider, 1977; Huttenlocher, 1967; Kosslyn, Cave, Provost & von Gierke, 1988; Lashley, 1951; Premack, 1975; Restle, 1970). Logically, once the knowledge embedded in a procedure is available as part of the system's data structures, it could be represented in a variety of formats. What the present research has shown is that at the first level of redescription the internal representation of the knowledge is specified as a sequentially fixed list, embodying the sequential constraint inherent at the procedural level. In other words, as could be seen from the changes introduced by the younger children as compared to the older group, it is clear that the sequential constraint holds even beyond the procedural level.

A sequential specification can be a limitation on any system. Work on mental imagery has demonstrated that a sequential procedure for recognizing a cube, for example, is far beyond our ability to operate on as a single integrated data structure. Yet we are only aware of such limitations when asked to compute something new that requires operation on the data structure as a whole (Hinton, 1979). However, a sequential constraint is not only a limitation on a system. If a domain is sequential by its very nature, then a sequential constraint in early learning can actually potentiate progress. Although sequence may restrict flexibility, it helps to get development off the ground by inputting representations into the mind in just those areas where sequence is important, for example early language, counting, drawing. If we take the case of early language, it might be objected that whilst sequence may be important for a relatively fixed word order language like English, this would not hold for an inflected language with free word order. However, data from Slobin on the acquisition of Russian (1966) show that even where the adult model does not provide fixed word order children initially get their language off the ground by using only one of the various possible word orders. In other words, they impose on themselves, presumably because it potentiates their learning, a temporary sequential constraint. In languages where the morphology is rich and receives full stress (e.g., Turkish, see Slobin, 1982), children may prefer this as an alternative route for potentiating their initial comprehension strategies. Nonetheless sequence seems to play an initially important role in potentiating production strategies. Furthermore, outside the area of language, it has been shown that the encoding of sequence often acts as a cognitive prop for young children in their attempts to attribute cause and intention (Dasser, Ulbaek, & Premack, 1989). Thus, sequential constraints both impede and potentiate learning. Yet, as the present study shows, even under a sequential constraint changes can and do occur.

I have argued that at the level of behavioural mastery procedures are compiled and automatized. Is this not a contradiction with Van Sommers' recent claim that children do not consistently repeat the same drawing (Van Sommers, 1984)? In my view, there is no contradiction. It is important to distinguish between tasks which involve highly practised procedures (house-drawing, man-drawing, etc.) which were purposefully chosen for the present study, versus tasks involving repeated attempts at drawing something new. In the present study, children had already reached behavioural mastery, whereas Van Sommers' work involved the study of children's repeated, partially successful attempts at producing drawings of a tennis shoe, a light bulb, a tape dispenser and a paper punch. Clearly, not only children but non-artist adults would have trouble drawing any of these and would show inconsistency across different attempts. As Freeman (1987) cogently argues, learning to draw something new involves allocating mental resources to both monitoring what is emerging on the page over time against a goal-directed plan and balancing the implementation of pre-planned decisions with on-the-spot repairs on the picture plane. By contrast, an already compiled house-drawing procedure is run off fast and automatically and, although repeated drawings may involve minor changes at the level of denotation (e.g., addition of a door knob, an extra window), initially they do not involve changes in sequential order.

Here and elsewhere I have argued that certain aspects of change are endogenously driven. Freeman (1980) offers another explanation for what impedes changes in drawings of men and houses which tend to remain "formula-driven", that is, stereotyped. He argues that drawing is a non-communicative act and that, unlike language, there is rather limited scope for ongoing social interaction to alter the course of the drawing. This would tend to imply that change is exogenously driven, since lack of social interaction and correction are invoked as a reason for why drawings remain formula-driven. However, even if drawings were changed due to feedback, this is only given exogenously on the drawing product, not on the drawing process itself. The child must build up and change sequential representations endogenously. Freeman is right in stressing that children and adults continue in normal circumstances to produce formula-driven drawings if they are not artists. However, such externalized depictions are not necessarily informative about potential internal capacities. The present experiment shows that given appropriate instructions even young children can change their formula-driven drawing procedures. There is an essential difference between external behaviour (the formula-driven drawings usually produced by non-artist children and adults) and internal representations which, as the present and previous research suggests, undergo developmental changes with respect to accessibility and flexibility. Like language where children go beyond behavioural mastery, that is, beyond communicative adequacy (Karmiloff-Smith, 1979a, b), change in drawing is also endogenously driven and not solely subject to external, communicative influences. It is part of the natural developmental process of representational redescription and progressive explicitation.

This is not to deny that external influences on children's drawing can be effective. I am not of course arguing that change is due *solely* to endogenous causes. Rather, when change is exogenously provoked, subsequent endogenously provoked representational change must still take place. Representational redescription and change is not to be equated with mere representational adjunction (i.e., adding a new representation on the basis of external stimuli). Drawing research successfully inducing change exogenously (Cox, 1985; Davis, 1985; Freeman, 1980; Pemberton & Nelson, 1987; Phillips, Inall & Lauder, 1985) has only demonstrated modest, if any, generalization of the results of such training. Thus, Pemberton and Nelson (1987) trained young children on various draw-a-man skills but only had "modest evidence that some generalization of the new drawing skills carried over to house drawing". Likewise, successful training on draw-a-cube did not transfer to draw-a-pyramid nor vice versa (Phillips et al., 1985). A further example comes from Cox (1985). She successfully trained children to change from object-centred to viewer-centred depictions but, as she herself notes, "the training procedures merely create a new entry in the child's repertoire for producing specific graphic outputs, given specific prompting inputs". Thus, when exogenous training is used, children are not inducing a general solution to a projection problem but merely building a separate structural description (Freeman, 1987). In other words, according to the model developed here, children are adding a new, independently stored procedure which will have to undergo representational redescription and explication – an endogenously provoked process – before becoming a data structure available to other parts of the system.

Most developmental work on children's drawing has focused on the progression from inadequate depictions to adult-like competence (e.g., Freeman & Cox, 1985; Goodnow, 1977). For example, to account for how children progressively become able to represent action in their hitherto static drawings of the human figure, Goodnow (1978) has argued that children first change so-called peripheral or accessory parts of the figure. These include, for Goodnow, legs, arms, and facial features. Thus, when asked to draw a man picking up a ball, young subjects draw a rigid, upright trunk to which they attach an elongated arm which can make contact with the ball. Only later in development do children change so-called core parts of the figure, for example draw the trunk of the body bending towards the ball. By peripheral and core, it would seem that Goodnow is referring to spatial distinctions (e.g., she refers to the trunk as "the centre of the figure to which other units are attached") rather than to conceptual distinctions. In the present study, by contrast, trunk, arms, legs and facial features are all taken to be part of the defining core characteristics of manhood, whereas hats, walking sticks, etc., are considered peripheral. The vast majority of children in the present study were all successful at making changes to core characteristics of manhood, househood and animalhood.

It could be that it is those very few subjects who were not successful in drawing an X that doesn't exist that are similar to Goodnow's younger subjects who failed to adequately represent a bending person. However, in the present study subjects were purposefully chosen at an age when in principle they would be successful at the task, and indeed 20 of the 22 younger subjects (as well as all of the older group) made changes to both peripheral and core elements as defined by Goodnow. Goodnow explains developmental change in terms of a movement in external depictions from periphery to core, which may indeed be an appropriate account of early drawing output progressively leading to behavioural mastery, that is, prior to the moment at which my experimental subjects were chosen. The present model goes beyond the observed changes in drawing output and explains general developmental change in terms of a movement from an internal representation specified as a sequentially fixed list of core features (embodying a constraint that was inherent in the procedural representation still available to the system), to an internal representation specified as a structured, yet flexibly ordered set of manipulate core features.

The theoretical framework used here is not only relevant to children's drawings, but has been used to account for aspects of children's theory building in physics (Karmiloff-Smith, 1984, 1988) and of lexico-morphological development in language (Karmiloff-Smith, 1979a, 1986). Some interesting conjectures have been offered in favour of a formal homology between certain syntactic structures in language and the development of action strategies (Goodson & Greenfield, 1975; Greenfield, Nelson & Saltzman, 1972; Huttenlocher, Eisenberg & Straus, 1968; Robert & Sinclair, 1974; Sinclair, 1971). Here I am not suggesting that the acquisition of syntax and the development of skills such as drawing are analogous processes – on the contrary. My view is that the basic syntactic component of language is innately specified and modular. So-called "learning" of sentential syntax is not constrained in my opinion by general cognitive factors. This would explain the data collected from retarded children with very low IQ but who can nonetheless produce fluent, syntactically complex language (Bellugi, 1987; Cromer, 1994). And there exist, of course, mentally retarded children and adults whose linguistic capacities are meagre but who are extraordinary artists (Hermelin & O'Connor, 1983; Selfe, 1985). However, innately specified linguistic and non-linguistic procedures, in the idiot-savant and in normal subjects, are not in my view available as data structures to other parts of the system. They are simply run.

To become available to cross-domain relationships, the knowledge embedded in procedures has to be redescribed and represented explicitly in central processing (Karmiloff-Smith, 1986). It is this step that I have argued is not available to the linguistic and artistic idiot-savant. The redescribed representations of normally developing children are available to central processing and form part of the basis for their spontaneous theory-building about the physical, social and linguistic environments (Karmiloff-Smith, 1979a, 1984, 1989). Once representations are dealt with centrally, they are constrained by general cognitive processes.

The new results of the present study can also be related to other aspects of language, a link to which my earlier research on more general aspects of representational change did not point. Indeed, the initial sequential constraint on representational redescription suggests a related explanation for data to be found in the literature on phonological awareness. In some interesting developmental work in this area (Bryant & Alegria, 1987), it has been shown that when children are asked to perform tasks involving the deletion of phonemes, they are initially more successful at deleting the final phoneme of a word, rather than the initial one. In the terms developed in this paper, initially children's phonemic representation is specified sequentially; they can put a stop function on the procedure but cannot yet insert anything once the procedure has been called. A similar empirical pattern can be found by comparing illiterate, newly literate, and literate adults. Morais, Alegria, and Content (1987) found that, whereas illiterate adults could not do the phonological awareness task at all, that is, they had not reached behavioural mastery, newly literate adults could only do one aspect of the task: that involving deletion of phonemes at the end of words, but not at the beginning of words. Thus, within the model developed here, it can be argued that once these adults had reached a degree of behavioural mastery in their literacy their initial redescription of the phonemic representations was constrained sequentially. These data are therefore suggestive of the same initial sequential constraint on representational redescription that I have been arguing for in this paper; that is, when adults first become literate they are constrained in the flexibility of their access to phonological knowledge.

Thus, an initial sequential constraint on the first level of redescription holds for both children and adults when knowledge is re-represented; that is, the process involves a phase in a reiterated cycle of representational change, and not a developmental stage only to be found in children.

The theoretical framework used here to account for representational changes underlying drawing output also suggests a link with the acquisition of musical skills. Take playing the piano as an example. Initially, there is a period during which a sequence of notes is laboriously practised; this is followed by a period during which the piece can be played automatically, but the automaticity is constrained by the fact that the learner can neither start in the middle of the piece nor play variations on a theme (Hermelin & O'Connor, 1989). The procedure is simply run off in its entirety. Subsequently, however, the learner can interrupt the piece and start at, say, the third bar without having to repeat the entire procedure from the outset. Finally the learner can play variations on a theme, changing various aspects of the sequential order, introducing insertions and so forth. Once again, the end result is representational flexibility and control.

Although not situated within the framework of representational redescription, sequential constraints on output have been documented in studies of seriation and hierarchical constructions (Cromer, 1983; Freeman, 1980; Gilliéron, 1976; Goodson & Greenfield, 1975; Greenfield, 1978; Greenfield et al., 1972; Greenfield & Schneider, 1977; Kilcher & Robert, 1977; Piaget & Inhelder, 1948). For example, in seriation tasks children can first only add elements to the ends of series, subsequently they can add elements to the beginning of series, and only much later can they introduce new elements within an already formed series. This holds both for simple seriation tasks with toddlers (Greenfield et al., 1972) and in more complex seriaton tasks with older children (Gilliéron, 1976; Piaget & Inhelder, 1948). Greenfield has clearly demonstrated that interruption and the insertion of subroutines is a problem that recurs at different moments in development and across a variety of linguistic and construction tasks. Analogous to the principle of interruption that operates at the surface structure level of language (Sever, 1970), Greenfield argues that interruption in action strategies should be considered as a surface structure dimension (Greenfield, 1978).

The present study highlighted two types of sequential constraint. One is that embedded in a rigidly ordered procedure which cannot yet be operated on or changed. This is consonant with Greenfield's arguments that in their initial efforts to master a new domain children follow a chaining strategy that is cognitively less demanding than strategies involving interruption (Greenfield, 1978; see, also, Ninio & Lieblich, 1976). These authors focus on constraints on strategies, without situating them within the broader context of representational redescription. My argument is that mastery in the output activated by such procedural representations constitutes a prerequisite to subsequent representational redescription (Karmiloff-Smith, 1979a, 1986), resulting initially in a second sequential constraint.

The sequential constraint seems to be part of a broader intra-representational rigidity which, when relaxed, constitutes one of several processes leading to inter-representational flexibility. It is this general inter-representational flexibility that was the focus of my earlier work (Karmiloff-Smith, 1979a, 1984, 1986). The present study has specified more clearly the constraints on internal representational change. Development appears to involve reiterated cycles of representational change, from the simple running of automatized procedures, to redescriptions of internal representations specified as a sequentially fixed list, and then to internal representations specified as a structured yet flexibly ordered set of features, that is, a manipulable concept. The sequential specification of a redescribed procedure constitutes a second phase, after behavioural mastery, in a complex cycle of internal redescription and explicitation, ultimately leading in some cases to conscious access and verbal report (Karmiloff-Smith, 1986). In my view, situating sequential constraints within this broader context of multiple representational levels, and linking redescription processes to cognitive flexibility and ultimate conscious access, offers a new, deeper account of developmental change.

Acknowledgments

I should like to express my thanks to the staff and pupils of Marlborough School, Harrow, and the King Alfred School, London, for their willing cooperation when I collected the data in their schools. Lesley Howard and Yara-Natasha Karmiloff are warmly thanked for acting as independent judges for the initial data analysis. A paper based on this research was presented at the Workshop on the Production of Drawings: Developmental Trends and Neurological Correlates, held at San Diego, January 1987. I would like to acknowledge helpful comments from the participants at that meeting, particularly Larry Fenson, Joan Stiles-Davis, Dennie Wolf, and Jean Mandler, who also provided feedback on the subsequent manuscript. I would also like to thank Mike Anderson, Susan Carey, Mani Das Gupta, Norman Freeman, Samuel Guttenplan, Mark Johnson, John Morton, Dick Neisser, Elizabeth Pemberton, David Premack, Neil Smith, Aaron Sloman, Liliana Tolchinsky-Landsmann and two anonymous reviewers for comments on an earlier draft.

Notes

1 It is important to note that the use of the term "representation" differs according to the focus of study (for discussion, see Mandler, 1983; Sperber, 1985). In the traditional drawing literature, "representation" is usually employed to refer to the externalized form that children put to paper, that is, the depiction. In this article, I will use the term "representation" solely in the sense of something internal to the child's mind.

2 It should further be noted that the category "animal that doesn't exist" was not as clear-cut as house and man. The reason for this is obvious since "animal" can be anything from a bird to an elephant, that is, involving totally different drawings. Had I abstracted the animal data and only analysed the house and man data, then agreement between judges and all relevant statistics would have been even clearer.

References

Anderson, M. (1988). Inspection time, information processing and the development of intelligence. *British Journal of Developmental Psychology*, *6*, 43–57.

Baillargeon, R. (1986). Representing the existence and the location of hidden objects: Object permanence in 6 and 8-month old infants. *Cognition*, *23*, 21–41.

Bellugi, U. (1987). Talk given at the MacArthur Workshop on the Production of Drawing: Developmental trends and neurological correlates. San Diego, January 1987.

Bever, T.G. (1970). The cognitive basis for linguistic structures. In J.R. Hayes (Ed.), *Cognition and language learning*. New York: Wiley.

Bialystok, E., & Olson, D.R. (1987). Spatial categories: The perception and conceptualization of spatial relations. In S. Hamad (Ed.), *Categorical perception* (pp. 511–531). Cambridge: Cambridge University Press.

Bolger, F. (1988). Children's Notational Competence. Unpublished PhD thesis, MRC Cognitive Development Unit & University College, London.

Bolger, F., & Karmiloff-Smith, A. (1990). The development of communicative competence: Are notational systems like language? *Archives de Psychologie*, *58*, 257–273.

Bruner, J.S. (1970). The growth and structure of skill. In K. Connolly (Ed.), *Mechanisms of motor development* (pp. 63–92). New York: Academic Press.

Bryant, P., & Alegria, J. (1987). *The transition to written language*. Paper presented at the European Science Foundation Workshop on Transition Mechanisms in Cognitive/Emotional Development. Grachen, Switzerland.

Catan, L. (1987). Literacy and cognition: A microgenetic study of the construction and transformation of rhythm representation during acquisition of musical literacy. Unpublished DPhil, Sussex University.

Chomsky, N. (1988). *Language and problems of knowledge: The Managua Lectures*. Cambridge, MA: MIT Press.

Cohen, S.R. (1935). The development of constraints on symbol-meaning structure in notation: Evidence from production, interpretation and forced-choice judgements. *Child Development*, *56*, 177–195.

Cox, M.V. (1985). One object behind another. Young children's use of array-specific or view-specific representations. In N.H. Freeman & M.V. Cox (Eds.), *Visual order: The nature and development of pictorial representation* (pp. 188–201). London: Cambridge University Press.

Cromer, R.F. (1983). Hierarchical planning disability in the drawings and constructions of a special group of severely aphasic children. *Brain and Cognition*, *2*, 144–164.

Cromer, R.F. (1994). A case study of dissociations between language and cognition. In H. Tager-Flueberg (Ed.), *Constraints on language acquisition: Studies of atypical children* (pp. 141–153). Hillsdale, NJ: Erlbaum.

Dasser, V., Ulbaeck, I., & Premack, D. (1989). The perception of intention. *Science*, *243*, 365–367.

Davis, A.M. (1985). The canonical bias: Young children's drawing of familiar objects. In N.H. Freeman & M.V. Cox (Eds.), *Visual order: The nature and development of pictorial representation* (pp. 202–213). London: Cambridge University Press.

Dean, A.L., Scherzer, E., & Chabaud, S. (1986). Sequential ordering in children's representations of rotation movements. *Journal of Experimental Child Psychology*, *42*, 99–114.

Diamond, A., & Gilbert, J. (1989). Development as progressive inhibitory control of action: Retrieval of a contiguous object. *Cognitive Development*, *4*, 127–152.

Freeman, N.H. (1980). *Strategies of representation in young children: Analysis of spatial skills and drawing processes*. London: Academic Press.

Freeman, N.H. (1987). Current problems in the development of representational picture production. *Archives de Psychologic*, *55*, 127–152.

Freeman, N.H., & Cox, M.V. (Eds.) (1985). *Visual order: The nature and development of pictorial representation*. London: Cambridge University Press.

Fuson, K., Richards, J., & Brians, D. (1982). The acquisition and elaboration of the number word sequence. In C.J. Brainerd (Ed.), *Children's logical and mathematical cognition* (pp. 33–92). New York: Springer-Verlag.

Gardner, H. (1980). *Artful scribbles: The significance of children's drawings*. New York: Basic Books.

Gilliéron, C. (1976). Décalages et sériation. *Archives de Psychologie*, *44*, Monographie 3.

Goodnow, J.J. (1977). *Children's drawing*. London: Fontana.

Goodnow, J.J. (1978). Visible thinking: Cognitive aspects of change in drawings. *Child Development*, *49*, 637–641.

Goodnow, J.J., & Levine, R.A. (1973). The grammar of action: Sequence and syntax in children's copying. *Cognitive Psychology*, *4*, 82–98.

Goodson, B.D., & Greenfield, P.M. (1975). The search for structural principles in children's manipulative play: A parallel with linguistic development. *Child Development*, *46*, 734–746.

Greenfield, P.M. (1978). Structural parallels between language and action in development. In A. Lock (Ed.), *Action, symbol and gesture: The emergence of language* (pp. 415–445). London: Academic Press.

Greenfield, P.M., Nelson, K., & Saltzman, E. (1972). The development of rulebound strategies for manipulating seriated cups: A parallel between action and grammar. *Cognitive Psychology, 3*, 291–310.

Greenfield, P.M., & Schneider, L. (1977). Building a tree structure: The development of hierarchical complexity and interrupted strategies in children's construction activity. *Developmental Psychology, 13*, 299–313.

Hermelin, B., & O'Connor, N. (1983). Flawed genius or clever Hans? *Psychological Medicine, 13*, 479–481.

Hermelin, B., & O'Connor, N. (1989). Intelligence and musical improvisation. *Psychological Medicine, 19*, 447–457.

Hinton, G.E. (1979). Some demonstration of the effect of structural descriptions in mental imagery. *Cognitive Science, 3*, 231–250.

Huttenlocher, J. (1967). Children's ability to order and orient objects. *Child Development, 38*, 1169–1176.

Huttenlocher, J., Eisenberg, K., & Straus, S. (1968). Comprehension: Relation between perceived actor and logical subject. *Journal of Verbal Learning and Verbal Behaviour, 7*, 527–530.

Johnson, M., Dziurawiec, S., Ellis, H., & Morton, J. (1991). Newborns' preferential tracking of face-like stimuli and its subsequent decline. *Cognition, 40*, 1–19.

Karmiloff-Smith, A. (1979a). *A functional approach to child language*. Cambridge University Press.

Karmiloff-Smith, A. (1979b). Micro- and macro-developmental changes in language acquisition and other representational systems. *Cognitive Science, 3*, 81–118.

Karmiloff-Smith, A. (1979c). Problem-solving procedures in children's construction and representation of closed railway circuits. *Archives de Psychologie, 1807*, 37–59.

Karmiloff-Smith, A. (1984). Children's problem-solving. In M.E. Lamb, A.L. Brown & B. Rogoff (Eds.), *Advances in developmental psychology, Vol. III* (pp. 39–90). Hillsdale, NJ: Erlbaum.

Karmiloff-Smith, A. (1985). A constructivist approach to modelling linguistic and cognitive development. *Archives de Psychologic, 53*, 113–126.

Karmiloff-Smith, A. (1986). From meta-processes to conscious access: Evidence from children's metalinguistic and repair data. *Cognition, 23*, 95–147.

Karmiloff-Smith, A. (1988). The child is a theoretician, not an inductivist. *Mind and Language, 3*, 1–13.

Karmiloff-Smith, A. (1989). Language and cognition: Modular versus non-modular. *Human Development, 32*, 272–275.

Karmiloff-Smith, A. (1992). *Beyond modularity: A developmental perspective on cognitive science*. Cambridge, MA: MIT Press/Bradford Books.

Karmiloff-Smith, A., & Inhelder, B. (1974). If you want to get ahead, get a theory. *Cognition, 3*, 195–212.

Karmiloff-Smith, A., Johnson, H., Grant, J., Jones M.-C., Karmiloff, Y.-N., Bartrip, J., & Cuckle, P. (1993). From sentential to discourse functions: Detection and explanation of speech repairs by children and adults. *Discourse Processes, 16*, 565–589.

Kilcher, H., & Robert, M. (1977). Procedures d'actions lors de constructions de pools et d'escaliers. *Archives de Psychologie, 173*, 53–83.

Kosslyn, S.M., Cave, C.B., Provost, D.A., & von Gierke, S.M. (1988). Sequential processes in image generation. *Cognitive Psychology, 20*, 319–343.

Kosslyn, S.M., Heldmeyer, K.H., & Locklear, E.P. (1977). Children's drawings as data about internal representations. *Journal of Experimental Child Psychology*, *23*, 191–211.

Lashley, K.S. (1951). The problem of serial order in behavior. In L.A. Jeffress (Ed.), *Cerebral mechanisms in behaviors: The Hixon symposium* (pp. 112–146). New York: Wiley.

Laszlo, J.I., & Broderick, P.A. (1985). The perceptual-motor skill of drawing. In N.H. Freeman & M.V. Cox (Eds.), *Visual order: The nature and development of pictorial representation* (pp. 356–370). London: Cambridge University Press.

Leslie, A.M., & Keeble, S. (1987). Do six-month-old infants perceive causality? *Cognition*, *25*, 265–288.

Luquet, G.H. (1927). *Le dessin enfantin*. Paris: Alcan.

Mandler, J.M. (1983). Representation. In J. Flavell & E. Markman (Eds.), *Handbook of child psychology, Vol. 3*. New York: Wiley.

Mandler, J.M. (1988). How to build a baby: On the development of an accessible representational system. *Cognitive Development*, *3*, 113–136.

Mehler, J., Jusczyk, P., Lambertz, G., Halsted, N., Bertoncini, J., & Amiel-Tison, C. (1988). A precursor of language acquisition in young infants. *Cognition*, *29*, 143–178.

Miliar, S. (1975). Visual experience or translation rules? Drawing the human figure by blind and sighted children. *Perception*, *4*, 363–371.

Moore, V. (1986). The relationships between children's drawings and preferences for alternative depictions of a familiar object. *Journal of Experimental Child Psychology*, *42*, 187–198.

Morais, J., Alegria, J., & Content, A. (1987). The relationships between segmental analysis and alphabetic literacy: An interactive view. *Cahiers de Psychologie Cognitive*, *7*, 415–438.

Ninio, A., & Lieblich, A. (1976). "The grammar of action": "Phrase structure" in children's copying. *Child Development*, *47*, 846–849.

Olson, D.R., & Bialystok, E. (1983). *Spatial cognition*. London: Erlbaum.

Pemberton, E.F. (1987). The drawing rules of children: Sequence and direction. *Bulletin of the Psychonomic Society*, *25*, 383–386.

Pemberton, E.F., & Nelson, K.E. (1987). Using interactive graphic challenges to foster young children's drawing ability. *Visual Arts Research*, *13*, 29–41.

Phillips, W.A., Inall, M., & Lauder, E. (1985). On the discovery, storage and use of graphic descriptions. In N.H. Freeman & M.V. Cox (Eds.), *Visual order: The nature and development of pictorial representation* (pp. 122–134). London: Cambridge University Press.

Piaget, J., & Inhelder, B. (1948). *La représentation de l'espace chez l'enfant*. Paris: Presses Universitaires de France.

Premack, D. (1975). Putting a face together. *Science*, *188*, 228–236.

Restle, F. (1970). Theory of serial pattern learning: Structural trees. *Psychological Review*, *77*, 481–495.

Robert, M., & Sinclair, H. (1974). Reglages actifs et actions de transformations. *Archives de Psychologie*, *167/168*, 425–458.

Rutkowska, J.C. (1987). Computational models and developmental psychology. In J.C. Rutkowska & C. Cook (Eds.), *Computation and development* (pp. 187–215). Chichester: Wiley.

Selfe, L. (1985). Anomalous drawing development: Some clinical studies. In N.H. Freeman & M.V. Cox (Eds.), *Visual order: The nature and development of pictorial representation* (pp. 135–154). London: Cambridge University Press.

Sinclair, H. (1971). Sensori-motor action patterns as the condition for the acquisition of syntax. In R. Huxley & E. Ingrams (Eds.), *Language acquisition: Models and methods*. New York: Academic Press.

Slobin, D.I. (1966). The acquisition of Russian as a native language: In F. Smith & C.A. Miller (Eds.), *The genesis of language: A psycholinguistic approach*. Cambridge, MA: MIT Press.

Slobin, D.I. (1982). Universal and particular in the acquisition of language. In E. Wanner & L.R. Gleitman (Eds.), *Language acquisition: The state of the art* (pp. 128–170). Cambridge: Cambridge University Press.

Spelke, E.S. (1982). Perceptual knowledge of objects in infancy. In J. Mehler, E. Walker, & M. Garrett (Eds.), *Perspectives on mental representation* (pp. 409–430). Hillsdale, NJ: Erlbaum.

Sperber, D. (1935). Anthropology and psychology: Towards an epidemiology of representations. *Man*, *20*, 74–89.

Stiles-Davies, J. (1987). Paper presented at the MacArthur Workshop on the Production of Drawing: Developmental trends and neurological correlates. San Diego, January 1987.

Van Sommers, P. (1984). *Drawing and cognition: Descriptive and experimental studies of graphic production processes*. London: Cambridge University Press.

Willats, J. (1977). How children learn to draw realistic pictures. *Quarterly Journal of Experimental Psychology*, *29*, 367–382.

3 Précis of *Beyond modularity: A developmental perspective on cognitive science*

Annette Karmiloff-Smith

It is less illogical than it first appears to speak of instincts for inventiveness.
(Marler 1991, p. 63)

1. Taking the developmental perspective seriously

Beyond modularity: A developmental perspective on cognitive science (Karmiloff-Smith 1992a) not only aims to reach developmental psychologists, but also strives to persuade cognitive scientists to treat cognitive development as a serious theoretical science contributing to the discussion of *how* the human mind/brain develops and is organized internally, and not merely as a cute empirical database addressing the question of the age at which external behavior can be observed. Nowadays much of the literature focuses on what cognitive science can offer the study of development. In *Beyond modularity*, I concentrate, on what a developmental perspective can offer cognitive science and attempt to pinpoint what is specifically human about human cognition.

As Piaget's conception of the sensorimotor infant is being severely undermined by new paradigms for studying infancy, the battle between nativism and constructivism once again rears its rather unconstructive head. In *Beyond modularity*, I do not choose between these two epistemological stances, one arguing for predominantly built-in, domain-specific knowledge, and the other for a minimum innate underpinning to subsequent domain general learning. Rather, I suggest that nativism (when redefined within a truly epigenetic perspective of genetic expression rather than genetic unfolding), on the one hand, and Piaget's constructivism, on the other, are complementary in fundamental ways, and that the ultimate theory of human cognition will encompass aspects of both. *Beyond modularity* is intended to excite the reader about the possibilities of a developmental perspective embracing both domain-specific predispositions and constructivism and to demonstrate that one can attribute various innate processes/structures to the human neonate without denying the crucial roles of the physical and sociocultural environments and without jeopardizing the deep-seated conviction that we are special – creative, cognitively flexible, capable of conscious reflection, novel invention, and occasional inordinate stupidity!

Developmental psychologists of the Piagetian school are loath to attribute domain-specific predispositions to the human infant, yet they would not hesitate to do so with respect to the ant, the spider, the bee, or the chimpanzee. Why would Nature have endowed every species except the human with some domain-specific predispositions? Yet, if it turns out that all species have such predispositions, that most can maintain a goal in the face of changing environmental conditions, and that most have the capacity for learning on the basis of interaction with conspecifics and the physical environment, what is special about human cognition? Is it simply that the *content* of knowledge differs between species? Is it language that makes humans special? Or, compared to other species, are there qualitatively different processes at work across many domains of the human mind? Does human cognitive change affect all domains of knowledge more or less simultaneously, or does development occur in a domain-specific fashion? These are some of the questions addressed in *Beyond modularity*.

I argue that domain-specific predispositions give development a small but significant kickstart by focusing the young infant's attention on proprietary inputs. The early period is followed by intricate interaction with environmental input which in turn critically affects brain development as subsequent learning takes place. But development does not stop at efficient learning. A fundamental aspect of human development is the hypothesized process by which information that is *in* a cognitive system becomes progressively explicit knowledge *to* that system. I call this the "representational redescription" hypothesis (henceforth RR). Support for the theoretical discussions of Chapter 1 is explored in Chapters 2 through 6, calling on empirical findings on the child as a linguist, a physicist, a mathematician, a psychologist, and a notator. Each chapter concentrates first on the initial state of the infant mind/brain and on subsequent domain-specific learning in infancy and early childhood, and then goes on to explore empirical data on older children's problem solving and theory building, with particular focus on evolving cognitive flexibility and metacognition. Throughout, I place particular emphasis on the status of representations underlying different capacities and on the multiple levels at which knowledge is stored and accessible.

In Chapters 7 and 8, I reconsider the reconciliation between nativism and Piaget's constructivism, and I discuss the need for more formal developmental models. Here, I compare aspects of the RR framework with connectionist simulations of development. The book ends with a final look at the RR framework and conjectures about the status of representations underlying the structure of behavior in nonhumans, who never become re-describers of the implicit knowledge embedded in their behavior, no matter how complex the behavior.

If our focus is on cognitive flexibility and conscious access to knowledge, why not explore the data from adult psychology? Surely adults are far more flexible cognitively than children, so what justifies a developmental perspective? Not, rest assured, the fact that child data are "cute"! One need only glance at the developmental literature to notice that many researchers are absorbed with the ages at which children reach cognitive milestones. Decades of developmental research were wasted, in my view, because the focus was entirely on lowering the age at which children could perform a task successfully, without concern for *how* they processed the information. I once began an article (Karmiloff-Smith 1981, p. 151) as follows: "The enticing yet awful fact about child development is that children develop! Awful, because it has provoked a plethora of studies, totally unmotivated theoretically, accepted for publication in certain types of journal because the results are 'significant' – significant *statistically*, since it is indeed easy to obtain differential effects between, say, 5 and 7 year olds, but questionable as to their significance *scientifically*." Some researchers, however, use the study of development as a theoretical tool for exploring the human mind/brain from a cognitive science perspective. We are not really interested in children per se but in human cognition in general, which we believe can be more fully understood via its development.

A developmental perspective is essential to the analysis of human cognition because understanding the predispositions of the human mind/brain, the constraints on subsequent learning, and *how representations change progressively over time* can provide subtle clues to representational format in the adult mind. The work of Spelke (1991), which I discuss in Chapter 3, has been particularly influential in pointing to the importance of a developmental perspective on cognitive science. For example, the processes for segmenting visual arrays into objects are overlaid, in preschool children and adult, by other processes for recognizing object categories. But by focusing on how very young infants segment visual arrays into objects before they are able to categorize certain object kinds, Spelke is able to generate new hypotheses about how the visual system may actually function beyond infancy and in adults.

Another area in which the developmental perspective can change our view of the adult mind concerns the status of different types of representations. Distinctions such as declarative/procedural, conscious/unconscious, explicit/implicit, and controlled/automatic, which are often used to explain cognitive processing in adults, turn out to involve far more than a dichotomy when explored within a developmental context. But in assuming a developmental perspective we must take the notion "developmental" seriously. Paradoxically, studies on neonates and infants are often not developmental at all. Like studies on adults, they frequently focus not on change but on real-time processing within steady-state systems. It is of course essential to determine the initial state of the human mind/brain, but the "developmental" notion goes beyond the specification of initial predispositions. It does not simply mean a focus on learning in children of different ages rather than the adult. When one makes theoretical use of development in cognitive science the specific age at which children can successfully perform a task is, to some extent, irrelevant.

A developmental perspective focuses on behavioral and representational change over time. I often use a later phase in a developmental sequence to understand the status of representations underlying earlier behavior – particularly in the interesting cases where child and adult behaviors are practically identical. This notion of *representational change over time* is the focus throughout *Beyond modularity*.

It is for all these reasons that I hold that a developmental perspective is essential to cognitive science's efforts to understand the human mind more fully.

2. Is the initial architecture of the infant mind/brain modular?

Fodor's 1983 book, *The modularity of mind*, made a significant impact on developmental theorizing by suggesting how the nativist thesis and the domain-specificity of cognition are relevant to constraints on the architecture of the human mind/brain. In *Beyond modularity*, I critically discuss Fodor's thesis at some length but, since it has been the subject of a BBS treatment (Fodor 1985) it is unnecessary to reiterate all the details in the present Précis. A brief summary suffices to recall that according to Fodor the mind/brain is made up of genetically specified, independently functioning, special-purpose "modules" (or input systems). Each functionally distinct module has its own dedicated processes and proprietary inputs. Information from the external environment first passes through a system of sensory transducers, which transform the data into formats that each special-purpose module can process. Each module, in turn, outputs data in a common format suitable for central, domain-general processing. The modules are deemed to be hard-wired (not assembled from more primitive processes), of fixed neural architecture, domain specific, fast, autonomous, mandatory, automatic, stimulus driven, giving rise to shallow outputs; they are informationally encapsulated and insensitive to central cognitive goals. For Fodor, it is the co-occurrence of all the properties that defines a module. Modules, then, are the parts of the human mind that are inflexible and unintelligent. They are the stupidity in the machine – but they are just what a young organism might need to get initial cognition off the ground speedily and efficiently.

Fodor posits a built-in dichotomy between what is computed blindly by the modules and what the organism "believes." It is in "central processing" that computations relevant to the human belief system are processed, by deriving top-down hypotheses about what the world is like from the interface between the outputs of modules and what is already stored in long-term memory. Fodor considers central processing, in contrast to modules, to be influenced by what the system already knows, and therefore to be relatively unencapsulated, slow, non-mandatory, controlled, often conscious, and influenced by global cognitive goals. Central processing receives outputs from each module which are automatically translated into a common representational format, a language of thought (Fodor 1975). Central processing, then, is general-purpose. It is devoted to the fixation of belief, the building up of encyclopedic knowledge, and the planning of intelligent action, in contrast to the special-purpose, domain-specific computations of modules.

Although I endorse the importance of some aspects of Fodor's thesis for understanding the human mind/brain, I do not maintain the notion that modules are prespecified in detail, and I question the strictness of the dichotomy that Fodor draws between modules and central processing. I also challenge his contention that the outputs of modules are automatically encoded into a single common language of thought. I focus on the argument that a crucial aspect of development involves the RR process of going beyond modularity.

3. Prespecified modules versus a process of gradual modularization

Fodor's detailed account of the encapsulation of modules focuses predominantly on their role in on-line processing. There is little discussion of ontogenesis. I draw a distinction between the notion of prespecified modules versus that of a process of "modularization" (which, I speculate, occurs repeatedly as the *product* of development). Here I differ from Fodor's strict nativist conception. I hypothesize that if the human mind/brain ends up with any modular structure, then this is the result of a process of modularization *as development proceeds*. My position takes account of the plasticity of early brain development (Johnson 1990; 1993; Neville 1991), suggesting that a fairly limited number of innately specified, domain-specific predispositions would be sufficient to constrain the classes of inputs that the infant mind computes. These predispositions can operate at many different levels and do not have to be limited to representational content (see Karmiloff-Smith 1992b for more recent discussion). It can thus be hypothesized that, *with time*, brain circuits are progressively selected for different domain-specific computations. In certain cases, relatively encapsulated modules would be formed as a product of development. In other cases, there would be more room for influence from other computations.

Only future research using on-line brain activation studies with neonates and young infants can distinguish between the two hypotheses. If Fodor's thesis of pre-specified modules is correct, such studies should show that, from the very outset (or the moment at which the infant shows sensitivity to particular forms of input), specific brain circuits are activated in response to domain-specific inputs. By contrast, if the modularization thesis is correct, activation levels should initially be relatively distributed across the brain, and only with time (and this could be a short or relatively long time during infancy, depending on the domain) would specific circuits be activated in response to domain-specific inputs. The modularization thesis allows us to speculate that, although there are maturationally constrained attention biases and domain-specific predispositions that channel the infant's early development, this endowment involves far more than mere triggering. Rather, it interacts richly with, and is in return affected by, the environmental input.

Research with other species also demonstrates the brain's plasticity. In studies of the rat, for example, Greenough et al. (1987) have shown that the brain's losses and gains of synapses are a function of different types of experience. Thus, when placed merely for exercise in a treadmill, the rat shows an increase in blood capillaries in the cerebellum, but a decrease in synapses (due to pruning of existing neural pathways, because of the lack of stimulation other than physical exercise). However, when the rat is placed in a rich environment that challenges it to learn, substantial increases in dendritic growth and synaptic connectivity are generated.

Despite my reservations regarding Fodor's modularity thesis, I, together with a number of cognitive developmentalists, believe that Fodor's thesis has pointed to where a domain-general view of development such as Piaget's is likely to be wrong. In *Beyond modularity*, however, I argue for a more dynamic view of development that Fodor's modularity of mind and I challenge Fodor's dismissal of the relevance of a developmental perspective on cognitive science. Moreover, I question Fodor's often cited claim that "the limits of modularity are also likely to be the limits of what we are going to be able to understand about the mind" (1983, p. 126). I argue that cognitive scientists can go beyond modularity to study the more creative aspects of human cognition. But my contention is that such an endeavor is greatly enhanced by a developmental perspective on the problem.

4. Development from a domain-general perspective

Fodor's nativist thesis is in sharp contrast with domain-general theories of learning, such as Piaget's constructivist epistemology, once so popular in the developmental literature. According to Piagetian theory neither processing nor storage is domain specific. Of course, implicitly at least, Piagetians acknowledge that there are different sensory transducers for vision, audition, touch, and so forth. They do not accept, however, that the transducers transform data into innately specified, domain-specific formats for modular processing. Rather, for Piagetians, all data are processed by the same mechanisms and development involves domain-general changes in representational structures.

By opposing the domain-general view to the domain specific explanation of development, I suggest that Piaget and behaviorism have much in common. Neither the Piagetian nor the behaviorist grants the infant any innate structures or domain-specific knowledge. Each grants only some domain-general, biologically specified processes: for the Piagetians, a set of sensory reflexes and three functional processes (assimilation, accommodation, and equilibration); for the behaviorists, inherited physiological sensory systems and a complex set of laws of association. These domain-general learning processes are held to apply across all areas of linguistic and nonlinguistic cognition. Piaget and the behaviorists thus concur on a number of conceptions about the initial state of the infant mind/brain. The behaviorists saw the infant as a *tabula rasa* with no built-in knowledge (Skinner 1953). Piaget's view of the young infant as assailed by "undifferentiated and chaotic" inputs (Piaget 1955) is substantially the same.

Needless to say, there are fundamental differences between these two schools. Piagetians view children as active information constructors; behaviorists view them as passive information storers. Piagetians conceive of development as involving fundamental stagelike changes in logical structure, whereas behaviorists invoke a progressive accumulation of knowledge. However, in the present state of developmental theorizing, Piagetians and behaviorists have much in common in their view of the neonate's "knowledge-empty" mind and their claims that domain-general learning explains subsequent development across all aspects of language and cognition.

5. Development from a domain-specific perspective

The domain-specific thesis projects a very different picture of the young infant. Rather than being assailed by incomprehensible, chaotic data from many competing sources, the neonate is seen as having domain-specific predispositions allowing it to process specific types of inputs. Contrary to the Piagetian or the behaviorist theses, the domain-specific thesis gives the infant a very good start. This does not, of course, mean that nothing changes during infancy and beyond; the infant has much to learn, but subsequent learning is guided by innately specified, domain-specific principles, and these principles determine how subsequent learning takes place (Gelman 1990; Spelke 1991).

Irrespective of whether they agree with Fodor's strict modularity thesis, many psychologists now consider development to be domain-specific. Indeed, much depends on what one understands by "domain," and it is important not to confuse domain with ''module.'' From the point of view of the child's mind, a domain is the set of representations sustaining a specific area of knowledge: language, number, physics, and so forth. A module is an information-processing unit that encapsulates that knowledge and the computations on it. Thus, considering development to be domain specific does not necessarily imply considering it modular. In other words, the storing and processing of information may be domain specific without being encapsulated, hardwired, mandatory, and so on. Throughout *Beyond modularity*, I argue for the domain specificity of development rather than modularity in the strict Fodorian sense. I retain the term "domain" to cover language, physics, mathematics, and so forth. I also distinguish "microdomains" such as gravity within the domain of physics and pronoun acquisition within the domain of language. These microdomains can be thought of as subcomponents within particular domains.

The need for this finer distinction of what constitutes a domain stems from the fact that I put forward a *phase* model of development, rather than a *stage* model. In a stage model, such as Piaget's, overarching changes occur more or less contemporaneously across different domains. One alternative view is that broad changes occur within a domain – for example, that a particular type of change occurs first with respect to language and later with respect to physics. The model discussed in *Beyond modularity* differs from both of these. It invokes *recurrent phase changes* at different times across different microdomains and repeatedly within each domain.

The domain specificity of cognitive systems is also suggested by developmental neuropsychology, that is the existence of children in whom one or more domains are spared or impaired. For example, high functioning autistic individuals show a serious deficit in communication and reasoning about mental states (theory of mind), [see Gopnik: "How We Know our Minds" *BBS* 16(1) 1993; Tomasello et al.: "Cultural Learning" *BBS* 16(3) 1993.] the rest of their cognition being relatively unimpaired (Frith 1989). Individuals with Williams syndrome, by contrast, display a very uneven cognitive profile in which language, face recognition, and theory of mind seem relatively spared, whereas number, spatial cognition, and problem solving are severely retarded (Bellugi et al. 1988; Karmiloff-Smith et al., 1995). Whether autism and Williams syndrome involve domain-specific representational deficits or computational deficits, or both, remains an open question. There are also numerous cases of idiot savants in whom only one domain (such as drawing or calender calculation) functions at a high level, while capacities are extremely restricted over the rest of the cognitive system (Hermelin & O'Connor 1986). Domain-general theorists have difficulty explaining such within-domain and across-domain dissociations.

Adult brain damage also points to domain specificity. It is remarkably difficult to find examples in the neuropsychological literature of an across-the-board, domain-general disorder (Marshall 1984), although a case could be made for an overall deficit in planning in patients with prefrontal damage (Shallice 1988). In many instances, however, disorders of higher cognitive functions, as a consequence of brain damage, are often domain-specific – that is, they affect only face recognition, number, language, or some other facility, leaving the other systems relatively intact.

So if adults manifest domain-specific damage, and if it can be shown that infants come into the world with some domain-specific predispositions, does that not mean that the nativists have won the debate over the developmentalists still ensconced on the theoretical shores of Lake Geneva (Piaget's former bastion of antinativism and antimodularity)? Not necessarily, for two reasons. First, most nativist accounts call on detailed genetic unfolding, simply triggered by environmental stimuli. An epigenetic view is very different (see the excellent discussion in Oyama 1985). Second, it is important to bear in mind that the greater the number of the fixed domain-specific properties of the infant mind/brain, the less creative and flexible the subsequent system would be (Chomsky 1988). Although the fixed constraints provide an initial adaptive advantage, there is a tradeoff between efficiency and automaticity, on the one hand, and relative inflexibility, on the other. This leads me to a crucial point: *The more complex the picture we ultimately build of the innately specified predispositions of the infant mind, the more important it becomes for us to explain the flexibility of subsequent cognitive development.* It is toward such an end – exploring the flexibility and creativity of the human mind beyond the initial state – that my work in language acquisition and cognitive development has been concentrated, in an attempt to determine both the domain-specific and the domain-general contributions to development. It is implausible that development will turn out to be entirely domain specific *or* entirely domain general. And, although I will need to invoke some initial constraints, development clearly involves a more dynamic process of interaction between mind/brain and environment than the strict nativist stance presupposes.

6. Reconciling nativism and Piaget's constructivism

What theory of development could encompass the dynamics of a rich process of interaction between mind/brain and environment? At first blush, a theory with a central focus on epigenesis and constructivism, like Piaget's, would seem the most appropriate. The notion of constructivism in Piaget's theory is the equivalent at the cognitive level of the notion of epigenesis at the level of gene expression. For Piaget, both gene expression and cognitive development are emergent products of a self-organizing system that is directly affected by its interaction with the environment. Fodor (1983, p. 33) uses the term "constructivism" very differently from Piaget. For Fodor, it is a form of empiricism, whereas Piaget argued that his constructivist genetic epistemology was an alternative to both nativism and empiricism. This general aspect of Piaget's theory, if more formalized, may well turn out to be appropriate for future explorations of the notion of progressive modularization discussed above. Much of the rest of Piaget's theory, however, has come under a great deal of criticism.

A growing number of cognitive developmentalists have become disenchanted with Piaget's account of the infant as a purely sensorimotor organism. For Piaget, the newborn has no domain-specific knowledge, merely sensory reflexes and the three domain-general processes of assimilation, accommodation, and equilibration. By contrast, the infancy research I discuss in the first part of Chapters 2 through 6 of *Beyond modularity* suggests that there is considerably more to the initial state of the mind/brain than Piaget's theory posits. But the exclusive focus of nativists like Fodor and Chomsky on biologically specified modules suggests that they think there is nothing of interest to say about development beyond modularity. Moreover, Fodor's concentration on input systems – he has far less to say about either output systems or central processing – does not help us to explore the ways in which children turn out to be active participants in the construction of their own knowledge.

Although for Chomsky (1988) and Spelke (1991) a nativist/modularity stance precludes constructivism, I argue that nativism and Piaget's epigenetic constructivism are not necessarily incompatible, with certain provisos. First, to Piaget's view one must add some innately specified predispositions that would give the epigenetic process a head start in each domain. This does not imply merely adding a little more domain-general structure than Piaget supposed. Rather, it means adding domain-specific biases to the initial endowment. But the second proviso for the marriage of constructivism and nativism is that the initial endowment involves far less detailed specifications than some nativists presuppose, and a more progressive process of modularization (as opposed to prespecified modules) where the structure of the input plays an essential role in the structure of the resulting module. Fodor does not, for instance, discuss the cases in which the operation of one of his prespecified modules cannot be triggered by its proprietary input (e.g., auditory input in the case of the congenitally deaf). We know that in such cases the brain selectively adapts and reconfigures itself to receive other (e.g., visuomanual) nonauditory inputs (Changeux 1985; Neville 1991; Poizner et al. 1987). Many cases of early brain damage indicate that there is far more plasticity in the brain than Fodor's strict modularity would imply. The brain is not prestructured with ready-made representations which are simply triggered by environmental stimuli; it is channeled to progressively *develop* representations via interaction with both the external environment and its own internal environment. Furthermore, it is important not to equate innateness with presence at birth or with the notion of a static genetic blueprint for maturation. Whatever innate component we invoke, it becomes part of our biological potential only through interaction with the environment; it is latent until it receives input (Johnson 1988; 1993; Marler 1991; Oyama 1985; Thelen 1989) and the input required is either relatively specific or simply in the form of environmental stimuli per se (Greenough et al. 1987; Johnson & Bolhuis 1991). The interaction with the input crucially in turn affects the development of the brain.

Nativists argue that development follows similar paths because all normal children start life with the same innately specified structures. The role of the environment is reduced to that of a mere trigger. [See Lightfoot: "The Child's Trigger Experience: Degree-0 Learnability" *BBS* 12(2) 1989; Crain: "Language Acquisition in the Absence of Experience" *BBS* 14(4) 1991.] But the fact that development proceeds in similar ways across normal children does not necessarily mean that development must be innately specified in detail, because it is *also* true that all children evolve in a species-typical environment (Johnson & Morton 1991) and we are discovering that environments are more structured than was originally thought (see Elman 1990; 1993). Thus, it is the *interaction* between similar innate constraints and similar environmental constraints that gives rise to common developmental paths.

The proposed reconciliation of nativism and constructivism will allow us to adhere to Piaget's epigenetic-constructivist view of the developmental process but to drop his insistence on domain generality in favor of a more domain-specific approach. Furthermore, the Piagetian focus on output systems (i.e., on the infant's and the child's *action on* the environment) is an important addition to the nativist's accent on input systems. But Piaget's strong antinativism and his arguments for across-the-board major structural stages no longer constitute a viable developmental framework.

The need to invoke domain specificity is apparent throughout *Beyond modularity*. For example, domain-general sensorimotor development alone cannot explain the acquisition of language. Syntax does not derive simply from exploratory problem solving with toys, as some Piagetians claim. [cf. interesting discussion by Greenfield "Language, Tools and Brain" *BBS* 14(4) 1991.] Lining up objects does not form the basis for word order. Trying to fit one toy inside another has nothing to do with embedded clauses. General sensorimotor activity alone cannot account for specifically linguistic constraints. If it could, then it would be difficult to see why chimpanzees, who manifest rich sensorimotor and representational abilities, do not acquire anything remotely resembling the complex structure of human language despite very extensive training (Premack 1986).

Despite these criticisms of Piaget's view of early infancy and my rejection of his stage view of development, I hope that *Beyond modularity* will persuade readers that important aspects of Piaget's epistemology should be salvaged, and that there is far more to cognitive development than the unfolding of a genetically specified program simply triggered by environmental stimuli. If we are to understand the human mind, our focus must stretch well beyond any innate specifications and embrace the interaction of both domain-specific constraints and domain-general processes.

7. The empirical data

Because of the space limitations of a Précis, I refer the reader to Chapters 2 through 6 in *Beyond modularity* for discussions of the empirical data and the literature referenced therein. New infancy research and the *representational status of infant knowledge* form the detailed focus of the first part of each chapter, showing the linguistic, physical, mathematical, psychological, and notational domain-specific constraints on early development. Future research may lead to reinterpretations of the present infancy data, but I remain convinced that we will have to invoke *some* domain-specific predispositions which initially constrain the infant mind/brain. For each cognitive domain, I go on to consider data suggesting that development involves much more than the domain-specific constraints. My research strategy has always been rather different from that of developmentalists who study a given capacity, from failure to partial success through to complete mastery. By contrast, I focus on an age group in each domain where the particular capacity under study is already proficient. I then attempt to trace subsequent representational change. The most important and subtle data in Chapters 2–6 are, in my view, those pointing to a level of representation in which knowledge is explicitly defined (i.e., represented differently from the information embedded in special-purpose domain-specific procedures of the earlier phase) but not yet available to conscious access and verbal report. Spontaneous repairs to linguistic output, unsuccessful problem solving subsequent to success, redundant behaviors, and so forth (data often ignored in developmental and adult research) are all used as vital clues to this phase of development.

At several points throughout *Beyond modularity*, I allude to abnormal development. Nature, alas, often presents the scientist with experiments of its own, in which different capacities are either spared or impaired. Such cases warrant study in their own right, but they also help us gain a deeper understanding of normal development and domain specificity/modularity. Again, for space reasons I merely allude to them here (for more recent detailed discussion, see Karmiloff-Smith 1992c).

Development involves, then, two complementary processes of progressive modularization and progressive explicitation. In the remainder of this Précis, I will concentrate on the second of these two processes, that is, on my hypothesis that development involves representational redescription, a process that increases the flexibility and manipulability of the knowledge stored in the mind, by turning information that is *in* the mind into progressively more explicit knowledge *to* the mind.

8. Beyond domain-specific constraints: how new knowledge gets into the mind

How does information get stored in the child's mind? I argue that there are several different ways. One is via innate specification as the result of evolutionary processes.

Predispositions can be either specific or non-specific (Johnson & Bolhuis 1991). In both cases, environmental input is of course necessary. Should an innate component be specified in detail (if it ever is), then it is likely that the environment acts simply as a trigger for the organism to select one parameter or circuit over others (Changeux 1985; Chomsky 1981; Piatelli-Palmerini 1989). By contrast, when a predisposition is specified merely as a bias or as a skeletal outline, then the environment acts as much more than a trigger; it influences the subsequent structure of the brain via a rich epigenetic interaction between the mind/brain and the physical/sociocultural environment (for discussions, see Johnson & Karmiloff-Smith 1992). The skeletal outline involves attention biases toward particular inputs and a certain number of predispositions constraining the computation of those inputs.

There are several other ways in which new information gets stored in the child's mind. One occurs when the child fails to reach a goal and must take information from the physical environment into account. New knowledge is also acquired when the child has to take into account and to represent information provided by the socio-cultural environment, often in the form of a direct linguistic statement. These are both external sources of change from environmental input, but there are also internal sources of change. One is illustrated by the above-mentioned process of modularization when input and output processing become progressively less influenced by other processes in the brain. This causes knowledge to become more encapsulated and less accessible to other systems. Another essential facet of cognitive change goes in the opposite direction, however, with knowledge becoming progressively more accessible.

My claim is that a specifically human way to gain knowledge is for the mind to exploit internally the information that it has already stored, by redescribing its representations or, more precisely, by iteratively rerepresenting in different representational formats what its internal representations represent. This is what I hypothesize is particular to human cognition (see details under "The process of representational redescription" below).

Finally, there is a form of knowledge change that is far more obviously restricted to the human species: explicit theory change, which involves conscious construction and exploration of analogies, thought experiments and real experiments, typical of older children and adults (Carey 1985; Klahr 1992; Kuhn et al. 1988). I argue, however, that this more obvious characteristic of human cognition is possible only on the basis of the more subtle prior representational redescription, which turns *implicit* information embedded in special-purpose procedures into *explicit* knowledge but is not yet available to conscious verbal report.

To give a more tangible feel for the theoretical discussion on which I am about to embark, let's consider the pathway to learning to play the piano. There is a first period during which a sequence of separate notes is laboriously practiced. The beginning pianist pays conscious attention to particular notes. There is a second period during which chunks of several notes are played together as blocks, until finally the whole piece can be played more or less automatically. In other words, the sequence gradually becomes proceduralized (see Anderson 1980). It is something like this that I call "reaching behavioral mastery." But the automaticity is constrained by the fact that the learner can neither start in the middle of the piece nor play variations on a theme (Hermelin & O'Connor 1989). The performance is generated, I hypothesize, by procedural representations which are simply run off in their entirety. There is little flexibility. At best, in a third period, the learner is able to play the *whole piece* softer, louder, slower, or faster. The pianist's "knowledge" is embedded in the procedural representations sustaining the execution. But most learners do not stop there. During a fourth period, the learner can interrupt the piece and start at, say, the third bar without having to go back to the beginning and repeat the entire procedure from the outset.

I hypothesize that this fourth period cannot take place on the basis of the automatized procedural representations. Rather, it involves a process of representational redescription such that the knowledge of the different notes and chords (rather than simply their run-off sequence) becomes available as manipulable data. It is only after a period of behavioral mastery that the pianist can generate variations on a theme, change sequential order of bars, introduce insertions from other pieces, and so forth. This differentiates, for instance, jazz improvisation from strict adherence to sheet music. The end result is representational flexibility and control, which allows for creativity. Also important is the fact that the earlier proceduralized capacity is not lost: for certain goals, pianists can call on the automatic skill; for others, they call on the more explicit representations that allow for flexibility and creativity. (Of course, the playing of some pianists remains simply at the procedural level.)

This movement from implicit information embedded in an efficient problem-solving procedure, to rendering the knowledge progressively more explicit, is a theme that recurs throughout *Beyond modularity*. And this, together with the process of modularization discussed earlier, is precisely what I think development is about. Children are not satisfied with success in learning to talk or to solve problems; they want to understand how they do these things. In seeking such understanding, they become little theorists and to do so they have to change the nature of their internal representations.

Development and learning, then, seem to take two complementary directions. On the one hand, they involve the gradual process of proceduralization and at times modularization (that is, rendering behavior more automatic and less accessible). On the other hand, they involve a process of "explicitation" and increasing accessibility (that is, explicitly representing information that is implicit in the procedural representations). Both are relevant to cognitive change, but the main focus of *Beyond modularity* is the process by which the representational "explicitation" which, I posit, occurs in a variety of linguistic and cognitive domains throughout development.

9. The process of representational redescription

For a number of years I have been trying to understand how internal representations change in the course of development, even when overt behavior may look identical. In this attempt, I have developed the hypothesis of a reiterative process of *representational redescription* (RR). First, I will make some general points about the hypothesis; then I will provide a summary.

The notion of RR attempts to account for the way in which children's representations become progressively more manipulable and flexible. Ultimately, this leads, in each domain at different times, to the emergence of conscious access to knowledge and children's theory building. RR involves a cyclical process by which information already present in the organism's independently functioning, special-purpose representations is made progressively available, via redescriptive processes, to other parts of the cognitive system, first within a domain and then sometimes across domains.

The RR process is posited to occur spontaneously as part of an internal drive toward the creation of intradomain and interdomain relationships. Although I stress the endogenous nature of representational redescription, clearly the process may at times also be triggered by external influences.

The actual *process* of RR is domain general, but it is crucially affected by the form and level of explicitness of the representations supporting particular domain-specific knowledge at a given time. When I state that RR is domain-general, I do not mean to imply that it involves a simultaneous change across domains. Rather, I mean that, within each domain, the RR process operates in a similar way.

Let us look now at the RR hypothesis in some detail. Development, I argue, involves three *recurrent* phases. During the first phase the child focuses predominantly on information from the external environment. This initial learning is data driven. Phase 1 culminates in consistently successful performance on whatever microdomain has reached that level. This is what I term "behavioral mastery." Behavioral mastery does not necessarily imply that the underlying representations are equivalent to the adult's, even though the behavioral output may be the same. The same performance (say, correctly producing a particular linguistic form, or managing to balance blocks on a narrow support) can be generated at various ages by very different representations. Later (phase 3) behavior may appear identical to phase 1 behavior. We thus need to draw a distinction between "behavioral change" (which sometimes gives rise to a U-shaped developmental curve) and "representational change" because behavioral mastery is not tantamount to the end point of the developmental progression in a given microdomain.

Phase 1 is followed by an internally driven phase during which the child no longer focuses on the external data. Rather, system-internal dynamics take over such that internal representations become the focus of change. In phase 2, the current state of the child's representations of knowledge in a microdomain predominate over information from the incoming data. The temporary disregard for features of the external environment during phase 2 can lead to new errors and inflexibilities. This can, but does not necessarily, give rise to a decrease in successful behavior – a U-shaped developmental curve. This is deterioration at the behavioral level, not at the representational level.

Finally, during phase 3, internal representations and external data are reconciled, and a balance is achieved between the quests for internal and external control. In the case of language, for example, a new mapping is made between input and output representations in order to restore correct usage.

But what about the format of the internal representations that sustain these reiterated phases? The RR framework argues for at least four levels at which knowledge is represented and re-represented. I have termed them Implicit (I), Explicit-I (E1), Explicit-2 (E2), and Explicit-3 (E3). The RR framework postulates different representational formats at different levels. At level I, representations are in the form of procedures or action patterns for responding to stimuli in the external environment. A number of constraints operate on the representational adjunctions that are formed at this level:

> Information is encoded in procedural form.
>
> The procedure-like encodings are sequentially specified.
>
> New representations are independently stored.
>
> Level-I representations are bracketed, and hence no intradomain or interdomain representational links can yet be formed.

Information embedded in level-I representations is therefore not available to other operators in the cognitive system. Thus, if two procedures or action patterns contain identical information, this potential interrepresentational commonality is not yet represented in the child's mind. A procedure *as a whole* is available as data to other operators; however, its *component parts* are not. It takes developmental time and representational redescription (see discussion of level El below) for component parts to become available for the marking of potential intradomain and interdomain relationships, a process which ultimately leads to interrepresentational flexibility and creative problem-solving capacities (see discussion of levels E2/E3). At this first level, however, the potential representational links and the information embedded in procedures or action patterns remain implicit. This gives rise to the ability to compute specific inputs in preferential ways and to respond rapidly and effectively to the environment. But the behavior generated from level-I representations is relatively inflexible.

Level-El representations are the result of redescription, into a new format, of the procedurally encoded representations at level-I. The redescriptions are abstractions and, unlike level-I representations, they are not bracketed (that is, the component parts are now open to potential intradomain and interdomain representational links). The El representations are reduced descriptions that lose many of the details of the procedurally encoded information. As a nice example of what I have in mind here, consider the details of the grated image delivered to the perceptual system of a person who sees a zebra (Mandler 1992). A redescription of this into "striped animal" (either linguistic or image-like) has lost much of the perceptual precision. To Mandler's discussion, I would add that the redescription allows the *cognitive* (as opposed to the *perceptual*) system to understand the analogy between an actual zebra and the road sign for a so-called "zebra crossing" (a European crosswalk with broad, regular, black and yellow stripes), although the zebra and the road sign deliver very different inputs to the *perceptual* system. A species without representational redescriptions would not make the analogy between the zebra and the zebra crossing sign. The redescribed representation is, on the one hand, simpler and less special purpose but, on the other, more flexible cognitively (because it is transportable to other goals and useable to make other inferences). Unlike perceptual representations, conceptual redescriptions are productive; they make possible the invention of new terms (e.g., "zebrin," the antibody which stains certain classes of cells in striped patterns).

Note that the original level-I representations remain intact in the child's mind and can continue to be called for particular cognitive goals which require speed and automaticity. The redescribed representations are used for other goals where explicit knowledge is required.

As representations are redescribed into the E1 format, we witness the beginnings of a flexible cognitive system upon which the child's nascent theories can subsequently be built. Level-E1 representations go beyond the constraints imposed at level I, where procedure-like representations are simply used in response to external stimuli. Once knowledge previously embedded in procedures is explicitly defined, the potential relationships between procedural components can then be marked and represented internally. Moreover, once redescription has taken place and explicit representations become manipulable, children can introduce violations to their data-driven, veridical descriptions of the world – violations which allow, for instance, for pretend play, false belief, and the use of counterfactuals.

It is important to stress that although E1 representations are available as data to the system, they are not available to conscious access and verbal report. Throughout the book I examine examples of the formation of explicit representations which are not yet accessible to conscious reflection and verbal report, but which are clearly beyond the procedural level. In general, developmentalists have not distinguished between implicitly stored knowledge and E1 representations in which knowledge *is* explicitly represented but is not yet consciously accessible. Rather, they have drawn a dichotomy between an undefined notion of something implicit in behavior (as if information were not represented in any form) and consciously accessible knowledge that can be stated in verbal form. According to the RR framework, the human representational system is far more complex than a mere dichotomy. It is particularly via a developmental perspective that one can pinpoint this multiplicity of levels of representational formats.

In the RR framework, conscious access and verbal report are possible only at levels beyond E1. At level E2, it is hypothesized, representations are available to conscious access but not to verbal report (which is possible only at level E3). Although for some theorists consciousness is reduced to verbal reportability, in the RR framework E2 representations are accessible to consciousness but they are in a representational code similar to that of the E1 representations of which they are redescriptions. Thus, for example, E1 spatial representations are recoded into consciously accessible E2 *spatial* representations. (We often draw diagrams of problems we cannot easily verbalize.)

At level E3, knowledge is recoded into a cross-system code. This common format is hypothesized to be close enough to natural language for easy translation into statable, communicable form. It is possible that some knowledge learned directly in linguistic form is immediately stored at level E3. Children learn a lot from verbal interaction with others, but knowledge may be stored in linguistic code and not yet linked to similar knowledge stored in other representational formats. Linguistic knowledge (e.g., a mathematical principle governing subtraction) often fails to constrain nonlinguistic knowledge (e.g., an algorithm used for actually doing subtraction) until both have been redescribed into a similar format, so that interrepresentational constraints can operate (Hennessy 1986).

The empirical examples throughout *Beyond modularity* illustrate levels I, E3, and particularly the subtleties of level El. In the book, I do not distinguish between levels E2 and E3, both of which, I believe, involve conscious access, because thus far research has not been directly focused on level E2 (conscious access without verbal report). Most, if not all, metacognitive studies focus on verbal report (i.e., level E3). Thus, E2 remains to be tested empirically. Nevertheless, I do not wish to foreclose the possibility of spatial, kinesthetic, and other *nonlinguistically encoded* representations that are available to conscious access, and it may well be that E2 and E3 redescriptional formats are both made directly on the basis of the El format, rather than E3 being a redescription of E2. This is discussed fully in Chapter l.

The end result of these various redescriptions is the existence in the mind of multiple representations of similar knowledge at different levels of detail and explicitness. This notion of multiple encoding is important; the development of the mind does not seem to be a drive for economy. Indeed, the human mind may turn out to be a very redundant store of knowledge and processes.

Let me stress again the concept of reiterative developmental phases. There is no such thing as a "phase E2 child." The child's representations are in different representational formats with respect to particular microdomains.

Although the process of representational redescription can occur on line, I suggest that it also takes place without ongoing analysis of incoming data or production of output. Thus, change can occur outside normal input/output relations, that is, simply as the product of system-internal dynamics, when there are no external pressures. Representational change *within* phases involves adding representations; here, negative feedback (failure, incompletion, inadequacy, mismatch between input and output, etc.) plays an important role, leading progressively to behavioral mastery. But in the transition *between* phases, it is hypothesized that *positive* feedback is essential to the onset of representational redescription. In other words, according to this success-based view of cognitive change, it is representations that have reached a stable state (the child having reached behavioral mastery) that are redescribed. Representational redescription is a process of "appropriating" stable states to extract the information they contain, which can then be used more flexibly for other purposes. Many of the studies discussed in *Beyond modularity*, and new data from Siegler and Crowley (1991), show that change often follows success, not only failure. In other words, children explore domain-specific environments beyond their successful interaction with them.

This is not to deny the importance of instability, failure, conflict, and competition as generators of other types of change (Bates & MacWhinney 1987;

Piaget 1967; Thelen 1989). It is worth reiterating this point. Competition can occur on line between different processes and can cause behavioral change, but the hypothesis I develop throughout *Beyond modularity* is that competition leading to representational change takes place after each of the potential competitors has been consolidated (i.e., is stable in its own right). In Chapter 3, for example, it is shown how counterexamples are not taken into account (do not have the status of a counterexample) until the child's theory about a particular microdomain has been consolidated. Similar examples are to be found in the history of science and in children's strategies of scientific experimentation (Klahr & Dunbar 1988; Kuhn et al. 1988; Kuhn & Phelps 1982; Schauble 1990), as well as across the various domains of knowledge discussed throughout *Beyond modularity*.

10. Are there domain-general processes at work?

Invoking domain-specific constraints on development does not deny the existence of some domain-general mechanisms. The infancy tasks explored in each chapter make it very clear that infants can call on complex inferential processes across different domains. Moreover, young infants go well beyond sensorimotor encodings and make use of domain-general processes such as representational redescription to recode sensorimotor input into accessible formats (see also Mandler 1992). Domain-general processes sustaining inference and representational redescription operate throughout development, but invoking general *processes* that are the same across different domains is not equivalent to invoking domain-general *stages of change*. It is the latter that *Beyond modularity* rejects.

Yet there might turn out to be *some* across-the-board domain-general changes also, perhaps linked to major maturation of particular regions of the brain (e.g. prefrontal cortex). One such change suggested by an abundance of empirical data seems to occur around 18 months of age. This holds for several domains, particularly with respect to holding two representations simultaneously in mind and representing hypothetical events in general (Meltzoff 1990; Perner 1991), rather than theory-of-mind computations in particular (Leslie 1992). Eighteen months is also the age Piaget singled out for a change in representational structure which allowed for the onset of pretend play, language, and mental imagery. The precise way in which Piaget accounted for such a change in terms of the closure of a purely sensorimotor period is likely to be wrong, but the conviction that something fundamental occurs around 18 months may turn out to be well-founded.

The other age at which an across-the-board, domain-general change may occur is somewhere around three and a half to four years. This age does not correspond to a stage change in Piagetian theory, but it seems to be when fundamental changes occur in various domains. Moreover, this is also roughly the age at which the human child differs radically from the chimpanzee. As Premack (1991, p. 164) put it, "a good rule of thumb has proved to be: if the child of three and a half years cannot do it, neither can the chimpanzee."

If it turns out that across-the-board, domain-general changes do occur, we may be able to use them as a diagnostic for fundamental neural changes in the brain, and vice versa. This of course remains an open question, but the flourishing new field of developmental cognitive neuroscience may soon provide some relevant answers. Even if some across-the-board changes were to hold, however, it is important to recall that their effects would be manifest somewhat differently across domains, since they would interact with domain-specific constraints. Development will not turn out to be *either* domain specific *or* domain general. It is clearly the intricate interaction of *both* – more domain-general than is presupposed by most nativist/modularity views of development, but more domain-specific than Piagetian theory envisages.

So, does Piagetian theory retain any role in developmental theorizing? To me, the answer is affirmative. Theories of cognitive development (and recent connectionist modeling of cognitive development [McClelland & Jenkins 1990; Parisi 1990; Plunkett & Sinha 1992], which I discuss in Chapter 8) continue to draw inspiration from Piaget's *epistemology* – his quest to understand emergent properties and his general stance with regard to epigenesis and the importance of the child's action on the environment. It is the details of his *psychological* description of across-the-board stagelike changes in logico-mathematical structure that are no longer viable. I believe that it is possible to retain the essence of Piagetian theory while doing away with stage and structure. The problem with Piaget's theory (and indeed, with the RR framework too), however, is that it is underspecified in comparison with, say, theories expressed as computer models. I now turn briefly to this issue.

11. Modeling development

One of the aims of *Beyond modularity* is to persuade cognitive scientists of the value of a developmental perspective for understanding the workings of the human mind. Yet, at the heart of much of the work in cognitive science is the use of computer models to test psychological theories. It is therefore essential to devote some space to a discussion of how the RR framework might be relevant to attempts to express developmental theories in the form of computer simulations.

What type of framework is RR? Throughout *Beyond modularity*, I describe RR in verbal terms. It is, as Klahr (1992) has put it, at the "soft-core" end of the modeling of cognitive development, the "hard-core" end being the implementation of theories as computer programs. Klahr's contrast captures an important distinction between a focus on general principles of development and a focus on the specification of precise mechanisms. Klahr argues that the very process of simulating development in the form of computer programs leads to insights about the mechanisms underlying developmental change, whereas verbal descriptions generally underspecify the mechanisms. I agree, but soft-core and hard-core approaches should not be considered mutually exclusive.

In my view, soft-core approaches often lead to a broader intuitive understanding of general principles of change, whereas both the information-processing use of the flow chart and the symbolic approach to computer simulation run the risk of reifying into one or more boxes or single-named operators what is in fact the product of a highly interactive system. Nonetheless, at the hard-core end of modeling there have been a number of interesting attempts to express developmental theories in various information-processing terms – for example, in the form of scripts (Nelson 1986; Schank & Abelson 1977), developmental contingency models (Morton 1986), and self-modifying production systems (Klahr et al. 1987). In Chapter 8, however, I take as my main example some recent connectionist simulations, since they seem to be closest to the spirit of epigenesis and constructivism (for fuller discussions, see Bates & Elman 1993; Clark & Karmiloff-Smith 1993; Elman et al., 1996; Karmiloff-Smith 1992b; 1992c; Karmiloff-Smith & Clark 1993; McClelland & Jenkins 1990; Parisi 1990; Plunkett & Sinha 1992). Connectionist simulations also address the problems I raise in *Beyond modularity* with respect to stage theories, in that they show that by incremental learning one can obtain stagelike shifts in overt behavior without the need for qualitatively different structures and mechanisms (McClelland & Jenkins 1990).

Although the connectionist framework has come under severe criticism (Pinker & Mehler 1988), a growing number of cognitive developmentalists see within this framework a considerable theoretical potential for explicating the more general tenets of Piaget's epistemology (e.g., Bates & Elman 1993; Bechtel & Abrahamsen 1991; Elman et al., 1996; Karmiloff-Smith 1992b; 1992c; Clark & Karmiloff-Smith 1993; Karmiloff-Smith & Clark 1993; McClelland & Jenkins 1990; Plunkett & Sinha 1992). Moreover, a number of features of the RR framework, developed quite independently in the 1970s and early 1980s, map interestingly onto features of recent connectionist simulations.

Chapter 8 of *Beyond modularity* describes the main features of connectionist models, but since a BBS treatment has dealt extensively with such models (Smolensky 1988), I will not repeat the description in this Précis. Instead, I will go on to explore directly the extent to which connectionist simulations can and cannot capture what I deem to be crucial to a model of developmental change. To the extent that they can, connectionism would offer the RR framework a powerful set of hard-core tools by applying the mathematical theory of complex dynamical systems to cognitive development (van Geehrt 1991). And to the extent that connectionist models fail to model development adequately, the RR framework suggests some crucial modifications.

Many of the details of phase 1 learning, which leads to behavioral mastery and level-I representations, turn out to be captured particularly well in a connectionist model. However, the very aspect of development on which *Beyond modularity* focuses – the process of representational redescription – is precisely what seems to be missing from connectionist simulations of development.

12. Connectionism: the starting state, the role of the input, and the process of representational redescription

Let us now look at some of the specific issues discussed throughout *Beyond modularity* and how they can be informed by, as well as inform, the connectionist framework.

12.1. The starting state

Most connectionist researchers adopt a non-nativist view as their research strategy. This makes it possible to explore the extent to which developmental phenomena can be simulated from a *tabula rasa* starting state – that is, from random weights and random activation levels, with no domain-specific knowledge. This has led some to interpret the results of connectionist modeling as strong evidence for the antinativist position, but there is nothing about the connectionist framework that precludes the introduction of initial biased weights and connections (i.e., the equivalents of innately specified predispositions as a result of evolution) rather than random weights and connections. Also, specific architectures, learning algorithms, learning rates, and so on which are part of the starting state, clearly affect how an input set is learned.

Various ways of simulating developmental change have been proposed. One is to start a network with a small number of hidden units and, as "development" proceeds, to recruit more and more units or an extra hidden layer to compress the data even further (Shultz 1991). This is rather like the neo-Piagetians' notion that processing capacity increases with age (Case 1985; Halford 1982). Other researchers (Bechtel & Abrahamsen 1991) have suggested the equivalent of "maturational" change, such that the network would start by using one learning algorithm (e.g., contrastive Hebbian learning) and, with maturation, come to use a different learning algorithm (e.g., backpropagation). Incremental learning has also been used, such that the network first sees only part of the input at a time, rather than the whole input set in one go (Elman 1990; Plunkett & Marchman 1991). These are all domain-general solutions to developmental change, but we are beginning to witness an increasing tendency on the part of connectionists to explore the ways in which domain-specific constraints might also shape learning. This is in my view, likely to be a future focus for connectionist models of development.

It might seem at present that connectionist models deny, either implicitly or explicitly, the need for domain-specific learning. In favor of domain generality, connectionists stress that their models use the *same* learning algorithms for different categories of input presented to different networks. But, in effect, architectures are fine-tuned to specific types of input. For example, a recurrent architecture is used for sequential input (see Elman 1990) whereas an associative network is used for concept learning (see Plunkett & Sinha 1992). To my knowledge, little work has been done on networks which progressively develop their own architecture as a function of the input they happen to process. Moreover, no single network has been presented with an array of inputs from *different* domains (e.g., language, spatial tasks, tasks involving physical principles). Networks designed to simulate language acquisition (e.g., Elman 1990; 1993) see only linguistic strings. A similar network could be used for physics input, but the very same network could not be used without totally upsetting the language learning that has already taken place unless it also continues to be trained on the original set. In other words, the fact that each network is dedicated to a specific type of input, in a specific learning task, with a specific architecture and learning algorithm, turns out to be equivalent to domain specificity in the human. Infants seem to process proprietary, domain-specific inputs separately, and so do networks. We will probably end up requiring multiple networks with different architectures and different learning algorithms.

A final point with respect to the starting state: networks are not "modules" in the sense of the distinction I drew between modules and a process of modularization. In fact, networks mimic the process of modularization because, with few or no built-in representational biases, it is only as learning proceeds that they *become* increasingly like special-purpose modules.

12.2. The role of the input

Although connectionist models have potential for developmental theorizing, they have several shortcomings. One concerns the input presented to networks. First, decisions about input representation are entirely external to the network and often are not motivated theoretically. Second, with some exceptions, connectionists have, until now, not really modeled development; they have modeled *tasks.* This becomes particularly apparent if we look at the example of the balance scale that is so popular in all kinds of computer modeling, including connectionist (Langley et al. 1987; McClelland & Jenkins 1990; Newell 1990; Shultz 1991; Siegler & Robinson 1982). The models have focused on children's performance on the balance-scale task, not on how children learn about general physical phenomena in real life (see also Shultz 1991 for discussion). Many children come to a balance scale experiment with no experience of balance scales, but this does not mean that they bring no relevant knowledge to the task. They may focus on weight in tasks using the traditional balance scale because weights are what the experimenter more obviously manipulates. But in other block balancing tasks not presented in the form of a balance scale, many young children ignore weight and focus solely on length. Children come to such tasks having already learned something about how rulers fall from tables, how seesaws work, and so forth. But a seesaw is not a balance scale. It does not have a neat line of equidistant pegs on which children of absolutely equal weight can be placed one on top of another! Development is not simply task-specific learning. It involves deriving knowledge from many sources and using that knowledge in a goal oriented way. Thus, in my view, far richer input vectors and the simulation of goal oriented behaviors are needed if we are to model the ways in which real children learn in real environments.

12.3. Behavioral mastery

Chapter 3, on the child as a physicist, and Chapter 6, on the child as a notator, give particularly clear examples of how a lengthy period of behavioral mastery precedes representational change. Indeed, throughout *Beyond modularity*, I argue that behavioral mastery is a prerequisite for representational change. An analysis of learning in a connectionist network, however, already reveals in the hidden units the existence of some representation of subsequent change *before* it is observable in the output. This suggests a way in which connectionist modeling might change the RR framework in that full behavioral mastery may not be a prerequisite to change; that is, representational change may start to occur prior to *overt* behavioral mastery.

12.4. Implicit to explicit representational change

It has often been difficult to convey, particularly to developmental psychologists, precisely what I meant by "level-I implicit representations." [See also Shanks & St. John: "Characteristics of Dissociable Human Learning Systems" *BBS* 17(3) 1994.] Researchers have often used the term "implicit" to explain away efficient behavior that appears "too early" for the tenets of a particular theory, but no definition of implicit has been offered. The connectionist framework may help to give a more precise definition. Indeed, some recent connectionist simulations of language learning (Elman 1990; 1993), for instance, are particularly illustrative of the status of implicit level-I representations. Elman's model is discussed fully in *Beyond modularity*. It demonstrates how grammatical function (noun/verb, transitive/intransitive verb, singular/plural, etc.) can be progressively inferred from statistical regularities of the input set and can be represented in the hidden units as learning proceeds. The full details of the learning process need not concern us here, rather, we should focus on the *status of the representations* that the network progressively builds. First, Elman shows that, as with most connectionist networks using nonlinear functions, a lengthy initial period is essential to learning. At first, the network's predictions are random. However, with time the network learns to predict, not necessarily the actual next word, but the correct *category* of word (noun vs. verb; if noun, animate vs. inanimate, edible vs. nonedible, etc.), as well as the correct subcategorization frame for the next verb (transitive or intransitive), and the correct number marking on both noun and verb (singular or plural). This cannot be done by mere association between adjacent surface elements. For example, whereas in the case of the simple string, a network could learn always to predict that strings without an "s" (plural verb) follow strings with an "s" (plural noun), it cannot do so for embedded relative clause strings. Here, a plural verb may follow a singular noun (e.g., "the boys that chase the *girl see* the dog"). In such cases, the network must make *structure-dependent* predictions. Thus, the network moves progressively from processing mere surface regularities to representing something more abstract, but without this being built in as a prespecified linguistic constraint.

This seemingly impressive grammatical knowledge is only implicit in the system's internal representations. Note, however, that this does not mean that the grammatical knowledge is not represented. As in the case of early learning in the child, I would argue that it is represented in level-I format. But it is we, as external theorists, who use level-E formats to label the trajectories through weight space as nouns, verbs, subjects, objects, intransitives, transitives, plurals, singulars, and so on. The network itself never goes beyond the formation of the equivalent of stable (but unlabeled) level-I representations. In other words, it does not spontaneously go beyond its efficient behavioral mastery. It does not redescribe the representations that are stored in its activation trajectories. Unlike the child, the network does not spontaneously "appropriate" the knowledge it represents about different linguistic categories. It cannot directly use the higher-level, more abstract knowledge for any other purpose than the one it was designed for, nor can it engage directly in internetwork knowledge transfer because its representations are input/task specific. The notion of, say, nounhood, always remains implicit in the network's system dynamics. The child's *initial* learning is like this, too. But, as several examples throughout *Beyond modularity* show, children go on to redescribe spontaneously their linguistic (and other) knowledge. This pervasive process of representational redescription gives rise to the manipulability and flexibility of the human representational system.

Now, it is not difficult to build a network, inspired by RR, that would redescribe stable states in weight space such that the implicit information represented in trajectories could be used as knowledge by the same or other networks. However, this would suggest a change in the architecture of the network, involving perhaps the creation of special nodes not implicated in other aspects of the on-line processing. Furthermore, the RR framework suggests that what is abstracted during the redescriptive process involves a loss of detail and a gain in accessibility. Thus, one would not want the entire trajectories of the network to be redescribed – only the product of the most important ones. (This would be equivalent to, say, labeling the phase-state portraits of the principal-component analysis.) The RR framework postulates that redescribed knowledge capturing abstract notions such as "verb" and "noun" must be in a format different from that of the original level-I representations. In other words, redescriptions would have to be in a representational format usable across networks which had previously processed *different* representations at the input level: hence the need for representational redescription into different (level E) formats. Simple copies of level-I representations would not be usable/transportable from one network to another because they would be too dependent on the specific features of their inputs.

In Chapter 2, I discuss a particularly relevant example of what progressive RR might look like in the human case. When three- to six-year-olds are asked to repeat the last word the experimenter had said before a story was interrupted, some of the youngest subjects (three years old) could not do the task at all, despite lengthy modeling and help from the experimenter. Yet their fluent language and their lack of segmentation errors suggest that they do represent formal word boundaries for the majority of words they use and understand, but that they are not yet ready to go beyond that behavioral mastery. There were other children (four to five years old) who could not do the task immediately but who, with one-off modeling for a few open-class words, were able *immediately* to extend the notion of "word" to *all* open-class and closed-class categories. Their level-I representations were ready for level-El redescription triggered by the experimenter from outside, but slightly older children (five to six years) who had never had a grammar lesson had spontaneously undergone the redescriptive process on their own. These showed immediate success, even on the practice story. Finally, six- to seven-year-olds' representations showed signs of having undergone further redescription into the E3 format; these children were able to access their knowledge consciously and to provide verbal explanations of what counts as a word and why. This process of *multiple* redescription of knowledge that becomes increasingly accessible to different parts of the system is an essential component of human development and one that connectionist modelers need to take into account.

It seems plausible that connectionist models can lend precision to an account of what I have called phase 1 learning – the phase that results in behavioral mastery (i.e., the period of rich interaction with the environment during which level-I representations are built and consolidated). However, there is much more to development than this. I have intimated at various points that connectionist simulations stop short of accounting for certain essential components of human development. Indeed, whereas behavioral mastery is the endpoint of learning in connectionist models, in the RR framework it is the starting point for new flexibility – that is, for generating redescriptions of implicitly defined level-I representations. Until now, connectionist models of development have had little to say about how to move from implicit representations to explicit ones, an essential process called for by RR. How could a network appropriate its own stable states? Clark (1989), Dennett (1993), and McClelland (1991) have argued that all that would have to be added to a connectionist network is another network that uses the equivalent of public language, implying that the only difference between implicit and explicit knowledge is that the latter is linguistically encoded. I have, however, provided numerous examples of children's knowledge that is explicitly represented, but with children unable to articulate it linguistically. The RR framework offers a far more complex view of multiple levels of representational redescription, of which language is but one manifestation. Finally, the fact that most connectionist models blend structure and content makes it difficult for the network to exploit knowledge components. Yet, in several chapters I show that children extract knowledge components from the procedural representations in which they are embedded, re-represent them, and use them in increasingly manipulable ways.

How representational redescription might be modeled in a connectionist network remains an open question. Can it be done simply by adding layers to the architecture of a single network, or by creating, say, a hierarchy of interconnected networks? Should a node, external to the online processing, be fed gradually with information from the developing internal representations when hidden units reach a certain threshold of stability? How can internet relations be introduced while keeping in mind the constraints suggested by RR regarding common transportable representational format? Or will we have to opt for hybrid models containing both parallel distributed processing and more classical sequential manipulation of discrete symbols (see discussions in Clark & Karmiloff-Smith 1993; Karmiloff-Smith 1987; 1992b; 1992c; Karmiloff-Smith & Clark 1993; Schneider 1987)? As connectionist networks become more complex, I think the issue of whether something is truly "hybrid" will lose relevance. Future developmental modeling must, in my view, simulate *both* the benefits of rapid processing via implicit representations and the benefits gained by further representational redescription – a process that I suggest makes possible human creativity (for a BBS treatment of creativity, see Boden: "Précis of: *The Creative Mind*" *BBS* 17(3) 1994).

13. Concluding remarks

I started *Beyond modularity* distinguishing between the representations that sustain complex behavior and the things that a given species can do with that complexity. My argument throughout has been that, far more pervasively even than that of its near cousin the chimpanzee, the human mind exploits its representational complexity by re-representing its implicit knowledge into many levels of explicit form. The knowledge thereby becomes applicable beyond the special-purpose goals for which it is normally used and representational links across different domains can be forged.

This is rarely if ever true of other species. The plover (discussed in Chapter 5), for example, displays a complex set of behaviors to keep competitors at bay – behaviors that, in human terms, would be called deceit. But these behaviors (keeping competitors away from their hatching eggs) are not available for other, even closely related, purposes (keeping competitors away from food). What about the chimpanzee, with whom we share close to 100% of our genetic makeup? Do chimpanzees, like children, play with *knowledge*, just as they play with physical objects and conspecifics? According to discussions I have had with Premack, there are no obvious indicators of representational redescription in the behavior of the chimpanzee. There are numerous examples of how the chimpanzee goes beyond a specified task; for example, when the task is to assemble the pieces of a puzzle of a chimp face, a chimpanzee might, after succeeding, add extra pieces as decoration to form a hat or a necklace (Premack 1975). But Premack could find no example that revealed that the chimpanzee spontaneously analyzes the components of its successful behavior in the way a child does. It is, of course, not immediately obvious how we would recognize representational redescription in the chimpanzee if it did exist. The higher levels of redescription (into, say, linguistic format) are obviously ruled out. We know, however, that in many instances children develop explicit representations (El) which lie between the implicit representations and the verbally reportable data. In the child, level El representational redescription is frequently manifest after overt behavioral mastery. The chimpanzee, by contrast, seems to be content to repeat its successes continuously; it does not go beyond behavioral mastery. Yet, throughout *Beyond modularity*, examples are explored of how human children spontaneously seek to understand their own cognition, and of how this leads to the sort of representational manipulability that eventually allows them to become folk linguists, physicists, mathematicians, psychologists, and notators.

My conjecture is that either the process of representational redescription is not available to other species or, if it is (perhaps to the chimpanzee), the higher-level codes into which representations are translated during redescription are very impoverished. It is conceivable that "language-trained" chimpanzees will show signs of representational redescription, but this would be due, not to the existence of a languagelike code per se, but to the possibility of redescription into any other more explicit code (for fuller discussion, see Karmiloff-Smith 1983).

RR is basically a hypothesis about the specifically human capacity to enrich itself from within, by exploiting knowledge already stored rather than by simply exploiting the human and physical environment. Intradomain and interdomain representational relations are the hallmark of a flexible and creative cognitive system. The pervasiveness of representational redescription is what makes human cognition specifically human. This is, of course, a challenge to ethologists and one I look forward to pursuing in the future. What indices should we be seeking in other species? What machinery would we have to add to the plover, the ant, the spider, the bee, or the chimpanzee to make the process of representational redescription possible?

In the final pages of *Beyond modularity*, I present a caricature drawing of the difference between humans and other species. In the top half of the caricature is drawn a human and an animal in reciprocal interaction with the external environment. In the bottom half, the drawing shows just the human figure with an arrow going around the head from one side to the other. This (rather silly) caricature is intended to illustrate that level-I representations exist as cognitive tools, allowing an organism (human or nonhuman) to act on the environment and to be affected by it in return. The second part of the figure is not meant to suggest that, in the human, knowledge goes in one ear and out the other! Rather, it is a reminder that, in the human, *internal representations* become objects of cognitive manipulation such that the mind extends well beyond its environment and is capable of creativity. Let me go so far as to say that the RR proess is, in Marler's (1991) terms, one of the human instincts for inventiveness.

In *Beyond modularity*, and even in this short Précis, I hope to have convinced the reader that the flourishing new domain of cognitive science needs to go beyond the traditional nativist-empiricist dichotomy that permeates much of the field, in favor of an epistemology that embraces both innate predispositions and constructivism. Cognitive science also has much to gain by going beyond modularity and taking developmental change seriously.

A Précis necessarily makes conceptual leaps, misses out on the richness of the empirical data, as well as on numerous references to relevant literature. It also, alas, leaves no room for the humor. Nevertheless, it has given a relatively complete idea of the theoretical issues raised in the book. I began this Précis with a quotation from Marler that I find particularly conducive to my thinking, and that I used as a colophon for one of the book chapters, but I began the actual book with a quotation from Fodor, and ended with the following one: "Deep down, I'm inclined to doubt that there is such a thing as cognitive development in the sense that developmental cognitive psychologists have in mind" (Fodor 1985, p. 35).

If this Précis has encouraged you to read the book in full, I hope that by the time you reach the end, deep down you will disagree with Fodor's statement and, with me, you will conclude that development goes far beyond the triggered unfolding of a genetic program, that where modularity occurs it is the result of a gradual process of modularization, and that representational redescription allows the human mind to go beyond modularity.

Acknowledgment

Many people have read and commented on *Beyond modularity* and they are thanked in the preface to the book. Here I would like to express my gratitude to my colleague, Geoff Hall, for having read and provided useful comments on this Précis.

References

Anderson, J. R. (1980) *Cognitive psychology and its implications*. Freeman.

Bates, E. & Elman, J. L. (1993) Connectionism and the study of change. In: *Brain development and cognition: A reader*, ed. M. H. Johnson. Blackwell.

Bates, E. & MacWhinney, B. (1987) Competition, variation and language learning. In: *Mechanisms of language acquisition*, ed. B. MacWhinney. Erlbaum.

Bechtel, W. & Abrahamsen, A. (1991) *Connectionism and the mind: An introduction to parallel processing in networks*. Blackwell.

Bellugi, U., Murks, S., Bihrle, A. M. & Sabo, H. (1988) Dissociation between language and cognitive functions in Williams syndrome. In: *Language development in exceptional circumstances*, ed. D. Bishop & K. Mogford. Churchill Livingstone.

Carey, S. (1985) *Conceptual change in childhood*. MIT Press.

Case, R. (1985) *Intellectual development: Birth to adulthood*. Academic Press.

Changeux, J. P. (1985) *Neuronal man: The biology of mind*. Pantheon.

Chomsky, N. (1981) *Lectures on government and binding*. Foris.

Chomsky, N. (1988) *Language and problems of knowledge*. MIT Press.

Clark, A. C. (1989) *Microcognition: Philosophy, cognitive science, and parallel distributed processing*. MIT Press.

Clark, A. C. & Karmiloff-Smith, A. (1993) The cognizer's innards: A psychological and philosophical perspective on the development of thought. *Mind and Language* 8(3):487–568.

Dennett, D. C. (1993) Learning and labeling. Peer commentary on Clark & Karmiloff-Smith "The cognizer's innards." *Mind and Language* 8(3):540–48.

Elman, J. L. (1990) Finding structure in time. *Cognitive Science* 14:179–211.

Elman, J. L. (1993) Learning and development in neural networks: The importance of starting small. *Cognition* 48(1):71–99.

Elman, J. L., Bates, E., Johnson, M. H., Karmiloff-Smith, A., Parisi, D. & Plunkett, K. (1996) *Rethinking innateness: A connectionist perspective on development*. MIT Press.

Fodor, J. A. (1983) *The modularity of mind*. MIT Press.

Fodor, J. A. (1985) Précis of *The modularity of mind*. *Behavioral and Brain Sciences* 8(1):1–46.

Frith, U. (1989) *Autism: Explaining the enigma*. Blackwell.

Gelman, R. (1990) Structural constraints on cognitive development. *Cognitive Science* 14:39.

Greenough, W. T., Black, J. E. & Wallace, C. S. (1987) Experience and brain development. *Child Development* 58:539–59.

Halford, G. S. (1982) *The development of thought.* Erlbaum.
Hennessy, S. (1986) The role of conceptual knowledge, in the acquisition of arithmetic algorithms. Ph.D. dissertation, University College London.
Hermelin, B. & O'Connor, N. (1986) Idiot savant calendrical calculators: Rules and regularities. *Psychological Medicine* 16:885–93.
Hermelin, B. & O'Connor, N. (1989) Intelligence and musical improvisation. *Psychological Medicine* 19:447–57.
Johnson, M. H. (1988) Memories of mother. *New Scientist* 18:60–62.
Johnson, M. H. (1990) Cortical maturation and the development of visual attention in early infancy. *Journal of Cognitive Neuroscience* 2:81–95.
Johnson, M. H. (1993) Constraints on cortical plasticity. In: *Brain development and cognition: A reader*, ed. M. H. Johnson. Blackwell.
Johnson, M. H. & Bolhuis, J. J. (1991) Imprinting, predispositions and filial preference in the chick. In: *Neural and behavioral plasticity*, ed. R. J. Andrew. Oxford University Press.
Johnson, M. H. & Karmiloff-Smith, A. (1992) Can neural selectionism be applied to cognitive development and its disorders? *New Ideas in Psychology* 10:35–46.
Johnson, M. H. & Morton, J. (1991) *Biology and cognitive development: The case of face recognition*. Blackwell.
Karmiloff-Smith, A. (1981) Getting developmental differences or studying child development? *Cognition* 10:151–58.
Karmiloff-Smith, A. (1983) A new abstract code or the new possibility of multiple codes? *Behavioral and Brain Sciences* 6(1):149–50.
Karmiloff-Smith, A. (1987) A developmental perspective on human consciousness. Invited Address, British Psychological Society Annual Conference, Sussex.
Karmiloff-Smith, A. (1992a) *Beyond modularity: A developmental perspective on cognitive science*. MIT Press.
Karmiloff-Smith, A. (1992b) Nature, nurture and PDP: Preposterous developmental postulates? *Connection Science* 4(3/4):253–69.
Karmiloff-Smith, A. (1992c) Abnormal behavioural phenotypes and the challenges they pose to connectionist models of development. Technical Reports in Parallel Distributed Processing and Cognitive Neuroscience, TR. PDP.CNS.92.7, Carnegie Mellon University.
Karmiloff-Smith, A. & Clark, A. (1993) What's special about the human mind/brain? A reply to Abrahamsen, Bechtel, Dennett, Plunkett, Scutt & O'Hara. *Mind and Language* 8(3):569–82.
Karmiloff-Smith, A., Klima, E., Bellugi, U., Grant, J. & Baron-Cohen, S. (1995) Is there a social interaction module? Language, face processing and theory of mind in subjects with Williams syndrome. *Journal of Cognitive Neuroscience* 7:196–208.
Klahr, D. (1992) Information-processing approaches to cognitive development. In: *Developmental psychology: An advanced textbook*, 3d ed., ed. M. H. Bornstein & M. E. Lamb. Erlbaum.
Klahr, D. & Dunbar, K. (1988) Dual search space during scientific reasoning. *Cognitive Science* 12:148.
Klahr, D., Langley, P. & Neches, R., eds. (1987) *Production system models of learning and development*. MIT Press.
Kuhn, D., Amsel, E. & O'Loughlin, M. (1988) *The development of scientific thinking skills*. Academic Press.
Kuhn, D. & Phelps, E. (1982) *The development of problem-solving strategics.* In: *Advances in child development and behavior*, vol. 17, ed. H. Reese. Academic Press.

Langley, P., Simon, H. A., Bradshaw, C. L. & Zytkow, J. M. (1987) *Scientific discovery: Computational explorations of the creative processes*. MIT Press.

Leslie, A. M. (1992) Pretense, autism and the theory of mind module. *Current Directions in Psychological Science* 1:18–21.

Mandler, J. M. (1992) How to build a baby II: Conceptual primitives. *Psychological Review* 99(4):587–604.

Marler, P. (1991) The instinct to learn. In: *Epigenesis of the mind: Essays in biology and knowledge*, ed. S. Carey & R. Gelman. Erlbaum.

Marshall, J. C. (1984) Multiple perspectives on modularity. *Cognition* 17:209–42.

McClelland, J. L. (1991) Paper given at meeting of the Society for Research in Child Development, Seattle.

McClelland, J. L. & Jenkins, E. (1990) Nature, nurture and connectionism: Implications for connectionist models for cognitive development. In: *Architectures for intelligence*, ed. K. van Lehn. Erlbaum.

Meltzoff, A. N. (1990) Towards a developmental cognitive science: The implications of cross-modal matching and imitation for the development of memory in infancy. *Annals of the New York Academy of Sciences* 608:1–37.

Morton, J. (1986) Developmental contingency modelling. In: *Theory building in developmental psychology*, ed. P. van Ceehrt. Elsevier.

Nelson, K. (1986) *Event knowledge, structure and function in development*. Erlbaum.

Neville, H. J. (1991) Neurobiology of cognitive and language processing: Effects of early experience. In: *Brain maturation and cognitive development: Comparative and cross-cultural perspectives*, ed. K. R. Gibson & A. C. Petersen. Aldine de Gruyter.

Newell, A. (1990) *Unified theories of cognition*. Harvard University Press.

Oyama, S. (1985) *The ontogeny of information: Developmental systems and evolution*. Cambridge University Press.

Parisi, D. (1990) Connectionism and Piaget's sensory-motor intelligence. Paper presented at conference on *Evolution and Cognition: The Heritage of Jean Piaget's Epistemology*, Bergamo, Italy.

Perner, J. (1991) *Understanding the representational mind*. MIT Press.

Piaget, J. (1955) *The child's construction of reality*. Routledge & Kegan Paul.

Piaget, J. (1967) *Biologie et connaissance*. Callimard.

Piatelli-Palmerini, M. (1989) Evolution, selection, and cognition: From "learning" to parameter setting in biology and the study of language. *Cognition* 31:1–44.

Pinker, S. & Mehler, J., eds. (1988) Connectionism and symbol systems: Special edition. *Cognition* 28.

Plunkett, K. & Marchman, V. (1991) U-shaped learning and frequency effects in a multi-layered perception: Implications for child language acquisition. *Cognition* 38:43–102.

Plunkett, K. & Sinha, C. (1992) Connectionism and developmental theory. *British Journal of Developmental Psychology* 10:209–54.

Poizner, H., Klima, E. S. & Bellugi, U. (1987) *What the hands reveal about the brain*. MIT Press.

Premack, D. (1975) Putting a face together. *Science* 188:228–36.

Premack, D. (1986) *Gavagail Or the future history of the animal language controversy*. MIT Press.

Premack, D. (1991) "Does the chimpanzee have a theory of mind?" revisited. In: *Machiavellian intelligence*, ed. R. Byrne & A. Whiten. Oxford Science Publications.

Schank, R. C. & Abelson, R. P. (1977) *Plans, goals and understanding: An inquiry into human knowledge structures*. Erlbaum.

Schauble, L. (1990) Belief revision in children: The role of prior knowledge and strategies for generating evidence. *Journal of Experimental Child Psychology* 1:31–57.

Schneider, W. (1987) Connectionism: Is it a paradigm shift for psychology? *Behaviour Research Methods, Instruments and Computers* 19(2):73–83.

Shallice, T. (1988) *From neuropsychology to mental structure*. Cambridge University Press.

Shultz, T. R. (1991) *Simulating stages of human cognitive development with connectionist models*. In: *Machine learning: Proceedings of the eighth international workshop*, ed. L. Birnbaum & G. Collins. Morgan Kaufmann.

Siegler, R. S. & Crowley, K. (1991) The microgenetic method: A direct means for studying cognitive development. *American Psychologist* 46(6):606–20.

Siegler, R. S. & Robinson, M. (1982) The development of numerical understanding. In: *Advances in child development and behavior*, vol. 16, ed. H. W. Reese & L. P. Lipsett. Academic Press.

Skinner, B. F. (1953) *Science and human behaviour*. Macmillan.

Smolensky, P. (1988) On the proper treatment of connectionism. *Behavioral and Brain Sciences* 11:1–74.

Spelke, E. S. (1991) Physical knowledge in infancy: Reflections on Piaget's theory. In: *Epigenesis of the mind: Essays in biology and knowledge*, ed. S. Carey & R. Gelman. Erlbaum.

Thelen, E. (1989) Self-organization in developmental processes: Can systems approaches work? In: *Systems and development. Minnesota symposium in child psychology*, vol. 22, ed. M. Gunnar & E. Thelen. Erlbaum.

Van Geehrt, P. (1991) A dynamic systems model of cognitive and language growth. *Psychological Review* 98:3–53.

Part II

From typical to atypical development

4 Development itself is the key to understanding developmental disorders

Annette Karmiloff-Smith

All scientists studying normal and atypical development – from the staunchest Chomskyan nativist to the most domain-general empiricist – agree that development involves contributions from both genes and environment. The gulf between the theories lies in how genes and environment are claimed to contribute to developmental outcomes. At some level, of course, we all concur in the existence of some degree of innate specification. The difference in positions concerns how rich and how domain-specific the innately specified component is, whether development is the result of predetermined epigenesis[1] (mere triggering) or probabilistic epigenesis[1], and what happens when things go wrong. These differences in position influence the focus of the questions asked (nature or nurture, on the one hand, versus the mechanisms of progressive developmental change, on the other) and the way in which developmental disorders are studied.

Let's briefly take the example of language. For the staunch nativist, a set of genes specifically targets domain-specific modules as the end product of their epigenesis (e.g. a syntactic module[2], a morphological module[3], or a more narrowly pre-specified module for, say, canonical linkage rules in grammar[4]). Under this non-developmental view, the environment simply acts as a trigger for identifying and setting (environmentally-derived) native-tongue realizations of (pre-specified) parameters of universal grammar. The child is born innately expecting nouns, verbs, canonical linking rules, agreement between asymmetrical sentence elements, and so forth, but not yet knowing how they are realized in her/his native tongue[5]. The deletion, reduplication or mispositioning of genes is assumed to result in very specific impairments in the endstate[3–6]. For the empiricist, by contrast, much of the structure necessary for building language and the rest of the human mind is discovered directly in the structure of the physical and social environment.

These two extremes are not the only options, however. The neuroconstructivist approach to normal and atypical development fully recognizes innate biological constraints but, unlike the staunch nativist, considers them to be initially less detailed and less domain-specific as far as higher-level cognitive functions are concerned. Rather, development itself is seen as playing a crucial role in shaping phenotypical outcomes, with the protracted period of postnatal growth as essential in influencing the resulting domain specificity of the developing neocortex[7,8]. A clearer way to capture this idea is to specify that the interaction is not in fact between genes and environment. Rather, on the gene side, the interaction lies in the outcome of the indirect, cascading effects of interacting genes and their environments and, on the environment side, the interaction comes from the infant's *progressive* selection and processing of different kinds of input. For both the strict nativist and the empiricist, the notion of 'environment' is a static one, whereas development (both normal and atypical) is of course dynamic. The child's way of processing environmental stimuli is likely to change repeatedly as a function of development, leading to the progressive formation of domain-specific representations.

Most nativists interested in language argue that what is innately specified are *representations* of universal grammar. Other theorists recognize that knowledge representations *per se* are unlikely to be pre-specified in neocortex (although see Ref. 9 for an alternative, selectionist view of pre-specified representations). Rather than representational innateness, they opt for dedicated domain-specific mechanisms within innately specified modules, the presumed absence of which in a developmental disorder will inform about their specific function in normal development[10,11]. Such arguments seem to be heavily influenced by so-called evolutionary psychology[12]. According to this view, phylogenesis has led to increasing pre-specification for ontogenesis, such that there are genetically-coded responses to evolutionary pressures, leading, through relatively predetermined epigenesis, to hardwired circuitry for language, theory of mind, and other specific forms of higher-level cognitive processing. In this 'Swiss army knife' view of the brain, domain specificity is the starting point of ontogenesis, with development relegated to a relatively secondary role. A different view is that although evolution has pre-specified many constraints on development, it has made the human neocortex increasingly flexible and open to learning during postnatal development. In other words, evolution is argued to have selected for adaptive outcomes and a strong capacity to learn, rather than prior knowledge[7]. Within such a perspective, it is more plausible to think in terms of a variety of what one might call domain-relevant mechanisms that might gradually *become* domain-specific as a result of processing different kinds of input.

What does such a distinction entail? First we need to draw a distinction between domain-specific and domain-general mechanisms. Take, for example, inhibition. For the domain-general theorist, when the inhibitory mechanism is impaired, it will affect all systems across the board. By contrast, for the domain-specific theorist, the infant brain will contain, say, an inhibitory process *A* for theory-of-mind computations, an inhibitory process *B* for language-relevant computations, and yet another for sensorimotor development, and so forth. For this position, when the theory-of-mind inhibitory process is impaired, it will affect solely theory-of-mind computations, but leave intact linguistic, sensorimotor, and other domains. It is a subtly different distinction that I wish to draw between domain-relevant and domain-specific mechanisms. Unlike the domain-general theorist, this position does not argue for domain-general mechanisms simply applied across all domains. Rather, it suggests that biological constraints on the developing brain might have produced a number of mechanisms that do not start out as strictly domain-specific, that is, dedicated to the exclusive processing of one and only one kind of input. Instead, a mechanism starts out as somewhat more relevant to one kind of input over others, but it is usable – albeit in a less efficient way – for other types of processing too. This allows for compensatory processing and makes development channelled but far less predetermined than the nativist view. Once a domain-relevant mechanism is repeatedly used to process a certain type of input, it becomes domain-specific as a result of its developmental history[7,13]. Then, in adulthood, it can be differentially impaired. For example, a learning mechanism that has a feedback loop will be more relevant to processing sequential input than to processing static, holistic input. With time such a mechanism would become progressively dedicated to processing, say, sequentially presented linguistic input. In other words, rather than evolution providing pre-specified representations, this change in perspective places the mechanisms of progressive ontogenetic change on centre stage.

The implications for developmental disorders

The neuroconstructivist modification in perspective crucially influences the way in which atypical development is considered. In this approach, the deletion, reduplication or mispositioning of genes will be expected to subtly change the course of developmental pathways, with stronger effects on some outcomes and weaker effects on others. A totally specific disorder will, *ex hypothesis*, be extremely unlikely, thereby changing the focus of research in pathology. Rather than solely aiming to identify a damaged module at the cognitive level, researchers are encouraged to seek more subtle effects beyond the seemingly unique one, as well as to question whether successful behaviour (the presumed 'intact' part of the brain) is reached by the same processes as in normal development. This change in perspective means that atypical development should not be considered in terms of a catalogue of impaired and intact functions, in which non-affected modules are considered to develop normally, independently of the others. Such claims are based on the static, adult neuropsychological model which is inappropriate for understanding the dynamics of developmental disorders[14,15] (see Box 4.1).

Box 4.1 The postulates of the static adult neuropsychological model and its application to developmental disorders

- The method of double dissociation is used to identify specialized functions: Patient 1 has function A intact and function B impaired, whereas for Patient 2 the opposite obtains.
- This leads to the conclusion that the brain is organized into specialized circuits or modules which can be differentially damaged.

(continued)

(continued)

Thus far, the argument might be valid with respect to the fully-formed adult brain (although for arguments against the reduction of double dissociation to autonomy of modules, see Refs a,b; and for those against modularity of adult processing, see Ref. c). The subsequent conclusions are, in my view, open to serious challenge:

- Similar dissociations are found in certain developmental disorders.
- This leads to the conclusion that modules are innately specified in the human brain, with impaired genes mapped to impaired modules, alongside otherwise normal brain development.
- Developmental disorders are then explained in terms of the juxtaposition of damaged and intact sets of modules.

This ignores both the probabilistic dynamics of gene expression during embryogenesis and of progressive brain development during postnatal growth. When one considers the dynamics of development, the notion of the juxtaposition of spared and impaired higher-level cognitive processes is challenged, suggesting that in some developmental disorders, ostensibly 'intact' performance might turn out to be achieved through different cognitive processes (see Box 4.5).

References

a Plaut, D. (1995) Double dissociations without modularity: evidence from connectionist neuropsychology *J. Clin. Exp. Neuropsychol.* 17, 291–331

b Van Orden, G.C., Jansen op de Haar, M. and Bosman, A.M.T. (1997) Complex dynamic systems also predict dissociations, but they do not reduce to autonomous components *Cognit. Neuropsychol.* 14, 131–165

c Marslen-Wilson, W.D. and Tyler, L.K. (1987) Against modularity, in *Modularity in Knowledge Representations and Natural Language Understanding* (Garfield, J.L., ed.), pp. 37–62, MIT Press

The neuroconstructivist approach highlights how tiny variations in the initial state could give rise to domain-specific differences in endstates[7,13,15] (see Box 4.2). With a shift in focus from dissociations to cross-syndrome associations, disorders might turn out to lie on more of a continuum than commonly thought. Thus, two very distinct phenotypical outcomes could start with only slightly differing parameters but, with development, the effects of this small difference might be far reaching. This contrasts with the notion that a whole cognitive module is initially impaired. Rather, phenotypical outcomes could stem from small differences in one or more of the following parameters: developmental timing, gene dosage, neuronal formation, neuronal migration, neuronal density, biochemical efficiency affecting firing thresholds, variations in transmitter types, dendritic arborization, synaptogenesis, and pruning. The effects of alterations in these initial parameters might also vary in strength at different developmental periods[14]. Furthermore, some problems might stem from lack of connections between brain regions or between the two hemispheres[16,17]. In some cases, like Down syndrome, cognitive problems could stem from a failure to progressively specialize or modularize as a function of development, whereas in others specialization might occur too rapidly leaving less opportunity for environmental constraints to play a role in shaping the developmental outcome. These are all indirect and at a much lower level than the notion of direct damage to innately-specified cognitive modules invoked by strict nativists to explain developmental disorders. It is these subtle differences that are likely to explain the range of phenotypical outcomes that atypical development can display. Such differences might affect the resulting organism at multiple levels.

Box 4.2 Single and multiple gene disorders, but no Swiss army knives

A report in the press recently heralded the discovery of a specific gene for hearing. The Science article[a] on which it was based, however, illustrates how indirect the effects of the gene are. Geneticists studying eight generations of a Costa Rican family found a 50% incidence of acquired deafness, with onset around age 10 and complete deafness by age 30. A single gene mutation was identified, with the last 52 amino acids in the gene's protein product misformed, and the first 1,213 amino acids formed correctly. This gene produces a protein that controls the assembly of actin. Actin organizes the tiny fibres found in cell plasma which determine a cell's structural properties, such as rigidity. Because the genetic impairment is tiny and the protein functions sufficiently well to control the assembly of actin in most parts of the body, no other deficits are observable. However, it turns out that hair cells are especially sensitive to loss of rigidity, such that even this tiny impairment has a huge effect on them, resulting in deafness. In other words, what might look like a specialized gene for a complex trait like hearing is, on closer examination, very indirect – hearing is dependent on the interaction of huge numbers of genes, one of which affects the rigidity of hair cells and has cascading effects on the others. A 'gene for hearing' might be a convenient shorthand, but it could be a very misleading one, impeding the researcher from seeking to understand the probabilistic dynamics of development.

A second illustration comes from a computational model of the development of the ventral and dorsal pathways of visual cortex. There are several things we know about these pathways. First, they operate on somewhat

(continued)

(continued)

different time schedules in early infancy: infants track novel objects (dorsal pathway) before they can categorize them (ventral pathway). Second, double dissociations exist in adult brain damage, such that patients can locate objects without being able to identify them, or vice versa[b]. This has led some neuropsychologists to argue that the two pathways must be innately specified. But is this conclusion necessary? Their specialization in adulthood could have emerged from development itself. A computational model illustrates how this might occur[c]. A simple three-layer feedforward network was used. At the hidden layer, two channels were fed with identical input (see figure). The only difference was the speed with which activation levels changed (channel A rapidly, channel B slowly). Despite processing identical inputs, channel A progressively came to represent where objects were (mimicking the dorsal pathway in the brain), whereas channel B came to represent what each object was (ventral pathway). These functions were not pre-specified in the network but emerged from its developmental history, caused by a small difference in a starting state parameter. Thus, when neuropsychologists find dissociations in brain-damaged adults in visual form agnosia, this does not mean that the 'where' and 'what' pathways are necessarily pre-specified in the infant neocortex for spatio/temporal information versus form/colour/shape information. A small difference simply in firing thresholds (which might be innate) could give rise to such specialized functions indirectly, via the gradual processing during early infancy of differences between moving versus static stimuli. And a lack of such a difference in firing thresholds could result in domain-specific abnormality in one of these pathways. Again, the shorthand of talking about innate 'where' and 'what' pathways could be seriously misleading. They might only *become* what they are after processing the input. This leads to an important speculation: domain-specific outcomes might not even be possible without the process of development itself.

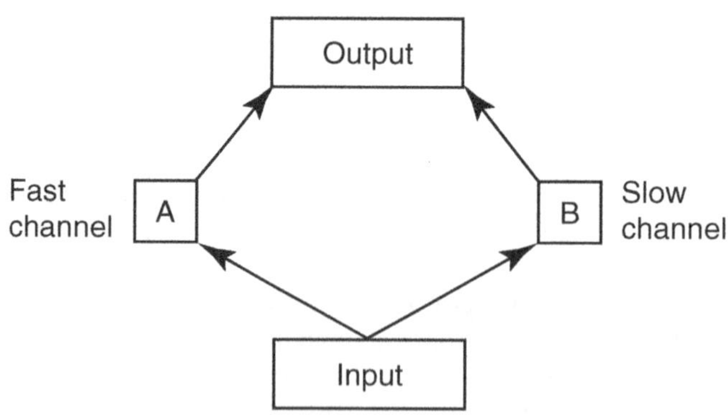

A simple three-layer feedforward network model of specialization in neural pathways. (See text for details.)

These two examples highlight the importance of giving serious consideration to very indirect causes of albeit very specific outcomes.

References

a Lynch, E.D. *et al.* (1997) Nonsyndromic deafness DFNA1 associated with mutation of a human homolog of the *Drosophila* gene *diaphanous Science* 278, 1315–1318

b Goodale, M.A. and Milner, A.D. (1992) Separate visual pathways for perception and action *Trends Neurosci.* 15, 20–25

c O'Reilly, R.C. and McClelland, J.L. (1992) The self-organization of spatially invariant representations *Technical Report PDP.CNS.92.5*, Carnegie Mellon University

These multiple levels – brain volume, regional anatomy, brain chemistry, hemispheric asymmetry, the temporal patterns of brain activity, physical characteristics and cognitive/ behavioural outcome – have recently been studied in some detail with respect to one neurodevelopmental disorder, Williams syndrome (see Boxes 4.3, 4.4 and 4.5). Consideration of the multiple two-way mappings from the biological to the cognitive levels leads to different hypotheses about so-called 'intact' abilities; that is, even where normal *behavioural* levels are found in a developmental disorder in a given domain, they might be achieved by different *cognitive* processes. This turns out to be the case for Williams syndrome, in which face processing and language are particularly proficient alongside other serious impairments, but the proficiency seems to be achieved through different cognitive processes (see Box 4.5).

Box 4.3 Williams syndrome: genetic and brain levels

Williams syndrome (WS) is caused by a microdeletion on the long arm of chromosome 7 at q.11,23 (Refs a,b). The genes on the deleted area have not all been identified, but they include:

- the elastin gene (*ELN*), not expressed in the brain, and thought to cause the vascular abnormalities;
- the *Limkinase1* gene (*LIMK1*) expressed in the brain, and claimed to cause the spatial deficits;
- the gene for DNA replication factor C2 (*RFC2*), and syntaxin1A (*STX1A*) which affects the way chemicals are released in the brain;
- the *frizzled* gene (*FZD3*), affecting the way in which cells signal to one another during development.

(continued)

(continued)

All patients with classic WS are hemizygous for *ELN, LIMK1, STX1A* and *RFC2*. While these discoveries seem to offer a neat mapping between genes and particular phenotypical outcomes, our recent study challenges these conclusions[c]. Three patients were identified with hemizygotic *ELN* and *LIMK1* deletions, two of whom also had *RFC2* deletions and one the *STX1A* deletion. However, none had the facial dysmorphology, the mental retardation or the specific spatio-constructive problems typical of people with Williams syndrome. The explanation of the WS phenotype clearly cannot be sought in simple gene/outcome mappings, but lies at the level of developmental timing and downstream effects of the complex interaction between all the deleted genes and the rest of the developing organism.

At the brain level, WS has been mainly described in terms of adult brains[d]. No work has yet been done on the developing infant brain. Some important discoveries about the fully-formed adult brain include:

- the WS brain is 80% of normal volume
- the total cerebral grey matter is significantly reduced
- there is abnormal layering, orientation, clustering and size of neurones
- the anterior regions are smaller than in normal controls but larger than in Down syndrome brains
- the dorsal hemispheres show cortical malformation
- the cerebrum is particularly small
- the limbic structures of the temporal lobe are small but proportionally similar to normal controls
- the frontal cortex displays a near normal proportional relation with posterior cortex, although both are reduced in size

Although limbic structures and frontal cortex are both proportionally similar in WS compared with normal brains, their functions show very different levels of impairment, with socio–affective behaviour being relatively good[e] and executive functions being particularly impaired[f]. Thus, the existence of normal anatomical proportions cannot be used to infer normal functions in the domains that they subserve in normal adults.

Our study using magnetic resonance spectroscopy has shown that brain biochemistry is also atypical in people with WS (Ref. g). Significant correlations were found between abnormal brain chemistry in the cerebellum and various neuropsychological tests, including Verbal and Performance IQ, British Picture Vocabulary Scale, and Ravens Progressive Matrices. The strongest correlation was with very poor results on a task measuring speed of processing, suggesting decreased neuronal efficiency in WS.

Finally, several studies have investigated brain activation in WS, particularly with respect to their domains of relative proficiency (language and face processing; see Box 4.5)[h]. Event-related potentials of individuals with WS show abnormal patterns for both face processing and language. More importantly, such patterns are found at no age across normal development, suggesting aberrant rather than delayed development in WS (Ref. h). Neither do people with WS show the progressive hemispheric asymmetries typical of normal development[h]. Furthermore, infants with WS spend far more time than controls focused on faces and language[i], suggesting that more of the developing brain might be devoted to processing such inputs.

In sum, brain volume, brain anatomy, brain chemistry, hemispheric asymmetry, and the temporal patterns of brain activity are all atypical in people with WS. How could the resulting cognitive system be described in terms of a normal brain with parts intact and parts impaired, as the popular view holds[j,k]? Rather, the brains of infants with WS develop differently from the outset, which has subtle, widespread repercussions at the cognitive level (see Box 4.5).

References

a Frangiskakis, J.M. *et al.* (1996) *LIM-kinase1* hemizygosity implicated in impaired visuospatial constructive cognition *Cell* 86, 59–69

b Tassabehji, M.K. *et al.* (1996) LIM-kinase detected in Williams syndrome *Nat. Genet.* 13, 272–273

c Tassabehji, M.K. *et al.* (1997) Genotype–phenotype correlations in Williams Syndrome *Am. J. Hum. Genet.* 61, 11

d Galaburda, A.M. *et al.* (1994) Cytoarchitectonic anomalies in a genetically based disorder: Williams syndrome *NeuroReport* 5, 753–757

e Karmiloff-Smith, A. *et al.* (1995) Is there a social module? Language, face processing and theory-of-mind in subjects with Williams syndrome *J. Cogn. Neurosci.* 7, 196–208

f Wang, P.P. *et al.* (1992) The specific neurobehavioral profile of WS is associated with neocerebellar hemispheric preservation *Neurology* 42, 1999–2002

g Rae, L. *et al.* (1998) Brain biochemistry in Williams syndrome: evidence for a role of the cerebellum in cognition? *Neurology* 51, 33–40

h Neville, H.J., Mills, D.L. and Bellugi, U. (1993) Effects of altered auditory sensitivity and age of language acquisition on the development of language-relevant neural systems: preliminary studies of Williams syndrome, in *Cognitive Deficits in Developmental Disorders: Implications for Brain Function* (Broman, S. and Grafman, J., eds), pp. 67–83, Erlbaum

i Mervis, C.B. *et al.* (1998) Williams syndrome: findings from an integrated program of research, in *Neurodevelopmental Disorders: Contributions to a New Framework from the Cognitive Neurosciences* (Tager-Flusberg, H., ed.), MIT Press

j Pinker, S. (1994) *The Language Instinct*, Harmondsworth, Penguin

k Bickerton, D. (1997) Constructivism, nativism and explanatory adequacy *Behav. Brain Sci.* 20, 557–558

Box 4.4 Clinical characteristics of the Williams syndrome phenotype

Williams syndrome (WS) is a rare genetic disorder that occurs in 1 in 20,000 live births. Its clinical features[a] include dysmorphic facies (see figures below), congenital heart and renal disorders due to a narrowing of the large arteries, musculo-skeletal abnormalities, growth retardation, hyperacusis, and infantile hypercalcaemia. The physical abnormalities are accompanied by moderate to severe mental retardation, a specific personality profile, very poor visuospatial constructive skills and relatively good language and face processing abilities (see Box 4.5).

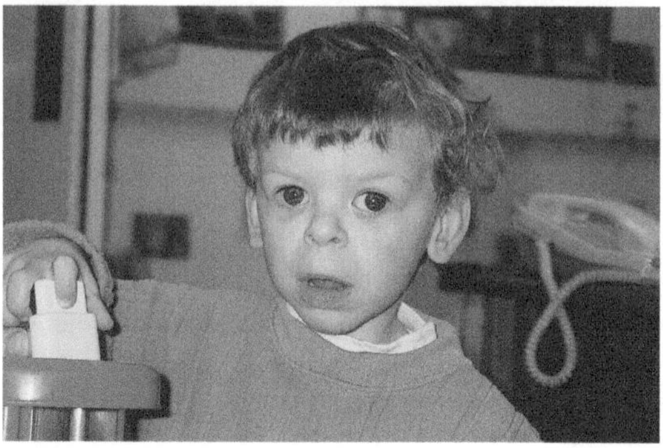

M.S., aged 2 years

The typical facial dysmorphology in WS, illustrated in three patients (photographs reproduced with permission of parents), aged 2 years, 10 years and 18 years, respectively. To be noted are the full cheeks, flared nostrils, wide mouth, full lips, pointed ears, and dental irregularities.

L.S., aged 10 years

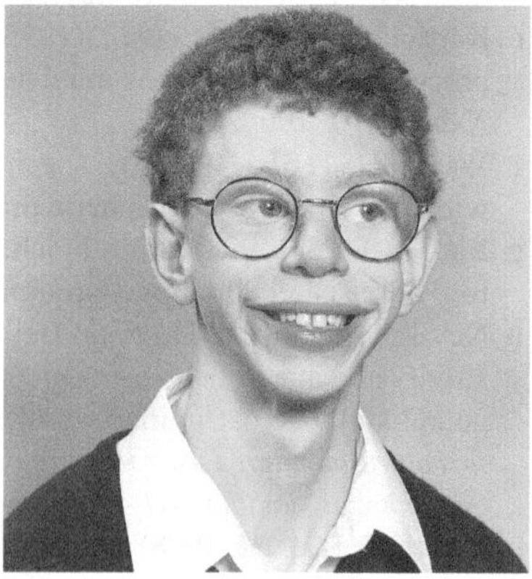

R.D., aged 18 years

Reference

a Udwin, O. and Dennis, J. (1995) Williams syndrome, in *Clinics in Developmental Medicine No. 138: Behavioural Phenotypes* (O'Brien, G. and Yule, W., eds), pp. 201–204, MacKeith Press, London

Box 4.5 Williams syndrome: the resulting cognitive–behavioural phenotype

Classic Williams syndrome (WS) has been characterized along the following lines (for more details, see Refs a–c):

- IQs mainly in the 50s (range: 45–87)
- serious deficits in spatio-constructive skills, but spatio-perceptual skills as would be predicted by Mental Age
- serious deficits in numerical cognition
- serious deficits in problem solving and planning
- intact syntactic capacities alongside aberrant semantics
- intact face processing capacities
- relatively spared social cognition skills.

The above conclusions stemmed mainly from standardized tests used to assess intact and impaired functions, an approach inspired theoretically by the adult neuropsychological model of deficit. However, even in cases where behavioural scores are equivalent to chronologically matched controls, it is essential to go beyond behavioural success and study the underlying cognitive processes in detail[d,e]. For example, our study of face-processing capacities of people with WS (Ref. e) showed that, although their scores were equivalent to normal controls, the way in which they solved the task was different. Whereas normal controls used predominantly configural (holistic) processing, the subjects with WS reached their good scores by using predominantly componential (feature-by-feature) processing. In other words, different *cognitive* processes led to similar *behavioural* outcomes. The notion that WS displays a normal, intact face-processing module is thereby challenged. Nonetheless, the neuroconstructivist view could accept that people with WS might have developed a face-processing module. However, it would be argued that, rather than simply being triggered, such a module – like the normal face-processing module – is the result of a developmental process of modularization, but emerging in this case from an atypical ontogenetic pathway.

A similar story obtains for WS language acquisition. Several studies now suggest that neither syntax nor semantics is entirely normal in WS, despite earlier claims to the contrary. First, there is a discrepancy between vocabulary Mental Age (MA) and syntactic MA, the former being considerably higher[f]. Second, high vocabulary scores in WS patients camouflage the fact that they learn the lexicon in a somewhat different way from normally developing children[g]. Third, they show dissociations within syntax itself, with problems in forming agreement between elements in phrase structure, difficulties in processing embedded relative clauses and subcategorization

(continued)

(continued)

frames (the distinction between transitive and intransitive verbs), and so forth[f,h,i]. Furthermore, even when language is fluent, Williams syndrome cannot be used to claim, as some have[j], that syntax develops independently of cognition. The use of IQ scores is very misleading in this respect. To state that a person has fluent language but an IQ of 51 indeed appears theoretically surprising and could lead to the conclusion that syntax develops in isolation from the rest of the brain. But to state that the same person has fluent language and an MA of 7 yrs changes the conclusion. In other words, those people with WS who have relatively fluent language might indeed have low IQs, but their MAs in non-verbal cognition, although seriously behind their chronological age, are usually well over 5, the age at which most language has been acquired in normally developing children.

In sum, not only are brain anatomy, brain chemistry, and temporal brain processes atypical, but Williams syndrome also displays an abnormal cognitive phenotype in which, even where behavioural scores are equivalent to those of normal controls, the cognitive processes by which such proficiency is achieved are different.

Our ongoing longitudinal behavioural and brain-imaging studies of atypical infants (with Janice Brown, Sarah Paterson, Marisa Gsödl, Michelle de Haan, Mark Johnson and others) already point to important differences in the initial state of WS patients compared with controls. The atypical groups' patterns are not one of juxtaposition of intact and impaired functions, as different end states might suggest. Interestingly, too, although WS linguistic performance ends up resembling normal language far more than Down syndrome performance, our preliminary results with infants show how important it is to distinguish the cognitive level from the behavioural level (see Box 4.6). Fluent linguistic behaviour might stem from different processes at the cognitive level of description. Our initial results suggest that Down syndrome language comprehension has a delayed but relatively normal developmental pathway in infancy, whereas WS language development seems to be deviant from the outset. It is only by focusing studies of developmental disorders at their roots in early infancy that we will ultimately be able to chart longitudinally the varying developmental pathways that progressively lead to different phenotypical outcomes.

References

a Udwin, O. and Yule, W. (1991) A cognitive and behavioural phenotype in Williams syndrome *J. Clin. Exp. Neuropsychol.* 13, 232–244

b Bellugi, U., Wang, P. and Jernigan, T.L. (1994) Williams syndrome: an unusual neuropsychological profile, in *Atypical Cognitive Deficits in Developmental Disorders: Implications for Brain Function* (Broman, S. and Grafman, J., eds), pp. 23–56, Erlbaum

c Mervis, C.B. *et al.* (1998) Williams syndrome: findings from an integrated program of research, in *Neurodevelopmental Disorders: Contributions to a New Framework from the Cognitive Neurosciences* (Tager-Flusberg, H., ed.), MIT Press

d Pennington, B. (1997) Using genetics to dissect cognition *Am. J. Hum. Genet.* 60, 13–16

e Karmiloff-Smith, A. (1997) Crucial differences between developmental cognitive neuroscience and adult neuropsychology *Dev. Neuropsychol.* 13, 513–524

f Karmiloff-Smith, A. *et al.* (1997) Language and Williams syndrome: how intact is 'intact'? *Child Dev.* 68, 246–262

g Stevens, T. and Karmiloff-Smith, A. (1997) Word learning in a special population: do individuals with Williams syndrome obey lexical constraints? *J. Child Lang.* 24, 737–765

h Karmiloff-Smith, A. *et al.* (1998) Linguistic dissociations in Williams syndrome: evaluating receptive syntax in on-line and off-line tasks *Neuropsychologia* 6, 342–351

i Volterra, V. *et al.* (1996) Linguistic abilities in Italian children with Williams syndrome *Cortex* 32, 67–83

j Bickerton, D, (1997) Constructivism, nativism and explanatory adequacy *Behav. Brain Sci.* 20, 557–558

Box 4.6 Models of developmental disorders of known genetic aetiology

The figure illustrates how the neuroconstructivist approach differs in its theoretical assumptions and resulting research strategies from both the nativist and empiricist accounts. Boxes and arrows are clearly not the most appropriate notation for a dynamic system, but the current representation hopefully captures some of the essential differences between neuroconstructivism and the other two theories. At the cognitive level, the neuroconstructivist approach stresses the difference between innate representations (invoked by most nativist linguists) and much lower-level innate computational and timing constraints from which representations progressively emerge as a function of development and of interaction with different types of environmental input. The multiple interactions between all levels, invoked by the neuroconstructivist approach, highlight why it is essential to start studies of developmental disorders in early infancy and then to trace the subsequent processes of development itself.

(continued)

(continued)

		Nativist
Theoretical assumptions	Cause	genetic defect
	Brain	specific deficit in prewired cortical circuit; plasticity solely as response to damage
	Cognitive	missing/damaged innate cognitive module
	Environment	environment static (acts as trigger only)
	Behavioural	domain-specific outcome
Research strategies	Seek cause	identify gene(s)
	Choose domain of study	focus on single, impaired higher-level cognitive modules
	Choose methodology	focus on cognitive tasks in impaired domain; search for selective impairments; brain imaging to highlight specific cortical areas involved; environmental input not studied
	Choose targeted population	study behaviour in endstate (middle childhood/adulthood); focus on phenotypes presenting specific or double dissociations

Empiricist	Neuroconstructivist
genetic defect of limited interest; main focus on environmental causes	genetic defect; widespread and/or specific deficits depending on how early in prenatal development perturbation occurs;
general brain deficit expected; plasticity solely as a passive response to input	perturbation to normal patterns of pre- and post-natal brain development; plasticity as basic feature of normal and atypical cortical development
not a distinct level	modules develop by a process of gradual modularization; distinguish innate representations (rare at cortical level) from lower-level computational devices and differential developmental timing
environment static (structures child's brain directly)	environment dynamic (changes as a function of infant's selection and processing of input)
domain-general outcome	specific and general outcomes both important; the later the gene expression, the more specific the impairment expected
identify environmental factors	identify timing of gene expression and interactions with other genetic and environmental events
focus on general processing efficiency and learning	identify lowest level of impairment and study its developmental effects on higher-level cognition re both proficiencies and impairments
IQ and other such tasks; training for behavioural change; investigate direct effects of environment	devise tasks to differentiate behaviour from cognitive processes; longitudinal brain imaging of both temporal and spatial changes; study changes in timing of environmental input
no specific age group targeted	study earliest possible markers of disorder in foetus and infancy; focus on differences and similarities across phenotypes

Are some developmental disorders truly specific?

Despite the arguments in the previous section, some developmental disorders (e.g. autism[18,19], Asperger syndrome[20], dyslexia[21], Turner's syndrome[22], Specific Language Impairment[14]) appear at first sight to involve very specific deficits at the cognitive level. Autism, for example, is argued to be the result of impairment of the domain-specific mechanism of metarepresentation, dedicated solely to the processing of social stimuli[10,19] – a deficit in the so-called 'theory-of-mind' module. When other, non-social impairments are noted, they are explained either in terms of secondary effects[10] or of an additional, unrelated cognitive impairment[23], with other parts of the brain assumed to be intact. A similar approach has been taken with respect to Specific Language Impairment (SLI). This phenotype suggests, by its very name, a specific linguistic deficit alongside otherwise intact intelligence, as if grammar developed in total isolation of the rest of the growing brain. Researchers differ as to what they claim the specific deficit to be: the inability to make canonical links from grammar to semantics[4], feature blindness with respect to morphology[3,24], and so forth (for comprehensive reviews, see Refs 14, 25). The common suggestion, however, is that there is a specific genetic underpinning to the derivation of certain grammatical rules, which is impaired in these forms of SLI but leaving the rest of development intact.

It is clear that disorders like autism and SLI have a genetic origin and that evolutionary pressures have contributed to whatever is innately specified. This is a truism. The question is whether, on the one hand, the deficit results from damage to a domain-specific starting point at the cognitive level, as a result of evolution specifying dedicated processing systems for grammar, theory of mind and so forth, or whether, on the other hand, evolution has specified more general constraints for higher-level cognition and there is a more indirect way for genetic defects to result in domain-specific outcomes as a function of development.

The case of SLI (Ref. 14) shows how this second alternative might hold. Developmental timing plays a crucial role. If, early on, the infant's processing of fast auditory transitions is even slightly delayed in maturation, then certain aspects of grammar might, with development, emerge as more impaired than others. Grammatical disorders would then be the indirect, developmental effect of a subtle, initial acoustic deficit. Such a position is supported by the fact that training solely at the acoustic level has been shown to have positive repercussions at the grammatical level[26]. However, some adolescents and adults with SLI do not display a processing deficit[3,4,25]. It is none the less possible that by later childhood or adulthood, an initial deficit in acoustic processing which had a huge effect at one point in development might no longer be detectable (owing, for example, to subsequent long-term compensation or to ceiling effects and the lack of sufficiently subtle measures; S. Rosen, pers. commun.), but its early effects could continue to have a significant impact. This stresses the importance of developmental timing in understanding developmental disorders. Although atypical processing of fast auditory transitions might not turn out to be the final cause of SLI, this view aptly illustrates how a less pre-specified approach to language can result in a language-specific representational impairment through the process of development itself. This is why a truly developmental approach is so crucial.

The neuroconstructivist account modifies the way a developmental disorder like SLI will be studied. It suggests that focus must be placed on at risk populations in early infancy, before the onset of language, and longitudinally thereafter, to ascertain whether the timing of subtle developmental processes is out of synchrony and grows in importance as the child starts to process more complex linguistic input. Furthermore, the neuroconstructivist approach predicts that because of the way genes interact in their developmental expression, we should seek co-occurring, more subtle impairments which might have nothing to do with language. In fact, it has been shown that people with language-related deficits, such as SLI or dyslexia, often display an impairment (albeit lesser) in various forms of motor control such as balance[27]. This indicates that we might not be dealing with an initially language-specific impairment, but a deficit that turns out to be more detrimental to spoken and/or written language over developmental time (i.e. caused by an earlier language-relevant deficit), but that also gives rise to (weaker) problems in other areas. There is unlikely to be such a thing as impaired 'genes for reading' or 'genes for grammar'. Rather, genetic impairments lead to a disruption in probabilistic epigenesis pushing individuals onto different developmental pathways which eventually result in reading or grammatical deficits[26–28].

The neuroconstructivist approach would seek the initial disruption in innate mechanisms such as level of firing thresholds, differences in inhibition, and so forth. These are clearly at a lower-level, less richly domain-specific form than is commonly invoked by strict nativists who argue for innately specified representations of universal grammar. Neuroconstructivists would seek domain-relevant computational biases and the effects of differential developmental timing[7]. This is because we hypothesize that, rather than bringing greater pre-specialization to neocortex, evolution has provided the human neocortex with a greater and more varied capacity to learn via the process of development itself[29]. This clearly requires innate constraints but, because of the unusually slow period of human postnatal brain development, the child's gradual processing of different types of input is likely to have a strong influence on the way in which neocortex structures itself.

Conclusions

One of the major problems with very specific accounts of developmental disorders of higher-level cognition is that so far no gene (or set of genes) has been identified that is expressed solely in a specific region of neocortex (see Ref. 30 for discussion). Yet, such theories claim that neocortex is pre-specified for functions such as theory of mind or language and that this is why they can dissociate in adulthood. This is the basis for most brain imaging studies. Some authors go as far as claiming that epigenetic selection acts on preformed synaptic substrates and that to learn is to stabilize pre-existing synaptic combinations and to eliminate the surplus[31]. By contrast, current knowledge suggests that genes that are expressed in neocortex tend to do so throughout most regions, resulting in a similar six-layer structure and a similar overall pattern of intrinsic connectivity[30]. Combinations of neuroanatomical features, cortical layers and brain cytoarchitectural regions are found to be remarkably similar in all regions of the brain from birth to 72 months. In other words, for quite some time the developmental patterns of different cytoarchitectural regions are indistinguishable from one another[32]. A single set of instructions might structure the different areas of neocortex, leaving the interaction with different environmental inputs to influence specific forms of synaptogenesis and dendritic arborization. In fact, neocortical specialization has already been shown to be very progressive across developmental time[33]. So if there is early genetic impairment, then it could be relatively widespread in the developing neocortex, even though its effects might be surprisingly differential in outcome. To be biologically and developmentally plausible, we must go beyond the more obvious deficit to seek far subtler effects on other aspects of the developing system. Even if future research were to uncover a specific regional pattern of neocortical gene expression – which is not ruled out by the position developed in this paper – the neuroconstructivist approach would force a reinterpretation of the meaning of localized gene expression, encouraging researchers to take serious account of the developmental time course. The systemic properties of ontogenesis and the developmental effects of the interconnectedness of brain regions, together with a structuring rather than merely triggering role for environmental input, would still be likely to result in a cascade of subtle deficits rather than a single, higher-level one.

Because both normal and abnormal development is progressive, a change of focus is essential in future research into pathology. Rather than concentrate on the study of disorders solely at their end state in school-aged children and adults, which is most commonly the case, it becomes essential to study disorders in early infancy, and longitudinally, to understand how alternative developmental pathways might lead to different phenotypical outcomes. Furthermore, if we accept that behavioural outcomes could stem from different cognitive processes, then matching control groups on the basis of behavioural scores, rather than underlying processes, might also be open to challenge.

One essential step towards a deeper understanding of developmental disorders is to model their various manifestations. In an important contribution to the field, Morton and Frith devised a structural framework for causal modelling within which to explore a variety of theories concerning different abnormal phenotypes[34]. Work of this nature is crucial in developing more constrained theories of developmental disorders. The authors present their discussion in terms of a framework rather than the embodiment of a particular theory. However, the 55 different models that they explore are all unidirectional in their causal chains, and so do not capture the basic assumptions of the neuroconstructivist approach. The figure in Box 4.6 illustrates how the neuroconstructivist approach differs from both the nativist and empiricist approaches to developmental psychopathology. It pinpoints the various theoretical assumptions discussed in this paper and the different research strategies to which they lead.

The complex dynamics of both normal and atypical development indicate, in my view, that the neuroconstructivist approach is the most viable theoretical framework within which to explore developmental disorders. These must be approached from early infancy onwards, and simultaneously at multiple levels: the genetic, the brain in its spatial and temporal dynamics, the cognitive, the environmental and the behavioural, as well as stressing the multiple two-way rather than unidirectional chains that interact all the way from genetic causes through to ultimate behavioural outcomes. This is because the dynamics of development itself are the key to understanding developmental disorders.

Outstanding questions

- Some argue that evolution has provided the human cortex with increasingly detailed pre-specification prior to ontogenetic development. To what extent can the ontogenetic data be accounted for in terms of evolution selecting for less specific factors, such as increased neocortical plasticity and a greater range of learning mechanisms, to ensure adaptive outcomes rather than prior knowledge? Is it more useful to entertain the possibility that the highest level of evolution is to pre-specify simply a number of domain-relevant mechanisms which, after processing specific aspects of the environment, *become* increasingly domain-specific, that is, specialized, during ontogenesis? How might this change our perspective on developmental disorders?
- What can we learn about subtle differences in the environmental input to atypically developing infants and children? In this respect, is it useful to replace the static notion of 'environment' by that of the 'child's progressive processing of environmental input'? To what extent does the infant/child contribute to its own subsequent brain specialization by selecting aspects of its environment to attend to at different times in development?
- How influential is subcortical specialization in the structuring of neocortex?
- Are developmental disorders really specific, or do they lie on a continuum, with seeming dissociations due to relatively small differences in developmental timing, gene dosage, neuronal formation, neuronal migration, neuronal density, biochemical efficiency affecting firing thresholds, variations in transmitter types, dendritic arborization, synaptogenesis, and pruning?

(continued)

(continued)

- Just as modularity theorists can show that specific disorders also predict more general impairments, so non-modularity theorists can show that dynamic systems predict dissociations that do not reduce to autonomous modules. Is the double-dissociation method necessarily the right tool for furthering our knowledge of developmental disorders?
- If we do discover a truly specific disorder of higher-level cognition with no other subtle impairments, how could this be explained without violating what is known about the probabilistic epigenetics of biological development? Can one region of neocortex develop abnormally with no effects on any other region?
- How do acquired developmental disorders differ from genetically-based disorders?
- If we take development seriously, is atypical ontogenesis necessarily a window on the structure/functioning of the normal mind/brain, as seems to be taken for granted by many of those studying developmental disorders?

Acknowledgements

I should like to thank Mike Anderson, Susan Carey, Mark Johnson and Steven Rose, as well as the anonymous reviewers, for comments on an earlier version of this paper.

References

1 Gottlieb, G. (1992) *Individual Development and Evolution: The Genesis of Novel Behavior*, Oxford University Press
2 Lightfoot, D.W. (1989) The child's trigger experience: degree–0 learnability *Behav. Brain Sci.* 12, 321–375
3 Gopnik, M. (1997) Language deficits and genetic factors *Trends Cognit. Sci.* 1, 5–9
4 Van der Lely, H. (1994) Canonical linking rules: forward versus reverse linking in normally developing and specifically language-impaired children *Cognition* 51, 29–72
5 Pinker, S. (1994) *The Language Instinct*, Harmondsworth, Penguin
6 Clahsen, H. (1989) The grammatical characterisation of developmental dysphasia *Linguistics* 27, 897–920
7 Elman, J.L. *et al.* (1996) *Rethinking Innateness: A Connectionist Perspective on Development*, MIT Press
8 Quartz, S.R. and Sejnowsky, T.J. (1997) A neural basis of cognitive development: a constructivist manifesto *Behav. Brain Sci.* 20, 537–556
9 Changeux, J.P. and Dehaene, S. (1989) Neuronal models of cognitive functions *Cognition* 33, 63–109

10 Frith, U. and Happé, F. (1998) Why specific developmental disorders are not specific: on-line and developmental effects in autism and dyslexia *Dev. Sci.* 1, 267–272

11 Baron-Cohen, S. (1994) How to build a baby that can read minds: cognitive mechanisms in mindreading *Cahiers de Psychol. Cognit.* 13, 513–552

12 Tooby, J. and Cosmides, L. (1990) On the universality of human nature and the uniqueness of the individual: the role of genetics and adaptation *J. Personal.* 58, 17–67

13 Karmiloff-Smith, A. (1995) Annotation: the extraordinary cognitive journey from foetus through infancy *J. Child Psychol. Child Psychiatry* 36, 1293–1313

14 Bishop, D.V.M. (1997) *Uncommon Understanding: Development and Disorders of Language Comprehension in Children*, Psychology Press

15 Karmiloff-Smith, A. (1997) Crucial differences between developmental cognitive neuroscience and adult neuropsychology *Dev. Neuropsychol.* 13, 513–524

16 Liegeois, F. and de Schonen, S. (1997) Simultaneous attention in the two visual hemifields and interhemispheric integration: a developmental finding on 20–26 month-old infants *Neuropsychologia* 35, 381–385

17 Mancini, J. *et al.* (1994) Face recognition in children with early right or left brain damage *Dev. Med. Child Neurol.* 36, 156–166

18 Frith, U. (1989) *Autism: Explaining the Enigma*, Blackwell Science

19 Leslie, A.M. (1992) Pretence, autism and the theory-of-mind module *Curr. Dir. Psychol. Sci.* 1, 18–21

20 Frith, U., ed. (1991) *Autism and Asperger Syndrome*, Cambridge University Press

21 Frith, C. and Frith, U. (1996) A biological marker for dyslexia *Nature* 382, 19–20

22 Skuse, D.H. *et al.* (1997) Evidence from Turner's syndrome of an imprinted X-linked locus affecting cognitive function *Nature* 387, 705–708

23 Happé, F.G.E. (1996) Studying weak central coherence at low levels: children with autism do not succumb to visual illusions (a research note) *J. Child Psychol. Psychiatry* 37, 873–877

24 Gopnik, M. (1990) Feature-blind grammar and dysphasia *Nature* 344, 715

25 Temple, C.M. (1997) Cognitive neuropsychology and its application to children *J. Child Psychol. Psychiatry* 38, 27–52

26 Tallal, P. *et al.* (1996) Language comprehension in language-learning impaired children improved with acoustically modified speech *Science* 271, 81–84

27 Fawcett, A.J., Nicolson, R.I. and Dean, P. (1996) Impaired performance of children with dyslexia on a range of cerebellar tasks *Ann. Dyslexia* 46, 259–283

28 Pennington, B. (1997) Using genetics to dissect cognition *Am. J. Hum.Genet.* 60, 13–16

29 Gerhart, J. and Kirschner, M. (1997) *Cells, Embryos and Evolution*, Blackwell Science

30 Johnson, M.H. (1997) *Developmental Cognitive Neuroscience*, Blackwell Science

31 Dehaene-Lambertz, G. and Dehaene S. (1997) In defence of learning by selection: neurobiology and behavioral evidence revisited *Behav. Brain Sci.* 20, 560–561

32 Shankle, W.R. *et al.* (1998) Developmental patterns in the cytoarchitecture of the human cerebral cortex from birth to six years examined by correspondence analysis *Proc. Natl. Acad. Sci. U. S. A.* 95, 4023–4038

33 Neville, H.J. (1991) Neurobiology of cognitive and language processing: effects of early experience, in *Brain Maturation and Cognitive Development: Comparative and Cross-Cultural Perspectives* (Gibson, K.R. and Petersen, A.C., eds), pp. 355–380, Aladine de Gruyter Press, New York

34 Morton, J. and Frith, U. (1995) Causal modelling: a structural approach to developmental psychopathology, in *Manual of Developmental Psychopathology* (Vol. 1) (Cicchetti, D. and Cohen, D.J., eds), pp. 357–390, John Wiley & Sons

5 Dethroning the myth

Cognitive dissociations and innate modularity in Williams syndrome

Annette Karmiloff-Smith, Janice H. Brown, Sarah Grice, and Sarah Paterson

Neurocognitive studies of developmental disorders never turn out to be as straightforward as they first promise. Studies of Williams syndrome (WS) are no exception. The pioneering work of Bellugi, Lichtenberger, Jones, Lai, and St. George (2000) seemed to point to some clear-cut dissociations in the cognitive architecture of WS. Language and face processing appeared to be preserved in the face of both general retardation and particularly serious problems with visuospatial cognition, number skills, planning, and problem solving (Bellugi, Wang, & Jernigan, 1994). Researchers in the field of WS have been cautious about these claims, couching them in terms of relative strengths and weaknesses rather than absolute ones (Bellugi et al., 2000; Karmiloff-Smith, 1998; Karmiloff-Smith et al., 1997; Klein & Mervis, 1999; Mervis, 1999; Vicari, Carlesimo, Brizzolara, & Pezzini, 1996; Volterra, Capirci, Pezzini, Sabbadini, & Vicari, 1996). By contrast, secondary sources regarding WS data, cited in writings by linguists, psychologists, and philosophers, have often used WS to bolster claims about innate and independently functioning modules, some of which are intact and others impaired (e.g., Bickerton, 1997; Pinker, 1994, 1999). This emanates from a view, held explicitly or implicitly, that behavioral deficits found in the phenotypic outcome of individuals with genetic disorders are direct windows on the initial state, that is, the innate modular structure of the cognitive system (Baron-Cohen, 1998; Leslie, 1992; Temple, 1997; see Karmiloff-Smith, 1998, for critical discussion). As Baron-Cohen (1998) put it,

> I suggest that the study of mental retardation would profit from the application of the framework of cognitive neuropsychology. In cognitive neuropsychology, one key question running through the investigator's mind is 'is this process or mechanism intact or impaired in this person'?

The notion that an ability is necessarily intact in a genetic disorder when behavior falls within the normal range fails to consider the psychological processes underlying overt behavior. This kind of reasoning negates the role of development in producing phenotypic outcomes and treats the end-state cognitive system as if it were a normal system with some components missing and others intact. In other words, it is based on the neuropsychology model of brain damage to previously normal adults and can, in our view, be very misleading when applied to developmental disorders. Further, as far as WS is concerned, the nativist literature frequently misrepresents the empirical findings, treating relative strengths as absolute strengths. In the first part of this article, data relating to the phenotypic outcome of two areas hailed as intact in WS—language and face processing—are examined. In the second part, we look at the early cognitive state in toddlers with WS and consider its relationship to the adult end state.

Language and Williams syndrome

In our view, it remains questionable as to whether any aspect of language—syntax, semantics, phonology, or pragmatics—is intact in WS. Yet a number of researchers have tried to demonstrate that language, in particular morphosyntax, is preserved in WS and functions independently of other cognitive systems. Rossen, Jones, Wang, and Klima (1995), for example, claimed that "Williams syndrome presents a remarkable juxtaposition of impaired and intact mental capacities: linguistic functioning is preserved in WS while problem solving ability and visuospatial cognition are impaired." Likewise, Pinker (1991) claimed that:

> Although IQ is measured at around 50, older children and adolescents with WS are described as hyperlinguistic with selective sparing of syntax, and grammatical abilities are close to normal in controlled testing. This is one of several kinds of dissociation in which language is preserved despite severe cognitive impairments.

Not all researchers make such sweeping claims, but many linguists of a Chomskyan persuasion nonetheless try to find an aspect of WS language that is spared and, by extension, innately specified. For example, Clahsen and Almazan (1998) argued for a double dissociation of innate mechanisms, on the basis of their claim that in WS lexical memory is impaired and syntax is intact, whereas in specific language impairment (SLI) the opposite obtains. These authors used evidence from a number of syntactic elicitation and comprehension tasks. These included tests of past tense formation, expressive language, and the interpretation of passive sentences and of anaphoric and reflexive pronouns. Performance of the individuals with WS on the latter two tasks was at ceiling. However, ceiling effects are notoriously difficult to interpret because they can simply suggest that a task is not sensitive enough. Furthermore, Clahsen and Almazan's arguments were based on a very small sample of children with WS ($n = 2$ for mental age [MA] 5 years and $n = 2$ for MA $= 7$ years), together with considerable interindividual variation among the few participants. Strong claims about the cognitive architecture of a syndrome cannot be made on the basis of such sparse data.

The main claim of the Clahsen and Almazan (1998) study was that individuals with WS have a specific deficit in forming irregular past tenses (e.g., creep–crept) but intact performance in forming the regular past tense (e.g., walk–walked). Because this important claim was based on such a small sample with individual variation, we carried out a much broader, in-depth study of past tense formation (Thomas et al., 2001), comparing the performance of 21 participants with WS on two past tense elicitation tasks with that of four typically developing control groups at ages 6 years, 8 years, 10 years, and adult. Given that WS language is seriously delayed initially, Thomas et al. (2001) argued that it is not sufficient to show that irregular past tense formation is poorer than regular past tense formation, because this is also true of some stages of typical development. Rather it is necessary to demonstrate that the level of past tense formation is poorer than would be expected in individuals with WS for their actual level of language development. The study showed that when performance was related to chronological age (CA) using regression analyses, individuals with WS showed a somewhat greater disparity between irregular and regular verbs compared to the controls. However, when verbal MA was controlled for, the WS group displayed no selective deficit in irregular past tense formation. Moreover, we could not replicate the Clahsen and Almazan (1998) control data. At no age did our controls show high levels of irregularization of novel verbs that rhyme with irregular verbs (see also van der Lely & Ullman [2001] for similar control data results to ours). Furthermore, our results also highlighted how potentially misleading small samples such as in the Clahsen and Almazan (1998) study can be. As individuals, a few of our participants with WS performed very poorly on both regular and irregular verbs, whereas a few others displayed very high performance on both. If these high performers had by chance constituted the very small *N* of the Clahsen and Almazan study, then the authors would have had to draw totally different conclusions from the ones drawn. Our findings on a much larger population of 21 individuals with WS are inconsistent with the view that people with WS are selectively impaired on irregular past tense forms. Indeed, as a group, there was no selective deficit for irregulars and the WS results could be placed on the typical developmental pathway found in younger individuals. The results were in fact consistent with the hypothesis that the WS language system is delayed because it has developed under different constraints. Mervis and her collaborators (e.g., Klein & Mervis, 1999) have also concluded that the best way to characterize WS language is that it is delayed, revealing patterns typical of younger children.

A number of findings now suggest, however, that the WS language system is not only delayed but also develops along a different trajectory compared to controls, with individuals with WS placing relatively more weight on phonological information and relatively less weight on semantic information. For example, during the early acquisition of language, the naming spurt in WS precedes fast-mapping ability, whereas in typical development these two are closely associated (Mervis & Bertrand, 1997). These same authors also showed that the naming spurt in WS does not coincide with exhaustive category sorting, an index of children's maturing semantic representations, which suggests that vocabulary growth relies less on semantics than in the typically developing case (Mervis & Bertrand, 1997). Further, although local semantic organization looks normal in WS in terms of priming effects (Tyler et al., 1997) and in terms of category fluency (Scott et al., 1995), global semantic organization remains at the level of young children and never reaches the mature state even in relatively high functioning adults with WS (Johnson & Carey, 1998).

A number of other studies of oral and written language also point to a reduced contribution of semantics in language development in WS. For example, Karmiloff-Smith et al. (1997) found that when participants with WS were monitoring sentences for a target word, they did not show sensitivity to subcategory violations, suggesting that in WS semantic information may become available too slowly to be integrated with the online processing of syntax. A recent study of reading in WS came to similar conclusions about the role of phonology over semantics. The group with WS displayed equal levels of reading for both concrete and abstract words (Laing, Hulme, Grant, & Karmiloff-Smith, 2001). By contrast, the controls found concrete, imageable words much easier to read. In addition, the study showed that imageability effects are weaker in people with WS. Finally, Grant et al. (1997) used the Children's Nonword Repetition task (Gathercole, Willis, Baddeley, & Emslie, 1994) with participants with WS. They showed that, despite a vocabulary test age of 8 years, when learning new words people with WS behaved like 4- to 5-year-olds and did not show the pattern seen from 6 years onward in the typically developing population. Like very young children, the participants with WS were less influenced by the semantics of the words that the nonce terms resembled and relied more on phonology. Taken together, these different studies suggest that, unlike typical development, semantics seems to place somewhat less of a constraint compared to phonology in the way in which WS language develops over time.

We have so far suggested that semantics may play a somewhat less important role in WS lexical development than in typical controls and that this aspect of WS language develops atypically. However, it remains possible that WS syntax is intact, as many have claimed (e.g., Bickerton, 1997; Clahsen & Almazan, 1998; Pinker, 1999). There are, however, a number of lines of evidence that cast doubt on this. First, vocabulary levels are usually better than syntactic levels in WS on various standardized tasks, and both are significantly below CA (Karmiloff-Smith et al., 1997). Second, even in very simple imitation tasks, participants with WS show impairment with complex syntactic structures like embedded relative clauses. A recent study by Grant, Valian, and Karmiloff-Smith (2002) showed that despite having a mean vocabulary test age of 9 years, the participants with WS performed significantly worse on relative clauses than the 6- and 7-year-old controls and worse than even the 5-year-olds on three of the four sentence types. Length of sentence did not explain the results because the shortest of the sentence types was the most difficult for the WS group who performed at ceiling on non-embedded filler sentences of varying length. These findings are inconsistent with the view that WS syntax is intact. Even in an area of relatively simple syntax–grammatical concord over sentence elements—which normal French-speaking children acquire easily and early—people with WS show impairment. Karmiloff-Smith et al. (1997) studied the ability of a group of French-speaking participants with WS to use grammatical gender agreement. The results showed that although the children with WS learned the local gender marker (correct article) for a nonce term easily (in fact, more easily than control children), their capacity for gender agreement across sentence elements such as agreement on adjectives or pronouns was seriously impaired. Even for known words, the WS group made double the number of errors of the young controls. This suggests that memory for local verbal material (article + noun) is good, but processing of sentential syntax (gender agreement across sentence elements) is not. Studies of Italian-speaking children have also revealed that grammatical gender is a particular problem, with children with WS displaying errors never encountered in typical development (Volterra et al., 1996). Several studies (e.g., Klein & Mervis, 1999) now suggest that the problems that people with WS have with semantics and syntax can often be camouflaged by their good verbal memory.

Despite these and numerous other linguistic data from studies of WS, the myth that WS morphosyntax is intact continues to thrive. This is clear from the following quotation from Pinker's (1999) recent book, where he contrasts individuals with SLI and WS, respectively: "The genes of one group of children impair their grammar while sparing their intelligence; the genes of another group of children impair their intelligence while sparing their grammar" (p. 262).

It is in our view theoretically misleading and empirically inaccurate to claim that grammar is spared in this clinical population. WS grammar is relatively good compared to some other clinical groups and relatively good compared to WS spatial deficits, but no better than their MA would predict. These are relative descriptions, not absolute ones. One of the crucial features of WS language is that in infancy and toddlerhood it is initially seriously delayed (Mervis, Morris, Bertrand, & Robinson, 1999; Mervis, Robinson, & Pani, 1999; Singer Harris, Bellugi, Bates, Jones, & Rossen, 1997). Now, if the WS infant brain presented with an intact morphosyntactic module, as many such quotations suggest, then this severe delay would surely be surprising. But given the empirical facts, it is not. The myth of intact WS language needs to be dethroned and buried once and for all. This does not mean that the WS cognitive architecture is uninteresting. On the contrary, we need to understand why the language of people with WS language is initially so delayed (Laing et al., 2002; Nazzi, Paterson, & Karmiloff-Smith, 2003) and why it develops atypically. We will look at the issue of early development, with respect to language, number, and spatial cognition, in the third part of this article. Prior to doing so, we consider another aspect of the WS cognitive architecture—face processing—that is also claimed to be intact.

Face processing skills in Williams syndrome

As with language, initial claims about face processing in WS suggested an innately specified face processing module that is intact. Indeed, Bellugi, Birhle, Jernigan, Trauner, and Doherty (1990) asserted, "we find in the WS population *normal* face processing capacities with at floor performance on spatial tasks," and Rossen et al. (1995) claimed to have found "*selective preservation* [italics added] of face recognition in Williams syndrome." There is no doubt that people with WS are very proficient at face processing. One might ask if face processing in adults with

WS is modular, and the reply could be affirmative, that is, it has become modularized with development. One might also ask: Is it an intact module? But this is the wrong question because it negates development and the possibility that the cognitive processes underlying proficient WS face processing are different from those of typically developing controls. Indeed, several studies (Deruelle, Mancini, Livet, Cassé-Perrot, & de Schonen, 1999; Karmiloff-Smith, 1998; Udwin & Yule, 1991) have replicated Bellugi's earlier work and revealed normal or near-normal behavioral scores on standardized tasks like the Benton Facial Recognition Test (Benton, Hamsher, Varney, & Spreen, 1983) and the Rivermead Behavioural Memory Test (Wilson, Cockburn, & Baddeley, 1985). But these same studies have seriously challenged the notion that the behavioral success displayed in WS face processing capacities is normal. It has been shown that whereas typically developing controls use predominantly configural processes to recognize faces, people with WS tend to use predominantly componential or featural processes and do less well when a task forces configural processing (Wang, Doherty, Rourke, & Bellugi, 1995). Under certain circumstances, they are capable of using global or configural processing, particularly in low-level perceptual tasks (Birhle, Bellugi, Delis, & Marks, 1989; Mervis et al., 1999; Pani, Mervis, & Robinson, 1999), but they show a stronger tendency toward featural processing in many low-level and higher level visuospatial tasks, including face processing.

In an elegant set of studies using faces, buildings, and geometric shapes, Deruelle et al. (1999) showed that when faces and buildings are inverted, typically developing controls display a significant inversion effect for faces (they are faster and more accurate for upright faces) but not for buildings. By contrast, although the performance of the group with WS decreased slightly with inverted faces, this decrease was not significantly greater than that observed for buildings. The lack of the face inversion effect is not attributable to a floor effect because the WS accuracy scores were similar to those of their MA matches who did exhibit an inversion effect with faces. Furthermore, although the WS group ranged from 7 to 23 years, there was no trend with age toward the typical pattern. This finding was also supported using another set of geometric stimuli. Deruelle et al. gave participants the choice between similarity on the basis of configuration or similarity on the basis of features. For example, a square composed of four tiny circles might be placed with a square composed of four tiny squares (same configuration, different features) or a rectangle composed of four tiny circles (same features, different configuration). Control participants of either the same CA or the same MA tended to choose patterns of the same configuration, whereas the WS group showed no such preference. With a match-to-sample design using a set of schematic faces in which either configuration or features were changed, the WS group did not differ in the number of errors made on local features, but showed severe deficits compared to the controls in the configural trials. The authors conclude that individuals with WS display a selective configural processing deficit compared to both CA and MA matches. Their face processing proficiency stems from a deviant developmental pathway and does not reveal the functioning of a so-called normal, intact module. So, it is not the case that people with WS have an intact face processing module and an impaired space processing module. Both follow atypical developmental trajectories.

Imaging studies focusing on the electrophysiology of face processing in WS also support the notion of a differently developing expertise rather than an intact module. In a face recognition (match/mismatch) event-related potentials (ERP) study of 18 adults with WS, Mills et al. (2000) found abnormalities in the early waveform (100 and 200 msec post stimulus onset) of each of the participants with WS. This was not found in any of the controls. The authors suggest that these differences index abnormalities in face perception that may be specific to WS. Another study also points to abnormalities in face processing in WS. Using high-density ERP and a simplified task of face perception, Grice et al. (2001) tested 18 individuals with WS (*M* CA = 21.4 years) and also found waveform differences compared to CA-matched controls that indicated both deviance and delay. The N170 face-sensitive component was abnormal in the WS group and, unlike controls, was not increased in amplitude to inverted faces. There was also less right lateralization than for controls. In addition, unlike the control group, there was no difference in the N170-equivalent component to human faces or monkey faces. This finding suggests that the individuals in the WS group are not specialized for human faces in the same way as are controls. These data again refute the idea of an 'intact' module. Rather, they suggest that people with WS have either an incomplete or a different form of modularization for face processing.

Early development in Williams syndrome

We now turn to early development with respect to these two areas of relative proficiency in WS language and face processing. Our aim (Paterson, 2000; Paterson, Brown, Gsödl, Johnson, & Karmiloff-Smith, 1999) is to challenge some of the deeply engrained assumptions in cognitive neuropsychology and developmental cognitive neuroscience about the use of developmental disorders for bolstering nativist claims. The assumption—which we will call the Modular Continuity Hypothesis—often remains implicit in writings, but is in fact part and parcel of the logic of the argument and stems, as we suggested in the Introduction, from adult neuropsychology models. It holds that the brain is organized into innate (genetically determined) mental/neural modules that have the same potential for dissociation across the human lifespan. In other words, it is assumed that there is a transparent relationship between phenotypic outcomes and genes, with the expectation that the same dissociations observed in the adult steady state hold during the period in which these abilities emerge.

Is the inference that the WS phenotypic end state supports the case for innate modularity justified? In other words, can one assume the state of early development simply from the pattern of proficiencies and impairments in the phenotypic outcome in the adult, without studying their developmental trajectories? It is known that WS and Down syndrome (DS) display different cognitive profiles in the end state (Jernigan, Bellugi, Sowell, Doherty, & Hesselink, 1993; Klein & Mervis, 1999; Wang, Doherty, Hesselink, & Bellugi, 1992), although, using more subtle measures, Klein and Mervis (1999) discovered a number of hitherto neglected similarities between WS and DS at 9 to 10 years of age. In adulthood, however, it remains clear that vocabulary levels of people with WS are better than those with DS and that both syndromes show serious impairment in the domain of number (Bellugi et al., 1994; Paterson, 2000).

Paterson (2000; Paterson et al., 1999) purposely chose two tasks—one language-related, one number-related—which could be designed to be as similar as possible for both very young children and adults. For number, numerosity judgments were required; for language, receptive vocabulary measures were taken. The domains of vocabulary and number were purposely chosen because in the phenotypic end state it had been claimed that individuals with WS show greater proficiency in vocabulary than individuals with DS, and that both syndromes are seriously impaired in number. If the phenotypic end state can be directly used to assume the pattern obtaining in infancy, then the infant profiles should resemble the adult profiles across these two syndromes. Paterson (2000) first examined adult abilities. She tested participants with WS and DS who were matched on CA and on MA from the British Ability Scales, $t(13) = 2.05, p > .06$. She showed that these adults had significantly different scores on a vocabulary test, the British Picture Vocabulary Scales (BPVS), with a smaller discrepancy between CA and test age on the BPVS for adults with WS than for those with DS, $t(6) = 2.55$, $p < .05$, as had been demonstrated in previous work. Numerosity judgment tasks had not been hitherto used with adults with either WS or DS. Participants were required to judge which of two numbers (either Arabic numerals 1–10 or dots displays) displayed on a computer screen is the larger. Reaction times and accuracy were measured. In the normal case, a distance effect is always apparent: Numbers very close (like 7 and 8) take longer for a decision as to which is the larger than numbers that are far apart (like 7 and 2). Paterson demonstrated that adults with WS and DS performed differently on the numerosity judgment tasks. The adults with DS, although slower overall, showed a clear-cut effect as evidenced by typically developing controls. By contrast, the adults with WS performed significantly worse than the matched adults with DS on several number tasks and, although there was a trend in the right direction, this WS group did not show the distance effect. There was a significant difference between the WS and DS groups for the discrepancy between reaction times to close and far pairs (Mann–Whitney $U = -11$, $p < .05$). So the phenotype in the adult end state was DS significantly worse than WS on vocabulary, WS significantly worse than DS on numerosity judgments.

An attempt was made to devise similar number tasks with adults and toddlers. In both cases, the tasks involved making a comparison between two numerosities. In the toddler case, an implicit same/different judgment was required, whereas the adults had to decide which of the numerosities was the larger. Likewise, vocabulary comprehension was measured in both adults and toddlers.

Paterson et al. (1999) used a preferential looking paradigm to examine numerosity and vocabulary in 65 toddlers between 13 and 36 months, divided into groups of toddlers with WS, atypical controls with DS matched for CA and MA on the

Bayley Infant Scales II (Bayley, 1993), typically developing MA controls (also matched on the Bayley), and typically developing CA controls. If the use of the so-called Modularity Continuity Hypothesis were justified, then these young children should show a similar profile of cognitive abilities and impairments to adults in each of the syndromes. However, this was not the case. The toddlers with WS and DS were equally impaired and performed significantly worse than CA controls on the language task, despite the fact that adults with WS were significantly better than the adults with DS. For vocabulary, then, both atypical groups of toddlers performed like the MA controls, that is, at approximately half their CA. By contrast, although the adults with WS were more impaired than the adults with DS with numerosity judgments, the toddlers with WS showed unimpaired performance on the numerosity judgment task. They performed like the CA controls, whereas the toddlers with DS were seriously impaired and did not even reach the level of the MA controls. Again, the pattern in early development differed considerably from that observed in adulthood. Caution must therefore be exercised when making claims about innate modules based on phenotypic outcomes. These data suggest either that the learning trajectories of the two syndromes are different in development or, in the language example, that children with DS are subject to increasing deficit in linguistic skills compared to their counterparts with WS, who retain a relatively stable pattern of delay throughout development. Whichever turns out to be the case, it is only via developmental studies following infants and toddlers from the initial state through childhood and adulthood that this question can be properly addressed. Alas, in WS, a syndrome characterized by initial feeding problems and failure to thrive, it is very hard to test infants in the very early phases of postnatal life. Even as late as 20 months, however, the toddler profile is different from the resulting adult profile. This again stresses the need to focus on the process of development itself when studying developmental disorders (Karmiloff-Smith, 1998) and that claims regarding starting states cannot necessarily be based on patterns found in phenotypic outcomes. In other words, although it is always possible that in some cases early developmental patterns turn out to show the same profile of abilities and impairments as the adult end state, this cannot be taken for granted without empirical verification. Furthermore, although the adult profile concerns higher level cognitive domains, it is probable that impairments in infancy are related to much lower level processing mechanisms.

With respect to language, we are left with an intriguing question as to why onset in WS is so delayed, given the relative proficiency in later life. We have argued that this may in part be due to an imbalance between semantics and phonology leading to weak semantic representations. It may also in part be due to abnormality of nonlinguistic precursors to language. For instance, Mervis and Bertrand (1997) showed that, unlike typical development, in WS naming precedes pointing. Thus, early naming in WS may be more like sound production and less like language production. Results from recent work in our lab also suggest that pointing and joint attention, which underpin certain aspects of normal language acquisition, are significantly reduced and atypical in toddlers with WS compared to MA and CA controls (Laing et al., in press). We are also examining early speech perception and have shown that infants with WS have deficits in early speech segmentation abilities (Nazzi et al., 2003). It is in our view crucial to examine the array of prelinguistic abilities that the typically developing child brings to the language-learning task. It is clear that throughout development, however, from the early stages through to the adult end state, WS language is not intact at any level that researchers have hitherto seriously examined. Let us reiterate, the myth of intact language should be buried and the search for intact modules ceased, so that more subtle research can be pursued to discover the developmental language trajectories followed by individuals with WS. The lack of intactness is unsurprising if we recall that the WS brain is qualitatively different from the normal brain in terms of brain anatomy (Bellugi, Lichtenberger, Mills, Galaburda, & Korenberg, 1999), brain chemistry (Rae et al., 1998), and computational processing (Grice et al., 2001; Mills et al., 2000). Nor is it therefore surprising that seemingly normal behavioral outcomes even in adults turn out to be underpinned by different linguistic processes from the normal case (Karmiloff-Smith, 1998).

What about face processing in early development? Can that provide clues to the atypical processing style used by adults with WS? First, it is known that normally developing infants already show a right hemisphere superiority for configural face processing from 4 to 5 months of age onward (Deruelle & de Schonen, 1998; de Schonen & Mathivet, 1990). So the right hemisphere bias in normal adults is already present early in infancy. Second, by 1 month of age, typically developing infants show a novelty preference for new faces over old faces in a preferential looking task. By 3 months of age, not only do they display a novelty preference, but they also show a prototype effect (de Haan, Johnson, Maurer, & Perrett, 2001). Take the following experimental situation. Four faces are displayed one after another and then the infant is given a choice between a fifth face (not previously seen by the infant, but a prototype morphed from the previous four faces) and one of the already-seen faces. In this situation, 3-month-olds (but not yet 1-month-olds) treat the morphed face as more familiar than the already seen face. This means that by 3 months, infants do not simply learn the details of exemplars, but build up a prototypical representation of the configuration of previously processed faces. In a pilot study, Brown (2000) found that infants with WS did not show the prototypical effect. This suggests that infants and toddlers with WS tend to learn exemplars and may lack the generalization processes necessary to form prototypes. If this preliminary finding holds, the WS lack of prototype extraction could well be due to a tendency early in development toward featural rather than configural processing. Because it has been shown that toddlers with WS spend more time than typically developing or DS controls fixated on faces (Mervis et al., 2003), the early infant processing style may explain the phenotypical outcome in WS adult face processing. It may also be a clue as to why infants with WS succeed in discriminating small numerosities compared to infants with DS: The former group's seemingly normal performance may actually rely on a focus on qualitative detail rather than quantity.

Yet again we need to bury the myth of what at first blush seemed like an intact face processing module in adults with WS. Face processing follows a different developmental trajectory in this clinical population.

It has always been recognized that children and adults with WS show clear behavioral deficits in visuospatial tasks outside face processing. Our lab has also pursued spatial cognition in infancy (see also Atkinson et al., 1997). In a study of saccade planning, Brown and colleagues (Brown, 2000; Brown et al., 2003) showed that toddlers with WS (with a mean CA of 29 months, range 23–37 months) have atypical spatial representations for planning visually guided actions. Saccades in healthy controls and in CA/MA-matched toddlers with DS (with a mean CA of 29 months, range 24–37 months) are executed within body-centered spatial coordinates. By contrast, toddlers with WS displayed evidence of deficits in saccade planning, suggesting in their case a greater reliance on subcortical processing mechanisms than the other groups. So once again, be it face processing or visuospatial processing, the WS brain proceeds along an atypical developmental pathway. Moreover, in both the prototype face processing and saccade planning studies, toddlers with WS displayed sticky fixation, that is, they looked longer at all the displays than participants with DS and the CA- and MA-matched typically developing controls. It is therefore possible that subsequent focus on features is the result of an early inability to disengage. To reiterate, it is not that one module—face processing—is spared and the other module—visuospatial processing—is impaired. Both domains develop atypically in WS.

Concluding comment

In our view, the notion of direct impairment to higher level cognitive modules is unlikely to explain the phenotypic outcome in WS or other genetic disorders. We anticipate that impairments will be in the form of lower level mechanisms traceable back to early infancy. There may be cases where infant and adult impairments turn out to be similar, but our new work stresses the importance of not taking for granted the idea that the infant start state will display the same profile as the adult end state. As we stated in the Introduction, neurocognitive studies of developmental disorders never turn out to be as straightforward as they first promise. We have shown that studies of WS are no exception, and that it is time that the myths of static, intact modules be dethroned in favor of studying the complex dynamics of developmental trajectories.

Acknowledgments

The studies reported in this article were funded by Programme Grant No. G9715642 and Project Grant No. 9809880 to A. K.-S. by the U.K. Medical Research Council, by a joint grant from the European Science Foundation, and by PhD studentships from the Medical Research Council and the Down's Syndrome Association.

References

Atkinson, J. A., King, J., Braddick, O. J., Nokes, L., Anker, S., & Braddick, F. (1997). A specific deficit of dorsal stream function in Williams syndrome. *NeuroReport*, *8*, 1919–1922.

Baron-Cohen, S. (1998). Modularity in developmental cognitive neuropsychology: Evidence from autism and Gilles de la Tourette syndrome. In J. A. Burack, R. M. Hodapp, & E. Zigler (Eds.), *Handbook of mental retardation and development* (pp. 335). Cambridge, England: Cambridge University Press.

Bayley, N. (1993). *Bayley Scales of Infant Development* (2nd ed.). San Antonio, TX: Psychological Corporation.

Bellugi, U., Birhle, A., Jernigan, T., Trauner, D., & Doherty, S. (1990). Neuropsychological, neurological, and neuroanatomical profile of Williams syndrome. *American Journal of Medical Genetics, 6*, 115–125.

Bellugi, U., Lichtenberger, L., Jones, W., Lai, Z., & St. George, M. (2000). The neurocognitive profile of Williams syndrome: A complex pattern of strengths and weaknesses. *Journal of Cognitive Neuroscience, 12*(1), 7–29.

Bellugi, U., Lichtenberger, L., Mills, D., Galaburda, A., & Korenberg, J. R. (1999). Bridging cognition, the brain and molecular genetics: Evidence from Williams syndrome. *Trends in Neurosciences, 22*(5), 197–207.

Bellugi, U., Wang, P. P., & Jernigan, T. (1994). Williams syndrome: An unusual neuropsychological profile. In S. H. Broman & J. Grafman (Eds.), *Atypical cognitive deficit in developmental disorders: Implications for brain function* (pp. 23–56). Hillsdale, NJ: Lawrence Erlbaum Associates, Inc.

Benton, A. L., Hamsher, K. de S., Varney, N. R., & Spreen, O. (1983). *Contributions to neuropsychological assessment*. New York: Oxford University Press.

Bickerton, D. (1997). Constructivism, nativism, and exploratory adequacy. *Behavioral and Brain Sciences, 20*, 557–558.

Birhle, J. M., Bellugi, U., Delis, D., & Marks, S. (1989). Seeing either the forest or the trees: Dissociation in visuospatial processing. *Brain and Cognition, 11*, 37–49.

Brown, J. (2000). *The development of visual cognition in infants with Williams and Down syndromes*. Unpublished doctoral thesis, University College London.

Brown, J., Johnson, M. H., Paterson, S., Gilmore, R., Gsödl, M., Longhi, E., et al. (2003). Spatial representation and attention in toddlers with Williams syndrome and Down syndrome. *Neuropsychologia, 41*, 1037–1046.

Clahsen, H., & Almazan, M. (1998). Syntax and morphology in Williams syndrome. *Cognition, 68*, 167–198.

de Haan, M., Johnson, M. H., Maurer, D., & Perrett, D. I. (2001). Recognition of individual faces and average face prototypes by 1- and 3-month-old infants. *Cognitive Development, 16*, 659–678.

Deruelle, C., & de Schonen, S. (1998). Do the right and the left hemispheres attend to the same visual information within a face in infancy? *Developmental Neuropsychology, 14*, 535–554.

Deruelle, C., Mancini, J., Livet, M. O., Cassé-Perrot, C., & de Schonen, S. (1999). Configural and local processing of faces in children with Williams syndrome. *Brain and Cognition, 41*, 276–298.

de Schonen, S., & Mathivet, E. (1990). Hemispheric asymmetry in a face discrimination task in infants. *Child Development, 61*, 1992–1205.

Gathercole, S. E., Willis, C. S., Baddeley, A. D., & Emslie, H. (1994). The children's test of nonword repetition: A test of phonological working memory. *Memory, 2*, 103–127.

Grant, J., Karmiloff-Smith, A., Gathercole, S. E., Paterson, S., Howlin, P., Davies, M., et al. (1997). Phonological short-term memory and its relationship to language in Williams syndrome. *Journal of Cognitive Neuropsychiatry, 2*(2), 81–99.

Grant, J., Valian, V., & Karmiloff-Smith, A. (2002). A study of relative clauses in Williams syndrome. *Journal of Child Language*, *29*, 403–416.

Grice, S., Spratling, M. W., Karmiloff-Smith, A., Halit, H., Csibra, G., de Haan, M., et al. (2001). Disordered visual processing and oscillatory brain activity in autism and Williams syndrome. *NeuroReport*, *12*, 2697–2700.

Jernigan, T. L., Bellugi, U., Sowell, E., Doherty, S., & Hesselink, J. R. (1993). Cerebral morphologic distinctions between Williams and Down syndromes. *Archives of Neurology*, *50*, 186–191.

Johnson, S., & Carey, S. (1998). Knowledge enrichment and conceptual change in folk biology: Evidence from Williams syndrome. *Cognitive Psychology*, *37*, 156–184.

Karmiloff-Smith, A. (1998). Development itself is the key to understanding developmental disorders. *Trends in Cognitive Sciences*, *2*, 389–398.

Karmiloff-Smith, A., Grant, J., Berthoud, I., Davies, M., Howlin, P., & Udwin, O. (1997). Language and Williams syndrome: How intact is "intact"? *Child Development*, *68*, 246–262.

Klein, B. P., & Mervis, C. B. (1999). Contrasting patterns of cognitive abilities of 9- and 10-year-olds with Williams syndrome or Down syndrome. *Developmental Neuropsychology*, *16*, 177–196.

Laing, E., Butterworth, G., Gsödl, M., Panagiota, G., Paterson, S., Longhi, E., et al. (2002). Preverbal communication in infants with Williams Syndrome. *Developmental Science*, *5*(2), 233–246.

Laing, E., Hulme, C., Grant, J., & Karmiloff-Smith, A. (2001). Learning to read in Williams syndrome: Looking beneath the surface of atypical reading development. *Journal of Child Psychology and Psychiatry*, *42*, 729–739.

Leslie, A. M. (1992). Pretence, autism, and the theory-of-mind-module. *Current Directions in Psychological Science*, *1*, 18–21.

Mervis, C. B. (1999). The Williams syndrome cognitive profile: Strengths, weakness, and interrelations among auditory short-term memory, language, and visuospatial constructive cognition. In E. Winograd, R. Fivush, & W. Hirst (Eds.), *Ecological approaches to cognition: Essays in honor of Ulric Neisser* (pp. 193–227). Mahwah, NJ: Lawrence Erlbaum Associates, Inc.

Mervis, C. B., & Bertrand, J. (1997). Developmental relations between cognition and language: Evidence from Williams syndrome. In L. B. Adamson & M. A. Romski (Eds.), *Research on communication and language disorders: Contributions to theories of language development* (pp. 75–106). New York: Brookes.

Mervis, C. B., Morris, C. A., Bertrand, J., & Robinson, B. F. (1999). Williams syndrome: Findings from an integrated program of research. In H. Tager-Flusberg (Ed.), *Neurodevelopmental disorders* (pp. 65–110). Cambridge, MA: MIT Press.

Mervis, C. B., Morris, C. A., Klein-Tasman, B. P., Bertrand, J., Kwitny, S., Appelbaum, L. G., et al. (2003). Additional characteristics of infants and toddlers with Williams syndrome during triadic interactions. *Developmental Neuropsychology*, *23*, 243–268.

Mervis, C. B., Robinson, B. F., & Pani, J. R. (1999). Cognitive and behavioral genetics '99: Visuospatial construction. *American Journal Human Genetics*, *65*, 1222–1229.

Mills, D. L., Alvarez, T. D., St. George, M., Appelbaum, L. G., Bellugi, U., & Neville, H. (2000). Electrophysiological studies of face processing in Williams syndrome. *Journal of Cognitive Neuroscience*, *12*(Suppl.), 47–64.

Nazzi, T., Paterson, S., & Karmiloff-Smith, A. (2003). Early word segmentation by infants and toddlers with Williams syndrome. *Infancy*, *4*, 251–271.

Pani, J. R., Mervis, C. B., & Robinson, B. F. (1999). Global spatial organization by individuals with Williams syndrome. *Psychological Science, 10*, 453–458.

Paterson, S. (2000). *The development of language and number understanding in Williams syndrome and Down syndrome: Evidence from the infant and mature phenotypes.* Unpublished doctoral thesis, University College London.

Paterson, S. J., Brown, J. H., Gsödl, M. K., Johnson, M. H., & Karmiloff-Smith, A. (1999). Cognitive modularity and genetic disorders. *Science, 286*, 2355–2358.

Pinker, S. (1991). Rules of language. *Science, 253*, 530–535.

Pinker, S. (1994). *The language instinct.* London: Penguin.

Pinker, S. (1999). *Words and rules.* London: Weidenfeld & Nicolson.

Rae, C., Karmiloff-Smith, A., Lee, M. A., Dixon, R. M., Blamire, Thompson, et al. (1998). Brain biochemistry in Williams syndrome: Evidence for a role of the cerebellum in cognition? *Neurology, 51*, 33–40.

Rossen, M., Jones, W., Wang, P. P., & Klima, E. S. (1995). Face processing: Remarkable sparing in Williams syndrome. *Genetic Counseling, 6*, 138–140.

Scott, P., Mervis, C. B., Bertrand, J., Klein, B. P., Armstrong, S. C., & Ford, A. L. (1995). *Semantic organization and word fluency in 9- and 10-year-old children with Williams syndrome.* Paper presented at the meeting of the Society for Research in Child Development, Indianapolis, IN.

Singer Harris, N. G., Bellugi, U., Bates, E., Jones, W., & Rossen, M. (1997). Contrasting profiles of language development in children with Williams and Down syndromes. *Developmental Neuropsychology, 13*, 345–370.

Temple, C. M. (1997). Cognitive neuropsychology and its applications to children. *Journal of Child Psychology and Psychiatry, 38*, 27–52.

Thomas, M. S. C., Grant, J., Barham, Z., Gsödl, M., Laing, E., Lakusta, L., et al. (2001). Past tense formation in Williams syndrome. *Language and Cognitive Processes, 2*(16), 143–176.

Tyler, L., Karmiloff-Smith, A., Voice, J. K., Stevens, T., Grant, J., Udwin, O., et al. (1997). Do individuals with Williams syndrome have bizarre semantics? Evidence for lexical organization using an on-line task. *Cortex, 33*, 515–527.

Udwin, O., & Yule, W. (1991). A cognitive and behavioural phenotype in Williams syndrome. *Journal of Clinical and Experimental Neuropsychology, 13*, 232–244.

van der Lely, H. K. J., & Ullman, M. T. (2001). Past tense morphology in specifically language-impaired and normally-developing children. *Language and Cognitive Processes, 16*(2), 177–217.

Vicari, S., Carlesimo, G., Brizzolara, D., & Pezzini, G. (1996). Short-term memory in children with Williams syndrome: A reduced contribution of lexical-semantic knowledge to word span. *Neuropsychologia, 34*, 919–925.

Volterra, V., Capirci, O., Pezzini, G, Sabbadini, L., & Vicari, S. (1996). Linguistic abilities in Italian children with Williams syndrome. *Cortex, 32*, 663–677.

Wang, P. P., Doherty, S., Hesselink, J. R., & Bellugi, U. (1992). Callosal morphology concurs with neurobehavioral and neuropathological findings in two neurodevelopmental disorders. *Archives of Neurology, 49*, 407–411.

Wang, P. P., Doherty, S., Rourke, S. B., & Bellugi, U. (1995). Unique profile of visuoperceptual skills in a genetic syndrome. *Brain and Cognition, 29*, 54–65.

Wilson, B., Cockburn, J., & Baddeley, A. (1985). *Rivermead Behavioural Memory Test.* Reading, England: Thames Valley Test Co.

6 Exploring the Williams syndrome face-processing debate

The importance of building developmental trajectories

Annette Karmiloff-Smith, Michael Thomas, Dagmara Annaz, Kate Humphreys, Sandra Ewing, Nicola Brace, Mike Van Duuren, Graham Pike, Sarah Grice, and Ruth Campbell

In this article, we investigate the emergence of face recognition abilities in a rare genetic developmental disorder, Williams syndrome. The capacity for species recognition is one of the most fundamental abilities across the animal kingdom. One might therefore expect this to be a strong candidate for an innate ability in the case of the human infant. Yet the past couple of decades have revealed, at both the behavioural and brain levels, that the recognition of faces is a very gradual developmental process in both humans and other species such as the chick (Johnson & Morton, 1991). Indeed, brain localisation and specialisation in the processing of human faces, i.e., the gradual modularisation of function over developmental time (Karmiloff-Smith, 1992, 1998), extends very progressively across the first 12 months of life and beyond (Johnson & de Haan, 2001). If infants start with anything resembling an innately specified template, it is unlikely to be face specific but rather in the form of a T-shape in which more information at the top of a stimulus parsed as an object is particularly attractive to the young infant's visual system (Simion, Macchi Cassia, Turati, & Valenza, 2001). With developmental time, however, the human face itself becomes increasingly the preferred stimulus (Johnson & Morton, 1991), enhanced not only by the massive input of faces but also by the fact that faces form a crucial site of attention for the social interactional patterns that develop over the first months of life.

Imaging experiments have shown that young infants' brains initially process upright human faces, inverted human faces, monkey faces and objects all in a relatively similar way across both hemispheres (Johnson & de Haan, 2001; de Haan, 2001). However, with development, brain processing of human upright faces becomes increasingly specialised and localised to the fusiform gyrus in the right hemisphere (Passarotti et al., 2003). Despite these developmental data pointing to very progressive specialisation and localisation of face processing, some theorists claim that the human brain is prespecified with an independently-functioning face-processing module. Such claims are based on the fact that *adult* patients can present with prosopagnosia, i.e., a selective inability to recognise familiar faces, despite showing no obvious impairments elsewhere (Bruyer et al., 1983; de Renzi, 1986; Farah, Levinston, & Klein, 1995; Temple, 1997). So, there is still a debate concerning the extent to which face recognition abilities are part of the hardwired functional architecture of the infant brain versus the extent to which these emerge in adults mainly as a product of development. Can developmental disorders address this question, particularly those where face recognition appears to exceed general cognitive ability, such as in Williams syndrome?

Williams syndrome

Williams syndrome (WS) is a genetic disorder in which some 25 genes are deleted on one copy of chromosome 7, leading to serious deficits in spatial cognition, number, planning and problem solving (see Donnai & Karmiloff-Smith, 2000, for full details). IQ scores are in the 50s to 60s range (Udwin & Yule, 1991). Of particular interest to cognitive neuroscientists is the fact that two domains – language and face processing – show particular behavioural proficiency compared to the general levels of intelligence reached by this clinical group. Indeed, WS scores on some language and face-processing tasks fall in the normal range. When such findings first arose, they were heralded as demonstrating that, in the case of face processing, for instance, WS presents with an 'intact' or 'preserved' face-processing module (e.g., Bellugi, Sabo, & Vaid, 1988; Bellugi, Wang, & Jernigan, 1994; Wang, Doherty, Rourke, & Bellugi, 1995; though see Bellugi, Lichtenberger, Mills, Galaburda, & Korenberg, 1999, for more recent discussion). While some have rejected these claims (Karmiloff-Smith, 1997, 1998; Deruelle, Mancini, Livet, Cassé-Perrot, & de Schonen, 1999), others maintain that people with the syndrome display normal face processing (e.g., Deruelle, Rondan, Mancini, & Livet, 2003; Tager-Flusberg, Plesa-Skwerer, Faja, & Joseph, 2003). This is of course tantamount to claiming that face processing *develops* normally in WS.

One of the problems with many of the WS face-processing studies is that terms like featural/piecemeal/componential/local/analytical versus configural/holistic/global/gestalt have been used interchangeably, as if they were synonymous, and thus have not been adequately specified. In this paper, we use the term 'featural' to refer to the ability to identify faces based on individual features (eyes, nose, mouth, chin), and the term 'configural' to refer to the ability to differentiate faces based on sensitivity to the spatial distances amongst internal features, i.e., second-order relational information. Configural face processing is associated with maturity of face recognition encoding and 'expert' recognition in adults. By contrast, the term 'holistic' is deemed to cover the gluing together of facial features (and hairline) into a gestalt, without necessarily conserving the spatial distances between features (Maurer, Le Grand, & Mondloch, 2002; Tanaka & Farah, 1993). In other words, the capacity to process information holistically does not involve the processing of second-order relational information. We start with a review of previous work on face processing in Williams syndrome, followed by three new experiments with this clinical population.

Previous WS face-processing studies

There are no experimental studies of face processing in infants with WS to complement the studies of healthy infants discussed in our introduction. However, some observational work, as well as experiments indirectly tapping face processing, revealed that infants with WS spend significantly more time focused on faces than on objects (Bellugi, Lichtenberger, Jones, Lai, & St. George, 2000; Laing et al., 2002; Mervis & Bertrand, 1997). This has led many authors to assume that the WS infant's inordinate attention to faces explains why adults with WS end up achieving good behavioural scores on some face-processing tasks. But does such early attention to faces necessarily lead to configural processing in older individuals with WS?

The initial claims that adolescents and adults with WS exhibit face recognition skills that are 'intact'/'spared' (i.e., developed normally) were based on findings that performance on the standardised face-processing tasks like the Benton Facial Recognition Test and the Rivermead Face Memory Task was at normal or near normal levels. However, several studies subsequently challenged the notion of an 'intact' face-processing module and suggested that people with WS achieve their normal scores by resorting to different strategies from controls. Karmiloff-Smith (1997) reported that on a face-matching task, adult participants with WS ($N = 10$) did not differ from chronological-age-matched controls with respect to featural analysis, but were significantly worse when items necessarily required configural analysis, i.e., taking account of second-order relations. These preliminary findings, the result of acknowledged post-hoc analyses, gained support from a later study by Deruelle et al. (1999). Twelve children and adults with WS, aged between 7 and 23, were compared against chronological-age (CA) and mental-aged (MA) matched controls in a task requiring participants to decide whether two pictures of faces were the same or different when presented in upright and inverted conditions (their second experiment). The clinical group was less subject to an inversion effect than the controls. The authors explained these results by a greater reliance of the WS participants on featural analysis in both the upright and inverted conditions, whereas the controls used predominantly featural processing for the inverted faces and configural processing for the upright faces. This led the authors to speculate that WS face processing is not merely delayed but follows a different developmental pathway. In a third experiment, Deruelle et al. (1999) investigated the processing of configurally and featurally modified schematic faces and geometric shapes. Yet again, the CA and MA matches produced significantly fewer errors than the WS group on configural items, but no differences emerged with respect to the featural ones. The 1999 Deruelle et al. study adds further support to the claim that people with WS are biased to process featural over configural information, regardless of the type of facial (real faces or schematic faces) or geometric stimuli.

Two recent papers have, however, challenged this now rather general conclusion and claimed that people with WS process faces in exactly the same way as controls (Deruelle et al., 2003; Tager-Flusberg et al., 2003).

Deruelle et al. (2003) sought to explore holistic face processing in WS. They compared 12 children and adolescents with WS (aged 6 to 17 years) against controls in their ability to match faces to either a low or high spatial frequency filtered target face. Two control groups were used, either matched individually on chronological age or on overall mental age. All groups tended to find face matching easier to a low spatially filtered target face (i.e., a face in which the broad patterns of light and dark were preserved but fine detail was lost) than a high spatially filtered face. WS performance fell between the CA and MA control groups but was not significantly different from either. While Deruelle et al. took these results to indicate that face-processing abilities develop normally in children with WS, the sensitivity of responses to the spatial frequency manipulation was unchanging with age across all the groups, despite the wide age range. This implies that, by the age of testing, any developmental change had already plateaued in terms of holistic face processing, making it impossible to assess the implications for the WS participants on the developmental trajectory.

Tager-Flusberg et al. (2003) have also recently argued in favour of normally developing face processing in WS. That study had the merit of using a considerably larger sample than previous work, including 47 adolescents and adults with WS (aged 12 to 36 years) and 39 CA-matched controls. They were tested on the standardised Benton Face Recognition Test used in previous studies, as well as on a part–whole paradigm. This latter task involved matching individual face parts in two conditions, either in isolation or in the context of a whole face. The authors predicted that if the WS group were less influenced by the overall context of a face, they should show a reduced difference between the two conditions, whereas the controls should be aided in the recognition of individual features by their presentation in the context of a face. Face orientation was also varied to assess whether the ability to use the whole-face context was disrupted by inversion to the same extent in the control and WS groups. While the overall accuracy was better in the CA-matched control group than in the WS group, the presence or absence of surrounding face context had the same effect for upright presentation on controls and the clinical group. Tager-Flusberg et al. present their results as challenging previous WS data that pointed to atypical face processing and argue that earlier studies were underpowered because of small *N*s. However, it is not clear that their task addresses the same aspect of face processing as previous studies. Their part–whole task (taken from Tanaka & Farah, 1993) concerns the processing of individual features recognised in isolation or in the context of a whole face. This taps, as the authors recognise, the processing of the face gestalt, i.e., first-order holistic processing, rather than second-order configural processing. Indeed, throughout their article, Tager-Flusberg et al. contrast featural processing with 'holistic' processing rather than with configural processing. Yet the Deruelle et al. (2003) study indicates that individuals with WS are not markedly impaired on holistic processing and none of the existing research, including our own, has claimed that individuals with WS are incapable of first-order holistic processing. The debate is about second-order configural processing. Of importance, too, is the fact that in the Deruelle et al. study holistic processing assessed by spatial frequency manipulations exhibited no developmental change across the age range employed by TagerFlusberg and colleagues. Similarly, when these researchers examined developmental change across their (wide) age range, they also found no correlation between age and performance in either the WS or CA groups. If the part–whole task targets holistic processing, and if holistic processing is at ceiling in both normal and clinical populations in the age ranges examined, then the conclusions that can be drawn regarding the typicality or atypicality of face-processing development in WS are obviously limited.

As noted, claims of atypicality in WS face processing revolve around the extent to which these individuals make use of *second-order configural relations* when recognising faces. This is a capacity that emerges over developmental time in healthy controls. Therefore, it is the inversion condition used by Tager-Flusberg et al. that is potentially more informative here, since inversion causes disruption particularly to configural processing (Diamond & Carey, 1986). Unfortunately, Tager-Flusberg and colleagues' WS data are uninterpretable in this regard, because the clinical group is at floor on inverted stimuli. By contrast, two previous studies from separate laboratories have found significantly less difference between upright and inverted face recognition in WS groups compared to controls (Deruelle et al., 1999; Rossen, Jones, Wang, & Klima, 1995), again supporting the claim that this clinical population is atypical with regard to configural processing. The possibility that inconsistent findings in the WS face-processing literature are a result of confounding holistic and configural processing is one to which we will return. For the moment, we focus on further investigating configural processing in WS face recognition.

The importance of developmental trajectories. Since the major theoretical dispute concerns whether face recognition develops normally in WS, it will be our contention that explanations must be couched in terms of developmental trajectories (see discussions in Karmiloff-Smith, 1998, and Thomas & Karmiloff-Smith, 2002). Indeed, this stance will influence our analytic techniques. It will cause us to move from comparisons of the WS group against individually-matched controls which we and other groups have used in the past (where the relation of performance to age is discarded in analyses once control participants are selected) to the construction of functions specifically linking performance with age. Our comparisons will relate performance to chronological age in both the control and clinical samples and, in the latter, also between our face-processing tasks and developmental stages on a number of standardised tests, including face recognition, visuospatial processing, and language (see Thomas et al., 2001, for a similar analytical approach). We believe that our new trajectory approach to disorders offers more insight with respect to the way in which development may have proceeded *over time* in a deviant fashion, even though the behavioural proficiency, measured by matching controls at a specific CA or MA, may end up similar to controls. Moreover, individual variability is as much a problem for individual matching as it is for building trajectories. Each participant exhibits individual variation from each group norm. In addition, we try to show in this paper that comparing trajectories has a marked advantage over individual matching with regard to MA comparisons.

In an individually matched comparison, everything rides on the choice of MA measure and this is typically theoretically laden. However, if one builds a task-specific typical developmental trajectory, one can then evaluate whether the atypical group fits on the typical developmental trajectory according to a range of metrics. These can be theoretically neutral (does each individual fit *anywhere* on the trajectory), or according to CA, or according to a variety of MA measures. Finally, where wide age ranges are a problem for studies matching on CA or MA and age is ignored in subsequent analyses, the wide age range can actually be exploited positively when building developmental trajectories.

Our aim in this article is threefold. In our first experiment we aim to produce clearer evidence of the configural processing deficit and reduced inversion effect in a WS group, by using real faces in a task specifically tailored to this purpose. In our second experiment, we concentrate on the inversion effect. We establish a cross-sectional, task-specific developmental trajectory for a wide age range of normal controls on a task that embeds the recognition of inverted faces in the naturalistic context of a storybook. We then derive and contrast the trajectory on this task for a group of individuals with WS. In Experiment 3, we concentrate on sensitivity to configural vs. featural transformations of schematic faces and geometric patterns, once more building and contrasting developmental trajectories for the typical and atypical groups. In contrast to the findings of Deruelle et al. (2003) and Tager-Flusberg et al. (2003), our tasks allow us to chart developmental change in performance across our age ranges in both groups. In each case, we will reveal patterns of atypicality in WS face recognition over developmental time, even when accuracy levels are broadly similar.

Hypotheses. Experiment 1: If face recognition in WS has developed normally, individuals with WS should show no difference in accuracy compared to controls in discriminating a target face from a featurally or configurally transformed version of the target; moreover, if WS face processing has developed normally, then performance should be similarly influenced by the nature of the transformation and by inversion.

Experiment 2: When required to recognise contextualised faces in a storybook task, presented in upright or inverted orientation, we expect controls to become increasingly accurate and rapid with age with respect to upright faces, but also to show increased sensitivity to inversion (since this disrupts configural processing). If face recognition in WS has developed normally, the clinical group should show the same pattern as the controls with increasing chronological age. By contrast, if the developmental trajectory is simply delayed, then performance should be predicted by developmental age on the standardised Benton face recognition test, or on a standardised test of visuospatial ability (but possibly not on a standardised test of vocabulary). Finally, if face processing in WS follows a deviant trajectory, then these predictions should not hold.

Experiment 3: We expect controls to demonstrate an emerging skill in detecting configural transformations in upright faces with increasing age. If face recognition in WS has developed normally, the clinical group should show the same pattern as the controls when matching schematic face and non-face stimuli transformed configurally or featurally. By contrast, if the developmental trajectory is merely delayed, then it should be predicted by developmental age on the Benton task, or on a standardised test of visuospatial ability. Finally, if face processing in WS follows a deviant trajectory, then these predictions should not hold.

Experiment 1: Investigating configural and featural processing of real faces

We begin by assessing the presence of differences in configural processing and in the inversion effect in WS using real faces in a test specifically designed for this purpose by Mondloch and colleagues (Mondloch, Le Grand, & Maurer, 2002).

Method

Participants.[1] Fourteen adult participants with WS were tested on this task. Two did not fully understand the instructions and their data were excluded from the analyses. The 12 remaining participants had a mean CA of 30;0 (SD: 11;11, range: 16;3–51;0). Language ability was assessed using the Peabody Picture Vocabulary test (Dunn & Dunn, 1981) for which their mean test age was 13;10 (SD: 6;7, range: 8;2–30;8). Visuospatial ability was assessed using the Pattern Construction subtest of the British Abilities Scale (BAS-II; Elliot, Smith, & McCulloch, 1996). The mean spatial test age of the WS group was 5;4 (SD: 1;7 range 3;7–8;9). Thus the WS group exhibited the characteristic disparity between these two abilities (language greater than visuospatial skill: paired *t*-test, $t = 5.42$, $df = 11$, $p < .001$), alongside overall delay. A control group was individually matched to each participant in the WS group, based on chronological age, gender and socioeconomic status. The choice of a chronological age match was based on the claims that face processing is an independently-functioning, intact ability in this clinical population, as well as to equate to the best extent possible for life experience with faces in the two groups. MA controls could have been interesting, too, but were not our main focus here. The CA matches were on average within 4.5 months of each of the participants with WS, with the mean CA of the control group being 29;11 (SD: 11;6, range 16;6–51;0). A comparison of the CAs of the control and WS groups revealed no significant difference (paired *t*-test, $t = .19$, $df = 11$, $p = .856$).

Stimuli. A photo of a real face (called Jane) was used to create featural and configural sets of new faces. In the featural set, new faces were created by replacing the original features (eyes and mouth) with the features of different faces. In the configural set, features were moved up or down within the face contour, or moved closer together or further apart in relation to the original positions of the features (for more detailed description of the task used with a different population, see Mondloch, Le Grand, & Maurer, 2002; note the 'contour' condition of that study was not employed here).

Procedure. The procedure employed a well-tested paradigm for directly differentiating between featural and configuring processing of real faces (Mondloch et al., 2002). Participants were presented sequentially with two faces and asked to determine whether the two faces were the same or different. Trials were blocked into upright and inverted trials, and within those, separate blocks where faces were featurally altered or configurally altered (referred to as 'spacing' in Mondloch et al.). Trials were blocked to encourage participants to adopt specific face-processing strategies (Mondloch et al., 2002). The testing session began with 12 practice trials, to ensure that all participants understood the instructions and meaning of the words 'same' and 'different'. During the task proper, each participant was presented on a computer laptop with 30 trials from the featural and configural sets respectively. For each participant, the upright block was always presented before the inverted block. The order of configural and featural blocks within these was counterbalanced. Each block consisted of 15 'same' and 15 'different' randomised trials. During each trial, the target face was presented for 400 ms and the second face, to which the participant had to respond on the keyboard with 'same' or 'different', was displayed until the response button was pressed. The inter-stimulus interval was 300 ms, a delay chosen to prevent apparent-motion cues from the presentation of a different face (Mondloch et al., 2002). Bright yellow Velcro pads were stuck on the two relevant keys to make it easy for participants to respond. For each trial a target face was followed by a test face that could either be identical to the target face or transformed configurally or featurally. The dependent variables were reaction time and accuracy.

For the analysis, we divided the task into two components: *Identity Recognition* (for all items where no change had been made between target and test face and the participant correctly responds 'same'), and *Difference Detection* (where the participant correctly spots that the test face differs from the target, either due to a configural or featural transformation, and responds 'different'). We consider the two sets of responses separately, because transformations are only relevant to difference detection.

Results

Identity Recognition. A comparison of accuracy levels in identity recognition revealed no significant difference between the groups (ANOVA: main effect of group: $F(1,22) = 1.38$, $p = .253$, $\eta^2_p = .059$). In addition, both groups performed equally well on upright and inverted faces. Prior to analysis, response time data were cropped so that outliers that fell two standard deviations away from each individual's mean time were eliminated. This removed 4.7% of the data points from the WS group and 4.4% of the data points from the CA control group. For identity recognition, individuals with WS tended to respond more slowly than CA controls, but this effect was not reliable ($F(1,22) = 3.38$, $p = .081$, $\eta^2_p = .132$). Where the WS were slower (in mean scores), they were also less accurate than the control group, suggesting that there were no speed–accuracy trade-offs at work.

Whether identity recognition trials fell within configurally transformed or featurally transformed blocks had no effect on performance (effect of transformation block: errors, $F(1,22) = 1.02$, $p = .323$, $\eta^2_p = .044$; response times, $F(1,22) = .43$, $p = .519$, $\eta^2_p = .019$). No significant interactions of transformation block emerged with any of the other variables, implying that trial blocking of featurally vs. configurally transformed faces did not induce specific face-processing strategies sufficient to affect identity recognition. The mean accuracy levels and response times are provided in Table 6.1.

Difference Detection. The difference detection condition includes the additional variable of manipulation type: configural or featural. Accuracy and response times for difference detection are also included in Table 6.1. Once more, there was no significant difference in accuracy levels between the groups (effect of group: $F(1,22) = 2.03$, $p = .168$, $\eta^2_p = .085$). Analysed in isolation, the CA control group exhibited a characteristic pattern in the difference detection task, whereby it turned out to be harder to detect configurally changed faces than featurally changed faces (main effect of transformation: $F(1,11) = 26.89$, $p < .001$, $\eta^2_p = .710$), and whereby inverting the face added to the difficulty only for configurally changed faces (interaction of transformation × orientation: $F(1,11) = 61.97$, $p < .001$, $\eta^2_p = .849$). Overall, the WS group experienced the same effects of transformation, i.e., configurally transformed faces were not additionally harder for the participants with WS (main effect of transformation in the WS group: $F(1,11) = 33.61$, $p < .001$, $\eta^2_p = .753$, between-group comparison, interaction of group × transformation: $F(1,22) = .57$, $p = .457$, $\eta^2_p = .025$). However, the clinical population did exhibit a differential effect of inversion on the face transformation compared to the control group. In particular, they demonstrated a larger inversion effect on featurally transformed faces than the CA control group and a smaller inversion effect on configurally transformed faces (between-group comparison, interaction of group × transformation × orientation: $F(1,22) = 14.73$, $p = .001$, $\eta^2_p = .401$). Inspection of Table 6.1 (lower panel) suggests that this interaction was driven most strongly by a greater disparity between WS and CA control groups in detecting configurally transformed upright faces. Indeed, in a direct comparison of detecting configural transformations in upright faces, the WS group were significantly worse than controls, but showed no difference when these stimuli were inverted (independent-sample *t*-tests comparing groups, Upright: $t(22) = 3.34$, $p = .003$; Inverted: $t(22) = .16$, $p = .878$). In other words, the normal configural expertise for upright faces found in the CA-matched controls was not apparent in the WS group, despite broadly equivalent overall levels of accuracy. The WS group responded more slowly than the CA control group but, as with Identity Recognition, this did not reach significance (main effect of group: $F(1,22) = 4.09$, $p = .056$, $\eta^2_p = .157$).

Discussion

The clinical group turned out to be as accurate as the CA controls on both identity recognition and difference detection and, although they tended to respond more slowly, the difference was not significant in either condition. By these measures alone, one might conclude that face recognition had developed normally in the WS group. However, the groups diverged in other important ways, in particular

Table 6.1 Means and standard errors (SE) for accuracy (%) and response times (ms) in Identity Recognition and Difference Detection

Identity Recognition Group	*Trial block*							
	'Featural'				*'Configural'*			
	Upright		*Inverted*		*Upright*		*Inverted*	
	Mean	*(SE)*	*Mean*	*(SE)*	*Mean*	*(SE)*	*Mean*	*(SE)*
WS								
Accuracy	72%	(6%)	67%	(10%)	81%	(4%)	74%	(9%)
RT	1702	(355)	1531	(249)	1630	(377)	1565	(306)
Control								
Accuracy	80%	(6%)	83%	(4%)	74%	(5%)	87%	(5%)
RT	880	(101)	1011	(136)	1115	(147)	992	(87)
Difference Detection Group	*Transformation*							
	Featural				*Configural*			
	Upright		*Inverted*		*Upright*		*Inverted*	
	Mean	*(SE)*	*Mean*	*(SE)*	*Mean*	*(SE)*	*Mean*	*(SE)*
WS								
Accuracy	86%	(5%)	74%	(7%)	51%	(6%)	31%	(8%)
RT	1701	366	1569	333	1766	371	1895	444
Control								
Accuracy	85%	(5%)	83%	(6%)	75%	(4%)	29%	(7%)
RT	873	73	874	62	1033	99	1136	112

on transformations in the difference detection task. While configural transformations were harder to detect than featural transformations, the key condition that separated the groups was performance on upright configural faces, where controls were significantly more accurate. Sensitivity to second-order configural differences in upright faces is a hallmark of face recognition expertise (Yin, 1969). It is most disrupted by inversion, and the WS group demonstrated a qualitatively different response to inversion that stemmed particularly from weaker performance on upright configurally transformed faces.

Experiment 2: Face recognition in a story-supported task

In Experiment 2, we consider the progressive developmental emergence of the inversion effect, using a task that embeds the recognition of inverted faces in the more naturalistic setting of a storybook. Here, we introduce a novel approach to controls, by building a full task-specific developmental trajectory.

Method

Participants. Seventeen adolescent and adult participants with WS were tested. Three participants failed to correctly identify either a single upright face or a single inverted face and were excluded from subsequent analyses. The 14 remaining participants with WS had a mean CA of 26;3 (SD: 11;11, range: 12;0–54;10). Language ability was assessed using the British Picture Vocabulary Scale (BPVS) (Dunn, Whetton, & Pintilie, 1997), for which the mean test age was 11;2 (SD: 3;6, range: 7;4–17;6). Visuospatial ability was assessed using the Pattern Construction subtest of the British Abilities Scale (Elliot et al., 1996). The mean test age of the WS group was 5;6 (SD: 1;2, range 3;4–8;9). Thus, this new WS group exhibited the characteristic disparity between these two abilities (language greater than visuospatial skill: paired t-test, $t = 7.51$, $df = 13$, $p < .001$), alongside overall delay. Participants were also given the Benton Face Recognition Test. Mean Benton score was 42.2 (SD: 4.5, range: 35–51), corresponding to performance within the normal adult range (41–54; Benton, Hamsher, Varney, & Spreen, 1983). Using the age norms from the Benton, these scores were translated into age equivalents (Benton et al., 1983), taking a ceiling score to be reached at 14 years. This gave the WS group a mean Benton age equivalent of 11;4 (SD: 2;7, range: 6;6–14;0).

Data from 111 control children were also analysed. These data were collected by Brace et al. (2001), with group means derived for separate age bins. We reanalysed the data for this sample, using each child's CA to build a task-specific cross-sectional developmental trajectory. The control group had a mean CA of 8;0 (SD: 2;7, range: 2;8–11;5). There were 12 children between 2;8 and 4;4, 20 children between 5;2 and 6;11, 26 children between 7;2 and 8;8, 28 children between 9;2 and 10;2, and 25 children between 11;1 and 11;5. This age range enabled us to build a full trajectory of typical developmental changes on this specific task.

Stimuli. The stimuli were taken from Brace et al. (2001) and were modified for use with a touch-screen monitor using Superlab 2.0. The stimuli consisted of two parts: a Storybook and a computer game. The Storybook was a hand-painted story about two boys, called Tom and Jamie. One of the boys is kidnapped by a witch and taken to her castle. The witch turns the boy into a variety of objects, such as a robot that retains only the boy's face, and hides him in amongst 8 other boys that she has kidnapped. The only way for the other boy to rescue his friend is to play a game of hide and seek in order to spot his friend amongst the other boys/objects, which are either upright or hung upside-down. In the first two pages of the book, pictures of Jamie and Tom are present, whereas in the next five pages the story continues without any pictures of the boys, to ensure that subsequent recognition of the faces is delayed by about three minutes. The hide and seek computer game includes upright and inverted pictures of one of the two target faces (Tom or Jamie) among 8 distracter faces. Two versions of the task were run with different target faces. Each participant saw one of the two versions (for further details, see Brace et al., 2001).

Procedure. In the first part of the study the experimenter (or the participant if s/he read easily) read a story aloud, during which the participant was asked to point to the pictures of the two boys and to repeat their names after the experimenter. On completion of the first part of the story, the participant was asked if s/he would like to play a computer game of finding the lost boy (Tom or Jamie). Eight trials were run, including two practice trials. For each trial, a picture was presented on the touch-screen with the target face hidden amongst 8 distractor faces of varying similarity to the target face. The position and orientation of the target face within the array of 9 faces was systematically varied. Once the detection game was completed, the story reading was continued to achieve a happy ending. Participants' data were only included if they correctly recognised at least one upright and one inverted instance of the target face. In most cases, performance accuracy was much better.

Results

The wide age and ability range of the WS and control groups was exploited to generate developmental trajectories on the story task, i.e., to create a function relating increase in performance (either accuracy or response time) against increasing age. For the WS group, 'age' was for each analysis either their chronological age, their Pattern Construction equivalent, their Benton equivalent or their BPVS equivalent. The WS developmental trajectory was compared against the developmental trajectory for the controls, constructed from over one hundred typically developing children between 2;8 years and 11;5 years.

WS performance on Benton Facial Recognition Test. First, we establish that the scores of this group of participants with WS generally fell 'in the normal range', according to a standardised test of face recognition. Figure 6.1 depicts the Benton scores for the WS group plotted against individuals' chronological age, on the one hand, and against their Pattern Construction age equivalent, on the other. This figure includes the 15 of the 17 participants for whom Benton scores were available. Scores on the Benton were also converted into a Benton age equivalent (Benton et al., 1983) for later use. Several points are of note. First, as in previous studies, many of the WS group fell within the normal range on the Benton task and, indeed, the overall WS group mean was in the normal range. Second, WS performance was nevertheless *delayed* compared to the typical developmental profile, so that scores-in-the-normal-range do not imply here entirely normal development. Third, while the WS scores broadly increased with age, this relationship was not significant ($r^2 = .000$, $p = .954$, or with 2 outliers removed, $r^2 = .153$, $p = .167$). This was because of the cross-sectional nature of the sample: severity of expression of the disorder varies independently of age. Fourth, the Benton scores were in excess of the level that would be predicted by the Pattern Construction ability of the WS group. Lastly, there was no correlation between performance on Benton and test age on the Pattern Construction subtest in the WS group ($r^2 = .000$, $p = .967$), suggesting that these two tasks tap (at least in part) different processes. While Brace et al. (2001) had no Benton and Pattern Construction data for their children, we collected indicative data in our laboratory for a sample of 21 healthy children between 3;6 and 11;2 (mean 6;9, SD 2;7) who performed both these tests. For these children, Pattern Construction test age strongly predicted Benton scores, with a correlation of $r = .873$ ($r^2 = .763$, $p < .001$).

The normal developmental trajectory. Trajectories were analysed using an analysis of co-variance (ANCOVA). This test requires the relationship between performance and age to be roughly linear. To linearise the relationships, accuracy was plotted against one-over-age squared (in months) (see Thomas et al., 2001, for details). The log of reaction time was plotted against the log of age (in months).

For the control sample, accuracy rates on upright and inverted faces (each out of 3) were compared to chronological age. Controls exhibited a significant improvement in accuracy with age ($F(1,109) = 27.01$, $p < .0001$) and a significant accuracy cost of recognising inverted faces ($F(1, 109) = 4.56$, $p = .035$). The size of the inversion effect did not alter significantly across the developmental profile ($F(1,109) = .153$, $p = .697$). Figure 6.2(a) depicts this relationship (note that, for clarity, accuracy is plotted against chronological age in this figure, rather than the transformed age variable used in the analysis). Chance performance in this face identification task was 11%.

Mean reaction times for upright and inverted face recognition on correct trials were compared to chronological age. Controls exhibited a significant reduction in reaction time with age ($F(1,109) = 38.50$, $p < .001$) and a significant time cost of recognising inverted faces ($F(1,109) = 4.50$, $p = .036$). Moreover, the cost of recognising inverted faces significantly increased with age, consistent with the emergence of configural faceprocessing expertise ($F(1,109) = 5.93$, $p = .016$). This trajectory is depicted in Figure 6.3(a).

WS developmental trajectory. For the relationship between performance and chronological age, direct comparisons between the WS and control groups must

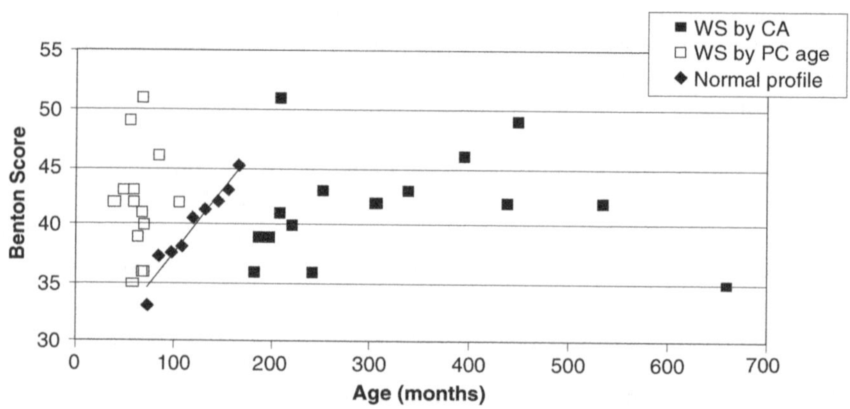

Figure 6.1 Benton face recognition scores for participants with WS ($N = 15$), plotted either against Chronological Age (CA) or against Pattern Construction (PC) age equivalent score. Also shown are normative scores from Benton age equivalent (Benton et al., 1983)

be interpreted with caution, because the samples have differing variability and are non-overlapping in terms of CA. The direct comparison revealed no overall significant group difference in either accuracy or reaction time when the performance of the WS group was compared to this much younger typically developing control group.

When considered on its own, the WS group revealed no significant relationship between accuracy or reaction time with increasing chronological age (accuracy: $F(1,12) = 1.13, p = .309$; RT: $F(1,12) = 2.33, p = .153$). Unlike the significance levels in the controls, there was only a trend in the direction of an inversion cost in the accuracy data ($F(1,12) = 4.34, p = .059$), and no effect in the RT data ($F(1,12) = .00$, $p = .999$). There was no indication that the inversion effect altered across chronological age (interaction of orientation and age: accuracy, $F(1,12) = 1.33, p = .271$; RT: $F(1,12) = .01, p = .908$). These trajectories are shown in Figures 6.2(b) and 6.3(b).

The next step was to explore whether any of the standardised measures – Benton, Pattern Construction, or BPVS – was a good predictor of performance on the Storybook task. Performance was compared against WS test age equivalents for each of these measures.

Performance on the Benton did not predict accuracy ($F(1,11) = .62, p = .447$) but did successfully predict reaction time on the Storybook task ($F(1,11) = 5.26$, $p = .043$; inversion effect non-significant: $F(1,12) = 3.23, p = .100$). By contrast, performance on the BPVS predicted neither accuracy nor reaction time. Performance on the Pattern Construction sub-test of the BAS-II did not predict reaction times but did successfully predict accuracy levels in the WS group (accuracy: $F(1,12) = 10.33, p = .007$; RT: $F(1,12) = .90, p = .362$). The trajectories are

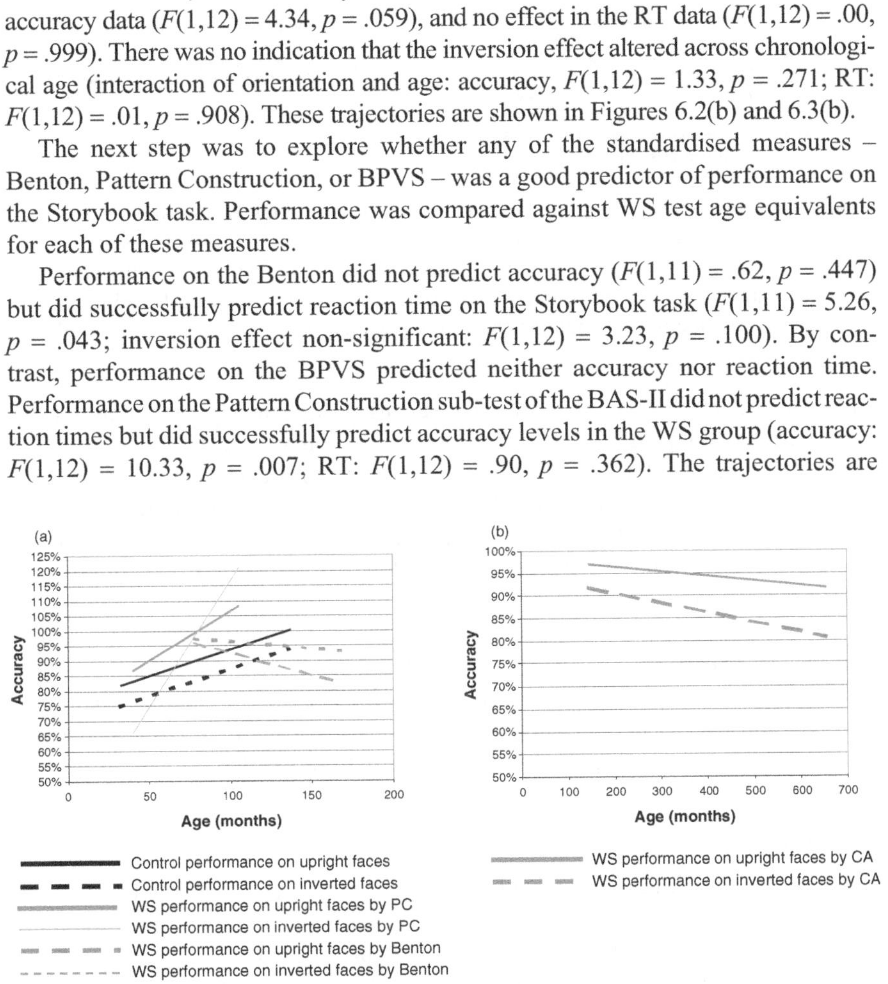

Figure 6.2 Developmental trajectories for accuracy on the Picture-book face recognition task: (a) trajectories for accuracy against age for controls and for the WS group plotted according to their Pattern Construction age equivalent and separately according to their Benton age equivalent; (b) accuracy against chronological age for the WS group

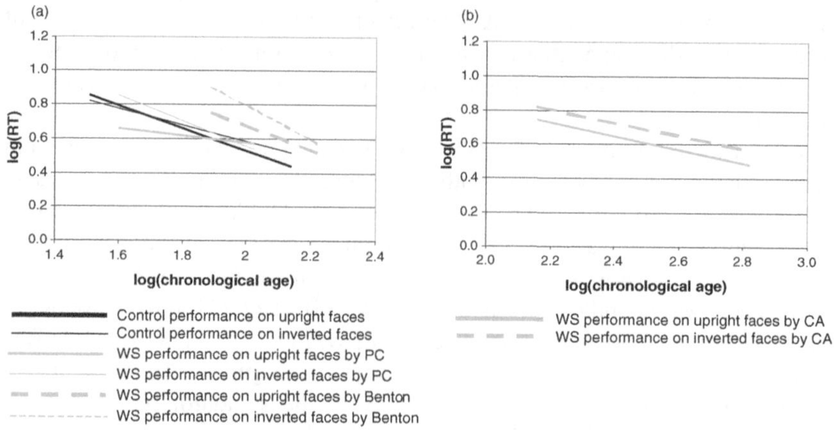

Figure 6.3 Developmental trajectories for response times on the Picture-book face recognition task: (a) response time against age for controls and for the WS group plotted according to their Pattern Construction age equivalent and separately according to their Benton age equivalent (log-log plot); (b) response time against chronological age for the WS group (log-log plot)

shown in Figures 6.2(a) and 6.3(a). The accuracy trajectory revealed an unusual pattern in the WS group. There was a marginally non-significant inversion effect in the WS group ($F(1,12) = 4.54, p = .055$) but a significant interaction whereby the inversion effect became *smaller* as Pattern Construction ability increased ($F(1,12) = 12.91, p = .004$). The reaction time data replicated this pattern but differences were not reliable (inversion effect: $F(1,12) = 1.32, p = .273$; interaction: $F(1,12) = 1.13, p = .308$).

Comparison to the control group revealed that WS accuracy on the Storybook task was in excess of what would be expected for Pattern Construction ability (main effect of group: $F(1,121) = 4.21, p = .042$). The differential modification of the inversion effect with increasing age was not significant in the combined analysis (3-way interaction of group by age by orientation: $F(1,121) = 2.78, p = .098$).

Discussion

As in previous studies, we found that WS Benton scores fell within normal range and better than would be expected by their performance on a standardised visuospatial constructive task. Experiment 2 also yielded novel findings, because we built a full trajectory of typical developmental changes over time for this particular task. Indeed, between the ages of 3 and 12, the normal developmental trajectory reveals increasing accuracy and faster response times for upright faces, as well as the progressive emergence of an inversion effect in terms of reaction times. Most theorists concur that this is the signature of an emerging specialisation for configural processing of upright faces. While the WS group did not differ from the control trajectory in terms of accuracy or speed of response, their developmental trajectory failed to show the progressive emergence of a face inversion effect. In other words, as was suggestive of the findings from Experiment 1, the WS *behavioural* proficiency on some face-processing tasks, e.g., the Benton, seems to stem from an atypical developmental trajectory. In terms of relating WS performance to their other skills, increasing ability on the Benton task predicted an increase in reaction time in the WS group, but again, no emergence of an inversion effect. Benton performance did not significantly predict accuracy on the Storybook task. Ability on BPVS bore no relation to increasing performance on our task. Increasing ability on Pattern Construction predicted an increase in accuracy in the WS group and a modification of the inversion effect, but the modification was unusually in the reverse direction: better Pattern Construction predicted a smaller inversion effect.

Experiment 3: Configural and featural processing of schematic stimuli

The aim of this experiment was to assess whether adults with WS show a configural or featural bias in their perceptual processing of schematic faces and geometric patterns. The use of schematic faces allows tighter control of stimulus attributes and the closer matching of face and non-face stimuli. Participants once again were required to make similarity judgements about transformed stimuli. In one condition, they judged which of two test patterns differed most from a previously presented target pattern, where one test pattern was identical to the target and one was transformed. This task is similar to the *Difference Detection* condition in Experiment 1. In a second condition, both test stimuli were transformed, one configurally, one featurally. This *Judgement Preference* task allowed us to assess the relative salience of the two types of transformation for the participants. In addition, the coexistence of normally developing performance on Difference Detection but atypical performance on Judgement Preference would point to a preferred processing strategy in WS rather than an underlying deficit.

Method

Participants. Twelve adolescents and adults with WS were tested on this task. Their mean CA was 27;1 (SD: 11;11, range: 15;1–52;3). Language ability was assessed using the British Picture Vocabulary Scale (Dunn et al., 1997), for which the mean test age was 12;2 (SD: 3;10, range: 7;0–17;6). Visuospatial ability was assessed using the Pattern Construction subtest of the British Abilities Scale. The mean spatial test age of the WS group was 5;8 (SD: 1;3, range 4;1–8;9). Thus as in the previous experiments, the new WS group exhibited the characteristic disparity between these two abilities (language greater than visuospatial skill: paired t-test, $t = 6.88$, df = 11, $p < .001$), along with overall delay. Performance on the Benton for this group yielded a mean of 42.0 (SD: 3.4, range: 35–47) corresponding to performance within the normal adult range (41–54; Benton, Sivan, Hamsher KdeS., Varney, & Spreen, 1994). Once more, the age norms from the Benton were used to convert these scores into age equivalents, taking a ceiling score to be reached at 14 years. Employing this method, the WS group had a mean Benton age equivalent of 11;3 (SD: 2;5, range: 6;6–14;0). For comparison with Experiment 1, once more Pattern Construction test age failed to reliably predict Benton score in this WS sample, Pearson correlation = .264 ($r^2 = .070, p = .408$).

Sixty-one control children, adolescents and adults, covering the mental and chronological age spans of the clinical group, were also tested in order to build a developmental trajectory specifically for this task. Their overall mean CA was 12;5 (SD: 9;3, range: 5;5–53;1). There were 12 children between 5;4 and 6;5, 12 children between 7;0 and 7;5, 12 children between 8;10 and 9;9, 13 children between 12;2 and 12;10, and 12 adolescent and adults between 14;11 and 53;1. For the children, BPVS data were also collected to ensure that they fell within the normal range.

Stimuli. Three sets of stimuli were displayed on a computer screen: schematic faces, scrambled faces and geometric shapes. The stimuli all comprised four black elements within a yellow circle of 7 cm. Two featurally modified and two configurally modified versions of each stimulus were created. For the schematic and scrambled faces, featural changes were made by replacing the eyes, since this is the most salient feature of a face: round eyes were replaced with squares or diamonds of a similar size as the original feature. By contrast, since all features have equivalent salience for geometric patterns, all four features were replaced to avoid disrupting symmetry. Configural changes were made by stretching or squashing the set of features towards or away from the centre by 20 pixels, thereby creating new, second-order configural relations between the features. Configural changes to the scrambled face could not be made by displacing the elements vertically without breaking the symmetry of the arrangement, so they were made by displacing all the elements horizontally towards or away from the centre of the pattern by 20 pixels.

Procedure. In each trial, a target pattern was presented followed by, or simultaneously with, two test patterns. In the *Difference Detection* task, one of the test patterns was identical to the target pattern while the other was a version that had undergone either a featural or a configural transformation. In the *Judgement Preference* task, both of the test patterns were transformed versions of the target pattern: one featurally transformed, the other configurally transformed. For both tasks, the participant had to decide as quickly as possible which test pattern (left or right) differed the most from the target pattern.

The stimuli consisted of two blocks of 48 trials. One block had sequential presentation, with the target presented in isolation, to be replaced by the two test patterns. The second block had simultaneous presentation, with target and two test patterns appearing on the screen at the same time. There were 16 schematic faces, 16 scrambled and 16 geometric pattern trials. The order of these blocks was the same for all participants. Within each of these blocks there were 8 difference detection and 8 judgement preference (4 configural and 4 featural) trials, which appeared in a randomised order. Participants indicated which image they thought was most different by pressing the response key on the same side as the picture. Velcro pads were attached to the two relevant keys on the computer keyboard to assist participants with remembering which keys should be pressed. Each participant was tested individually and given 8 practice trials. For the Difference Detection trials the dependent variables were accuracy of response and response time, whereas for Judgement Preference trials it was the number of featural responses.

Results

As in the previous experiment, the results were analysed by building and comparing task-specific crosssectional developmental trajectories for the control group and the WS group. For the WS group, the trajectory linking age and performance employed a variety of age measures: either their CA, their Benton age equivalent, their Pattern Construction age equivalent, or their BPVS age equivalent. As before, analysis of covariance was used to compare developmental trajectories. Unless otherwise noted, these involved the same data transformations to improve linearity discussed for Experiment 2.

The typical developmental trajectory. A comparison of control accuracy levels for all stimuli (face-like, scrambled, geometric), transformation types (featural vs. configural), and presentation conditions (simultaneous vs. sequential) against age was carried out. Presentation condition had no main effect ($F(1,58) = .21, p = .648$) and the same held for an overall analysis of response times ($F(1,58) = 1.07, p = .305$). There did appear to be a face-specific effect of simultaneous presentation, a point to which we will return shortly. For the remainder of the analyses, performance was averaged over simultaneous and sequential presentation conditions. A comparison of the two non-face-like patterns revealed that scrambled face features were harder than geometric patterns (accuracy: $F(1,58) = 3.96, p = .051$; RT: $F(1,58) = 1.92, p = .171$) but there were no interactions with other variables. For the remainder of the analyses, we will focus on comparisons between face-like stimuli and geometric patterns.

Difference Detection. The relationship between accuracy and age for the typically developing controls on face-like stimuli is depicted in Figure 6.4(a). An ANCOVA revealed significant improvement in accuracy with age ($F(1,59) = 4.88, p = .031$). There was no differential response to face-like stimuli and geometric patterns ($F(1,59) = .74, p = .392$), although there was an indication that performance on geometric patterns increased more rapidly with age (interaction of stimulus type and age: $F(1,59) = 3.95, p = .051$). Transformation type had no overall effect, but this turned out to be a consequence of averaging across presentation conditions.

A comparison of the accuracy data in the simultaneous vs. sequentially presented conditions revealed one unexpected effect. In the simultaneous condition, the controls responded more accurately to configurally transformed stimuli than featurally transformed stimuli. This held only for face-like stimuli and not for geometric patterns ($F(1,58) = 4.21$, $p = .045$) and was not present in the sequential conditions (interaction with condition: $F(1,58) = 3.96$, $p = .050$). An analysis of the sequential condition on its own revealed an interaction of transformation type with age, such that detection of configural transformations was less accurate than featural transformations, but the disparity decreased with age (interaction of transformation and age: $F(1,59) = 6.37$, $p = .014$). This effect was the same for both faces and geometric patterns. It is therefore possible that under the low-memory load conditions of simultaneous presentation, configural expertise for face processing emerges more easily in typically developing children than for sequential processing.

An analysis of reaction times revealed that responses became faster with age ($F(1,59) = 47.36$, $p < .001$), shown in Figure 6.4(b). Configural transformations were detected significantly more slowly than featural transformations but this disparity disappeared with age (main effect of transformation: $F(1,59) = 9.96$, $p = .003$; interaction with age: $F(1,59) = 6.90$, $p = .011$).

Judgement Preference. Which transformation type was more salient to typically developing children? Comparison of preference data was restricted to accuracy, because when participants' preferences were exclusively for one transformation type, no response times were available for the non-preferred transformations. Figure 6.5(a) demonstrates how preferences change with age. The relationship between choice type and age was best fitted by a linear relationship, and so choice was compared against untransformed chronological age. The analysis was carried out for a single choice type, since configural vs. featural choices co-specify each other in the forced choice paradigm. An ANCOVA revealed a significant effect of age on choice type ($F(1,59) = 11.35$, $p = .001$) whereby in typical development, individuals increasingly see configurally transformed stimuli as more different from the target and decreasingly choose featurally transformed stimuli. Let us now turn to the trajectory of the clinical group.

The WS developmental trajectory. Difference Detection. Did the WS group demonstrate a normal facility for recognising each transformation type? Dealing with accuracy first, a between-group comparison of WS developmental trajectory with the typical trajectory revealed no overall effect of group ($F(1,69) = .216$, $p = .643$). The trajectories are shown in Figure 6.4(a). Importantly, however, the WS group exhibited worse performance on configurally transformed stimuli while the control group did not (interaction of group and transformation type: $F(1,69) = 8.27$, $p = .005$).

Moreover, when the trajectory of the WS group was constructed according to their Benton test age equivalent, a comparison with controls revealed that the disparity in configural processing in WS persisted ($F(1,69 = 8.07$, $p = .006$), depicted in Figure 6.4(b). In neither case is this pattern modified by presentation condition. Importantly, then, for their level of performance on a standardised face recognition task (which generally fell in the normal adult range), the WS group exhibited a differential pattern of response to featural vs. configural transformations.

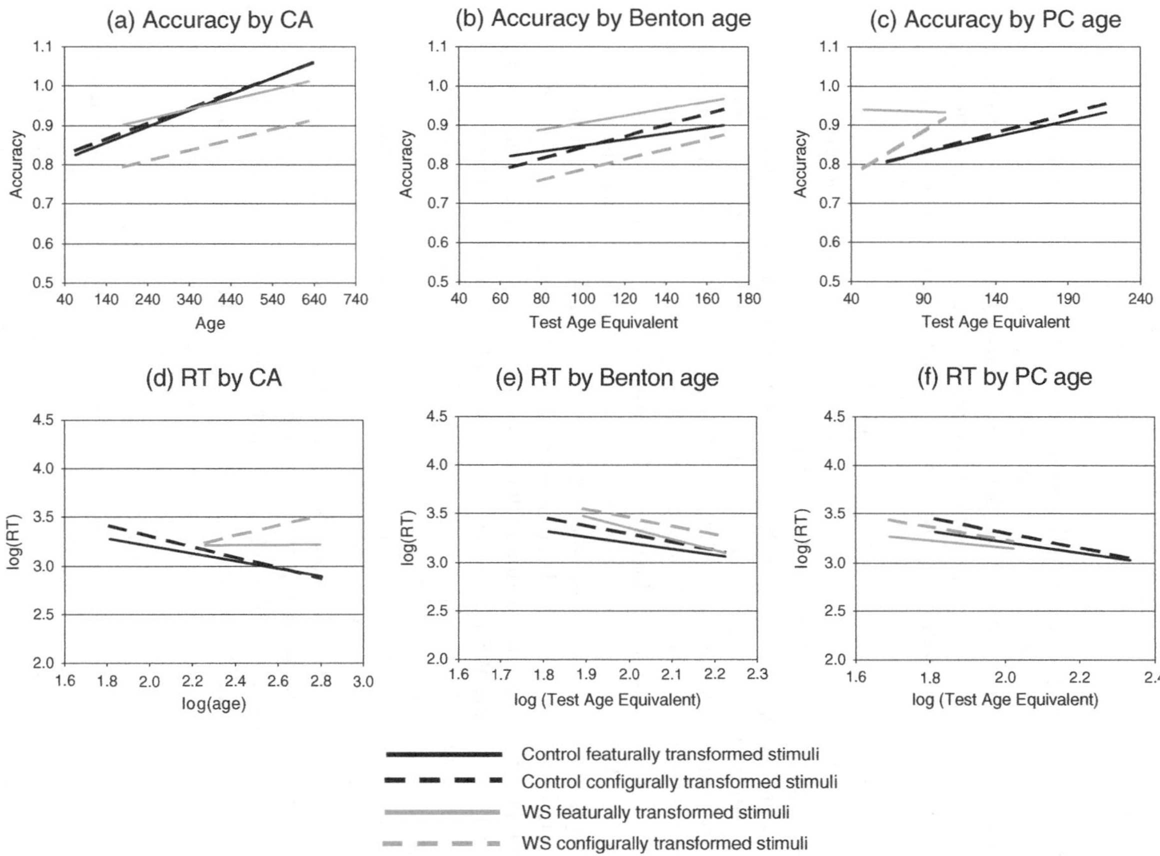

Figure 6.4 Cross-sectional developmental trajectories for the WS and control groups on the schematic faces task, for detecting featural vs. configural transformations. Trajectories for accuracy and reaction time across age are plotted according to the chronological age of the participants (CA), Benton face recognition test age equivalent (ceiling age 14;0), or Pattern Construction (PC) test age equivalent (ceiling age 18;0). See text for details

A further comparison was carried out constructing the WS trajectory according to their test age on the Pattern Construction sub-test of the BAS (Elliot et al., 1996), depicted in Figure 6.4(c). In this case, the configural deficit now disappears ($F(1,69) = .21, p = .652$). The only significant difference between the trajectories is that the WS group shows a larger initial deficit in and subsequent steeper improvement for the geometric patterns than for faces, causing an interaction of group, stimulus type, and age ($F(1,69) = 5.56, p = .021$).

In the control group, we saw high accuracy on configurally transformed face-like stimuli in the simultaneous presentation condition alone. Examination of the WS performance in this condition yielded no such face-specific effect: configural transformation detection lagged behind featural, as it did with geometrical patterns (effect of transformation: $F(1,10) = 5.87, p = .036$; interaction with stimulus type: $F(1,10) = .25, p = .632$). Moreover, the effect also held whether accuracy was plotted against CA or Benton test age equivalent.

An analysis of response times against age in the WS group generated the same configural deficit found in the accuracy data (interaction of transformation type and group: $F(1,69) = 5.79, p = .019$), in Figure 6.4(d). WS responses were slower overall, and did not show the decrease in RT with age of the control trajectory (main effect of group: $F(1,69) = 8.06, p = .006$; interaction with age: $F(1,69) = 10.09, p = .002$). However, these disparities became non-significant when RTs were plotted according to Benton test age, depicted in Figure 6.4(e). Plotting the WS trajectory according to Pattern Construction ability also caused the WS group to be indistinguishable from the normal trajectory, in Figure 6.4(f). However, somewhat unexpectedly, plotting performance against BPVS age equivalent produced a strong interaction with transformation type, such that increasing vocabulary age in the WS group (but not the control group) was associated with a divergence in RTs for recognising featurally and configurally transformed stimuli, with configural recognition slowing ($F(1,69) = 10.85, p = .002$). While this pattern appeared in the response times for both face-like stimuli and geometrical patterns, it did not appear in the accuracy data.

Judgement Preference. Did the WS group reveal the same relative salience of transformation type as the typically developing controls? Figures 6.5(a) to (c) summarise the responses of the WS group in deciding whether a configurally or featurally transformed stimulus was more different than the target. These are plotted against CA, Benton test age, and Pattern Construction test age respectively. The WS group demonstrated no alteration in choice with CA ($F(1,10) = .02$, $p = .880$) or Benton test age ($F(1,10) = .42, p = .534$; controls: $F(1,59) = 8.31$, $p = .005$). Plotting the WS performance according level of Pattern Construction ability produces a more typical-looking pattern, although the effect of age on choice does not yet approach significance ($F(1,10) = 1.91, p = .197$). The implication here is that sensitivity to the configural–featural dimension in WS is in line with Pattern Construction ability; yet this dimension is not the one exploited when participants with WS achieve their high face recognition scores in standardised tasks like the Benton.

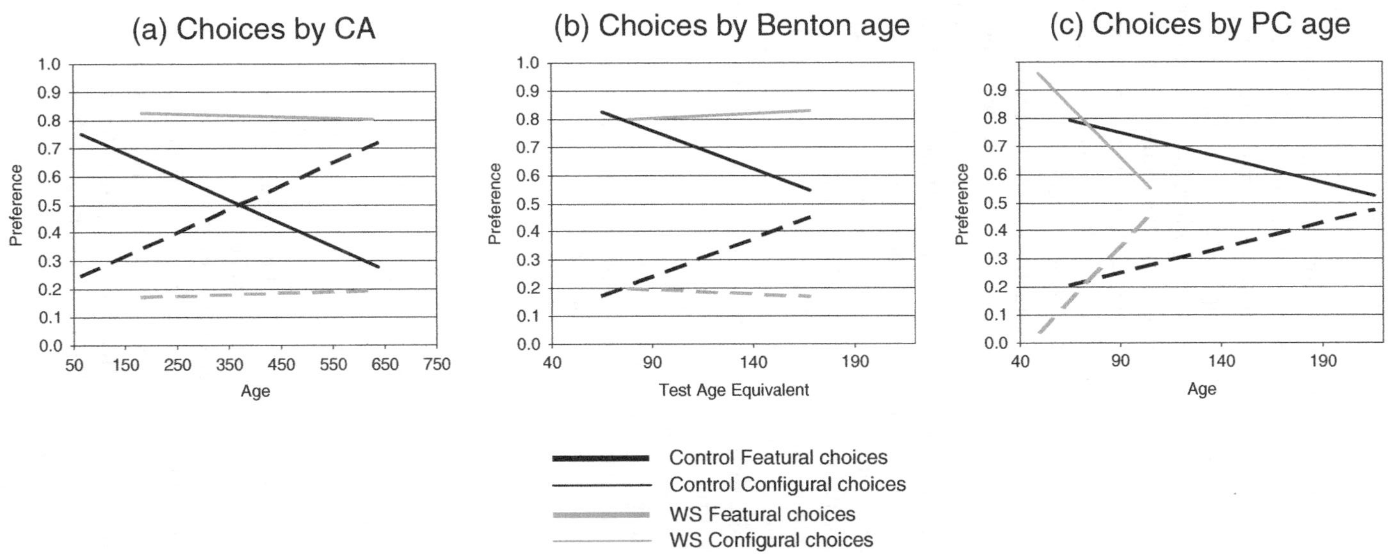

Figure 6.5 Cross-sectional developmental trajectories for the WS and control groups on preferences for featurally vs. configurally transformed face schematics, in a forced choice task to determine which stimulus is most different from the target. Trajectories are plotted according to the (a) chronological age of the participants (CA), (b) Benton face recognition test age equivalent (ceiling age 14;0), or (c) Pattern Construction (PC) test age equivalent (ceiling age 18;0). See text for details

Discussion

Although in Experiment 1 scores were poorer in the configural than in the featural trials in the upright condition, in this third experiment configural processing turned out to be easier than featural processing in upright condition. Why is this? A possible explanation is that the transformation types had different relative salience in the two tasks, i.e., configural transformations were more obvious with the schematic stimuli (stretched or compressed faces) than featural transformations (diamonds instead of squares for eyes), whereas in the Jane real faces, the configural changes involve quite subtle rearrangements compared to the more obvious change of different eyes in a face. Hence the importance of avoiding premature conclusions from a single study. Our focus, however, is on change over time in the sensitivity to the two transformation types, and particularly in the cross-group comparison, leading to several important differences between the WS group and the controls. First, the clinical group display a developmental delay in configural processing for their CA, but importantly, this also holds with respect to their level of face recognition performance on the Benton, which suggests atypical underlying processes. Second, when memory load is completely reduced due to simultaneous presentation of the target and test stimuli to be compared, then the controls, but *not* the participants with WS, display a face-specific sensitivity to configural transformations. Third, the clinical population is significantly slower than the controls, with a particular deficit in RTs for configurally transformed stimuli. While this holds for chronological age, the trajectory of RTs is not distinguishable from the normal trajectory when plotted according to their Benton or Pattern Construction age equivalents. Plotting the WS data according to their BPVS language test age does point to some indication of verbally mediated strategies that have been identified in other areas like number (Ansari et al., 2003), suggesting that the WS individuals may use their language proficiency to bootstrap other domains.

General discussion

What have we learnt from these three experiments? In our first experiment with real faces, we hypothesised that if face processing in WS had developed normally, then individuals with the syndrome should show no difference in accuracy or response time in discriminating a target face from a featurally or configurally transformed version of the target. At first blush, our overall results suggest this to be the case: the clinical group was as accurate as the controls on both identity recognition and difference detection, albeit somewhat slower. However, a key condition separated the groups' performance; for upright configural faces, the controls were significantly more accurate than the WS group. Yet, sensitivity to second-order configural differences in upright faces is the hallmark of face-processing expertise (Yin, 1969), lacking in the WS group. In our second experiment with real faces embedded in a story, we hypothesised that if face processing in WS had developed normally, then like the controls they would become increasingly accurate and rapid with age with respect to upright faces, but also show increased sensitivity to inversion, which disrupts configural processing. Our results showed that although again the WS group did not differ from the controls in terms of accuracy or speed of response, their developmental trajectory failed to show progressive emergence of the face inversion effect, again lacking the hallmark of face-processing expertise (Yin, 1969). Moreover, despite normal scores on the Benton, these latter did not predict accuracy on the storybook task. Finally, in our third experiment with schematic faces, we hypothesised that if face processing in WS had developed normally, then like controls they would demonstrate an emerging skill in detecting configural transformations in upright faces with increasing age. Our results showed not only a delay in configural processing with respect to CA, but importantly with respect to their level of face-processing performance on the Benton, suggesting not only delay but atypicality. Moreover, when memory load was reduced in the simultaneous presentation condition, the controls, but *not* the participants with WS, showed an increase in their sensitivity to configural transformations in faces.

A number of our findings, particularly the lack of progressive emergence of the inversion effect, only became obvious from the comparison of the developmental trajectories. Plotting the WS data with respect to their levels over time on several other developmental criteria (standardised measures of face processing, pattern construction or language) brought forth differences than were not detectible in accuracy or speed alone. Comparisons of behavioural scores at specific ages (CA or MA) often suggested no difference between WS and controls. But these are static comparisons that do not elucidate the trajectory by which people reach their proficiency. So, in our view, there is a distinct advantage of building task-specific developmental trajectories. In general, many studies of developmental disorders fall within the theoretical framework of adult neuropsychology. In such an approach researchers ask whether an ability in an atypical group is 'intact' or 'impaired' and draw their inferences on the basis of whether the clinical group does or does not differ from normal controls matched, say, on mental age. Delay is often ignored or implicitly dismissed as irrelevant, with statements such as 'the clinical group did not differ significantly from the controls', omitting to recall in the discussion that the MA-controls were, say, 20 years younger than the atypical participants! Here and elsewhere we have argued that delay cannot be simply ignored because the dynamics of a developing system over time are vital influences on final outcome (Karmiloff-Smith, Scerif, & Ansari, 2003). But this doesn't merely hold for mental-age-matched controls. Even if a clinical population reaches the same scores as their chronological controls, it is still an open question as to whether they display those *behavioural* scores via the same *cognitive* processes as the controls and whether the trajectory by which they moved from childhood to adulthood followed the same *developmental trajectory* as controls (see discussion in Karmiloff-Smith, 1998). In other words, the vital issue for an in-depth comparison of two groups is whether the developmental trajectory shows the same pattern *over time*. Merely demonstrating the equivalence of two groups at Time Z tells us about Times X and Y and thus nothing of the route by which each group reached that level. Furthermore, even when Benton scores fell within the normal range, our trajectories showed that WS performance was nevertheless delayed compared to the typical trajectory, meaning that even 'scores-in-the-normal-range' does not imply entirely normal development. And in many cases, Benton scores for face processing in WS did not predict success levels on configural processing in our face-processing tasks.

We have argued in this paper that building full normal developmental trajectories of each specific task, and subsequently plotting the atypical trajectory on the trajectory, is a more informative way in which to address developmental questions. What we deem to be particularly interesting in our studies is that the broad pattern of scores in the end state was often not reliably distinguishable from chronological age, and yet the trajectory of development was atypical. In addition, by placing the clinical group at different points on the typically developmental trajectory of different standardised measures, we overcome the problem of having to recruit numerous different individually matched control groups for each and every standardised measure. In sum, our approach focuses on change over time rather than performance at a particular moment in development.

The important question for developmental disorders must always be, in our view, 'does it (face processing, language, number, and the like) *develop* normally or atypically'? We have tested this by asking: 'Is face recognition in WS in step with developmental markers established in the control sample?' While a truly longitudinal approach would obviously be ideal (but take some two decades!), our cross-sectional task-specific trajectories of a very large number of controls addresses this question more directly than groups matched statically on either mental or chronological age. For the practical purposes of the present set of experiments, and because of the claims in the literature that we were attempting to address, our youngest participants were 12 years of age. However, our lab is currently working on the featural/configural face-processing distinction in infants, toddlers and children, to complete the trajectories of both typically developing controls and those with developmental disorders. These are clearly very labour-intensive studies.

In conclusion, we agree that the extant literature has identified a proficiency with respect to holistic processing in WS (Deruelle et al., 2003; Tager-Flusberg et al., 2003). But, contrary to the claims of these authors, this work is not inconsistent with our claim that second-order configural processing is indeed impaired in WS in both face processing and general visuospatial processing. Our work measuring brain potentials (Grice et al., 2003) also points to particularly deficient integration of features into a configural whole in WS, suggesting that both face processing and visuospatial processing suffer from similar deficits. Yet, for two decades, the literature has claimed that face processing and visuospatial processing are independent of one another in WS, with the former 'spared' and the latter seriously impaired (Bellugi et al., 1988, 1994). Our findings suggest that this may not be the case. Although scores on the Benton were better than predicted by Pattern Construction scores, it was these latter that were more in line with our face-processing experimental tasks targeting directly the featural/configural distinction. And, whereas people with WS show improvements with age for the Benton, the same improvements are not apparent for tests where configural processing is essential. When configural processing is crucial, people with WS show a deficit (Deruelle et al., 1999), but when global/holistic processing is needed such as in the Navon task, then the WS resemble typically developing controls (Farran, Jarrold, & Gathercole, 2003). It is *second-order configural processing*, demonstrated by the lack of an emergent inversion effect, that yields an atypical developmental trajectory in this clinical population. In our view, spatial cognition is simply more vulnerable to second-order configural impairments in WS development, and many face-processing tasks can be solved by featural or holistic strategies, thereby camouflaging any configural deficit. In other words, while scores in one domain (face processing) may outstrip scores in the other domain (visuospatial cognition), both domains may be affected by similar deficient processes but one reveals this impairment more subtly than the other. Seeming dissociations in the outcome, then, do not necessarily entail dissociations all the way along the developmental pathway (Karmiloff-Smith, 1998).

In conclusion, we argue that the developmental approach taken here, highlighting the importance of building developmental trajectories, is an essential, additional methodology for uncovering the subtleties of the causes of developmental disorders in general, and of face processing in particular.

Acknowledgements

We should like to thank the Williams Syndrome Foundation, UK, for putting us in touch with families and particularly all the clinical and typically developing participants for their contribution. This research was supported by MRC Programme Grant No. G9715642 NIH Project Grant R21TW06761-01 to AK-S. We especially thank Daphne Maurer and Cathy Mondloch of MacMaster University, Canada, for making the Jane Faces Task available to us.

Note

1 All participants with WS across the three experiments (a different opportunity sample each time because of the great distances) had been diagnosed clinically and by means of the FISH probe for the deletion of the elastin gene. Because of the rarity of Williams syndrome and the size of the United Kingdom, numbers are necessarily somewhat low, ranging from 12 to 17 participants with WS per experiment. However, this is well above many of the published papers on this syndrome and is comparable, for instance, to the study of Deruelle et al. (2003), which was viewed by these authors as sufficient to make claims about 'normal' development in WS face processing.

References

Ansari, D., Donlan, C., Thomas, M., Ewing, S., Peen, T., & Karmiloff-Smith, A. (2003). What makes counting count? Verbal and visuo-spatial contributions to typical and atypical number development. *Journal of Experimental Child Psychology*, *85*, 50–62.

Bellugi, U.L., Lichtenberger, L., Jones, W., Lai, Z., & St. George, M. (2000). I. The neurocognitive profile of Williams Syndrome: A complex pattern of strengths and weaknesses. *Journal of Cognitive Neuroscience*, *12*(Suppl 1), 7–29.

Bellugi, U., Lichtenberger, L., Mills, D., Galaburda, A., & Korenberg, J.R. (1999). Bridging cognition, brain and molecular genetics: Evidence from Williams syndrome. *Trends in Neurosciences*, *5*, 197–208.

Bellugi, U., Sabo, H., & Vaid, J. (1988). Spatial deficits in children with Williams Syndrome. In J. Stiles-Davis & M. Kritchevsky (Eds.), *Spatial cognition: Brain bases and development*. Hillsdale, NJ: Lawrence Erlbaum Associates, Inc.

Bellugi, U., Wang, P.P., & Jernigan, T.L. (1994). Williams syndrome: An unusual neuropsychological profile. In S.H. Broman & J. Grafman (Eds.), *Atypical cognitive deficits in developmental disorders: Implications for brain function* (pp. 23–56). Hillsdale, NJ: Lawrence Erlbaum Associates, Inc.

Benton, A.L., Hamsher, K.S., Varney, N.R., & Spreen, O. (1983). *Contributions to neuropsychological assessment: Tests*. New York: Oxford University Press.

Benton, A.L., Sivan, A.B., Hamsher K. deS., Varney, N., & Spreen, O. (1994). *Contributions to neuropsychological assessment: A clinical manual*. New York: Oxford University Press.

Brace, N.A., Hole, G.J., Kemp, R., Pike, G., Duuren, M., & Norgate, L. (2001). Developmental changes in the effect of inversion: Using a picture book to investigate face recognition. *Perception*, *30*, 85–94.

Bruyer, R., Laterre, C., Seron, X., Feyereisen, P., Strypstein, E., Pierrard, E., & Rectem, D. (1983). A case of prosopagnosia with some preserved covert remembrance of familiar faces. *Brain and Cognition*, *2*, 257–284.

de Haan, M. (2001). The neuropsychology of face processing during infancy and childhood. In C.A. Nelson & M. Luciana (Eds.), *The handbook of developmental cognitive neuroscience* (pp. 381–398). Cambridge, MA: MIT Press.

de Renzi, E. (1986). Current issues in prosopagnosia. In H.D. Ellis, M.A. Jeeves, F. Newcombe, & A.W. Young (Eds.), *Aspects of face processing*. Dordrecht: Martinis Nijhoff.

Deruelle, C., Mancini, J., Livet, M., Cassé-Perrot, C., & de Schonen, S. (1999). Configural and local processing of faces in children with Williams syndrome. *Brain and Cognition*, *41*, 276–298.

Deruelle, C., Rondan, C., Mancini, J., & Livet, M. (2003). Exploring face processing in Williams syndrome. *Cognitie, Creier, Comportanent*, *7*, 157–171.

Diamond, R., & Carey, S. (1986). Why faces are and are not special: An effect of expertise. *Journal of Experimental Psychology General*, *115*, 107–117.

Donnai, D., & Karmiloff-Smith, A. (2000). Williams syndrome: From genotype through to the cognitive phenotype. *American Journal of Medical Genetics: Seminars in Medical Genetics*, *97*, 164–171.

Dunn L.M., & Dunn L.M. (1981). *Peabody Picture Vocabulary Test–Revised*. Minnesota: American Guidance Service.

Dunn, L.M., Whetton, C., & Pintilie, D. (1997). *British Picture Vocabulary Scale*. Windsor, UK: NFER-Nelson.

Elliot, C.D., Smith, P., & McCulloch, K. (1996). *British Ability Scales*. NFER-Nelson, Windsor, UK.

Farah, M.J., Levinson, K.L., & Klein, K.L. (1995). Face perception and within-category discrimination in prosopagnosia. *Neuropsychologia*, *33*, 661–674.

Farran, E.K., Jarrold, C., & Gathercole, S.E. (2003). Divided attention, selective attention and drawing: Processing preferences in Williams syndrome are dependent on the task administered. *Neuropsychologia, 41*, 676–687.

Grice, S.J., de Haan, M., Halit, H., Johnson, M.H., Csibra, G., Grant, J., & Karmiloff-Smith, A. (2003). ERP abnormalities of visual perception in Williams syndrome. *NeuroReport, 14*, 1773–1777.

Johnson, M.H., & de Haan, M. (2001). Developing cortical specialization for visual-cognitive function: The case of face recognition. In J.L. McClelland & R.S. Siegler (Eds.), *Mechanisms of cognitive development: Behavioral and neural perspectives. Carnegie Mellon symposia on cognition* (pp. 253–270). Mahwah, NJ: Lawrence Erlbaum Associates, Inc.

Johnson, M.H., & Morton, J. (1991). *Biology and cognitive development: The case of face recognition*. Oxford (UK) and Cambridge (USA): Blackwell.

Karmiloff-Smith, A. (1992). *Beyond modularity: A developmental perspective on cognitive science*. Cambridge MA: MIT Press.

Karmiloff-Smith, A. (1997). Crucial differences between developmental cognitive neuroscience and adult neuropsychology. *Developmental Neuropsychology, 13*, 513–524.

Karmiloff-Smith, A. (1998). Development itself is the key to understanding developmental disorders. *Trends in Cognitive Sciences, 2*, 389–398.

Karmiloff-Smith, A., Grant, J., Berthoud, I., Davies, M., Howlin, P., & Udwin, O. (1997). Language and Williams Syndrome: How intact is 'intact'? *Child Development, 68*, 246–262.

Karmiloff-Smith, A., Scerif, G., & Ansari, D. (2003). Double dissociations in developmental disorders? Theoretically misconceived, empirically dubious. *Cortex, 39*, 161–163.

Laing, E., Butterworth, G., Ansari, D., Gsödl, M., Longhi, E., Panagiotaki, G., Paterson, S., & Karmiloff-Smith, A. (2002). Atypical development of language and social communication in toddlers with Williams syndrome. *Developmental Science, 5*, 233–246.

Maurer, D., Le Grand, R., & Mondloch, C.J. (2002). The many faces of configural processing. *Trends in Cognitive Sciences, 6*, 255–260.

Mervis, C.B., & Bertrand, J. (1997). Developmental relations between cognition and language: Evidence from Williams syndrome. In L.B. Adamson & M.A. Romski (Eds.), *Research on communication and language disorders: Contributions to theories of language development* (pp. 75–106). New York: Brookes.

Mondloch, C.J., Le Grand, R., & Maurer, D. (2002). Configural face processing develops more slowly than featural face processing. *Perception, 31*, 553–566.

Passarotti, A.M., Paul, B.M., Joseph, R., Bussiere, J.R., Buxton, R.B., Wong, E.C., & Stiles, J. (2003). The development of face and location processing: An fMRI study. *Developmental Science, 6*, 100–117.

Rossen, M.L., Jones, W., Wang, P.P., & Klima, E.S. (1995). Face processing: Remarkable sparing in Williams syndrome. Special Issue, *Genetic Counseling, 6*, 138–140.

Simion, F., Macchi Cassia, V., Turati, C., & Valenza, E. (2001). The origins of face perception: Specific versus non-specific mechanisms. *Infant and Child Development, 10*, 59–65.

Tager-Flusberg, H., Plesa-Skwerer, D., Faja, S., & Joseph, R.M. (2003). People with Williams syndrome process faces holistically. *Cognition, 89*, 11–24.

Tanaka, J. W., & Farah, M. J. (1993). Parts and wholes in face recognition. *Quarterly Journal of Experimental Psychology, 46*(2), 225–245.

Temple, C. (1997). *Developmental cognitive neuropsychology*. Hove: Psychology Press.

Thomas, M.S.C., Grant, J., Barham, Z., Gsödl, M., Laing, E., Lakusta, L., Tyler, L.K., Grice, S., Paterson, S., & Karmiloff-Smith, A. (2001). Past tense formation in Williams syndrome. *Language and Cognitive Processes*, *16*, 143–176.

Thomas, M.S.C., & Karmiloff-Smith, A. (2002). Are developmental disorders like cases of adult brain damage? Implications from connectionist modelling. *Behavioural and Brain Sciences*, *25*, 727–750.

Udwin, O., & Yule, W. (1991). A cognitive and behavioural phenotype in Williams syndrome. *Journal of Clinical and Experimental Neuropsychology*, *13*, 232–244.

Yin, R.K. (1969). Looking at upside-down faces. *Journal of Experimental Psychology*, *81*, 141–145.

Wang, P.P., Doherty, S., Rourke, S.B., & Bellugi, U. (1995). Unique profile of visuo-perceptual skills in a genetic syndrome. *Brain and Cognition*, *29*, 54–65.

Part III

Genetics and computational modelling approaches

7 Different approaches to relating genotype to phenotype in developmental disorders

Annette Karmiloff-Smith, Gaia Scerif, and Michael Thomas

Introduction

The recent sequencing of the human genome provides the hope that substantial progress now can be made with respect to the relation between genes and cognition. However, many of the empirical tools at our disposal have serious limitations in uncovering the links between genotype and phenotype. In this article, our aim is threefold. First, we attempt to rule out overly simplistic theories of genotype–phenotype relations sometimes found in psychological literature. Second, we examine three current empirical approaches to investigating this relation—quantitative genetics, molecular genetics, and animal models. Third, we stress the importance of the contribution of developmental computational neuroscience in building a realistic account of the way in which gene expression may affect the construction of the computational circuits that—via an extended process of development—give rise to the adult cognitive system.

We begin by identifying a trend in some disciplines to employ overly simple analyses of the relationship between genes and phenotypic outcomes, and in particular, to reduce this relationship to simple one-to-one mappings. Linguists, philosophers, and even psychologists often can be found using the dangerous shorthand of "a gene (or set of genes) for *X*," where *X* is a purported higher level cognitive module such as face processing, grammar, number, or so on. Claims abound in the psychological and linguistic literature about the specific contribution of genes to cognitive outcomes, as the following examples illustrate: (a) "[The human mind] is equipped with a body of genetically determined information specific to Universal Grammar" (Smith & Tsimpli, 1995, p. 31); "(b) it is uncontroversial that the development [of Universal Grammar] is essentially guided by a biological, genetically determined program" (Wexler, 1996, p. 117); and "(c) the mind is likely to contain blueprints for grammatical rules . . . and a special set of genes that help wire [it] in place" (Pinker, 1994, p. 45).

We focus our quotations on the domain of language because this is where much of the debate has centered. However, similar claims have been made with respect to number (Butterworth, 1999), to face processing (Bellugi, Lichtenberger, Jones, Lai, & St. George, 1999; Rossen et al., 1994), and to other cognitive domains, as illustrated in the following quotation by Butterworth (1999):

> These three abilities: to recognize numerosities, to detect changes in numerosity caused by adding or taking away from a collection, and ordering numbers by size, are the biologically basic numerical capacities, the ones that are embedded in our innate Number Module.
>
> (p. 162)

Two issues are at stake: how *direct* the relation between genes and cognitive processes may be, and how *specific*. It is uncontroversial that a single gene product cannot construct cognition (although some appear tempted by this idea because the lack of a single gene product can sometimes *impair* cognition). The issue of *directness* relates to how precise a role any group of genes will have in determining the structure and content of any subsequent cognitive module. It is our contention that no combination of gene effects will alone determine a cognitive function. Necessarily, the environment plays a causal role in generating the ultimate cognitive structures, whether that environment constitutes the biochemical environment affecting cell differentiation, the prenatal nutritional environment affecting development of the fetus, or the environment of the external world with which the individual interacts during the process of cognitive development. There obviously can be no *direct* link between genes and successful cognition.

The issue of *specificity* relates to the idea that genes, whether one or several, code for structures that are entirely specific to a particular cognitive domain. Consider, for example, the following quote by Pinker (1994):

> The *grammar genes* [italics added] would be stretches of DNA that code for proteins, or trigger the transcription of proteins, in certain times and places in the brain, that guide, attract, or glue neurons into networks that, in combination with the synaptic tuning that takes place during learning, are necessary to compute the solution to some grammatical problem (like choosing an affix or a word).
>
> (p. 322)

The deliberate stipulation that genes are “grammar” genes seems to serve the claim that these genes code for information specific to the domain of grammar. Without such a qualification, the previous quote would simply read as a proposal that genes code for a brain that can learn language.

Our contention is that claims for such specificity are unwarranted given the empirical data and the prevalence of many-to-many mappings in relating genes to cognition. To the extent that genes are involved in the causal chain of several cognitive domains, it will be less likely that they code anything specific to a single domain. And they are unlikely given that spatial distributions of gene expression in the brain are rarely narrowly confined to subsequent areas of functional specialization in the adult brain.

However, it is important to understand the origin of claims that postulate *direct, specific, one-to-one mappings* between genes and cognition. Such claims are usually made on the basis of two important sources of data: adult neuropsychology and developmental disorders. At first blush, these data often seem to point to independently functioning cognitive modules (identified by cognitive neuropsychology in the adult) that can be selectively impaired or preserved in genetic developmental disorders. On the basis of these data, it is not uncommon to find statements like the following by Pinker (1999):

> Overall, the genetic double dissociation is striking, suggesting that language is both a specialisation of the brain and that it depends on generative rules that are visible in the ability to compute regular forms. The genes of one group of children [Specific Language Impairment] impair their grammar while sparing their intelligence; the genes of another group of children [Williams syndrome] impair their intelligence while sparing their grammar.
>
> (p. 262)

In this article, we argue that such direct mapping between genes and higher level cognitive outcomes is highly questionable. Genes are likely to affect much lower level mechanisms than "grammar." In the following section, we look at various methods available to establish relations between genes and behavior, illustrated with the specific example of Fragile X syndrome. We then briefly present our in-depth cognitive and computational studies of another developmental disorder, Williams syndrome, to illustrate a developmental neuroconstructivist approach to genotype/phenotype relations.

Methods for relating genotype to phenotypic outcome

Quantitative genetics

The method. Epidemiological studies of human genetics focus on discovering the extent to which genetic and environmental factors influence individual differences in a particular trait. These can involve physical traits such as height and weight, personality traits such as aggressiveness and altruism, or cognitive traits such as intelligence, novelty seeking, and memory. Researchers pinpoint a trait for which there is interesting population variation, e.g., IQ, and then search for a correlating genetic variation in the population under study. Of course, the discovery that something is highly heritable, i.e., influenced by genes, does not mean that the trait is not also strongly influenced by environmental factors.

There are two types of possible genetic influence: additive, in which the effects of each gene are simply accumulated to influence the final trait, and nonadditive, where gene effects are multiplicative. Although multiplicative effects are far more likely, heritability estimates are normally based only on additive genetic variance (see discussion in Thapar & McGuffin, 2000). Note that the heritability calculations are relevant at the population level, not at the individual level. Thus, for example, a statement that trait *X* (e.g., IQ) has a heritability estimate of 50% does not imply that 50% of any particular person's IQ is explained by their genes. Rather, the figure refers to the proportion of the *variation* of IQ in the population as a whole that can be imputed to genetic effects. It also is important to recall that children not only inherit half of each of their parents' genes, they also are exposed to environments that are molded by their parents' genetic make-up and by the children's own influence on their environments. Such indirect effects are known as genotype–environment correlations, and illustrate that evidence of heritability does not in itself implicate direct or specific causal relations between genes and cognitive traits.

In methodological terms, researchers studying heritability employ huge sample sizes in the general population and focus on family, twin, and adoption methods with smaller numbers. Of course, while stating that something "runs in families" may indicate a genetic influence, this conclusion cannot be taken for granted because environment may be a causal factor, either alone or together with susceptible genes. It is rare that a specific cognitive trait can be explained by a single genetic variation in the population. Rather, cognitive traits typically involve complex patterns of inheritance involving many genes, each accounting for quite a tiny percentage of the behavioral variance, e.g., as little as 1 or 2% (Plomin, DeFries, McClean, & McGuffin, 2001), in combination with environmental factors.

In an attempt to separate the influence of genes and environment, researchers have used twin and adoption methods, comparing monozygotic (MZ) and dyzygotic (DZ) twins either reared together or apart. If the MZ twin pairs reared apart show a higher correlation than DZ twin pairs, this usually indicates a genetic influence. Even in this case, however, caution is warranted because adoption often is into similar families as those of the original parent. Note, too, that some environmental factors have an influence on twins that make them more similar (the shared environment) whereas others exaggerate the difference between twins (the nonshared environment).

Developmental disorders: evaluating the quantitative genetics approach. Turning now to developmental disorders, it is true that if one of a pair of MZ twins—whether reared together or apart—develops autism or dyslexia, the other twin is at greater risk than in the case of DZ twins. This suggests a genetic component to the disorders. Interestingly, however, the risk is far from being 100%. Heritability figures based on MZ twins for autism and dyslexia are 60 and 65%, respectively (Plomin et al., 2001), suggesting that environmental factors play an important role. Noteworthy, too, is the fact that concordance rates for schizophrenia are much higher when MZ twins have shared the same placenta (Davis, Phelps, & Brancha, 1995). Thus, environmental factors such as prenatal nutrition also play a significant part in determining the extent to which genetic risk factors are actually expressed. Indeed, genes and environment have an interactive influence, such that particular environments can exaggerate genetic differences (Rutter, 2000). But within disorders such as dyslexia and autism, mere heritability estimates are far from telling us which of the mutated genes are responsible for the elevated risk. Rather, at this stage, we simply know that genetic factors are implicated. With other genetic syndromes, the likelihood of both MZ twins having the disorder is much closer to 100%, as for example, in Williams syndrome and Down syndrome. However, even in the latter case, the much greater heritability does not mean that we can automatically relate mutation of specific genes directly to phenotypic traits.

Finally, it is worth stressing that quantitative genetics only can report on *variability*. Its methods are unable to investigate the relation between genes and cognition where there is little or no allelic variability in genes or in cognitive outcomes.

Molecular genetics

The method. The second approach we discuss targets the identification of specific genes. A candidate gene approach is used when genetic variation can be traced back to the protein function for which a particular gene codes. One especially well-known example is the case of variant alleles found in the number of 16 amino acid repeats in the so-called dopamine D4 receptor (D4DR). In general, people vary as to whether they have 2, 4, or 7 repeats, and this difference has been implicated in behaviors such as novelty seeking (Benjamin et al., 1996). Differences in repeats impact on dopamine binding, so this neurotransmitter variation could implicate allelic differences contributing to variation in phenotypic outcome.

However, even when a *single* gene is implicated in a disorder, there is no simple mapping to phenotypic outcome. This is because, in most cases, the gene's effect is widespread, having many cognitive (and physical) effects. To illustrate this point, let us consider the example of Fragile X syndrome.

Example of a molecular genetics approach to genotype/phenotype relations: Fragile X. Fragile X syndrome is one of the most common forms of inherited mental retardation, with a prevalence of 1 in 4,000 males and 1 in 6,000 females (de Vries et al., 1997). Clinically, the syndrome presents with variable levels of ability ranging from mild to severe mental retardation, with abnormal facial features (prominent jaw and large ears), subtle connective tissue abnormalities, and macroorchidism in males. However, the physical morphology is often less diagnostic of the syndrome than the individual's cognitive profile (Turk, 1998). The cognitive profile in late childhood and adulthood is characterized by weaknesses in attention (Munir, Cornish, & Wilding, 2000), visuospatial cognition (Cornish, Munir, & Cross, 1999), and short-term memory and sequential information processing, along with (relative) strengths in language, long-term memory, and holistic information processing (Freund & Reiss, 1991). In addition, many individuals with Fragile X display hyperactive/attention deficit disorder, hyperacusis, and autisticlike behaviors (Hagerman & Cronister, 1996).

Fragile X is interesting in the current context because, in addition to a characteristic phenotypic outcome, the underlying genetic anomaly also is reasonably well understood. It will become clear that despite knowledge of both the genotype and the adult phenotype, a cognitive developmental perspective is still essential to uncover the complex developmental relationship between genotype and phenotype in this disorder. This is because an understanding of the molecular, cellular, and system pathophysiology of the syndrome points to *experience-dependent* synaptic plasticity as critical in determining phenotypic outcome (Churchill et al., 2002).

This has implications for understanding the syndrome at the cognitive level. First, given that experience and learning are key factors in shaping the structure of the brain, the effects on cognition must be understood in the context of a dynamically developing cognitive system rather than merely in terms of the relation of the anomalous genotype to the adult phenotype. Focus on the adult system alone will not help us understand how restrictions in low-level synaptic plasticity could result in the pattern of deficits seen. Instead, we must consider the way in which normal developmental processes would be warped if cognitive development were attempted with a system whose plasticity is restricted.

Second, given the role of this type of synaptic plasticity in establishing neural networks across the developing brain, all circuits in which this low-level process is involved will develop atypically to some extent. However, some cognitive domains may rely less crucially on this particular low-level property, and they will thus display less overt impairment. In other words, as with other syndromes, development itself will be a crucial factor in governing atypical phenotypic outcome across and within domains of both relative strength and weakness (Karmiloff-Smith, 1998).

Let us consider the underlying genetic anomaly in Fragile X, and how this alters low-level neural properties. The vast majority of cases of Fragile X syndrome are due to an expansion of the CGG repeat in the untranslated 5' region of the Fragile X mental retardation-1 (FMR1) gene. Among normal individuals, this CGG repeat is highly variable in length and content. The normal repeat size varies from 7 to 60, with 30 repeats being the level most commonly found in the general population. In most affected Fragile X individuals, CGG repeats are massively expanded, ranging from more than 200 repeats up to several thousands (Jin & Warren, 2000). This results in silencing of the FMR1 gene. The lack of expression of the Fragile X mental retardation protein (FMRP) is the *sole genetic contribution* to the Fragile X phenotype (Verkerk et al., 1991).

Greenough and collaborators (e.g., Churchill et al., 2002; Greenough et al., 2001) present strong evidence for a role of FMRP in processes underlying morphological synaptic changes in response to glutamatergic stimulation. They suggest that FMRP is not necessary for initial neuronal outgrowth, but is crucial for the refinement of dendritic spine morphology, a crucial neural correlate of changes linked to both development and learning. Let us look briefly at development to understand how dynamic and complex this role may be.

FMRP is highly expressed in both adult and fetal brain tissues (Devys, Lutz, Rouyer, Bellocq, & Mandel, 1993). Early in fetal development, FMR1 gene expression is high throughout the brain, and particularly high in the hippocampus, cerebellum, and nucleus basalis (Devys et al., 1993). The levels are considerably greater than in the adult. FMRP does not act in isolation: It interacts with at least two proteins that are very similar to it in structure (Zhang et al., 1995). In human adult cerebellum and cerebral cortex, FMRP and these proteins are co-localized. In the fetal brain, however, they are not: FMRP is located in the cytoplasm as in the adult whereas one of the two collaborating proteins also is strongly expressed in the fetal nuclei (Tamanini et al., 1997). This suggests that the collaborative functions of FMRP may vary from undifferentiated fetal neurons to differentiated adult neurons. Furthermore, the pathway in which FMRP plays a role, triggered by stimulation of the metabotropic glutamate receptors type 1, is more active in young animals than in adults (e.g., Flavin, Daw, Gregory, & Reid, 1996), pointing to the possibility of differential roles of FMRP functioning (and malfunctioning) across developmental time.

Therefore, the important role of FMRP in experience-dependent plasticity only can be properly understood within a truly developmental context. The complex interaction of FMRP with other proteins across development suggests that the silencing of the FMR1 gene alone initiates a series of imbalances that have cascading effects on other elements of the developmental pathway at differing times in development.

In the next section, we discuss the advantages and disadvantages of animal models as an increasingly prevalent tool for understanding such complex cascades. In addition, we review the loss-of-function approach with the example of knockout mouse models of Fragile X syndrome itself.

Animal models

The method. Selective breeding of natural traits and the creation of transgenic animals (e.g., mice that have had genes knocked out, or altered so that gene products are under- or overexpressed) allow scientists to study the effects of genetic change at different stages of embriogenesis and postnatal development. Transgenic models (altering the genetic make-up of a species) have hitherto mainly concentrated on rodents—in particular, the mouse. This is because the mouse breeds very rapidly and shows a high degree of evolutionary conservatism of many developmentally important genes. Conservation of specific genes across species does not necessarily mean, of course, that sequence or timing of gene expression are equivalent in mice and man (Fougerousse et al., 2000). Moreover, murine embriogenesis and postnatal life are considerably shorter than in the human case, with experience-dependent processes playing a much greater role in specifying the microcircuitry of the human neocortex. Thus, developmental processes may play a much greater role in specifying the phenotypic outcome in the human than in equivalent mouse models.

Induced changes in an animal's genetic make-up can be produced in several ways (Flint, 1996; Heinz, 2000; Hunter, Nolan, & Brown, 2000; Kempermann, Kuhn, & Gage, 1997), the main examples of which are selective breeding of naturally occurring traits, selective breeding of animals exposed to radiation, drugs, specific diets, and enriched or impoverished environments, or breeding of animals in whom specific genes have been knocked out or under/over-expressed. Selective breeding of normal variation in traits capitalizes on naturally occurring individual differences of a particular trait. For example, a group of animals may be divided into those with high novelty exploration and those with low exploratory behavior.

The groups are then interbred separately across a number of generations until the offspring all display the group trait. This experimental group then undergoes a number of genetic and behavioral tests. The other strategy is to modify the amount of a particular gene product or the product itself and then to assess the effect of the mutagenesis on the animal's responses in behavioral tasks.

Example of a mouse model of a developmental disorder: Fragile X. In human brain development, the lack of FMR1 transcription has widespread effects. FMR1 knockout mice display some of the cognitive and behavioral characteristics of the human syndrome (Churchill et al., 2002), such as hyperreactivity to stimuli (Chen & Toth, 2001) and difficulties with visuospatial spatial learning and working memory. However, these deficits are specific to *certain strains* of knockout mice only, pointing to genetic background effects (Dobkin et al., 2000). Again, this serves to undermine the notion of simple one-to-one mappings from a single gene dysfunction to phenotype, even when simply considering rodents.

Irwin et al. (2001) found that the morphology of dendrites in knockout mice was atypical and resembled immature cortex or the effects of sensory deprivation, with a large number of long and thin spines as opposed to the thicker and shorter ones characteristic of adulthood and rearing in rich environments. Postmortem studies of a small number of humans with Fragile X syndrome have confirmed the atypical dendritic morphology suggested by the mouse models in all cortical tissues sampled (Hinton, Brown, Wisniewski, & Rudelli, 1995; Irwin et al., 2001).

Churchill et al. (2002) discuss the similarities and differences between murine and human data. The extent of the dendritic abnormality is more limited in knockout mice than in humans. Furthermore, in contrast with human data, the effects on spine morphology are transient in rodents, being most marked at 1 week of age but disappearing at 4 weeks (Nimchinsky, Oberlander, & Svoboda, 2001). Churchill et al. explain these important cross-species differences in terms of the divergent developmental timing between human and rodent as well as different levels of environmental stimulation to which humans and laboratory mice are exposed. Both arguments suggest that, as in humans, work with mouse models requires an approach that takes into account changes over developmental time and dynamic interactions between developing mice and their environment.

Strengths and weaknesses of mouse models. One of the obvious advantages of mouse models is that the human and murine genomes are very similar, so that many human genes have mouse counterparts. Since mice breed very rapidly and plentifully, linkage analysis often is faster than in humans and provides a smaller candidate region than in the human genome. Many organ systems of mouse and man also are very similar, so that expression analysis of known or candidate genes can be done in the laboratory with the justified expectation that it will be similar in the human case. A particular advantage is that scientists can study gene expression throughout murine embryogenesis and early postnatal life, which makes it possible to chart *where* and *when* a mutant gene is expressed.

However, as specific genes in humans are mapped to specific genes in mice, there is an unfortunate tendency to take the *static* unit of a gene as a valid theoretical construct. Yet, the gene only has meaning within the complex dynamics of development involving multiple gene–gene/gene–environment interactions (Gerhart & Kirschner, 1997; Keller, 2000). Differences in the developmental trajectories of various species are just as important as similarities in the structure of their genes since function derives from development over time. As mentioned earlier, in contrast to the shorter period of murine embryogenesis and postnatal life, the formation and consolidation of much of the microcircuitry of the human neocortex takes place postnatally. Consequently, the importance of the external environment in shaping gene expression and brain structure/function is likely to be greater in the human case than in the mouse. Thus, while human genes have many orthologues in the mouse, expression patterns in terms of both spatial and time-dependent processes differ significantly between the two species (Fougerousse et al., 2000). Although specific genes may be similar, interactions between genes as well as with the internal and external environments may be different. Even identical single genes may have different functions across different species within the development of the total organism. Many knockout models of genes expressed in the brain have resulted in no obvious behavioral consequences of any kind, supporting the view of genetic redundancy (Keverne, 1997), which may not be the same in mice and man. It is quite possible that while one copy of a gene knocked out in the mouse has no effect, the presence of both alleles is vital for normal human development. Alternatively, the deletion of a gene in the mouse may be lethal whereas haploinsufficiency (i.e., the presence of a single copy of a gene rather than both alleles) may be tolerated in the human case. Equally, environmental conditions and training can alter the way in which genes are expressed. In sum, generalizations from mouse to man need to be examined with great caution, and there are no simple mappings between genes and outcome at any level of analysis.

Another factor relevant to the problems of generalizing from mouse to man is the fact that the mouse repertoire of measurable behavior is limited and even then, not always empirically investigated to the full. When exploring something equivalent to intelligence, most researchers focus on the mouse's spatial memory in the water maze. How comparable are enhanced murine behaviors in the water maze (which is not even a natural environment for the mouse) to improvements in, say, human memory in all its multiple forms? Other measurements less often used, but perhaps more homologous to human behavior, might be speed of mental processing or motor reaction time. In other words, good genetics requires an accurate and detailed characterization of cognitive outcome—what one might call "good phenotypics!"

Apart from theoretical difficulties in extrapolating from the mouse to the human case, there also are methodological issues to be resolved in mouse models. It becomes clear that results from mouse studies cannot be taken at face value unless replicated numerous times across different conditions. This has been particularly evident when results differ even across ostensibly identical conditions. Crabbe, Wahlston, and Dudek (1999) set up a comparison of results from three different laboratories with serotonin neurotransmitter knockout mice. Each laboratory had identical strains of mice, with the experiments starting at the same time on the same day and under the same laboratory conditions as well as the same mouse feed and the same battery of postmutagenesis behavioral tests (including the water maze). The results were surprising. Compared to wild-type littermates, one laboratory's mice showed more activity in the maze, the second laboratory less activity, and the third no difference in activity. These results only can be explained by minute differences in handling, the odor of the handlers, or the composition of the water supply. Recall that the strains used in each of the three laboratories were identical, and thus individual differences across groups were similar and therefore cannot explain the empirical disparities here. If such tiny differences such as handling or water composition can affect whether the serotonin knockout has an effect on subsequent behavioral outcome, considerable caution must be exercised when extrapolating from the mouse model to the human case.

Finally, we return to a more general issue to which we alluded in our Introduction. There can be dangerous slippage when reporting on mouse models and extrapolating to the human case. Terms such as gene *X contributes to* outcome *Y* (one of many indirect causes) become easily translated into *X causes Y* (the only direct cause). The fact that complex systems such as human intelligence can be easily disrupted by deficiencies in a single gene does not validate the opposite claim that the normal function of the gene is solely responsible for the phenotypic trait.

In conclusion, there is no denying that animal models of the genetics of human behavior have greatly advanced our understanding of gene expression and brain development in developmental disorders. However, it is essential to recognize that behavioral outcome is far removed from gene expression, that there is a reciprocal and dynamic relationship between genes, environment, and behavior, and that extrapolations to the human case from even closely related species must be made with considerable caution.

Genes and cognition: how plausible are direct relations

The developmental disorder Fragile X has attracted a lot of attention from cognitive neuroscientists because as a single gene disorder it promised to present a relatively simple case of direct gene/cognition mapping. For example, Kaufmann, Abrams, Chen, and Reiss (1999) found correlations between FMRP expression and IQ. Menon, Kwon, Eliez, Taylor, and Reiss (2000) investigated correlations between FMR1 gene expression and brain activation measured using functional magnetic resonance imaging during a working memory task. Both measures of FMR1 gene expression correlated with activity in the right inferior frontal, middle frontal gyrus (left and right), and supramarginal gyrus (left and right, parietal lobe), but not with activity in the left inferior frontal gyrus and superior parietal lobe.

There are, however, a number of reasons to be cautious in interpreting such otherwise-intriguing correlations. First, clear correlations between protein expression and cognitive functioning are not unequivocally found even in this well-understood syndrome. For example, Cornish et al. (1999) found no evidence of a correlation between activation ratio (i.e., proportion of FMR1 genes that are not silenced) in young girls with Fragile X and their spatial performance (for further evidence, see Cornish, Munir, & Cross, 2001). Second, understanding the neurophysiology of FMRP expression suggests that even robust correlations only represent markers of indirect cascading events rather than of one-to-one mappings. Third, the Kaufmann et al. (1999) and Menon et al. (2000) studies did not focus on *developmental* differences in correlations between FMRP expression and cognition across participants, despite the complex role of FMRP in the process of development itself. However, when Bayley, Hatton, Tassone, Skinner, & Taylor (2001) examined the development of 53 young children with the syndrome (23–98 months of age), they found that FMRP expression accounted for a small but significant variance in the level, but not the rate of development. Correlations between FMRP expression and cognition thus received weak support, but crucially suggested the involvement of other factors in understanding early development in Fragile X syndrome.

So how directly does FMRP expression affect cognition? First, FMRP is involved in experience-dependent plasticity, a core process in development and learning. Therefore, approaches to cognition in Fragile X syndrome must encompass a developmental picture. Second, despite higher FMRP concentration in certain areas, FMRP is expressed ubiquitously in the typically developing brain. Thus, Fragile X syndrome should be characterized by effects on the development of the whole brain. In conclusion, *all* cognitive domains are likely to have *developed* atypically to some extent, and the focus on certain domains of very apparent deficit should never overshadow atypicalities, however subtle, in others. In sum, even in a single gene disorder, direct genotype–phenotype mappings are highly questionable. And such reasoning applies equally to developmental disorders caused by mutations of multiple genes and their cascading effects on the developing system.

Genes and cognition: an indirect approach

The computational level

Let us assume that we have actually discovered "a gene (y) for x," where presence or absence of gene y accounts for variability in behavior x in a developmental disorder (or presence/absence of gene y accounts for variation of behavior x in a mouse model; or different alleles of gene y account for variation in behavior x in the normal population). The product of gene y cannot alone be responsible for the cognitive processes underlying behavior x. Instead, gene y will likely be part of a group of genes that code for molecular processes that construct the brain, in an overall process that itself relies on activity-dependent changes to construct microcircuitry, and perhaps even macro areas of functional specialization in the adult cognitive system. What can it mean, then, that gene y correlates with behavior x?

To answer this question, we must turn to an intermediate level of description, one that falls in between the low-level properties of the brain (such as the synaptic plasticity discussed in the case of Fragile X), and the high-level behaviors that, in the human at least, very often only consolidate after a protracted period of postnatal development. The cognitive level imports computational principles from biological circuits and builds them into more abstract models that can make contact with the cognitive phenomena of interest. Since development is a key contributor to the causal pathway between genetic mutation and cognitive deficit, it is essential that models studying genotype–phenotype relations are truly developmental in nature. Research carried out over the last 15 years with the *connectionist* modeling paradigm provides such a framework within which to examine disruptions to or variations within trajectories of cognitive development (for reviews, see Elman et al., 1996; Thomas & Karmiloff-Smith, 2002).

Connectionist models are computational systems loosely based on principles of neural information processing. They comprise simple processing units connected together into networks. Each processing unit has associated with it an activation level, analogous to the firing rate of a neuron. Units facilitate or inhibit the activity of their neighbors depending on the strength of the connection between the units. In models of cognitive development, initial computational architectures are exposed to an environment (internal or external, depending on their level within the system). Using a learning algorithm, the network changes its structure (in terms of connectivity patterns or strengths) to encode cognitive domains, and to learn mappings corresponding to appropriate behaviors.

In extending these models to account for patterns of atypical development or individual variation, it is important to note that connectionist networks incorporate a range of *initial computational constraints*. These affect both the types of problem that the system can learn and the way in which learning will take place (Thomas & Karmiloff-Smith, 2001, 2002, 2003). These constraints include the architecture of the network, its learning algorithm, its activation dynamics, and the representations it uses to encode the cognitive domain. In generalizing these models to atypical development (including disorders of a specifically genetic origin), it is assumed that the underlying biological anomaly serves to change the initial computational constraints of the learning system. When the system then undergoes a process of development using these constraints, the outcome can be a system showing behavioral impairments. However, impairments are not a necessary outcome since not all problem domains will weigh equally heavily on all computational constraints within the system: Some domains may be reasonably successfully acquired even in an atypical system. In this case, the only way to show that such an apparently "intact" cognitive system was atypical would be to probe the fine-grained characteristics of its processing.

Example of the indirect approach to a multigene disorder: Williams syndrome

We illustrate this approach with regard to a particular disorder that has been the focus of much research in our laboratory, Williams syndrome (WS). WS is a rare, neurodevelopmental disorder occurring in approximately 1 in 20,000 live births, caused by a deletion of 17 genes on chromosome 7q11.23 (Tassabehji et al., 1999). It results in specific physical, cognitive, and behavioral abnormalities, with relatively good verbal, face-processing, and social skills along with deficient visuospatial, numerical, and problem-solving abilities (Donnai & Karmiloff-Smith, 2000; Howlin, Davies, Udwin, 1998, Mervis, Morris, Bertrand, & Robinson, 1999; Paterson, Brown, Gsödl, Johnson, & Karmiloff-Smith, 1999). Some researchers have characterized WS as a juxtaposition of impaired and intact mental capacities (Rossen et al., 1994), in which language, face-processing, and social skills are viewed as the intact components, and number, problem-solving, and visuospatial cognition the impaired components.

Part of the research interest in this disorder stems from the fact that the underlying genetic basis is becoming increasingly well understood (Donnai & Karmiloff-Smith, 2000). While some researchers have attempted to link specific genes in the deleted region to specific behavioral deficits (e.g., Bellugi et al., 1999), detailed investigation of the supposedly intact abilities has revealed that in every case, the cognitive processes appear atypical and to be subserved by atypical neural processes. For example, face recognition was initially reported as a "spared" ability in WS on the basis that scores on standardized tests fell within the normal range (Bellugi, Wang, & Jernigan, 1994; Udwin & Yule, 1991). However, closer examination of the items within the standardized tests on which individuals with WS performed well and those on which they performed poorly suggested that their recognition of faces proceeded atypically. Specifically, individuals with WS were better at recognizing faces which could be identified by single features than those which required computation of configurations of features; control participants showed no such distinction (Karmiloff-Smith, 1997; Deruelle, Mancini, Livet, Cassé-Perrot, de Schonen 1999). Subsequent experimentation with artificially created stimuli confirmed this difference (Humphreys, Ewing, & Karmiloff-Smith, 2002, April). Although Jones et al. (as cited in Bellugi et al., 1999) reported a correlation between WS performance on standardized face-recognition tasks and the volume of gray matter in inferior posterior medial cortex, electrophysiological brain-imaging studies have indicated anomalous underlying processing. Mills et al. (2000) found reduced sensitivity in event-related potential waveform components to inverted faces compared to normal faces in WS as well as an absence of the progressive developmental pattern of right-hemisphere localization found in typically developing controls. Moreover, based on a detailed analysis of gamma frequencies in waveforms during face recognition, Grice et al. (2001) revealed patterns consistent with atypical processes of perceptual grouping in their participants with WS. In short, when examined in detail, a superficially intact ability was found to be associated with quite atypical cognitive and brain processes.

A similar story can be told for language, another aspect of the WS cognitive profile often referred to as intact. The apparent successful acquisition of language in the face of low IQ has been adopted by some to motivate claims for the developmental independence of language from general cognition (Pinker, 1994). Once more, however, detailed investigation has demonstrated atypicalities in many areas of language including vocabulary, grammar, pragmatics, and the precursors to language development in infants (Karmiloff-Smith et al., 1997; Paterson et al., 1999; see Thomas & Karmiloff-Smith, 2001, for a review). For instance, Thomas et al. (2001) demonstrated that the developmental trajectory of acquisition of morphology (learning how to change word forms to modify their meanings) in WS was not only delayed but displayed qualitative differences compared to controls. Other studies have suggested a difficulty in acquiring items that violate grammatical regularities as well (Clahsen & Almazan, 1998; Zukowski, 2001).

Importantly, for verbal morphology, much work exists demonstrating how connectionist computational models can account for the trajectory of development in normal children. These models use neural networks to learn the relation between verb stems, their meanings, and their inflected forms. Perhaps a model with atypical computational constraints might account for the WS profile of development. But which constraints should we alter?

A growing body of literature suggests that the relative balance between the use of phonological information (i.e., the sounds of words) and semantic information (i.e., their meaning) may be different in WS. Once more, evidence for atypical brain processes has been uncovered. Using an event-related potential paradigm, Neville, Mills, and colleagues (Neville, Holcomb, & Mills, 1989; Neville, Mills, & Bellugi, 1994) found that individuals with WS had activation responses to auditory stimuli that were less refractory and more excitable than those found in controls, a difference which did not extend to the visual modality. Neville et al. (1994) suggested that the hypersensitivity of the auditory system may be related to atypical language development in WS.

More generally, we are beginning to have an explanation that in WS, genetic influences operate to affect the *trajectory of development* via an alteration in the relative quality or accessibility of different types of information that normally enable successful language development in children. Here is an example illustrating the indirect route through which genes are likely to contribute to impairments. For this particular domain, however, the empirical evidence is sometimes contradictory, and a clear theory has yet to emerge. To clarify the viability of different theoretical accounts, Thomas and Karmiloff-Smith (2001) employed a connectionist model of the typical development of inflectional morphology. They systematically compared existing hypotheses by altering the initial computational constraints of the model in line with each account and examining its adequacy in accounting for the WS data. The model was able to rule as unlikely some explanations (e.g., that in WS, inflectional morphology is acquired purely on the basis of word sounds), and to point to more viable explanations (word sounds are represented atypically; there are problems integrating information about a word's sound and its meaning.) In addition, the model demonstrated for the first time precisely how different computational constraints interact in a developmental system: The atypical trajectory found in WS may arise from more than one altered constraint.

Conclusion

In this article, we have explored genotype/phenotype relations, particularly in regard to two syndromes in which both genes and behavioral outcomes are well documented. Whether a single gene disorder, as in the case of Fragile X, or a contiguous multiple gene disorder, as in the case of Williams syndrome, the relations between genotype and phenotype were shown to be very indirect and complex. Even in the case of supposedly intact abilities, we found that detailed empirical investigation revealed atypical cognitive and brain processes underlying a superficially preserved ability. This supports the idea that from a low-level consideration of how genes contribute to the developmental process, it is unlikely that we will find specific outcomes in terms of impaired and preserved cognitive modules. Computational models of development form an intermediate level at which hypotheses may be generated concerning the link between low-level neurocomputational differences and high-level cognitive outcomes. This is an explanatory strategy that respects the inevitable indirectness of the causal relation between genotype and phenotype and takes seriously the process of development itself.

References

Bayley, D. B., Hatton, D. D., Tassone, F., Skinner, M., & Taylor, A. K. (2001). Variability in FMRP and early development in males with fragile X syndrome. American Journal on Mental Retardation, 106, 16–27.

Bellugi, U., Lichtenberger, L., Mills, D., Galaburda, A., & Korenberg, J. R. (1999). Bridging cognition, the brain, and molecular genetics: Evidence from Williams syndrome. Trends in Neurosciences, 22, 197–207.

Bellugi, U., Marks, S., Bihrle, A., & Sabo, H. (1988). Dissociation between language and cognitive functions in Williams syndrome. In D. Bishop & K. Mogford (Eds.), Language development in exceptional circumstances (pp. 177–189). London: Churchill Livingstone.

Bellugi, U., Wang, P., & Jernigan, T. L. (1994). Williams syndrome: An unusual neuropsychological profile. In S. Broman & J. Grafman (Eds.), Atypical cognitive deficits in developmental disorders: Implications for brain function (pp. 23–56). Hillsdale, NJ: Erlbaum.

Benjamin, J., Li, L., Patterson, C., Greenberg, B. D., Murphy, D. L., & Hamer, D. H. (1996). Populations and familial association between the D4 dopamine receptor gene and measures of novelty seeking. Nature Genetics, 12, 81–84.

Butterworth, B. (1999). The mathematical brain. New York: Macmillan.

Chen, L., & Toth, M. (2001). Fragile X mice develop sensory hyperreactivity to auditory stimuli. Neuroscience, 103, 1043–1050.

Churchill, J. D., Grossman, A. W., Irwin, S. A., Galvez, R., Klintsova, A. Y., Weiler, I. J., & Greenough, W. T. (2002). A converging methods approach to Fragile X syndrome. Developmental Science.

Clahsen, H., & Almazan, M. (1998). Syntax and morphology in Williams syndrome. Cognition, 68, 167–198.

Cornish, K. M., Munir, F., & Cross, G. (1999). Spatial cognition in males with Fragile X syndrome: Evidence for a neuropsychological phenotype. Cortex, 35, 263–271.

Cornish, K. M., Munir, F., & Cross, G. (2001). Differential impact of the FMR-1 full mutation on memory and attention functioning: A neuropsychological perspective. Journal of Cognitive Neuroscience, 13, 144–151.

Crabbe, J. C., Wahlsten, D., & Dudek, B. C. (1999). Genetics of mouse behavior. Science, 284, 1670–1672.

Davis, J. O., Phelps, J. A., & Brancha, H. S. (1995). Prenatal development of monozygotic twins and corcordance for schizophrenia. Schizophrenia Bulletin, 21, 357–366.

Deruelle, C., Mancini, J., Livet, M. O., Cassé-Perrot, C., & de Schonen, S. (1999). Configural and local processing of faces in children with Williams Syndrome. Brain and Cognition, 41, 276–298.

De Vries, B. B., van den Ouweland, A. M., et al. (1997). Screening and diagnosis for the fragile X syndrome among the mentally retarded: An epidemiological and psychological survey. Collaborative Fragile X Study Group. American Journal of Human Genetics, 61, 660–667.

Devys, D., Lutz, Y., Rouyer, N., Bellocq, J. P., & Mandel, J. L. (1993). The FMR1 protein is cytoplasmic, most abundant in neurons, and appears normal in carriers of a fragile X premutation. Nature Genetics, 4, 335–340.

Dobkin, C., Rabe, A., Dumas, R., El Idrissi, A., Haubenstock, H., & Brown, W. T. (2000). FMR1 Knockout mouse has a distinctive strain-specific learning impairment. Neuroscience, 100, 423–429.

Donnai, D., & Karmiloff-Smith, A. (2000). Williams syndrome: From genotype through to the cognitive phenotype. American Journal of Medical Genetics: Seminars in Medical Genetics, 97, 164–171.

Elman, J. L., Bates, E. A., Johnson, M. H., Karmiloff-Smith, A., Parisi, D., & Plunkett, K. (1996). Rethinking innateness: A connectionist perspective on development. Cambridge, MA: MIT Press.

Flavin, H. J., Daw, N. W., Gregory, D. S., & Reid, S. N. (1996). Glutamate receptors and development of the visual cortex: Effect of metabotropic glutamate receptors. Progress in Brain Research, 108, 263–272.

Flint, J. (1996). Annotation: Behavioural phenotypes: A window on the biology of behavior. Journal of Child Psychology and Psychiatry, 37, 4, 355–367.

Fougerousse, F., Bullen, P., Herasse, M., Lindsay, S., Richard, I., Wilson, D., Suel, L., Durand, M., Robson, S., Abitbol, M., Beckmann, J., & Strachan, T. (2000). Human–mouse differences in the embryonic expression patterns of development control genes and disease genes. Human Molecular Genetics, 9, 165–173.

Freund, L., & Reiss, A. L. (1991). Cognitive profiles associated with the fragile X syndrome in males and females. American Journal of Medical Genetics, 38, 542–547.

Gerhart, J., & Kirschner, M. (1997). Cells, embryos, and evolution. Oxford, England: Blackwell.

Greenough, W. T., Klintsova, A. Y., Irwin, S. A., Galvez, R., Bates, K. E., & Weiler, I. J. (2001). Synaptic regulation of protein synthesis and the fragile X protein. Proceedings of the National Academy of Sciences, USA, 98, 7101–7106.

Grice, S., Spratling, M. W., Karmiloff-Smith, A., Halit, H., Csibra, G., de Haan, M., & Johnson, M. H. (2001). Disordered visual processing and oscillatory brain activity in autism and Williams syndrome. NeuroReport, 12, 2697–2700.

Hagerman, R. J., & Cronister, A. (1996). Fragile X syndrome: Diagnosis, treatment, and research. Baltimore: Johns Hopkins University Press.

Heinz, N. (2000). Analysis of mammalian central nervous system gene expression and function using bacterial artificial chromosome-mediated transgenesis. Human Molecular Genetics, 9, 937–943.

Hinton, V. J., Brown, W. T., Wisniewski, D., & Rudelli, R. D. (1995). Analysis of neocortex in three males with the fragile X syndrome. American Journal of Medical Genetics, 41, 239–294.

Howlin, P., Davies, M., & Udwin, O. (1998). Cognitive functioning in adults with Williams syndrome. Journal of Child Psychology and Psychiatry, 39, 183–189.

Humphreys, K., Ewing, S., & Karmiloff-Smith, A. (2002, April). Face processing in Williams syndrome: Infant precursors in developmental disorders. Paper presented at the International Conference on Infant Studies, Toronto.

Hunter, A. J., Nolan, P. M., & Brown, S. D. M. (2000). Towards new models of disease and physiology in the neurosciences: The role of induced and naturally occurring mutations. Human Molecular Genetics, 9, 893–900.

Irwin, S. A., Patel, B., Idupulapati, M., Harris, J. B., Cristostomo, R., Larsen, B. P., Kooy, F., Willems, P. J., Cras, P., Kozlowski, P. B., Swain, R. A., Weiler, I. J., & Greenough, W. T. (2001). Abnormal dendritic spine characteristics in the temporal and visual cortices of patients with fragile X syndrome: A quantitative examination. American Journal of Medical Genetics, 98, 161–167.

Jin, P., & Warren, S. T. (2000). Understanding the molecular basis of fragile X syndrome. Human Molecular Genetics, 9, 901–908.

Karmiloff-Smith, A. (1997). Crucial differences between developmental cognitive neuroscience and adult neuropsychology. Developmental Neuropsychology, 13, 513–524.

Karmiloff-Smith, A. (1998). Development itself is the key to understanding developmental disorders. Trends in Cognitive Sciences, 2, 389–398.

Karmiloff-Smith, A., Grant, J., Berthoud, I., Davies, M., Howlin, P., & Udwin, O. (1997). Language and Williams syndrome: How intact is "intact"? Child Development, 68, 246–262.

Kaufmann, W. E., Abrams, M. T., Chen, W., & Reiss, A. L. (1999). Genotype, molecular phenotype, and cognitive phenotype: Correlations in Fragile X syndrome. American Journal of Medical Genetics, 83, 286–295.

Keller, E. F. (2000). The century of the gene. Cambridge, MA: Harvard University Press.

Kempermann, G., Kuhn, H. G., & Gage, F. H. (1997). More hippocampal neurons in adult mice living in an enriched environment. Nature, 386, 493–495.

Keverne, E. B. (1997). An evaluation of what the mouse knockout experiments are telling us about mammalian behaviour. BioEssays, 19, 1091–1098.

Menon, V., Kwon, H., Eliez, S., Taylor, A. K., & Reiss, A. L. (2000). Functional brain activation during cognition is related to FMR1 gene expression. Brain Research, 877, 367–370.

Mervis, C. B., Morris, C. A., Bertrand, J., & Robinson, B. F. (1999). William syndrome: Findings from an integrated program of research. In H. Tager-Flusberg (Ed.), Neurodevelopmental disorders (pp. 65–110). Cambridge, MA: MIT Press.

Mills, D. L., Alvarez, D., St. George, M., Appelbaum, G., Bellugi, U., & Neville, H. (2000). Electrophysiological studies of face processing in Williams syndrome. Journal of Cognitive Neuroscience, 12(Suppl), 47–64.

Munir, F., Cornish, K. M., & Wilding, J. (2000). A neuropsychological profile of attention deficits in young males with fragile X syndrome. Neuropsychologia, 38, 1261–1270.

Neville, H. J., Holcomb, P. J., & Mills, D. M. (1989). Auditory, sensory, and language processing in Williams syndrome: An ERP study. Journal of Clinical and Experimental Neuropsychology, 11, 52.

Neville, H. J., Mills, D. L., & Bellugi, U. (1994). Effects of altered auditory sensitivity and age of language acquisition on the development of language-relevant neural systems: Preliminary studies of Williams syndrome. In S. Broman & J. Grafman (Eds.), Atypical cognitive deficits in developmental disorders: Implications for brain function (pp. 67–83). Hillsdale, NJ: Erlbaum.

Nimchinsky, E. A., Oberlander, A. M., & Svoboda, K. (2001). Abnormal development of dendritic spines in FMR1 knockout mice. Journal of Neuroscience, 21, 5139–5146.

Paterson, S. J., Brown, J. H., Gsödl, M. K., Johnson, M. H., & Karmiloff-Smith, A. (1999). Cognitive modularity and genetic disorders. Science, 286, 2355–2358.

Pinker, S. (1994). The language instinct. New York: Penguin.

Pinker, S. (1999). Words and rules. London: Weidenfeld & Nicolson.

Plomin, R., DeFries, J., McClean, M., & McGuffin, P. (2001). Behavioural genetics (4th ed.). New York: Freeman.

Rossen, M., Klima, E. S., Bellugi, U., Bihrle, A., & Jones, W. (1994). Interaction between language and cognition: Evidence from Williams syndrome. In J. H. Beitchman, N. Cohen, M. Konstantareas, & R. Tannock (Eds.), Language learning and behaviour (pp. 367–392). New York: Cambridge University Press.

Rutter, M. (2000). Psychosocial influences: Critiques, findings, and research needs. Development and Psychopathology, 12, 375–405.

Smith, N. V., & Tsimpli, I. M. (1995). The Mind of a Savant: Language learning and modularity. Malden, MA: Blackwell.

Tamanini, F., Willemsen, R., van Unen, R., Bontekoe, C., Galjaard, H., Oostra, B. A., & Hoogeveen, A. T. (1997). Differential expression of FMR1, FXR1, and FXR2 proteins in human and brain testis. Human Molecular Genetics, 6, 1315–1322.

Tassabehji, M., Metcalfe, K., Karmiloff-Smith, A., Carette, M. J., Grant, J., Dennis, N., Reardon, W., Splitt, M., Read, A. P., & Donnai, D. (1999). Williams syndrome: Use of chromosomal microdeletions as a tool to dissect cognitive and physical phenotypes. American Journal of Human Genetics, 64, 118–125.

Thapar, A., & McGuffin, P. (2000). Quantitative genetics. In M. G. Gelder, J. Lopez-Ibor, & N. Andreasen (Eds.), Oxford textbook of psychiatry. Oxford, England: Oxford University Press.

Thomas, M. S. C., Grant, J., Gsödl, M., Laing, E., Barham, Z., Lakusta, L., Tyler, L. K., Grice, S., Paterson, S., & Karmiloff-Smith, A. (2001). Past tense formation in Williams syndrome. Language and Cognitive Processes, 16, 143–176.

Thomas, M. S. C., & Karmiloff-Smith, A. (2001). Modeling language acquisition in atypical phenotypes. Manuscript submitted for publication.

Thomas, M. S. C., & Karmiloff-Smith, A. (2002). Modelling typical and atypical cognitive development. In U. Goswami (Ed.), Handbook of childhood development. Oxford, England: Blackwell.

Thomas, M. S. C., & Karmiloff-Smith, A. (2003). Connectionist models of development, developmental disorders, and individual differences. In R. J. Sternberg, J. Lautrey, & T. Lubart (Eds.), Models of intelligence for the next millennium. Washington, DC: American Psychological Association.

Turk, J. (1998). Fragile X syndrome and attentional deficits. Journal of Applied Research in Intellectual Disabilities, 11, 175–191.

Udwin, O., & Yule, W. (1991). A cognitive and behavioural phenotype in Williams syndrome. Journal of Clinical and Experimental Neuropsychology, 13, 232–244.

Verkerk, A. J. M. H., Pienetti, M., Sutcliffe, J. S., Fu, Y.-H., Kuhl, D. P. A., Pizzuti, A., Reiner, O., Richard, S., Victoria, M. F., Zhang, F., Eussen, B. E., Van Ommen, G.-J. B., Blonden, L. A. J., Riggins, G. J., Chestain, J. L., Kurst, C. B., Galjaard, H., Caskey, C. T., Nelson, D. L., Oostra, B. A., & Warren, S. T. (1991). Identification of a gene (FMR-1) containing a CGG repeat coincident with a breakpoint cluster region exhibiting length variation in fragile X syndrome. Cell, 65, 905–914.

Wexler, K. (1996). The development of inflection in a biologically based theory of language. In M. L. Rice (Ed.), Towards a genetics of language acquisition. Hillsdale, NJ: Lawrence Erlbaum Associates.

Zhang, Y., O'Connor, J. P., Siomi, M. C., Srinivasan, S., Dutra, A., Nussbaum, R. L., & Dreyfuss, G. (1995). The fragile X mental retardation syndrome protein interacts with novel homologs FXR1 and FXR2. EMBO Journal, 14, 2401–2408.

Zukowski, A. (2001). Uncovering grammatical competence in children with Williams syndrome. Unpublished doctoral dissertation, Boston University.

8 Using case study comparisons to explore genotype-phenotype correlations in Williams-Beuren syndrome

Annette Karmiloff-Smith, Julia Grant, Sandra Ewing, Martin J. Carette, Kay Metcalfe, Dian Donnai, Andrew P. Read, and May Tassabehji

Williams-Beuren syndrome (WBS, MIM 194050) is a rare condition, with striking physical and behavioural features,[1–3] which occurs in 1/20 000–1/50 000 live births. Cases are generally sporadic; however, familial cases with an autosomal dominant mode of inheritance have been reported. It results in a complex phenotype with physical, cognitive, and behavioural aspects that include an uneven cognitive profile (WBSCP), with verbal tasks outstripping spatial tasks, and overall IQs in the 50–60 range. Physically, WBS phenotypes include a dysmorphic face, congenital heart disease (typically supravalvular aortic stenosis (SVAS)), growth retardation, hyperacusis, premature ageing, and often infantile hypercalcaemia. These features are caused by deletion of the Williams-Beuren syndrome critical region (WBSCR) at chromosomal position 7q11.23 on either the maternal or paternal chromosome 7. The deletion is thought to arise from recombination between misaligned repeat sequences flanking the WBSCR during meiosis. The breakpoints cluster within these repeat regions, so that most WBS patients have similar deletions of approximately 1.5 Mb. A few WBS patients have, however, been reported with smaller deletions (<1 Mb).[3 4] Patients with partial deletions of the WBSCR (that include the elastin gene) and SVAS as the only resulting phenotype have also been described.[5] No credible cases of WBS without the deletion have so far been reported, suggesting that haploinsufficiency for a single gene will not explain the phenotype. Nineteen genes have so far been described in the WBSCR, yet only elastin hemizygosity has been confidently associated with any aspect of the WBS phenotype, namely SVAS, hernias, and possibly premature ageing. It would therefore appear that, alone or in combination, some of the remaining genes in the deleted region are responsible for the other features of WBS.

Relations between genotype and phenotype in WBS are mainly studied at the group level with rather gross measures of behavioural outcome. Yet, much is to be gained by more in depth cognitive studies. In our earlier work,[5] we identified some SVAS patients who were deleted for both elastin (*ELN*) and *LIMK1* genes, and our findings confirmed that hemizygosity for *ELN* causes SVAS and some of the connective tissue phenotypes (for example, hernias). The role of *LIMK1* in WBS is more ambiguous. *LIMK1* encodes a cytoplasmic protein kinase, expressed at high level in neurones, that phosphorylates cofilin (an actin depolymerising factor) and regulates actin cytoskeletal reorganisation.[6 7] Since defects in actin turnover could affect axonal guidance during development of the central nervous system, *LIMK1* is a good candidate for the mental aspects of the WBS phenotype, and *LIMK1* hemizygosity has been implicated in impaired visuospatial constructive cognition.[8] However, psychometric testing of our SVAS patients with small deletions encompassing the *LIMK1* gene showed no evidence of the WBSCP.[5]

In this paper, we take Williams-Beuren syndrome as a model for cognitive profiling and examine two cases in some detail at the physical, cognitive, and molecular level. We compare the profile of one unusually high functioning patient with WBS to one SVAS patient who has a large deletion within the WBSCR. Somatic cell hybrids containing the deleted chromosome 7 were used to assess the extent of the deletions in these patients, so that genotype comparisons could be made. Analysis of such cases highlights typical differences in cognitive profiles between normal controls and all patients with WBS, whatever their intellectual level.

Materials and methods

Somatic cell hybrids

Hybrid cell lines were isolated after fusion of lymphoblastoid cells from the patients with mouse BW5147 cells as described previously.[5] The presence of a single chromosome 7 in all cell lines was verified by microsatellite typing using *LIMK1GT*, D7S1870, and D7S669. The hybrids containing the normal and deleted chromosome 7 homologues were distinguished by PCR analysis of elastin exon 34 and *LIMK1GT*[10] with D7S653 as a non-deleted control.

Deletion mapping of hybrids by PCR

Primers for the genes mapping to the WBSCR were designed for PCR analysis of somatic cell hybrids. Either exon 11 of the *CFTR* gene (CFX11) or the microsatellite marker D7S669, which map outside the deleted region, were included as internal PCR controls depending on the size of the WBS PCR products tested. Negative controls included a water blank and a mouse total genomic DNA reaction for each primer set; 50 ng of DNA, 10 pmol of each primer, and 0.5 U *Taq* polymerase (BCL) were used with the manufacturer's buffer in a 20 μl reaction. PCR conditions were: two minutes denaturation at 94°C, followed by 30 cycles of 94°C for one minute, 54–65°C for one minute, 72°C for one minute, with a final five minute extension at 72°C. Primer sequences and conditions are summarised in Table 8.1.

Cognitive-behavioural assessment

Psychometric testing was performed using the British Abilities Scales II (BAS II).[11] We used six core subtests (Matrices, Quantitative Reasoning, Similarities,

Table 8.1 WSCR gene primer sequences

Gene	*Primer sequence (5′-3′)*	*Annealing temperature*	*Size of product (bp)*
FKBP6 X6	F CTCTTGACCATCTGCCTTCCC R CCTGGGTGTTTATTCCCAAGTCAC	60°C	310
BCL7B	F CGCGGTCAGAAAGCTAGCACC R ACTGCTGCCTGGAGGTCACAG	60°C	302
STX1A	F TCGCCTAGAAGCCACCCAAAC R CTGCCTGGGTCTGCTCCTCGC	60°C	280
ELN X2	F TCCATGTAATTGTGGGTTTTGCC R CAATGTTCCTACCTTCTGTAGTG	60°C	256
ELN X34	F GATTAGAGCCGAAACTGAGAG R AGGTTACAGCAGGGCGAGAGC	60°C	261
LIMK1GT[10]	F AGTCTTCTTTGCGGGCTATGTTA R TGGGGCAGGAGAATGATGTG	60°C	180
LIMK1 3′	F CCGACTGAGCCAGGGCCACTC R AGGTTACAGCAGGGCGAGAGC	65°C	241
WBSCR1 X2	F CCCGCGGCAGTGCTGGTGGCCAT R GCCACTTAGACCAGGCAAATGTT	60°C	350
WBSCR5 5′	F TCATAGCTGAGCCTGTCCGGC R AGGCTTACCTGAGAGTCCAGGGT	60°C	200
RFC2 3′	F GTGGCCAGTTAGAGCAGAGAC R GTCCCAGAAGCAAACATGCAAGT	60°C	500
CYLN2	F AAGAGAAATCCCTGTCGGATC R TTGTCAGGGCAGCTCCTCATG	60°C	172
GTF2IRD 1	F AATGGCCAATGTACATGGTGG R GCCTTGGTGGCAGGAATATAG	54°C	204
GTF2I X1	F CTTCTTACTTCTCCTGCACAG R AAATCAACCTTATCTACAGTG	60°C	131
GTF2I X10	F AGCTTCCAAATAGAAGCGTTGTA R TTCCCATAGGCTTTATTAATCAG	60°C	160
GTF2I 3′UTR	F C TACATAACCT AGATAACCTA AC R TATGCAGGGGGTTCAGATGGACA	60°C	170
NCF1 X2	F CCTTTCTGCAATCCAGGACAACC R ATTTCACCAGGAACATGTACACC	60°C	200
NCF1 X6	F GGGGACGTGGTGGAGGTCGTA R CCACAGGGTGCACACTAAGAC	60°C	210
CFX11	F CAACTGTGGTTAAAGCAATAGTGT R GCACAGATTCTGAGTAACCATAAT	60°C	400
D7S669	F ATGCAACCTACCCTCAAATG R TACGGTTTACCCACATTGCTAT	60°C	120

Word Definitions, Recall of Designs, and Pattern Construction) plus Digit Recall. For the WBS patient who is over 18 years, we used the norms for the oldest age group in the standardisation sample (17 years 6 months–17 years 11 months). This is consistent with the procedure used in previous research.[8] We also used the Peabody Picture Vocabulary Test,[12] the Benton Facial Recognition Task, and the

Benton Line Orientation Task,[13] as well as a series of experimental tasks measuring language, memory, face processing, and number.

Results

Clinical assessment of WBS and SVAS patients

Case 1 (WBS-223) is a 43 year old woman (dob 29.11.56) with Williams-Beuren syndrome who is considerably higher functioning than normally found in this syndrome. She has the typical WBS facial dysmorphology, with bilateral stellate patterns of irises and mild strabismus. Characteristic of the syndrome, she is small in stature, has a midsystolic murmur in the aortic area, suffers from hyperacusis and anxiety, and has a somewhat hoarse, monotonous voice. As a child, she suffered from hypercalcaemia and had typical hand-eye coordination difficulties. Like most patients with WBS, she is inappropriately friendly with strangers, cannot relate to peers, and in general has difficulties judging the pragmatics of social situations. She displays considerable emotional immaturity.

Case 2 (WBS-21) is a normal 11 year old girl (dob 26.6.89, aged 7 at the time of testing) who underwent surgery at 4 years of age for severe SVAS and peripheral pulmonary arterial stenosis (described in Tassabehji *et al*[5]). Mentally, she is above average. Her mother tongue is English, but at the time of examination she was attending mainstream school in France and functioning bilingually with lessons conducted in both languages. Developmental milestones are all within normal limits; she is of normal height and does not have the dysmorphic facial features of Williams-Beuren syndrome. She has no documented history of hypercalcaemia, hyperacusis, or joint problems. She displays normal interaction with adults and peers.

Case 2 was chosen for direct comparisons with case 1 in this study because: (1) she has an unusually large deletion for an SVAS patient and (2) she was perfectly matched to case 1 on verbal scores.

Molecular definition of deletions

Somatic cell hybrids were generated from lymphoblastoid cells from these two patients whereby the normal and deleted chromosome 7 homologues were separated for deletion mapping studies (two different deleted chromosome 7 hybrids were obtained and tested for each patient). Hybrids containing the deleted chromosome 7 were tested by PCR amplification for the presence of the genes spanning the region between *FKBP6* and *NCF1* (Table 8.1) within the WBS critical region. Primers specific for the genes *FKBP6, GTF2I*, and *NCF1*, which map to the duplicons flanking the WBS deletion breakpoints, were designed to encompass base changes (single nucleotide polymorphisms) specific to the duplicon under investigation. The markers CF exon 11 and D7S669, mapping outside the deleted region, were included as positive controls in the PCR reactions. Mouse DNA was also included as a control to show that the PCR amplification products were human specific.

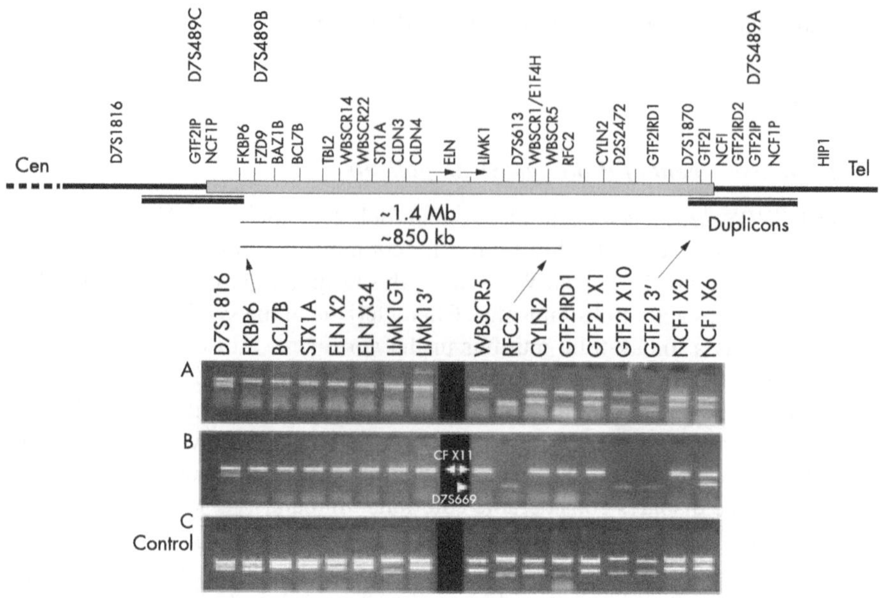

Figure 8.1 Deletion mapping of cases 1 and 2. Diagram showing a map of the WBSCR and genes deleted in the patients (diagram not to scale). PCR analysis of somatic cell hybrids from the deleted chromosome 7 homologues of cases 1 and 2. Panel A: case 2; B: case 1; C: normal control. Control primers were included in the reactions as internal non-deleted controls; CFX11 (top band) in lanes 1–9, 11–13, 16, 17, and D7S669 (bottom band) in lanes 10, 14, 15). Case 2 is deleted from *FKBP6* to *RFC2*; case 1 is deleted from *FKBP6* to part of *NCF1*.

Preliminary molecular analysis of case 2 has been previously reported.[5] However, since that time extensive mapping efforts have defined new genes in the region which have been included in our continuing fine mapping of the deletion status of this and other SVAS patients. The results (Figure 8.1) show that case 2 has a large deletion (approximately 850 kb) encompassing 14 of the defined WBS genes including the whole of the WBS critical region proximal to *ELN.* Despite her high functioning, case 1 with Williams-Beuren syndrome has a typical WBS deletion. This includes 18 of the described genes in the WBSCR (we confirmed deletion of *FKBP6, BCL7B, STX1A, ELN, LIMK1, WBSCR1* (*E1F4H*), *WBSCR5* (*WBSCR15*), *RFC2, CYLN2, GTF2IRD1*, and *GTF2I*; the remainder of the 18 genes lie between pairs of deleted genes) and part of *NCF1* (exon 2 is deleted but not exon 6). The deletion spans a genomic region of approximately 1.4 Mb (Figure 8.1).

Cognitive profile of case 2

In response to evidence from a study suggesting that *LIMK1* haploinsufficiency contributes to the spatial impairment in WBS,[8] we carried out cognitive profiling of four SVAS patients all with deletions of at least *ELN* and *LIMK1* and found no evidence in any of them of the linguistic/spatial imbalance typical of patients with WBS.[5] There was no facial dysmorphology in any of these SVAS patients. More recent inspection of photographs of two of the SVAS patients at different periods in infancy, childhood, and adolescence through to adulthood (data not shown) showed no facial features reminiscent of the facial dysmorphology typical of WBS. This excludes a contribution of *ELN* alone to this latter phenotype.

Case 2, the patient with the largest deletion, was the highest functioning of these four SVAS patients, displaying an above average, even cognitive profile, with no indication of a spatial impairment.[5] This is evident from her scores on the British Abilities Scales II (BAS II). BAS II standard scores have a mean of 100 and a standard deviation of 15. Average scores for a typically developing child are therefore around 100 (classification labels and centiles for BAS II verbal, non-verbal reasoning, and spatial scores are shown in Table 8.2). Case 2 had a verbal standard score of 110, a non-verbal reasoning score of 118, and a spatial score of 115. In particular, she scored above average on the Pattern Construction subtest of the BAS II, while scores of WBS patients are typically at floor (that is, the lowest possible level) on this test. This highlights the fact that haploinsufficiency of *LIMK1* alone cannot contribute to the WBS spatial impairments since, like all WBS patients described to date, Case 2 is hemizygous for this gene.

Cognitive profile of case 1

Over the past 10 years we have carried out in depth cognitive profiling of over 100 WBS patients ranging from age 9 months to 53 years.[14–17] Case 1 is the highest functioning patient tested to date. On the Wechsler Adult Intelligence Scale, she had a full scale IQ of 93 and a verbal IQ of 99 (both close to the average score in the normal population of 100) and a performance IQ of 86 (at the lower end of the normal range). Although these measures do not bring out very strikingly the discrepancy between her verbal and spatial scores, other tests do highlight the typical pattern of her WBS profile. On the British Abilities Scale II, she had an impressive verbal standard score of 112, but a non-verbal reasoning score of 64 and a spatial score of 55, typical of the low levels seen in patients with WBS (see Table 8.2 for classification of BAS II scores). Her verbal score was significantly higher than any WBS patient we have tested, as was her score on the Peabody Picture Vocabulary Test (standard score of 107 where the average is 100). On language specific experimental tasks, case 1 scored almost at ceiling (that is, the highest possible level), compared with other WBS patients who score around the equivalent of their mental age, albeit always better than their spatial performances. The inspection time of case 1 (amount of time required to inspect a display to make a decision) was significantly longer than normal controls, but shorter than the majority of people with WBS. All experimental tasks of verbal memory showed high scores in this patient, much higher than in other WBS patients. On the Benton Facial Recognition task she scored within the normal range, typical of many people with WBS. However,

Table 8.2 Descriptive classification labels and centiles for BAS II verbal, non-verbal reasoning, and spatial scores[11]

Scores (mean=100, SD=15)	*Category*	*Centiles*
130 and above	Very high	98th–99th
120–129	High	91st–97th
110–119	Above average	75th–90th
90–109	Average	25th–74th
80–89	Below average	9th–24th
70–79	Low	3rd–8th
69 and below	Very low	1st–2nd

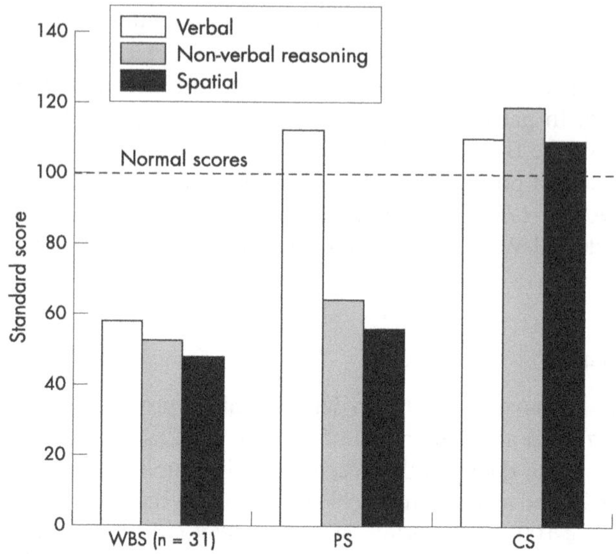

Figure 8.2 Comparison on British Abilities Scale-II of typical WBS patients (WBS), case 1 (PS), and case 2 (CS) on verbal (SD 10.29), non-verbal reasoning (SD 5.87), and spatial scores (SD 2.19). The dotted line represents normal control scores.

like most people with WBS she scored at floor on the Benton Line Orientation Task, attesting once more to her spatial problems.

Figure 8.2 shows how, notwithstanding the possibility of clearly matching these two patients on their verbal scores, the patterns of their cognitive profiles differed significantly. Despite above average scores for the syndrome, case 1 resembled the typical uneven profile of Williams-Beuren syndrome. In contrast, the SVAS patient (case 2) displayed an even profile across both language and spatial measures.

Discussion

Unravelling the relationship between genes and the cognitive/behavioural components of Williams-Beuren syndrome is a complex task. We have approached this by carrying out detailed cognitive assessments on a large number of subjects with WBS, to identify those with a somewhat different cognitive profile from the classical cases. These have been compared with subjects who have partial deletions in the same region that have resulted in only single, non-cognitive features of Williams-Beuren syndrome, SVAS in the present case. Since the uneven profile is a near universal feature of Williams- Beuren syndrome and the 7q11.23 deletion is the only genetic factor common to all WBS patients, it is reasonable to assume that the determinants of the WBS cognitive profile map within the WBS critical region.

Comparing the two cases reported here, they have similar high verbal test scores and have many of the same genes deleted, yet case 1 has the typical WBS cognitive profile, while case 2 does not, high scores of case 2 were evenly distributed across verbal and spatial tasks, whereas in case 1, although verbal scores were as high as those of case 2, spatial scores (and non-verbal reasoning scores) were very poor and typical of WBS. The comparison suggests that the features of WBS apart from SVAS are caused by deletion of genes in the *CYLN2–NCF1* region at the telomeric end of the WBS critical region.

It has been suggested[18] that case 2 might be mosaic, so that the deletion is not present in the cells of her CNS. This suggestion is impossible to disprove, since her deletion, as in virtually all WBS patients, is de novo, and no laboratory test can ever totally exclude mosaicism in somebody with a de novo change. We think the suggestion is implausible for three reasons. First, mosaicism would most likely arise by mitotic recombination, which occurs at approximately 10^{-4} times the frequency of the meiotic recombination that produces the typical WBS deletions. Second, the deletion is present in both her lymphocytes and vessel walls, which would imply a very early embryonic origin of the deletion. Finally, case 2 is not our only patient with a *LIMK1* deletion but no WBS cognitive profile; we have previously described two others.[5] Thus, we doubt that case 2 is a mosaic, and together with our previously described cases, we think that she shows that deletion of *LIMK1* does not of itself produce the WBS cognitive profile. It remains possible that the profile results from deletion of *LIMK1* together with deletion of one or more of the genes from the part of the WBS critical region that is not deleted in case 2.

Our genotyping results do not explain why case 1 is so high functioning: her deletion is not clearly different from those in typical WBS patients. One plausible explanation is the contribution made by her parents. They have well above average IQs, as do her sibs. Therefore her verbal score of 112 could be the result of her high biological potential and thus still involve a typical WBS deficit. However, detailed characterisation of her telomeric breakpoint might indicate a genetic cause; our findings suggest that genes at the telomeric end of the WBS deletion are likely to be important in causing the WBS cognitive profile.

Further studies require the identification and in depth cognitive profiling of other subjects with different sized deletions in the WBSCR. Detailed molecular and clinical characterisation of subjects with variations on the classical WBS phenotypes or classical WBS deletions are important tools for dissecting the roles of each of the genes, within the WBS critical region, in the different aspects of this fascinating developmental disorder.

Acknowledgements

We are grateful to the patients involved in the study for their cooperation. MT was supported by the Wellcome Trust (grant No 061183). AK-S was supported by MRC Programme Grant No G9715642. MC was supported by The Birth Defects Foundation.

References

1 Donnai D, Karmiloff-Smith A. Williams syndrome: from genotype through to the cognitive phenotype. *Semin Med Genet* 2000;**97**:164–71.
2 Morris CA. The natural history of Williams syndrome: physical characteristics. *J Pediatr* 1988;**113**:318–26.
3 Osborne LR. Williams-Beuren syndrome: unravelling the mysteries of a microdeletion disorder. *Mol Genet Metab* 1999;**67**:1–10.
4 Botta A, Novelli G, Mari A, Novelli A, Sabani M, Korenberg J, Osborne LR, Digilio MC, Giannotti A, Dallapiccola B. Detection of an atypical 7q11.23 deletion in Williams syndrome patients which does not include the STX1A and FZD3 genes. *J Med Genet* 1999;**36**:478–80.
5 Tassabehji M, Metcalfe K, Karmiloff-Smith A, Carette MJ, Grant J, Dennis N, Reardon W, Splitt M, Read AP, Donnai D. Williams syndrome: use of chromosomal microdeletions as a tool to dissect cognitive and physical phenotypes. *Am J Hum Genet* 1999;**64**:118–25.
6 Tassabehji M, Metcalfe K, Fergusson WD, Carette MJA, Dore JK, Donnai D, Read AP, Proschel C, Gutowski NJ, Mao X, Sheer D. LIM-kinase deleted in Williams syndrome. *Nat Genet* 1996;**13**:272–3.
7 Yang N, Higuchi O, Ohashi K, Nagata K, Wada A, Kangawa K, Nishida E, Mizuno K. Cofilin phosphorylation by LIM-kinase 1 and is role in Rac-mediated actin reorganization. *Nature* 1998;**393**:809–12.
8 Frangiskakis JM, Ewart A, Morris CA, Mervis CB, Bertrand J, Robinson BF, Klein BP, Ensing G, Everett LA, Green ED, Proschel C, Gutowski NJ, Noble M, Atkinson DL, Odelberg SJ, Keating MT. LIM-kinase1 hemizygosity implicated in impaired visuospatial constructive cognition. *Cell* 1996;**86**:59–69.
9 Arber S, Barbayannis FA, Hanser H, Schneider C, Stanyon CA, Bernard O, Caroni P. Regulation of actin dynamics through phosphorylation of cofilin by LIM-kinase. *Nature* 1998;**393**:805–9.
10 Mari A, Amati F, Conti E, Bengala M, Novelli G, Dallapiccola B. A highly polymorphic CA/GT repeat (LIMK1GT) within the Williams syndrome critical region. *Clin Genet* 1998;**53**:226–7.
11 Elliot CD Smith P, McCulloch K. *British Ability Scales II*. Windsor: NFER-Nelson, 1996.

12 Dunn LM, Dunn LM. Peabody Picture Vocabulary Test Revised. Nashville, TN: American Guidance, 1982.
13 Benton AL, Hamsher KdS, Varney NR, Spreen O. *Contributions to neuropsychological assessment*. New York: Oxford University Press, 1983.
14 Karmiloff-Smith **A**. Development itself is the key to understanding developmental disorders. *Trends Cogn Sci* 1998;**2**:389–98.
15 Paterson SJ, Brown JH, Gsödl MK, Johnson MH, Karmiloff-Smith A. Cognitive modularity and genetic disorders. *Science* 1999;**286**:2355–8.
16 Karmiloff-Smith A, Brown JH, Grice S, Paterson S. Dethroning the myth: cognitive dissociations and innate modularity in Williams syndrome. *Dev Neuropsychol* 2003;**23**:227–42.
17 Grice S, Spratling MW, Karmiloff-Smith A, Halit H, Csibra G, de Haan M, Johnson MH. Disordered visual processing and oscillatory brain activity in autism and Williams syndrome. *NeuroReport* 2001;**12**:2697–700.
18 Francke U. Williams-Beuren syndrome: genes and mechanisms. *Hum Mol Genet* 1999;**8**:1947–54.

9 Mechanisms of developmental regression in autism and the broader phenotype

A neural network modeling approach

Michael S. C. Thomas, Victoria C. P. Knowland, and Annette Karmiloff-Smith

In this article, we present a neurocomputational model of behavioral regression in autism. The primary aim of the model was to explore candidate mechanisms that could cause a decline in performance in an experience-dependent learning system, following an initial phase of normal-looking development. Many developmental disorders are characterized by varieties of delay, sometimes occurring unevenly across different cognitive domains. The disorders can be characterized by the term *delay* because behaviors in affected domains in older children resemble those of younger typically developing children. Trajectories of development that cannot be characterized as delayed but are clearly atypical turn out to be relatively rare and presumably imply more radical differences in the underlying neural constraints. Developmental regression is amongst the most atypical patterns observed, and its causes are currently unknown (Baird et al., 2008; Molloy et al., 2006).

The inspiration for the current model was a recent hypothesis by Pickles et al. (2009) that pertained to regression in the form of loss of language in the early development of children with autism. Pickles et al. argued that language loss is highly specific to autistic spectrum disorder (ASD) and is unlike linguistic deficits found, for instance, in children with specific language impairment (SLI). Although only a subgroup of children with autism show regression (regression was observed in 15% of the Pickles et al. sample), the authors speculated that the underlying abnormality may be more prevalent than the raw data suggest, because cases of potential language loss may be hidden in children whose language development is delayed. The children exhibiting language loss in the ASD sample studied were indeed those with the fastest developing language. The implication we draw from this hypothesis is that factors causing variation in the rate of language development are independent of those causing variation in the timing of the mechanism that causes regression. If language development occurs more slowly, there will be little or no overt language behavior at the point in development when the mechanism that causes regression tends to occur. This implication led us to explore candidate neurodevelopmental mechanisms that share three properties: (a) They operate after the onset of experience-dependent development; (b) their timing, while potentially varying between individuals, does so in a manner that is relatively orthogonal to the developmental process; and (c) they have the potential to impair functionality should they operate atypically. The mechanism we considered was synaptic pruning. Specifically, we considered the idea that regression in autism is caused by *overaggressive* synaptic pruning (Johnson & Karmiloff-Smith, 1992). This would serve to damage functional circuits, thereby causing overt behavior to worsen over time. In comparison, the normal process of progressive elimination of unused neural resources consolidates proficient behavior over time.

Developmental regression in children with autism

Developmental regression is observed in only a subset of children with autism. Estimates range from 20%–40%, with skills typically lost between 15 and 24 months of age (Richler et al., 2006). There is possibly a higher incidence of regression in core autism than in the broader spectrum disorder (Baird et al., 2008). Following regression, there is usually some level of recovery of function. To date, most investigations have been based on retrospective parental reports, which indicate the loss of children's social and communication skills during the second year of life. The most systematic study of regression has focused on word loss. Although in most cases, word loss co-occurs with the loss of social communicative skills (such as eye contact, gestures, reciprocal games like peek-a-boo, and sometimes a loss of play and fine motor skills; Pickles et al., 2009), the disappearance of words that a child had previously produced is a particularly salient event for parents. Richler et al. (2006, p. 302) provided one operational definition for classifying children in the word loss group:

> if s/he had spontaneously used at least three meaningful words (aside from "mama" and "dada") on a daily basis for at least 1 month, and then had stopped using *all* words for at least 1 month, prior to 36 months of age.

The current issues of debate in this field are whether regression forms a distinct subtype of autism or reflects an aberrant mechanism characterizing the full disorder, the degree to which development is normal or atypical prior to the onset of regression, and whether the presence of regression in a child with autism indicates poorer ultimate outcome (Baird et al., 2008; Davidovitch, Glick, Holtzman, Tirosh, & Safir, 2000; Fombonne & Chakrabarti, 2001; Goldberg et al., 2003; Lord, Shulman, & DiLavore, 2004; Molloy et al., 2006; Pickles et al., 2009; Siperstein & Volkmar, 2004; Werner, Dawson, Munson, & Osterling, 2005). For each of these points, the evidence is mixed. There is some indication that the later regression occurs before the 3-year diagnostic cutoff for autism, the poorer the prognosis (Pickles et al., 2009). Where regression occurs after 3 years of age, by definition this is referred to as childhood disintegrative disorder (CDD) rather than autism. CDD has a poorer prognosis still (e.g., Hill & Rosenbloom, 1986). Moreover, the relation of regression in autism to CDD remains unclear. Overall, regression in autism is marked by its *variability*: in the nature of development prior to regression, in the age of onset, in the speed of the loss of behaviors, and in the eventual level of recovery (e.g., Goldberg et al., 2003; Lord et al., 2004; Rogers, 2009).

Connectivity and autism

Early brain development is characterized by a period of exuberant growth in connectivity, followed by the pruning back of unused or weak connections (Cowan, Fawcett, O'Leary, & Stanfield, 1984; Huttenlocher, 2002; Stiles, 2008). This allows the brain maximum plasticity to adapt to the environment in which it finds itself and then, by removing unused connectivity, to save on the metabolic costs of supporting resources for plasticity after such adaptation has taken place. Associated with this growth-followed-by-pruning is the idea of sensitive periods in development, where the plasticity of the cognitive system is initially heightened (Huttenlocher & Dabholkar, 1997; see Huttenlocher, 2002; Thomas & Johnson, 2008, for discussion). Synapses are one of the main neural structures responsible for changing functional connectivity in the brain, with synaptogenesis and synaptic pruning corresponding to the growth and cutting back of resources for connectivity. Evidence suggests that the formation and elimination of synapses is in fact a continuous process, and the reduction in uncommitted synapses with age is a change in the balance of formation and elimination (Hua & Smith, 2004). The reduction appears to be a global constraint and has been found in all the areas of the mammalian cortex that have been studied (Stiles, 2008). However, the exact timing across brain areas is heterogeneous in humans (Huttenlocher & Dabholkar, 1997). Although there are likely to be individual differences in the timing of the onset of synaptic pruning, the necessary longitudinal data in humans to confirm this are currently lacking (studies of more macro-level measures, such as gray matter volume, are suggestive of such variability; see, e.g., Schumann et al., 2010). The thesis we pursue here is that overaggressive synaptic pruning is responsible for regression but that the onset of pruning is within the normal time window. The fact that the decline in social communicative skills does not occur until the second year is therefore explained by the (normal) timing of pruning events in brain development.

There have been a number of hypotheses that problems with connectivity may underlie autism as a whole (e.g., Abrahams & Geschwind, 2008; Belmonte et al., 2004; Johnson & Karmiloff-Smith, 1992; Just, Cherkassky, Keller, & Minshew, 2004; see Wass, 2011, for a recent review). These accounts have been supported by new findings using diffusion tensor imaging (e.g., Ben Bashat et al., 2007; Frazier & Hardan, 2009) that reveal abnormal structural connectivity in autism (i.e., abnormalities in the white matter structures that are thought to represent the "wiring" of the brain; though see Káradóttir, Hamilton, Bakiri, & Attwell, 2008). Accounts have also been supported by findings from functional magnetic resonance imaging that demonstrate reduced functional connectivity in individuals with ASD (e.g., Koshino et al., 2008), indicated by reduced correlations in task-related activity between nodes in a functional network of brain regions. Other studies have also pointed to an overreliance on some forms of connectivity, such as short-range over long-range connectivity (Belmonte et al., 2004) or thalamo–cortico over cortico–cortico connectivity (Koshino et al., 2008). These proposals are sometimes linked to cognitive-level accounts of behavioral deficits in autism, such as weak central coherence (Happé, 1999) and executive function deficits (Ozonoff, Strayer, McMahon, & Filloux, 1994). Connectivity-based accounts still need to clarify whether the atypicality observed has temporal primacy in the development of autism or whether the connectivity abnormalities observed are downstream of other developmental abnormalities. Moreover, abnormal connectivity is not unique to autism: It has been observed in other conditions as diverse as schizophrenia (Pachou et al., 2008), HIV/AIDS (Melrose, Tinaz, Castelo, Courtney, & Stern, 2008), and dyslexia (Richards & Berninger, 2008).

Three empirical phenomena

Before introducing the computational methods to investigate the hypothesis of overaggressive pruning, we mention three additional empirical phenomena pertaining to autism as a whole. These will become relevant when we discuss the modeling results. First, recent work has assessed whether delays in language development in autism share a common cause with delays in language development in the nonautistic population (Bishop, 2010; Folstein & Mankoski, 2000; Vernes et al., 2008). For example, a common gene variant on Chromosome 7 was found to occur more frequently both in individuals with autism and those with SLI, compared with controls (Vernes et al., 2008). Studies of rare genetic mutations associated with syndromes that exhibit comorbid autistic traits have also suggested that these mutations do not selectively cause autism but are also associated with global developmental delay or language delay, once more implicating a common cause of separate disorders (Abrahams & Geschwind, 2008).

Second, it has been observed that early in development, overall brain size is larger in children with autism than in typically developing controls; across development, cross-sectional studies indicate that brain size then returns to within the normal range. In a meta review of relevant literature, Redcay and Courchesne (2005, p. 1) concluded that the data suggest "a period of pathological brain growth and arrest in autism that is largely restricted to the first years of life, before the typical age of clinical identification." The brain size data led Frith (2003) to speculate that the overgrowth was caused by a failure of the normal pruning process, which was then associated with poor functioning of certain neural circuits. However, the brain size data are puzzling in two respects: In typical development, there is a weak but positive correlation between brain size and intelligence (of between +.1 and +.4; e.g., in a meta-analysis of more than 1,530 people, McDaniel, 2005, reported a correlation of .33 between in vivo brain volume and intelligence). Why should a bigger brain be advantageous when it comes to typical development but then be associated with a developmental disorder such as autism? Furthermore, why should the relative pattern of brain size in autism compared with controls change across developmental time? Indeed, Courchesne et al. (2007) proposed that in autism, brain overgrowth at the beginning of life might be accompanied by slowing or arrest of growth during early childhood and, in some individuals, a third atypical phase of degeneration in later life. Despite these puzzles, some connectivity-based accounts of autism have identified brain size differences as a primary cause of the behavioral impairments (e.g., Lewis & Elman, 2008; Stanfield et al., 2008).

Third, although autism is now viewed primarily as a genetic disorder, researchers have identified a form of "quasi-autism" occurring in children who have experienced extreme deprivation (e.g., Rutter et al., 1999, 2007). This phenomenon was observed in adoptees from Romanian orphanages in the 1990s and followed longitudinally. The affected children showed disinhibited attachment disorder but also cognitive deficits in mental flexibility and idiosyncratic interests symptomatic of autism. The patterns were variable across children, with the effects being typically milder and yielding better outcome than in ASD. Because assignment of the children to the orphanages was not based on any preexisting mental condition, and because the incidence of quasi-autism at 10% was much higher in the adoptees than the incidence in the general population of autism spectrum disorder (approximately 1%; Baird et al., 2006), the cause of the disorder in the adoptee case appears to be environmental. Nevertheless, it did not produce quasi-autism in all children exposed to the deprived environment, which also remains to be explained.

Computational models and autism

Several neurocomputational models have been put forward to explain the origins of behavioral deficits in autism. These have focused either on category formation, atypical neural codes, or connectivity disruptions. Using *self-organizing maps*, Gustafsson (1997) proposed that autism results from an imbalance between short-range excitatory and long-range inhibitory connections on cortical maps, whereby too much inhibition results in the emergence of overdetailed features. Using *associator networks*, Cohen (1994, 1998) argued that autism results from a surfeit of internal resources causing overfitting of the data and therefore the encoding of too much detail. In the framework of *adaptive resonance theory*, Grossberg and Seidman (2006) put forward a similar idea that an oversensitive novelty parameter causes the allocation of too many representational resources during category formation and therefore overdetailed categories. Allied to this, they proposed unstable dynamics between cortical and limbic systems under conditions of novelty, producing extreme emotional responses to change. Focusing on *neural codes*, McClelland (2000) proposed that autism arises from too conjunctive/insufficiently componential representations. Simmons et al. (2007) viewed the neural codes in sensory systems as containing elevated levels of noise. Beversdorf, Narayanan, Hillier, and Hughes (2007) speculated that sparse connectivity in a network model of semantic memory would produce decreased use of context. Finally, using an *associator network*, Lewis and Elman (2008) demonstrated that early brain overgrowth would particularly impact those functions that relied on long-range or integrative connections. This plethora of modeling efforts focused on different aspects of the autism phenotype, but their explanations are difficult to generalize to other aspects of the broader autism spectrum. By contrast, the simulations presented in the current article attempt to encompass both autism itself and the broader autism spectrum.

The current simulations employed associative artificial neural networks and began with an adventitious finding emanating from work on population modeling. In population modeling, large numbers of artificial neural networks (ANNs) are exposed to a learning problem. Individual differences are included in the parameters of the ANNs, altering their learning properties, as well as in the learning environments to which the networks are exposed. Population modeling allows for the study of individual differences within a development framework (Thomas, Forrester, & Ronald, 2016) and, by extension, the origins of variability in developmental disorders. Thomas, Forrester, and Ronald (2016) employed population modeling to explore genetic and environmental contributions to language development. The ANNs they used contained 14 computational parameters that could alter the networks' learning capacity (see Method section). Each parameter was initially benchmarked to assess the range of variation that would accommodate developmental outcomes spanning failure through to success. The benchmarking constrained the range of parameter variation that would subsequently be encoded into the population. Following the Pickles et al. (2009) proposal that timing of regression and rate of development might dissociate, we revisited the benchmarking conditions. For 13 of the 14 parameters, suboptimal settings resulted only in a slowing of the rate of development. One parameter, however, produced patterns of developmental regression. This parameter related to the pruning of connectivity.

The framework employed by Thomas, Forrester, and Ronald (2016) incorporated parameters analogous to several neural functions. These included how the neural network was built (number of layers, internal units, and connections), its dynamics (processing noise, threshold functions), how it was maintained (weight decay and pruning), and how it adapted through experience (learning rate, momentum). In terms of connectivity, the initial overgrowth of connections was not simulated (see Shultz, 2003, for modeling approaches relevant to this phase of development). Instead, each individual's starting level of connectivity was specified. After a certain variable period of development, pruning of unused connectivity began. Pruning was guided by three parameters, for which the settings could vary between individuals. One parameter determined when in development pruning would commence. The second parameter was a threshold that determined how small a connection (excitatory or inhibitory) should be before it was judged that the connection was unused. In associator networks, small connections mean that the activity of the sending unit cannot markedly alter the activity of the receiving unit, and so cannot significantly contribute to function.[1] A third parameter specified the probability that a connection judged as unused would be permanently pruned. It was the second parameter, the *pruning threshold*, that was found to cause regression when set to extreme values. If the threshold was set high, so that large weights were judged to be unused and legitimate targets of pruning, then the pruning process could damage previously established functional circuits. In turn, this could cause impairments in behavior.

The following simulations took advantage of population modeling to assess the impact of atypical settings of the pruning threshold parameter on producing patterns of regression in the developmental trajectories of connectionist associator networks. Because networks contained population-wide individual differences in the other 13 neurocomputational parameters as well as in the composition of the learning environment, we were able to consider possible sources of variation in the onset of regression, its severity, and the prognosis for recovery. We report the results for three populations of 1,000 network models: (a) a *low-risk* population, in which the pruning threshold parameter varied within the normal range, along with all other parameters; (b) a *high-risk* population, in which the pruning threshold parameter was allowed to vary to much higher levels, while all other parameters varied in the normal range; and (c) an *environmental-risk* population, in which all parameters varied in the normal range but the environment could in principle be very impoverished. The goal of the simulations was to consider three principal questions: (a) How do atypical settings of the pruning threshold parameter relate to incidence of regression in the population? (b) To what extent do the incidence and characteristics of regression depend on variation in other neurocomputational parameters? And, (c) Could an extremely impoverished environment also cause regression without the presence of atypical pruning threshold settings?

Method

We first introduce the target learning problem, then the basic network architecture. Next we describe how individual variability was included in network parameters and the training set. Finally, we describe the three populations for which results are discussed.

Target learning problem

This was a qualitative and exploratory model, and for the purposes of this article, we consider the training set only as an abstract mapping problem (see Thomas, Forrester, & Ronald, 2016, for its psychological origin in the domain of language development). The mapping problem was quasi-regular, in that it included a predominant regularity, which could be generalized to novel input patterns, along with a set of exception patterns. The learning environment was designed to assess the role of similarity, type frequency, and token frequency in development. Through these properties, the domain was taken to be representative of some of the mapping problems that the cognitive system faces, including category formation and language development. The mapping problem was defined over 90 input units and 100 output units, using binary coded representations. The training set comprised 508 patterns. This was complemented by a generalization set of 410 patterns.

The predominant regularity required the network to reproduce the input pattern on the first 90 units of the output layer and then add a binary code on the last 10 units of the output layer. There were 410 regular patterns in the training set. The regular pattern had a high type frequency and formed a consistent set of mappings, and so is referred to as *easy*. The generalization ability of each network was tested on 410 novel patterns that were similar to the *easy* patterns, in that they shared 60 of the 90 input elements. This set is referred to as *generalization*. There were three different classes of exception pattern in the training set, which fell on a continuum of (dis)similarity from the predominant regularity: (a) Reproduce the input but do not add the final code. There were 20 of these patterns. (b) Reproduce only a portion of the input and again do not add the final code. There were 68 of these patterns. (c) Associate an arbitrary binary pattern with the input and again do not add the final code. There were 10 of these patterns. The first exception type was most similar to predominant regularity, the third type the least similar. All three were in the minority in the training set; that is, they possessed a lower type frequency than the predominant regularity. The combination of dissimilarity and low type frequency creates a continuum of difficulty. We refer to the first exception type as *hard* and the second as *harder*. Finally, the arbitrary mappings were sufficiently difficult that, to be learned at all, they needed to be repeated in the training set. They therefore provide an opportunity to assess whether greater practice provides immunity to regression or allows better recovery from regression. The third pattern type, then, is referred to as *hardest-practiced*. Together, the five pattern types allowed us to assess whether regression interacted with task difficulty.

Basic architecture

The simulations employed connectionist pattern associator networks trained using the supervised backpropagation learning algorithm. This type of architecture has been employed in a number of cognitive-level models of development, for example, infant categorization, child vocabulary acquisition, semantic memory, morphosyntax acquisition, and reading development (see Mareschal & Thomas, 2007, for a review).

Variations in the learning environment

The full training set was considered to be the ideal learning environment. For each individual, a subset of this training set was stochastically selected, to represent the family conditions in which each simulated child was being raised. Each individual was assigned a family quotient, which was a number between 0 and 1. The value was used as a probability to sample from the ideal training set. Thus for an individual with a family quotient value of .75, each of the 508 training patterns had a 75% chance of being included in that individual's training set. Family quotients were sampled randomly depending on the range selected for the population. We used either the range 0.6 to 1.0 for typical populations or the range 0 to 1.0 for an environmental-risk population. In the latter case, individuals could potentially be exposed to a learning environment containing very few training patterns.

Variations in network learning capacity

Fourteen neurocomputational parameters were allowed to vary between individuals, serving to alter the learning capacity of each network. The available parameter settings allowed for more than 2,000 billion unique combinations. Detailed descriptions of the computational role of each parameter can be found in Thomas, Forrester, and Ronald (2016). Here, we broadly categorize them by function and indicate the range used. The parameters were as follows: *Network construction*: Architecture (two-layer network, three-layer network incorporating a layer of hidden units, or a fully connected network incorporating a layer of hidden units and also direct input–output connections); number of hidden units (10 to 500); range for initial connection weight randomization (±0.01 to ±3.00); sparseness of initial connectivity between layers (50% to 100% connectivity). *Network activation*: unit threshold function (sigmoid temperatures between 0.0625 and 4); processing noise (0 to 6); response accuracy threshold (.0025 to .5). *Network adaptation*: backpropagation error metric (Euclidean distance or cross-entropy); learning rate (.005 to .5); momentum (0 to .75). *Network maintenance*: weight decay (0 to 2×10^{-5} per pattern presentation); pruning onset (0 to 1,000 epochs); pruning probability (0 to 1); pruning threshold (low-regression-risk population: 0.1 to 1.5; high-regression-risk population: 0.1 to 4.0).

Creation of a population

Each parameter had a probability distribution created during the calibration phase. The distribution determined how likely it was that an individual would have a given value for that parameter. Parameter values producing medium performance were more likely than those producing very good or very poor performance. Table 9.1 shows the probability distribution for the pruning threshold parameter for low-regression-risk and high-regression-risk populations (distributions for all parameters are available in Thomas, Forrester, & Ronald, 2016). The low-risk population exhibits the normal distribution used for all parameters, with intermediate values being more common. The high-risk population had equal numbers of individuals with increasingly large pruning thresholds (11.1% of individuals at each value).

For each individual, the 14 parameters were independently sampled from each distribution. Next, a family quotient value was generated in the appropriate range for that population, and the quotient was then used to create the individual's bespoke family training set. Then the network was initiated with random weight values (in the range determined by the individual's weight range parameter) and trained for 1,000 epochs, where one epoch was an exposure to all the patterns in the individual's training set presented in random order. Performance was measured on the five pattern types (*easy, generalization, hard, harder, hardest-practiced*)

Table 9.1 Probability distribution used to determine the pruning threshold parameter value for individuals in the low-regression-risk and high-regression-risk populations

Probability	*0.1*	*0.2*	*0.3*	*0.4*	*0.5*	*0.75*	*1.0*	*1.25*	*1.5*	*2.0*	*2.5*	*3.0*	*3.5*	*4.0*
Low-risk population (%)	0.1	1.0	4.4	11.7	65.6	11.7	4.4	1.0	0.1					
High-risk population (%)	11.1					11.1	11.1		11.1	11.1	11.1	11.1	11.1	11.1

Note. In the low-risk population, the median value was more frequent and extreme values were rarer. In the high-risk population, each of the values had equal probability. When pruning commenced, connections with magnitude less than the threshold were vulnerable to pruning. The most common value for initially randomized weights before training commenced was in the range ±0.5.

at each epoch, according to the full training set and the generalization set. The process was repeated for 1,000 individuals to create a population.

Three populations were considered. First, we created a population at low risk for regression, exposed to relatively good learning environments (family quotients in the range of .6 to 1). Maximum pruning thresholds were 1.5. Next, we created a population at high risk for regression. For 13 of the 14 neurocomputational parameters, values were sampled from the same probability distributions. For the pruning threshold parameter, values were sampled from a flat probability distribution that included much higher threshold values (see Table 9.1). Note that because initial, random weight values were typically around ±0.5, a pruning threshold exceeding 0.5 would place many connections at risk of pruning. However, because pruning did not commence until an epoch specified by each individual's onset parameter, early experience could serve to strengthen connection weights before pruning commenced, reducing the risk of connection loss. Atypical pruning thresholds up to 4.0 were included in the high-risk population. Finally, an environmental-risk population was created. This used the same network parameter sets as the low-risk population but exposed these individuals to potentially much more impoverished learning environments. The family quotient range for the environmental-risk population was 0 to 1.

Results

Measuring developmental regression

We plotted each of the 1,000 individual developmental trajectories in the high-risk population and coded them by hand for whether they exhibited developmental regression. Regression was defined as a noticeable drop in performance over development in one or more of the five behavioral measures (*easy, generalization, hard, harder, hardest-practiced*).[2] Figure 9.1 depicts sample trajectories for four typically developing networks and four networks showing regression. We found that it was not possible to automate the classification of regression because, whether regression was present or not, development was very often nonmonotonic (i.e., sometimes it got worse before it got better). Regular and exception pattern types could interfere with each other during development, causing performance on one or the other to temporarily decline. In addition, one of the neurocomputational parameters was the level of internal processing noise, which could cause performance to oscillate between measurement points. In individuals with noisy processing, performance could show large oscillations. A judgment of the presence of regression was made against the degree of developmental variation exhibited by that network. To ensure consistency, a random sample of 20% of the trajectories was rated by a second coder who was blind to the ratings of the first coder. Both coders were blind to the parameter set and environmental conditions of each individual, including the actual onset of the pruning process. Interrater reliabilities for onset and size of regression ranged from $r = .81$ to .98 (all $ps < .001$).

When regression was observed for a given pattern type, six measurements were made: the level of performance just prior to the onset of regression; the epoch at which regression occurred; the size of the drop in accuracy; the number of epochs over which that drop occurred; the rate of recovery (five qualitative categories were used: no recovery, slow recovery, medium recovery, fast recovery, and almost instant recovery); and the final level of performance at the end of training (1,000 epochs). On the basis of the size of the drop in accuracy, we defined four levels of severity of regression: Level 1, corresponding to a drop in accuracy between 0% and 20%; Level 2, corresponding to a drop in accuracy of 20% to 40%; Level 3, corresponding to a drop in accuracy between 40% and 60%; and Level 4, corresponding to a drop in accuracy of 60% to 100%. For the high-risk population, 641 cases of regression were recorded. In the low-risk population, there were 46 cases. In the environmental-risk population, there were 67 cases.

Regression and variability

Figure 9.1 illustrates the large variations found in developmental trajectories in the typically developing individuals (by which, in this context, we mean networks not showing regression). Variations in computational parameters and learning environments produced differences in the rate of development, the smoothness of developmental trajectories, and the uniformity of performance increases across different mapping types. Cases of regression, also shown in Figure 9.1, similarly exhibited a great deal of variability. Variations were observed in the onset of regression, its severity, its specificity to pattern type, the subsequent rate of recovery, and the final level of recovery. Although Figure 9.1 demonstrates clear cases of regression, there were also less obvious patterns. These included a slow decline in performance; slight dips in performance in all pattern types that, given the variability in the trajectory of development, would not constitute regression except for

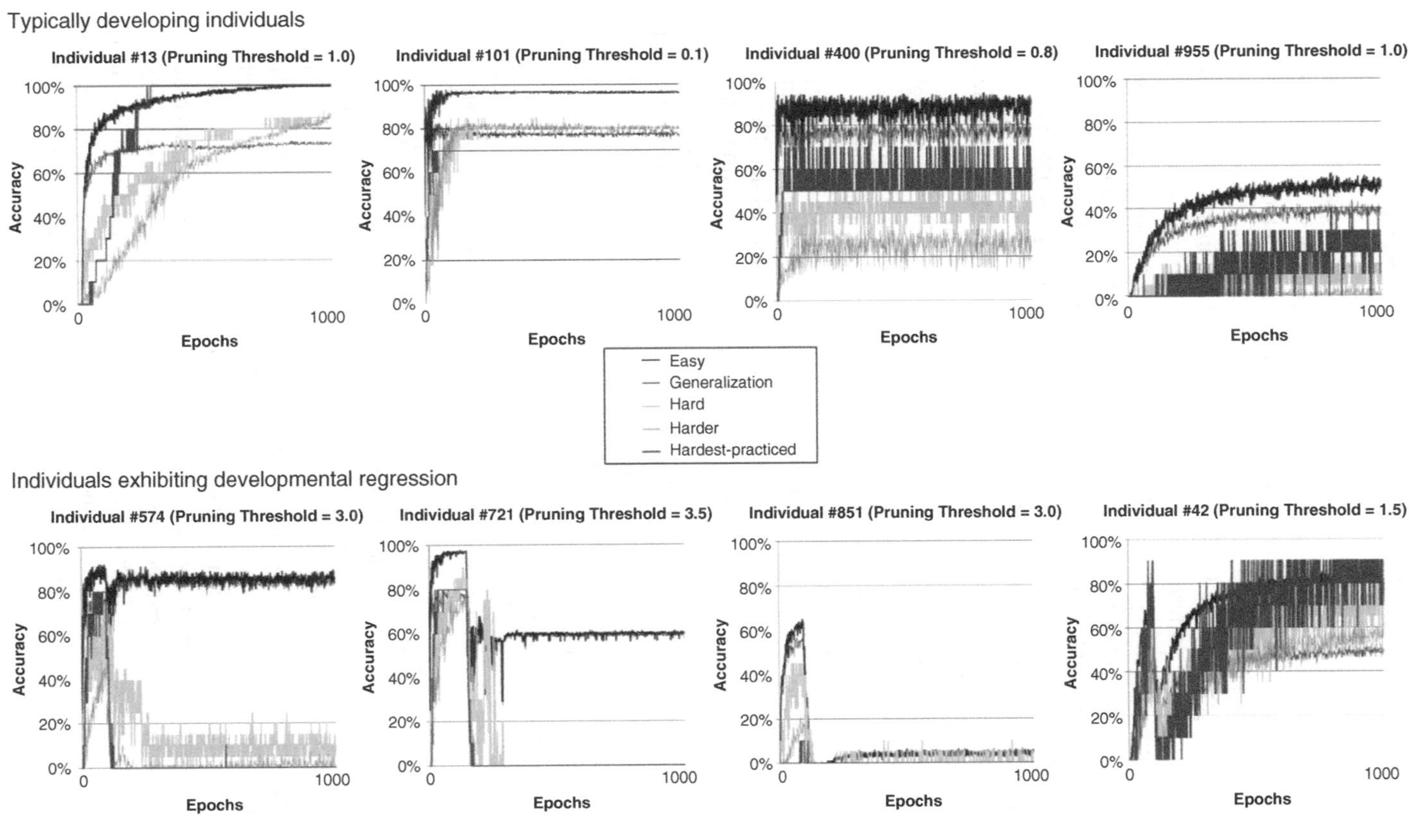

Figure 9.1 Example developmental trajectories for four typically developing individuals and four individuals exhibiting regression. Each plot includes the pruning threshold parameter setting for that individual.

the simultaneous appearance in all pattern types; and regression in early developing patterns with development in the other patterns occurring only as the early developing patterns recovered.

The onset of regression in the high-risk population showed a normal distribution, with a mean of 106 epochs and a standard deviation of 56 epochs. Counting all cases of regression in the five behavioral metrics among the 641 individuals, 16% were at Severity Level 1, 20% at Severity Level 2, 24% at Severity Level 3, and 40% at Severity Level 4. Where regression occurred, in 22% of cases it was found across all five pattern types, whereas in 78% of cases it was found only in subsets. Again, collapsing across all cases of regression, 51% of cases showed no recovery, 6% slow recovery, 19% medium recovery, 18% fast recovery, and 6% very fast recovery. The variability observed in the typically developing networks was generated by the implemented parameter and learning environment variations. It seems reasonable to conclude that the variation observed in the nature of regression arose from the same cause: population-wide individual variation (see Thomas, Knowland, & Karmiloff-Smith, 2011, for discussion).

Of course, analytically, we know that the pruning threshold was the sole process that caused developmental regression in these simulations. And we know that the only difference between the low-risk and high-risk populations was in the sampling of the pruning threshold parameter values: The increases in the size of the threshold shown in Table 9.1 led to a 14-fold increase in the incidence of regression between the low-risk and high-risk populations. The pruning threshold is thus obviously the cause of regression in these networks. However, it is interesting to establish exactly how increases in the pruning threshold parameter affected the incidence of developmental regression. The discovery of mechanisms is clearly a major point of the simulations. Figure 9.2 plots this relationship, depicting the cumulative probability of exhibiting regression at each severity level for each level of the pruning threshold parameter. The panel on the left plots the incidence of regression in the most robust behavior (*easy*), whereas the panel on the right plots the incidence for the most vulnerable behavior (i.e., if any one of the five showed regression). For each panel, the first line shows the incidence at Severity Level 1 (the mildest), the second line Severity Levels 1 and 2 combined, the third line Severity Levels 1, 2, and 3 combined, and so forth. The difference between adjacent lines shows how many cases are present at each severity level. Two points from this figure are of note. First, the relationship between pruning threshold and regression was *probabilistic*. Even with more extreme values of the pruning threshold parameter, there was no guarantee that regression would be observed. For example, at the most extreme threshold value of 4.0, 4.3% of those individuals (five networks) showed no evidence of regression at any level of severity in any behavior. Second, the relationship between incidence and parameter value was *nonlinear*, jumping up after a threshold of 1.0 was reached; and the exact pattern of the relationship was modulated by the robustness of the target behavior. Such nonlinear relationships between parameter variations and behavior are a common characteristic of nonlinear processing systems like neural networks.

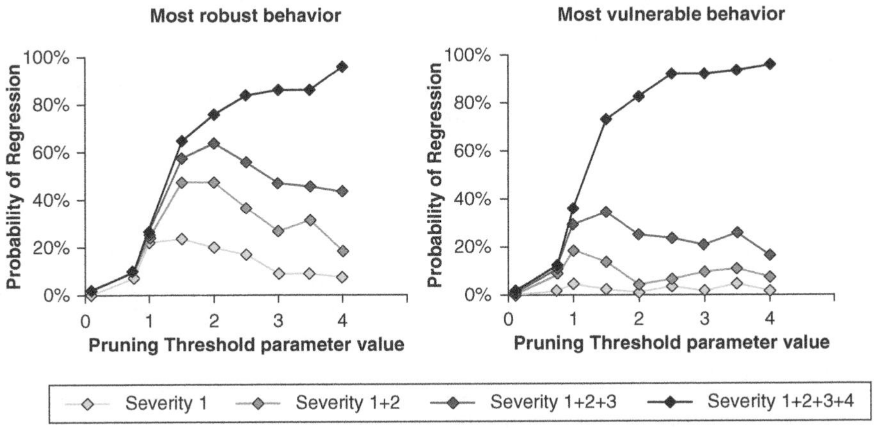

Figure 9.2 The cumulative probability of regression per severity level plotted against the value of the pruning threshold parameter, for the most robust behavior (*easy* patterns) and the most vulnerable behavior (presence of regression in any pattern type). Regression was defined on the basis of behavior (1 = *least severe*, 4 = *most severe*).

Next we sought to unpack the precise role of population-wide variation in producing this probabilistic outcome: What were the protective and risk factors? We used the statistical technique of stepwise logistic regression (forward Wald method) to evaluate which neurocomputational parameters predicted the presence or absence of regression (including, in this case, any developmental regression observed in any behavior). We also included each individual's family quotient value in the statistical model. Table 9.2 shows the results of this analysis, listing the parameters in decreasing size of the variance in outcome that they explained.

As expected, the pruning threshold value predicted most of the variance in outcome. Six further parameters then served as protective or risk factors. They fell into three types: (a) The pruning probability parameter determined the likelihood of a connection being pruned if it was sufficiently small. A very low probability directly ameliorated the negative effects of a high pruning threshold, whereas a high probability exacerbated it. (b) The processing unit threshold function and the momentum were both parameters that altered how quickly connection weights grew during learning. If weights grew slowly, their small size rendered them more vulnerable to pruning. (c) Three parameters affected the number of connections in the network. First, sparseness determined how many connections were initially created between any two layers of processing units. Second, the number of hidden units also contributed to a greater number of connections. In both cases, these connections operated in parallel. Roughly speaking, if there are twice as many connections wired up in parallel, then the connections need to be only half the magnitude to produce the same effect at the output. Large numbers of parallel connections therefore increase the risk of pruning because they reduce connection

Table 9.2 Statistical stepwise logistic regression analysis for neurocomputational parameters that modulate probability of developmental regression in the high-risk population

Parameter	*−2 log likelihood of the model*	*Nagelkerke R^2 change*	*Significance of model*
Pruning threshold	734.8	.597	<.001
Unit threshold function	642.2	.068	<.001
Architecture	624.9	.012	<.001
Pruning probability	611.2	.010	<.001
Hidden unit number	603.7	.005	<.001
Sparseness	598.9	.003	.029
Momentum	594.8	.003	.042
Family quotient (environment)[a]	—	—	.593

a Not included in model. The *p* value shows significance at the seventh step.

size. Third, the architecture determined how many layers of weights were arranged in series. When additional weights are arranged in series, as in the three-layer and fully connected networks compared with the two-layer networks, there is a further risk for developing connections with small sizes. Connections between input and hidden units are more remote from the error signal that is driving learning. They therefore change more slowly and retain a smaller size for longer (see Thomas & McClelland, 2008, for an algebraic account). Lower layers in multilayer networks are therefore more at risk of pruning.

In terms of the mapping to actual neural constraints, we should be clear about the level of abstractness intended. To take the last example of lower layers in the network, we do not assume this to offer a direct parallel to the six layers of the neocortex or to lower level processing in the perceptual stream; rather, we assume it to demonstrate that neurocomputational constraints that serve to modulate connection magnitude in the normal case will become implicated as risk or protective factors for an atypical process that operates on connection size.

At this stage we can draw two preliminary conclusions. The first is that developmental regression showed a probabilistic relationship to its cause (large values of the pruning threshold parameter) because of the interaction with population-wide individual variation in other neurocomputational parameters. Only one of the six risk factors directly modulated the pruning process. The other five modulated the risk of regression by acting on the size of connections achieved during the early phase of development prior to the onset of pruning. Larger connections were less vulnerable to pruning. The second preliminary conclusion is that variability arose through protective and risk factors acting via the *common causal pathway of connectivity*.

Regression was also observed in the low-risk and environmental-risk populations. A similar statistical analysis suggested that the presence of regression was once more mostly predicted by the pruning threshold parameter, even when it took on smaller values (the parameter explained approximately 20% of the variance for each population). The population-wide individual variation that conspired to generate regression in the low-risk population comprised the number of hidden units (7.7% of the variance), the learning rate (5.6%), the unit threshold function (4.1%), and the learning algorithm (3.8%). In terms of mechanism, these factors conspired to encourage very small weights and so make even a modest pruning threshold damaging to network structure and function. The environmental-risk analysis produced similar results, with the addition of one further factor: Family quotient now explained 2.1% of the variance.

Specificity was a marked characteristic of regression in the simulations, with the majority of cases impacting on selective behaviors. We used one-way analyses of variance (ANOVAs), with pattern type as a single five-level factor, to investigate which aspects of regression exhibited the strongest effects of specificity. Effects were found in all the measures we took, including the timing of onset, $F(4, 3194) = 3.03$, $p = .017$, $\eta^2_p = .004$; the size of the drop in accuracy, $F(4, 3194) = 80.1$, $p < .001$, $\eta^2_p = .091$; the duration over which regression took place, $F(4, 3194) = 23.3$, $p < .001$, $\eta^2_p = .028$; the rate of recovery, $F(4, 3194) = 106.7$, $p < .001$, $\eta^2_p = .118$; and the final level of performance, $F(4, 3194) = 242.5$, $p < .001$, $\eta^2_p = .233$. Specificity was most apparent in the drop size, the rate of recovery, and the final level of recovered performance. It was least apparent in the timing of onset of regression. In all these cases, vulnerability echoed the difficulty of the pattern type. The three types of exception patterns were lost more easily and recovered more poorly. High type frequency and consistency of behaviors were protective factors against regression. Idiosyncratic behaviors, even highly practiced ones, were more vulnerable to loss. In sum, although neurocomputational parameters were general to the system, their effects on behavior (via a developmental process) were uneven.

A series of statistical linear regression (SLR) analyses was carried out to see which computational parameters modulated the onset of regression, the drop size, the speed of decline, the rate of recovery, and the final level. The onset was relatively impervious to the effects of learning, with the pruning onset parameter explaining most of the variance. This indeed reflected our initial thesis that the timing of the cause of regression should be relatively independent from factors causing variation in learning. The speed with which behavior declined also pertained mainly to the constraints of the pruning process. By contrast, the size of the drop in behavior, the recovery rate, and the final outcome were mutually determined by many of the factors involved in experience-dependent change, as well as by the details of the pruning process. Features of regression modulated by several causal factors would be expected to show greater variability in the population. Notably, in all these analyses, variations in the environment featured only in the final level of performance following recovery and even in this case, explained only around 1% of the variance. For the high-risk population, then, variation in the quality of the environment had little influence on the characteristics of regression. These characteristics were instead influenced by intrinsic properties.

One salient empirical issue in the autism literature is the relationship between the age at which regression occurs and the prognosis for the child, with reports suggesting that later onset may be associated with poorer prognosis (e.g., Pickles et al., 2009). In the simulations, we investigated whether the final outcome level was altered by differences in the timing of onset. We compared the size of recovery for 118 cases of regression occurring before 50 epochs of training with the size of recovery for 112 cases occurring after 140 epochs of training. We assessed recovery for the *easy* patterns and the *harder* patterns and measured recovery based on the accuracy difference at the end of training (1,000 epochs) compared with the peak performance prior to regression. A value of zero would indicate that behavior had returned to its preregression peak. Positive numbers would indicate further progress beyond the preregression peak. Negative numbers would indicate a lasting deficit. The results are shown in Figure 9.3. The evidence indicates that in the model, later regression was indeed associated with poorer outcome, and this effect was independent of the vulnerability of the behavior; main effect of timing: $F(1, 432) = 13.4$, $p < .001$, $\eta^2_p = .030$; main effect of vulnerability, $F(1, 432) = 20.8$, $p < .001$, $\eta^2_p = .046$; interaction, $p = .877$. To some extent, this might be explained by the shorter time available for recovery in the later onset group. However, in most cases there was sufficient training time for recovered performance to reach asymptotic levels. Moreover, the value of the pruning threshold parameter was reliably higher in the late onset group compared with the early onset group (means of 2.74 vs. 2.45), $t(228) = 2.189$, $p = .021$. This suggests that for regression to occur later in development, when connection weights were typically stronger, it had to be caused by an even more aggressive pruning process.

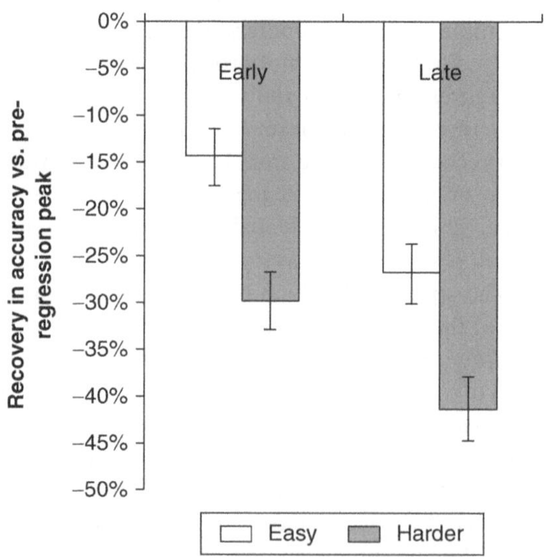

Figure 9.3 Recovery level compared with preregression peak, for *easy* and *harder* patterns, split by timing of regression (early = before 50 epochs, $n = 112$; late = after 140 epochs, $n = 118$). Error bars show the standard error of the mean.

Links to the broader autism phenotype

In this section we report three findings from the simulations that are relevant if developmental regression is in fact an overt manifestation of a mechanism that also underlies the broader phenotype of autism (as per the hypothesis of Pickles et al., 2009). These findings take the behavioral manifestation of regression as the marker of the atypical process responsible for the wider phenotype. We later discuss under what conditions overaggressive pruning would lead to a failure to progress developmentally (as occurs in the wider autism phenotype) rather than development followed by regression.

First, for the low-risk population, we used an SLR analysis to evaluate which parameters predicted individual differences in the rate at which development occurred. We used the dependent variable of performance on the *harder* pattern type after 50 epochs of training, as this was the most sensitive measure. Table 9.3 lists a subset of the factors explaining reliable amounts of variance at the .05 level. These were the factors that made development faster or slower. In the low-risk population, variation in the pruning process predicted very little of the variance in rate of development, with pruning onset and probability not significant predictors at the .05 level and the pruning threshold explaining only 0.3% of the variance. This reflects the fact that in its normal operation, pruning just removed unused connectivity resources. Comparison of Tables 9.2 and 9.3 indicates that several of the computational parameters that served as risk factors for regression also served as direct causes of variations in the rate of development. If we take the former to stand for autism and the latter to stand for language delay, this model provides one means to explain why there might be some shared common gene variants between autism and SLI (Vernes et al., 2008). Under this view, the genes would contribute to variation in a neurocomputational parameter that was a *direct cause* of SLI but only a *risk factor* for autism. We can classify such parameters as risk factors in the second case because they do not cause autism (here, regression) provided the

Table 9.3 A subset of the computational parameters that predicted rate of development in the low-risk population (for comparison with Table 9.2)

Parameter	*R^2 change*	*Significance*
Pruning threshold	.003	.014
Unit threshold function	.057	<.001
Architecture	.055	<.001
Pruning probability[a]	—	.096
Hidden unit number	.018	<.001
Sparseness	.008	<.001
Momentum	.028	<.001
Family quotient (environment)	.023	<.001

Note. Values show the R^2 change taken from a statistical stepwise linear regression analysis. The learning rate parameter explained most of the variance in rate of development (R^2 change = .113).

a Not included in model. The *p* value shows significance at the seventh step.

pruning process is not overaggressive. Rare mutations linked with both autism and global delay (mental retardation) might be related in the same way.

Comparison of Tables 9.2 and 9.3 also yielded another interesting result. The number of hidden units and the sparseness of connectivity were predictors of both regression and developmental rate in the same direction. That is, more hidden units made it both more likely that an individual would experience regression (if the pruning process was overaggressive) and more likely that an individual would develop at a faster rate (if the pruning process was normal). Similarly, more dense initial connectivity made it more likely that an individual would experience regression (if the pruning process was overaggressive) but also more likely that an individual would develop more quickly (if the pruning process was normal). This is a surprising yet important demonstration that a neurocomputational parameter can be positively correlated with outcome in the typically developing population but negatively correlated with outcome in a disordered population. As we pointed out earlier, exactly this paradox arises in the positive relationship between brain size and intelligence in the typically developing population, against the larger brain sizes observed in early development in children with autism. As we saw above, whereas parallel resources increase computational power, they also encourage smaller connection sizes that are more at risk of being pruned.[3]

Empirically, it is also puzzling that larger brain size is a feature only of early development in autism (Redcay & Courchesne, 2005). Such a pattern encouraged Courchesne et al. (2007) to propose that from early childhood onward in autism, there might be slowing or arrest of brain growth; this would explain the absence of a difference compared with controls in older individuals with autism. The connectionist networks employed in the current simulations are relatively abstract and obviously bear only an analogous relationship to actual neural circuits. Nevertheless, if one postulated that the number of connections in an artificial neural network is analogous to brain size, an assessment of how connection numbers changed across development might be informative. Figure 9.4 displays these data for the high-risk population, comparing the number of connections at various points in development for individuals exhibiting regression (split by the level of severity) with typically developing controls. All individuals showed initially high levels of connectivity that declined following the onset of pruning. However, in line with the fact that high levels of initial connectivity elevate the risk for regression, Figure 9.4 also shows that for networks yielding the most severe level of regression, there were initially more connections than in the control population. Once the (overaggressive) pruning process began, the number of connections in this severely affected group fell below the level found in the control group. Elevated network size in the group with severest regression was only a feature of early development. Figure 9.4 shows that regression also occurred in smaller networks at less severe levels.

The link between these simulation results and the brain size data for autism is, of course, speculative. The simulations have the limitation of predicting that there should be shrinkage in overall network size with age, whereas this pattern

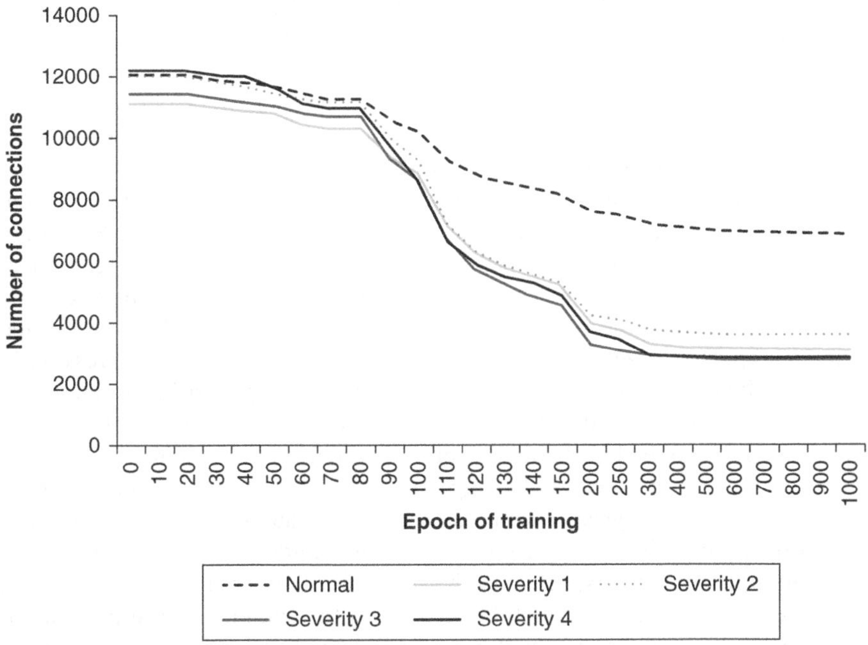

Figure 9.4 The mean number of connections in networks across development, shown for typically developing individuals and individuals exhibiting each level of severity of regression. The insert shows the early crossover for individuals with the severest level of regression, with initially higher and later lower numbers of connections compared with controls.

is observed only for gray matter volume, while white matter volume increases across development (Giedd et al., 1999; Paus et al., 2001). Nonetheless, the simulation results would reconcile both (a) how brain size could have the opposite correlation with outcome in a typically developing population compared with a disordered population, and (b) how the larger brain size in autism could be a feature only of early development. This account differs from those that have identified brain size as a primary cause of the behavioral deficits in autism. In the current simulations, the larger network size in affected individuals was not a direct cause of deficit but an artifact of sampling in a behaviorally defined disorder: Because network size was a risk factor for regression, individuals with large networks were overrepresented in the regression group compared with controls. Moreover, because network size was only a risk factor for regression rather than a direct cause, there was a great deal of overlap in the network sizes found in typical and disordered networks. This pattern is also found for studies comparing brain size of children with and without autism (e.g., Schumann et al., 2010). Such a degree of overlap tends to undermine the potential role of brain size as a direct cause of the phenotype.

Third, we considered whether extremely impoverished environments could increase the likelihood of regression in a population that shared the same computational parameters as the low-risk population. Figure 9.5 compares the incidence of regression at each severity level for the low-risk and the environmental-risk populations. Twenty-one additional cases of regression were observed in the environmental-risk population, a 45% increase in population risk. These new cases exhibited regression with mainly mild or medium severity and with good ultimate outcome. Recovery levels, comparing final outcome with preregression accuracy peak, yielded means of +13.6% for *easy* and +8.0% for *harder* pattern types; means for the high-risk population were –24.9% and –36.8%, respectively. The additional cases corresponded to individuals exposed to impoverished environments, with a mean family quotient value of .32 (i.e., only a third of the training set). The mean family quotient value for the 46 cases of regression in the low-risk population was .78. Mechanistically, the impoverished training sets caused these networks to develop smaller than usual connection weights, making them vulnerable to the less aggressive pruning process present in this population. The pattern of results is certainly suggestive of the "quasi-autism" identified by Rutter et al. (2007). Quasi-autism was seemingly caused by extreme environmental deprivation but was not universal to the children who experienced this deprivation. From the perspective of the simulations, two points are noteworthy. First, the environmental effect still operated via the common causal pathway of connectivity. Second, as indicated in an earlier analysis, variations in the pruning threshold parameter still explained most of the incidence of regression in the environmental-risk population. That is, not all individuals were affected by the impoverished environment because, in affected cases, it also required marginally elevated underlying risk for aggressive synaptic pruning. Poor environment only exaggerated underlying risk that would have remained latent in a normal environment. For both the simulations and the cases of quasi-autism reported by Rutter et al., the impairments were less severe and the outcome more positive than that observed for many core cases of autism.

These three findings provide a parsimonious explanation of several empirical phenomena in the broader autism phenotype. However they rest, of course, on the assumption that regression can be linked to the broader autistic phenotype. Autism is more often characterized by a failure to progress than by regression. Under what circumstances could overaggressive pruning cause failure to progress, rather than development followed by regression? We believe this link can be made if the mechanism damaging neural circuits is the same in the two cases but its timing is different. Under this view, autism will occur without regression if developmentally the overt behavior has not yet appeared by the time pruning begins. This may be either because the emergence of the overt behavior is itself delayed (as per the hypothesis of Pickles et al., 2009) or because there are individual differences in the timing of onset of pruning. Earlier occurring pruning will damage circuits before they have had time to give rise to many overt behaviors.

Indeed, the idea of individual differences provides a way to link mechanistically a number of phenomena hitherto treated separately: autism without regression, the

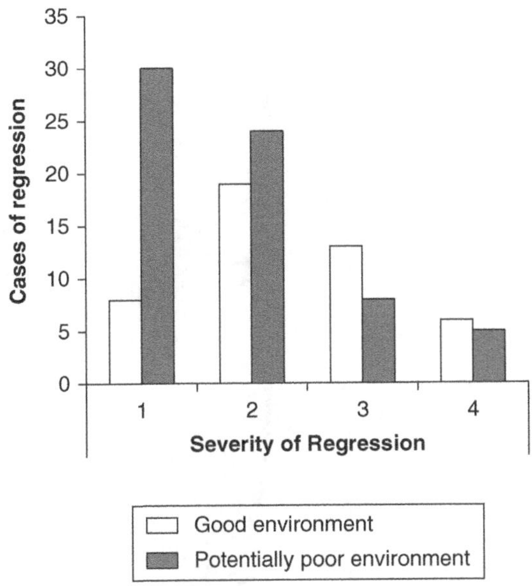

Figure 9.5 The incidence of regression split by severity level, for low-risk and environmental-risk populations.

regressive subtype, and some cases of childhood disintegrative disorder where regression occurs after the age of 3 years. In the first case, the aggressive pruning occurs before many overt behaviors are apparent. In the second case, it occurs after some salient behaviors have emerged (such as vocabulary development and social interactions). In the third case, the aggressive pruning occurs after 3 years of age. The later it appears, the more extreme pruning would need to be, in order to damage the more established functional circuits of older children, explaining the poorer prognosis of children with CDD.

In our final simulation analysis, we investigated whether some cases that were not rated as instances of regression but that exhibited delay or a developmental plateau might in fact have been caused by overaggressive pruning that had occurred early in development. We identified several candidate cases in the high-risk population based on a combination of behavioral delay and either a high pruning threshold or early pruning onset parameter value. These analyses are different in kind from the preceding analyses because cases were identified by a combination of behavior and a priori knowledge of the individual's neurocomputational parameter set. Four candidate individuals are illustrated in Figure 9.6, with the trajectories illustrating delay and plateau shown in the upper row. To verify the contribution of the pruning process, these networks were rerun with identical parameters and environmental conditions, with the exception of the pruning threshold parameter, which was lowered to a value of 0.1. Pruning would therefore occur only for very small connections. The lower row in Figure 9.6

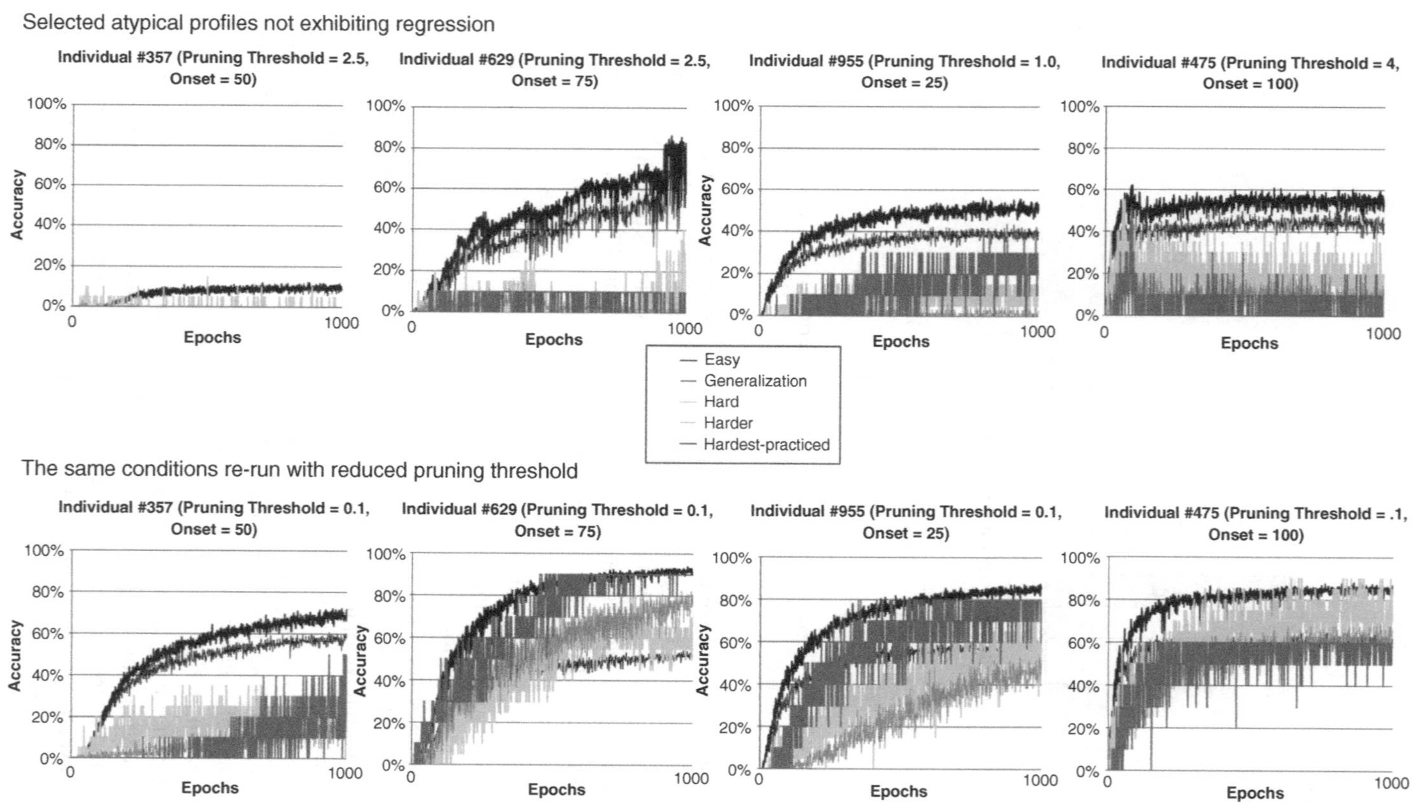

Figure 9.6 Top row: Trajectories of individuals who exhibited a pattern of delay or plateau rather than a clear pattern of regression, and where early aggressive pruning was implicated as a cause. Bottom row: the same networks rerun with identical parameters and environmental conditions except for the pruning threshold parameter, which was reduced to 0.1. Stronger performance confirmed the potential role of early pruning in causing delays and plateaus in development.

demonstrates the trajectories for each individual under these conditions. With this one parameter altered, these cases yielded much more successful developmental outcomes, thereby implicating overaggressive pruning as a cause of the delay. (Other cases of delay identified in the population were not altered by changing the pruning threshold parameter.) In three of the four illustrated cases, the onset of pruning was earlier than that found in regression (at 50, 75, and 25 epochs, compared with the regression mean of 106). Pruning thresholds were high for two of these cases (2.5), but for the third and earliest occurring case, the threshold was only 1.0. The fourth case experienced pruning onset at 100 epochs but had a high threshold of 4.0. These case studies offer cautious support that delay rather than regression can result from overaggressive pruning if it occurs earlier in development. The fourth case shows that a plateau in development rather than regression is a possible consequence of later occurring pruning at more aggressive levels.

There were a number of more extreme cases where development failed completely. We identified 21 such cases in the high-risk population, where no learning was apparent (which we refer to as *flatliners*). For these networks, the mean onset of pruning was 70 epochs and the mean pruning threshold was 2.7. Once more, we reran these networks with the sole change of a reduction in the pruning threshold parameter to 0.1. In 15 cases, the networks now showed some degree of development, whereas in six others there was no change. The mean trajectory averaging across these 15 cases of "recovered development" is shown in Figure 9.7 (right panel), with the mean trajectory from all typically developing (i.e., nonregression) networks shown for comparison (left panel). The mean typically developing trajectory includes the 21 flatliners. These extreme cases demonstrate a number of points. First, early overaggressive pruning can contribute to a failure to progress

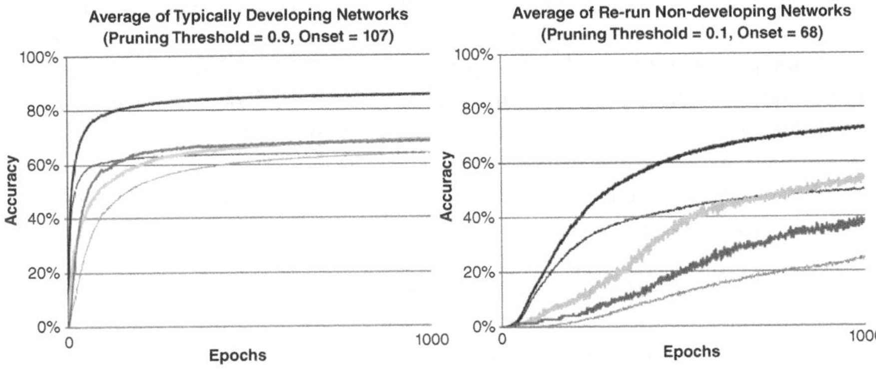

Figure 9.7 Left panel: Average trajectories for all individuals not classified as showing regression ($n = 359$). Right panel: Average trajectories for individuals in whom development failed completely, but who showed some level of development when the networks were rerun with the pruning threshold parameter reduced to 0.1 ($n = 15$). The pattern of delay indicates that failure was due to a combination of aggressive pruning and underlying slow development.

in an experience-dependent learning system. Second, the failure to progress can have other neurocomputational causes than pruning, corresponding to a critical accumulation of risk factors for delay. Third, as Figure 9.7 illustrates, in cases of failure, had the overaggressive pruning process not operated, development would have been delayed in any case. That is, the failure to progress in the 15 cases resulted from a "double hit" of delay and overaggressive pruning. The simulation result provides computational support for Pickles et al.'s (2009) hypothesis that cases of regression may represent faster developing cognitive systems, with the same mechanism causing slower developing cognitive systems to fail to progress.

Although this final analysis can only be provisional due to its post hoc nature, it nevertheless provides support for the hypothesis that regression and the wider autism phenotype may be linked by a common underlying mechanism, with the more usual autism pattern occurring when there is earlier overaggressive pruning or slower underlying development.

General discussion

Our account of regression in autism extends the approach of placing the developmental process at the heart of the explanation of developmental deficits (Karmiloff-Smith, 1998, 2009) and using implemented neurocomputational models to specify the details of that process (Mareschal et al., 2007; Thomas & Karmiloff-Smith, 2002). It is novel in its use of *population modeling*, where large numbers of individuals are simulated to capture the contribution of intrinsic and extrinsic sources of variation on behavior (neurocomputational parameters and the learning environment, respectively). This technique permitted the investigation of *heterogeneity* in regression and the influence of *risk factors* and *protective factors* in modulating the relationship between disorder cause and deficit outcome. Such factors could not be described as directly causal because, importantly, they also varied in unaffected individuals. We were therefore able to model the subsequent probabilistic relationship between cause and effect in a mechanistic rather than statistical model. Bishop (2006) recently advocated a causal framework for developmental deficits based on protective and risk factors. Although this framework is familiar in medicine, it stands in contrast to previous approaches in neuropsychology that have appealed to dissociation methodology, seeking to identify necessary and sufficient conditions for developmental deficits to arise. We believe that the use of population modeling to explore the statistical distribution of possible developmental trajectories given particular intrinsic conditions and particular environments has much to offer in understanding the causes of individual variation in behavior and that the same technique could be used to explore the origins of other developmental disorders.

The main findings of the current simulations can be summarized as follows. We hypothesized that the loss of previously established behaviors in early childhood observed in some children with autism is the result of overaggressive synaptic pruning. A normal threshold led to the pruning of connections without a negative impact on development. Setting the threshold too high allowed established functional circuits to be pruned, thereby damaging behavior. The simulations showed that (a) the pruning threshold parameter bore only a probabilistic relationship to the behavioral manifestation of regression; (b) the relationship was also nonlinear, so that variations in the parameter up to a certain point had little effect, but over a certain level increasingly led to regression; (c) the probabilistic nature of regression was due to an interaction of the pruning threshold parameter with population-wide variation in other computational parameters that could serve as risk or protective factors; (d) such factors produced heterogeneity in many of the characteristics of regression, including the timing of onset, the severity, the behavioral specificity, and the recovery; and (e) late onset regression had a poorer prognosis for recovery. Both the latter characteristics have been noted in the empirical literature on autism (Goldberg et al., 2003; Lord et al., 2004; Rogers, 2009). The heterogeneity arose because computational effects converged on the common causal pathway of connectivity size; (f) some computational parameters that were only risk factors for regression were the direct cause of developmental delay. This would provide an explanation of the finding that some common gene variants have been found that are more frequent in both autism and SLI (Vernes et al., 2008); (g) a larger number of parallel connections produced more powerful learning when pruning operated normally but increased the risk of regression when pruning was overaggressive. This would provide an explanation of why larger brain size is correlated with greater intelligence in the typically developing population but is also associated with increased risk of autism (McDaniel, 2005; Redcay & Courchesne, 2005). Large brain size would not be a cause of autism, as some have claimed, but merely a risk factor for overaggressive pruning; (h) an extremely impoverished learning environment exaggerated the risk that regression would occur in a low-risk population, because in such an environment, networks developed small connections that were more at risk of pruning. Such regression was milder and with better prognosis for recovery. This would explain why Rutter et al. (1999, 2007) identified a condition of "quasi-autism," affecting some but not all children exposed to extreme physical and social deprivation while in Romanian orphanages. Finally, (i) supporting the contention that overaggressive pruning might also underlie the broader autism phenotype, we found that if pruning commenced early, or development was delayed for other neurocomputational reasons, overaggressive pruning could result in patterns of delay, plateau, or failure to develop.

The proposed mechanistic explanation of developmental regression reconciles a number of disparate and sometimes paradoxical findings. It reconciles how cognitive abilities can decline after the onset of development; how the decline can occur while an adaptive mechanism, which is always seeking to improve the child's adaptive fit to his or her environment, continues to operate; and how the cognitive system can then show some level of recovery. It reconciles how regression in autism can have late onset yet have nothing to do with environmental factors (such as parenting): In the high-risk population with normal environmental variation, there was little effect of variations in experience. It is worth noting that the presence of recovery following regression is less easy to explain than one might imagine: How can an atypical process with a late onset be severe enough to cause an overt decline in behavior yet then allow the cognitive system to exhibit recovery—has the atypical process suddenly ceased to operate? The current hypothesis has a straightforward explanation of recovery in these children. Overaggressive pruning removes connections that encode established behaviors, so causing the decline. But eventually, all connections that fall beneath the pruning threshold will have been pruned. The cognitive system can then use those that remain to acquire abilities as best it can. Importantly here, in our simulations, the atypical mechanism causing the decline in behavior never ceased to operate—once activated, pruning was active through each network's life span—yet in many cases recovery followed regression nonetheless. The model reconciles paradoxical findings, in particular demonstrating how a neurocomputational parameter can be positively correlated with outcome in the typically developing population but negatively correlated with outcome in a developmentally disordered population.

Biological mechanisms and heritability

Although the causal process underlying developmental regression in autism is currently unknown, there has already been speculation that gene-based mechanisms may impair the anatomical remodeling of the brain, altering synaptic growth and pruning during the second year of life (Baird et al., 2008; Carper & Courchesne, 2005). In the broader autism phenotype, hypotheses concerning synaptic pruning and remodeling are being investigated via genetic disorders of known cause that show elevated incidence of the symptomatology of autism, such as Rett and Fragile X syndromes (Glaze, 2004; Kelleher & Bear, 2008). Although ASDs show high heritability (see Ronald & Hoekstra, 2011, for a review), a large percentage of this heritability remains unaccounted for, with candidate genes explaining little phenotypic variability in genome-wide association studies. The majority of cases of autism are believed to result from probabilistic genetic interactions, with multiple common variants of small effect contributing marginally to the behavioral phenotype (Abrahams & Geschwind, 2008). However, around 10%–20% of cases can be accounted for by known genetic effects, including (transmitted or de novo) medium-effect mutations or copy number variations (Sebat et al., 2007). Continued discoveries of specific mutations (Awadalla et al., 2010; O'Roak et al., 2011) suggest that estimates of their contribution to heritability may be adjusted in the future. The complex genetic picture raises the important question of how a large number of single mutations, or the interplay between many common variants, can each give rise to a very similar phenotype; for although a great deal of behavioral heterogeneity is seen in autism, the diagnostic commonality between individuals suggests a common underlying cause.

If cases with different genetic causes share a neurobiological basis, then that process, anomalous in autism, must rely on a wide variety of genes that also contribute to typical development. Atypical pruning is a plausible candidate mechanism from this perspective. Courchesne et al. (2007) noted that although there has been speculation that the cause of autism lies at the synapse (Garber, 2007), there have been few quantitative studies that have investigated cortical synapses in children with autism. The regulation of synaptic function depends on potentially thousands of genes (Rouleau, 2011), the expression of which is likely to change most dramatically during developmental periods of modifications in synaptic structure. Many of the genes identified as being associated with autism are also known to be involved in the regulation of synaptic function, or to control the expression of these genes. For example, in individuals with an ASD, transmitted or de novo mutations have been found in a number of genes that are involved in synaptogenesis, neurotransmitter release, or pruning, including Synapsin 1 (Fassio et al., 2011), SynGAP1 (Hamdan et al., 2011), SHANK3 (Bozdagi et al., 2010; Durand et al., 2006), and NLGN4 (Laumonnier et al., 2004); moreover, some of these are X-linked (Fassio et al., 2011; Piton et al., 2010).

The current proposal implicates the pruning of connectivity as the common causal pathway and also the mechanism by which both risk and protective factors can operate. The model is consistent with a genetic account in which variation in risk and protective factors is the result of the common gene variants, whereas the cause of overaggressive pruning may either be the accumulation of risk from common variants (as in the low-risk population; see Table 9.1) or the targeting of this process via mutations that increase population risk (as in the high-risk population). Because in this view the risk factors and the cause of overaggressive pruning can in principle be inherited independently, this predicts that some biological markers of autism may be observed in siblings or other individuals who nevertheless do not present with the disorder. Such a pattern has been observed both for common gene variants (Scott-Van Zeeland et al., 2010) and for variations in white matter structure (Barnea-Goraly, Lotspeich, & Reiss, 2010). Similarly, the model predicts that if brain size is a risk factor and independently heritable from the direct cause of autism, siblings of affected individuals may also show larger than average brain size; but in this case, without overaggressive pruning, our model predicts that it should persist in siblings across development. This remains to be verified empirically.

Modeling limitations

As with all modeling, the work presented here has some limitations. Theoretically, several of the findings depend on the assumption that regression indexes mechanisms at work also in the broader autism phenotype. Although our results support the viability of this link, regression could of course constitute a subtype, requiring a separate mechanistic explanation of the broader phenotype. Additionally, the current proposal is that in regression, autistic symptoms have later onset because they do not emerge until pruning begins. This would predict that phases of development prior to regression should be normal, but whether early development is indeed normal prior to regression is the subject of continuing debate (Luyster et al., 2005; Pickles et al., 2009; Wilson, Djukic, Shinnar, Dharmani, & Rapin, 2003). In terms of the simulations themselves, the modeling is both abstract and high level. Although we used a computational architecture that has been employed in a number of models of cognitive development, it obviously bears only an analogous relationship to the properties of actual neural circuits. For example, we did not simulate the early phase of synaptogenesis (the growth of connections). Other constructivist neural network models would be required to investigate the possibility of anomalies in this earlier phase (Shultz, 2003). Moreover, as mentioned earlier, in real neural circuits, pruning itself is a change in the balance of two concurrent processes of synapse formation and elimination (Hua & Smith, 2004). The model used the supervised learning algorithm of backpropagation, which is only indirectly biologically plausible (see Thomas & McClelland, 2008, for discussion). And we relied upon the metric of connection size to determine whether a connection was unused. In neural circuits, it is possible to conceive of other properties guiding pruning, such as how recently or often a synapse has been utilized.

Furthermore, in common with all accounts that posit the cause of autism as a low-level computational anomaly, it remains to be demonstrated why such an anomaly should lead to the particular triad of deficits in communication, socialization, and a restricted repertoire of behaviors that seem to be syndrome-specific to autism. The assumption is usually that these cognitive domains must rely on the computational property that is compromised in autism, but this remains to be demonstrated. In the case of a pruning account, one might posit that the pruning process differentially affects different types of connections. If the overaggressive pruning process particularly impacted long-range connectivity over short-range connectivity, then the current hypothesis would fit into existing (dis)connectivity hypotheses about autism and its associated cognitive formulations (e.g., Courchesne & Pierce, 2005; Happé, 1999; Ozonoff et al., 1994; Rippon, Brock, Brown, & Boucher, 2007; Williams & Casanova, 2010), which posit that the triad are cognitive domains that require the integration of nonlocally available cues or interactions between remote brain regions for the development of typical behavior.

We described the learning problem employed in our simulations in abstract terms. The results indicated that internally consistent behaviors with high type frequency were more robust to regression than idiosyncratic/exceptional behaviors, even if the latter were highly practiced. Future simulations would need to incorporate features of target cognitive domains to show how they interact with compromised connectivity and lead to domain-specific phenotypic outcomes. Other low-level deficits should produce other phenotypic outcomes, such as global delay or language impairment. Lastly, any full account needs to consider the extended developmental trajectory, incorporating the adaptive response of the individual to changes in processing properties, proactive control of behavior, and emotional regulation (see Grossberg & Seidman, 2006, for a computational account of the latter).

Novel predictions

The model generates a prediction that is not found in any current theory of autism. Our central hypothesis is that regression is triggered by atypical synaptic pruning. In humans, data suggest that the timing of synaptic pruning is different across brain areas, with primary sensory and motor areas experiencing the earliest pruning, followed by temporal and parietal associative areas, and lastly frontal cortex (Huttenlocher, 2002; Huttenlocher & Dabholkar, 1997). Behaviors are not typically generated by the operation of a single brain area. Nevertheless, to the extent that behaviors rely differentially on certain brain areas, our prediction is that the order of appearance of the behavioral symptoms of autism should follow the onset of pruning in relevant brain areas. Thus, we hypothesize that sensory and motor anomalies should appear first. This novel prediction contradicts the usual claim that social deficits (e.g., in communicative eye gaze behavior) are the first overt symptoms to emerge in autism.

It is likely that retrospective parental reports will be insufficiently sensitive to test our hypothesis, because very early sensory and motor anomalies may be subtle. Instead, prospective studies examining the early development of infants at risk for autism are better suited to probe for the earliest atypical behaviors for children who subsequently turn out to present with autism. Several such studies are underway, but it is premature to draw strong conclusions. The preliminary evidence, however, is suggestive. Rogers (2009) reviewed the findings to date from studies of infant siblings of children with autism, noting the surprising lack of overt behaviors at 6 months of age that would point to later autism and highlighting the actual presence of social behaviors in these infants, alongside atypicalities in other areas. Indeed, referring to findings from Bryson et al. (2007) on nine infants who subsequently developed autism, Rogers noted that the earliest atypicalities were in two areas: delayed motor development and unusual visual interest or reactivity to objects. Further data are required, but the indication is that deficits in sensory and motor behaviors may precede social impairments, consistent with the fact that pruning takes place earlier in the sensory and motor brain systems, and thus supporting our hypothesis.

Intervention

Finally, are there any implications for intervention based on the hypothesis we have developed? Several types of intervention might be conceived that differ from those currently pursued in developmental disorder remediation approaches in general. Rather than target domain-specific deficits known to be part of a syndrome's profile (e.g., social communication in autism), intervention might target very basic-level processes that subsequently have a cascading impact on domain-specific outcomes (Karmiloff-Smith, 2009). These would include a very early behavioral intervention to enhance connectivity prior to the onset of pruning, a pharmacological intervention to lessen the severity of pruning, and very early visuo-motor training rather than focusing on communicative deficits. Baird et al. (2008) recently concluded that it was unknown whether regressive processes are influenced by environmental factors. Our simulations of autism showed that environmental stimulation had an asymmetric role: Although a very impoverished environment could elevate risk, a good environment was insufficient to prevent loss of function.

However, we did not consider the possible effects of increased stimulation of at-risk systems. Turning to autism itself, a speculative and optimistic vision from our current simulations would be that risk status for aggressive synaptic pruning could be identified on the basis of genotype and a pharmacological intervention applied in early infancy to normalize the pruning process.

Acknowledgments

This research was supported by Economic and Social Research Council (ESRC) Grant RES-062-23-2721, Medical Research Council Grant G0300188, and a Leverhulme Study Abroad Fellowship to Michael S. C. Thomas held at the University of Chicago. We would like to thank Tony Charman, Sam Wass, Mark Johnson, Andrew Pickles, and Neil Forrester for helpful discussions and Anna Fedor for her help with coding. The ideas presented here were partly developed during the ESRC workshop "Language and Social Understanding in Developmental Disorders" organized by Gina Conti-Ramsden in October 2009.

Notes

1 The same assumption may not hold in recurrent networks, because cycling activation may exaggerate the contribution of a small connection weight to subsequent function.

2 Raters were given the following definition:

> Regression is present when any one of the pattern types shows a systematic drop in performance at any point in development. This may range from a temporary dip in one pattern type to a complete collapse in performance across all types. The dip should be noticeable compared to the developmental variation exhibited by that individual.

3 Not all parameters showed the paradoxical correlations: The unit threshold function contributed to risk of regression in the high-risk population and risk of developmental delay in the low-risk population.

References

Abrahams, B. S., & Geschwind, D. H. (2008). Advances in autism genetics: On the threshold of a new neurobiology. *Nature Reviews Genetics*, *9*, 341–355. doi:10.1038/nrg2346

Awadalla, P., Gauthier, J., Myers, R. A., Casals, F., Hamdan, F. F., Griffing, A. R., . . . Rouleau, G. A. (2010). Direct measure of the de novo mutation rate in autism and schizophrenia cohorts. *American Journal of Human Genetics*, *87*, 316–324. doi:10.1016/j.ajhg.2010.07.019

Baird, G., Charman, T., Pickles, A., Chandler, S., Loucas, T., Meldrum, D., . . . Simonoff, E. (2008). Regression, developmental trajectory and association problems in disorders in the autism spectrum: The SNAP study. *Journal of Autism and Developmental Disorders*, *38*, 1827–1836. doi:10.1007/s10803-008-0571-9

Baird, G., Simonoff, E., Pickles, A., Chandler, S., Loucas, T., Meldrum, D., & Charman, T. (2006). Prevalence of disorders of the autism spectrum in a population cohort of children in South Thames: The Special Needs and Autism Project (SNAP). *Lancet*, *368*, 210–215. doi:10.1016/S0140-6736(06)69041-7

Barnea-Goraly, N., Lotspeich, L. J., & Reiss, A. L. (2010). Similar white matter aberrations in children with autism and their unaffected siblings. *Archives of General Psychiatry, 67*, 1052–1060. doi:10.1001/archgenpsychiatry.2010.123

Belmonte, M. K., Allen, G., Beckel-Mitchener, A., Boulanger, L. M., Carper, R. A., & Webb, S. J. (2004). Autism and abnormal development of brain connectivity. *Journal of Neuroscience, 24*, 9228–9231. doi:10.1523/JNEUROSCI.3340-04.2004

Ben Bashat, D., Kronfeld-Duenias, V., Zachor, D. A., Ekstein, P. M., Hendler, T., Tarrasch, R., . . . Ben Sira, L. (2007). Accelerated maturation of white matter in young children with autism: A high b value DWI study. *NeuroImage, 37*, 40–47. doi:10.1016/j.neuroimage.2007.04.060

Beversdorf, D. Q., Narayanan, A., Hillier, A., & Hughes, J. D. (2007). Network model of decreased context utilization in autism spectrum disorder. *Journal of Autism and Developmental Disorders, 37*, 1040–1048. doi:10.1007/s10803-006-0242-7

Bishop, D. V. M. (2006). Developmental cognitive genetics: How psychology can inform genetics and vice versa. *Quarterly Journal of Experimental Psychology, 59*, 1153–1168. doi:10.1080/17470210500489372

Bishop, D. V. M. (2010). Overlaps between autism and language impairment: Phenomimicry or shared etiology? *Behavior Genetics, 40*, 618– 629. doi:10.1007/s10519-010-9381-x

Bozdagi, O., Sakurai, T., Papapetrou, D., Wang, X., Dickstein, D. L., Takahashi, N., . . . Buxbaum, J. D. (2010). Haploinsufficiency of the autism-associated Shank3 gene leads to deficits in synaptic function, social interaction, and social communication. *Molecular Autism, 1*, 15. doi:10.1186/2040-2392-1-15

Bryson, S. E., Zwaigenbaum, L., Brian, J., Roberts, W., Szatmari, P., Rombough, V., & McDermott, C. (2007). A prospective case series of high-risk infants who developed autism. *Journal of Autism and Developmental Disorders, 37*, 12–24. doi:10.1007/s10803-006-0328-2

Carper, R. A., & Courchesne, E. (2005). Localized enlargement of the frontal cortex in early autism. *Biological Psychiatry, 57*, 126–133. doi:10.1016/j.biopsych.2004.11.005

Cohen, I. L. (1994). An artificial neural network analogue of learning in autism. *Biological Psychiatry, 36*, 5–20. doi:10.1016/0006-3223(94)90057-4

Cohen, I. L. (1998). Neural network analysis of learning in autism. In D. J. Stein & J. Ludik (Eds.), *Neural networks and psychopathology* (pp. 274–315). New York, NY: Cambridge University Press. doi:10.1017/CBO9780511547195.012

Courchesne, E., & Pierce, K. (2005). Why the frontal cortex in autism might be talking only to itself: Local over-connectivity but long-distance disconnection. *Current Opinion in Neurobiology, 15*, 225–230. doi: 10.1016/j.conb.2005.03.001

Courchesne, E., Pierce, K., Schumann, C. M., Redcay, E., Buckwalter, J. A., Kennedy, D. P., & Morgan, J. (2007). Mapping early brain development in autism. *Neuron, 56*, 399–413. doi:10.1016/j.neuron.2007.10.016

Cowan, W. M., Fawcett, J. W., O'Leary, D. D. M., & Stanfield, B. B. (1984, September 21). Regressive events in neurogenesis. *Science, 225*, 1258–1265. doi:10.1126/science.6474175

Davidovitch, M., Glick, L., Holtzman, G., Tirosh, E., & Safir, M. P. (2000). Developmental regression in autism: Maternal perception. *Journal of Autism and Developmental Disorders, 30*, 113–119. doi:10.1023/A:1005403421141

Durand, C. M., Betancur, C., Boeckers, T. M., Bockmann, J., Chaste, P., Fauchereau, F., . . . Bourgeron, T. (2006). Mutations in the gene encoding the synaptic scaffolding protein SHANK3 are associated with autism spectrum disorders. *Nature Genetics, 39*, 25–27. doi:10.1038/ng1933

Fassio, A., Patry, L., Congia, S., Onofri, F., Piton, A., Gauthier, J., . . . Cossette, P. (2011). SYN1 loss-of-function mutations in autism and partial epilepsy cause impaired synaptic function. *Human Molecular Genetics*, *20*, 2297–2307. doi:10.1093/hmg/ddr122

Folstein, S. E., & Mankoski, R. E. (2000). Chromosome 7q: Where autism meets language disorder? *American Journal of Human Genetics*, *67*, 278–281. doi:10.1086/303034

Fombonne, E., & Chakrabarti, S. (2001). No evidence for a new variant of measles-mumps-rubella-induced autism. *Pediatrics*, *108*, E58. doi: 10.1542/peds.108.4.e58

Frazier, T. W., & Hardan, A. Y. (2009). A meta-analysis of the corpus callosum in autism. *Biological Psychiatry*, *66*, 935–941. doi:10.1016/j.biopsych.2009.07.022

Frith, C. D. (2003). What do imaging studies tell us about the neural basis of autism? In G. Bock & J. Goode (Eds.), *Autism: Neural basis and treatment possibilities: Novartis Foundation Symposium 251* (pp. 149–176). Chichester, England: Wiley. doi:10.1002/0470869380.ch10

Garber, K. (2007, July 13). Autism's cause may reside in abnormalities at the synapse. *Science*, *317*, 190–191. doi:10.1126/science.317.5835.190

Giedd, J. N., Blumenthal, J., Jeffries, N. O., Castellanos, F. X., Liu, H., Zijdenbos, A., . . . Rappaport, J. L. (1999). Brain development during childhood and adolescence: A longitudinal MRI study. *Nature Neuroscience*, *2*, 861–863. doi:10.1038/13158

Glaze, D. G. (2004). Rett syndrome: Of girls and mice—lessons for regression in autism. *Mental Retardation and Developmental Disabilities Research Reviews*, *10*, 154–158. doi:10.1002/mrdd.20030

Goldberg, W. A., Osann, K., Filipek, P. A., Laulhere, T., Jarvis, L., Modahl, C., . . . Spence, M. A. (2003). Language and other regression: Assessment and timing. *Journal of Autism and Developmental Disorders*, *33*, 607–616. doi:10.1023/B:JADD.0000005998.47370.ef

Grossberg, S., & Seidman, D. (2006). Neural dynamics of autistic behaviors: Cognitive, emotional, and timing substrates. *Psychological Review*, *113*, 483–525. doi:10.1037/0033-295X.113.3.483

Gustafsson, L. (1997). Inadequate cortical feature maps: A neural circuit theory of autism. *Biological Psychiatry*, *42*, 1138–1147. doi:10.1016/S0006-3223(97)00141-8

Hamdan, F. F., Daoud, H., Piton, A., Gauthier, J., Dobrzeniecka, S., Krebs, M. O., . . . Michaud, J. L. (2011). De novo SYNGAP1 mutations in nonsyndromic intellectual disability and autism. *Biological Psychiatry*, *69*, 898–901. doi:10.1016/j.biopsych.2010.11.015

Happé, F. (1999). Autism: Cognitive deficit or cognitive style? *Trends in Cognitive Sciences*, *3*, 216–222. doi:10.1016/S1364-6613(99)01318-2

Hill, A. E., & Rosenbloom, L. (1986). Disintegrative psychosis of childhood: Teenage follow-up. *Developmental Medicine & Child Neurology*, *28*, 34–40. doi:10.1111/j.1469-8749.1986.tb03827.x

Hua, J. Y., & Smith, S. J. (2004). Neural activity and the dynamics of central nervous system development. *Nature Neuroscience*, *7*, 327–332. doi:10.1038/nn1218

Huttenlocher, P. R. (2002). *Neural plasticity: The effects of environment on the development of the cerebral cortex*. Cambridge, MA: Harvard University Press.

Huttenlocher, P. R., & Dabholkar, A. S. (1997). Regional differences in synaptogenesis in human cerebral cortex. *Journal of Comparative Neurology*, *387*, 167–178. doi:10.1002/(SICI)1096-9861(19971020)387:2<167::AID-CNE1>3.0.CO;2-Z

Johnson, M. H., & Karmiloff-Smith, A. (1992). Can neural selectionism be applied to cognitive development and its disorders? *New Ideas in Psychology*, *10*, 35–46. doi:10.1016/0732-118X(92)90046-3

Just, M. A., Cherkassky, V. L., Keller, T. A., & Minshew, N. J. (2004). Cortical activation and synchronization during sentence comprehension in high-functioning autism: Evidence of underconnectivity. *Brain: A Journal of Neurology, 127*, 1811–1821. doi:10.1093/brain/awh199

Káradóttir, R., Hamilton, N. B., Bakiri, Y., & Attwell, D. (2008). Spiking and nonspiking classes of oligodendrocyte precursor glia in CNS white matter. *Nature Neuroscience, 11*, 450–456. doi:10.1038/nn2060

Karmiloff-Smith, A. (1998). Development itself is the key to understanding developmental disorders. *Trends in Cognitive Sciences, 2*, 389–398. doi:10.1016/S1364-6613(98)01230-3

Karmiloff-Smith, A. (2009). Nativism versus neuroconstructivism: Rethinking the study of developmental disorders. *Developmental Psychology, 45*, 56–63.

Kelleher, R. J., & Bear, M. F. (2008). The autistic neuron: Troubled translation? *Cell, 135*, 401–406. doi:10.1016/j.cell.2008.10.017

Koshino, H., Kana, R. K., Keller, T. A., Cherkassky, V. L., Minshew, N. J., & Just, M. A. (2008). fMRI investigation of working memory for faces in autism: Visual coding and underconnectivity with frontal areas. *Cerebral Cortex, 18*, 289–300. doi:10.1093/cercor/bhm054

Laumonnier, F., Bonnet-Brilhault, F., Gomot, M., Blanc, R., David, A., Moizard, M. P., . . . Briault, S. (2004). X-linked mental retardation and autism are associated with a mutation in the NLGN4 gene, a member of the neuroligin family. *American Journal of Human Genetics, 74*, 552–557. doi:10.1086/382137

Lewis, J. D., & Elman, J. L. (2008). Growth-related neural reorganization and the autism phenotype: A test of the hypothesis that altered brain growth leads to altered connectivity. *Developmental Science, 11*, 135–155. doi:10.1111/j.1467-7687.2007.00634.x

Lord, C., Shulman, C., & DiLavore, P. (2004). Regression and word loss in autistic spectrum disorders. *Journal of Child Psychology and Psychiatry, 45*, 936–955. doi:10.1111/j.1469-7610.2004.t01-1-00287.x

Luyster, R., Richler, J., Risi, S., Hsu, W. L., Dawson, G., Bernier, R., . . . Lord, C. (2005). Early regression in social communication in autism spectrum disorders: A CPEA study. *Developmental Neuropsychology, 27*, 311–336. doi:10.1207/s15326942dn2703_2

Mareschal, D., Johnson, M., Sirios, S., Spratling, M., Thomas, M. S. C., & Westermann, G. (2007). *Neuroconstructivism: How the brain constructs cognition*. Oxford, England: Oxford University Press.

Mareschal, D., & Thomas M. S. C. (2007). Computational modeling in developmental psychology. *IEEE Transactions on Evolutionary Computation (Special Issue on Autonomous Mental Development), 11*, 137–150. doi:10.1109/TEVC.2006.890232

McClelland, J. L. (2000). The basis of hyperspecificity in autism: A preliminary suggestion based on properties of neural nets. *Journal of Autism and Developmental Disorders, 30*, 497–502. doi:10.1023/A:1005576229109

McDaniel, M. A. (2005). Big-brained people are smarter: A meta-analysis of the relationship between in vivo brain volume and intelligence. *Intelligence, 33*, 337–346. doi:10.1016/j.intell.2004.11.005

Melrose, R. J., Tinaz, S., Castelo, J. M. B., Courtney, M. G., & Stern, C. E. (2008). Compromised fronto-striatal functioning in HIV: An fMRI investigation of semantic event sequencing. *Behavioural Brain Research, 188*, 337–347. doi:10.1016/j.bbr.2007.11.021

Molloy, C. A., Morrow, A. L., Meinzen-Derr, J., Dawson, G., Bernier, R., Dunn, M., . . . Lord, C. (2006). Familial autoimmune thyroid disease as a risk factor for regression in children with autism spectrum disorder: A CPEA study. *Journal of Autism and Developmental Disorders*, *36*, 317–324. doi:10.1007/s10803-005-0071-0

O'Roak, B. J., Deriziotis, P., Lee, C., Vives, L., Schwartz, J. J., Girirajan, S., . . . Eichler, E. E. (2011). Exome sequencing in sporadic autism spectrum disorders identifies severe de novo mutations. *Nature Genetics*, *43*, 585–589. doi:10.1038/ng.835

Ozonoff, S., Strayer, D. L., McMahon, W. M., & Filloux, F. (1994). Executive function abilities in autism and Tourette syndrome: An information processing approach. *Journal of Child Psychology and Psychiatry*, *35*, 1015–1032. doi:10.1111/j.1469-7610.1994.tb01807.x

Pachou, E., Vourkas, M., Simos, P., Smit, D., Stam, C. J., Tsirka, V., & Micheloyannis, S. (2008). Working memory in schizophrenia: An EEG study using power spectrum and coherence analysis to estimate cortical activation and network behavior. *Brain Topography*, *21*, 128–137. doi:10.1007/s10548-008-0062-5

Paus, T., Collins, D. L., Evans, A. C., Leonard, G., Pike, B., & Zijdenbos, A. (2001). Maturation of white matter in the human brain: A review of magnetic resonance studies. *Brain Research Bulletin*, *54*, 255–266. doi:10.1016/S0361-9230(00)00434-2

Pickles, A., Simonoff, E., Conti-Ramsden, G., Falcaro, M., Simkin, Z., Charman, T., . . . Baird, G. (2009). Loss of language in early development of autism and specific language impairment. *Journal of Child Psychology and Psychiatry*, *50*, 843–852. doi:10.1111/j.14697610.2008.02032.x

Piton, A., Gauthier, J., Hamdan, F. F., Lafrenière, R. G., Yang, Y., Henrion, E., . . . Rouleau, G. A. (2010). Systematic resequencing of X-chromosome synaptic genes in autism spectrum disorder and schizophrenia. *Molecular Psychiatry*, *16*, 867–880. doi:10.1038/mp.2010.54

Redcay, E., & Courchesne, E. (2005). When is the brain enlarged in autism? A meta-analysis of all brain size reports. *Biological Psychiatry*, *58*, 1–9. doi:10.1016/j.biopsych.2005.03.026

Richards, T. L., & Berninger, V. W. (2008). Abnormal fMRI connectivity in children with dyslexia during a phoneme task: Before but not after treatment. *Journal of Neurolinguistics*, *21*, 294–304. doi:10.1016/j.jneuroling.2007.07.002

Richler, J., Luyster, R., Risi, S., Hsu, W.-L., Dawson, G., Bernier, R., . . . Lord, C. (2006). Is there a "regressive phenotype" of autism spectrum disorder associated with the measles-mumps-rubella vaccine? A CPEA study. *Journal of Autism and Developmental Disorders*, *36*, 299–316. doi:10.1007/s10803-005-0070-1

Rippon, G., Brock, J., Brown, C., & Boucher, J. (2007). Disordered connectivity in the autistic brain: Challenges for the "new psychophysiology." *International Journal of Psychophysiology*, *63*, 164–172. doi:10.1016/j.ijpsycho.2006.03.012

Rogers, S. J. (2009). What are infant siblings teaching us about autism in infancy? *Autism Research*, *2*, 125–137. doi:10.1002/aur.81

Ronald, A., & Hoekstra, R. A. (2011). Autism spectrum disorders and autistic traits: A decade of new twin studies. *American Journal of Medical Genetics Part B*. Advance online publication.

Rouleau, G. (2011, April). *Genomic studies in neurodevelopmental disorders*. Paper presented at the conference Wiring the Brain: Making Connections, Powerscourt, County Wicklow, Ireland.

Rutter, M., Anderson-Wood, J., Beckett, C., Bredenkamp, D., Castle, J., Goothues, C., . . . O'Connor, T. (1999). Quasi-autistic patterns following severe early global privation. *Journal of Child Psychology and Psychiatry*, *40*, 537–549. doi:10.1111/1469-7610.00472

Rutter, M., Kreppner, J., Croft, C., Murin, M., Colvert, E., Beckett, C., . . . Sonuga-Barke, E. (2007). Early adolescent outcomes of institutionally deprived and non-deprived adoptees: III. Quasi-autism. *Journal of Child Psychology and Psychiatry*, *48*, 1200–1207. doi:10.1111/j.14697610.2007.01792.x

Schumann, C. M., Bloss, C. S., Carter Barnes, C., Wideman, G. M., Carper, R. A., Akshoomoff, N., . . . Courchesne, E. (2010). Longitudinal magnetic resonance imaging study of cortical development through early childhood in autism. *Journal of Neuroscience*, *30*, 4419–4427. doi: 10.1523/JNEUROSCI.5714-09.2010

Scott-Van Zeeland, A. A., Abrahams, B. S., Alvarez-Retuerto, A. I., Sonnenblick, L. I., Rudie, J. D., Ghahremani, D., . . . Bookheimer, S. Y. (2010). Altered functional connectivity in frontal lobe circuits is associated with variation in the autism risk gene CNTNAP2. *Science Translation Medicine*, *2*, 56ra80.

Sebat, J., Lakshmi, B., Malhotra, D., Troge, J., Lese-Martin, C., Walsh, T., . . . Wigler, M. (2007, April 20). Strong association of de novo copy number mutations with autism. *Science*, *316*, 445–449. doi:10.1126/science.1138659

Shultz, T. R. (2003). *Computational developmental psychology*. Cambridge, MA: MIT Press.

Simmons, D. R., McKay, L., McAleer, P., Toal, E., Robertson, A., & Pollick, F. E. (2007). Neural noise and autism spectrum disorders [Abstract]. *Perception*, *36*(Suppl.), 119–120.

Siperstein, R., & Volkmar, F. (2004). Brief report: Parental reporting of regression in children with pervasive d\evelopmental disorders. *Journal of Autism and Developmental Disorders*, *34*, 731–734. doi:10.1007/s10803-004-5294-y

Stanfield, A. C., McIntosh, A. M., Spencer, M. D., Philip, R., Gaur, S., & Lawrie, S. (2008). Towards a neuroanatomy of autism: A systematic review and meta-analysis of structural magnetic resonance imaging studies. *European Psychiatry*, *23*, 289–299. doi:10.1016/j.eurpsy.2007.05.006

Stiles, J. (2008). *The fundamentals of brain development*. Cambridge, MA: Harvard University Press.

Thomas, M. S. C., Forrester, N. A., & Ronald, A. (2016). Multi-scale modeling of gene-behavior associations in an artificial neural network model of cognitive development. *Cognitive Science*, *40*, 51–99.

Thomas, M. S. C., & Johnson, M. H. (2008). New advances in understanding sensitive periods in brain development. *Current Directions in Psychological Science*, *17*, 1–5. doi:10.1111/j.1467-8721.2008.00537.x

Thomas, M. S. C., & Karmiloff-Smith, A. (2002). Are developmental disorders like cases of adult brain damage? Implications from connectionist modelling. *Behavioral and Brain Sciences*, *25*, 727–787. doi: 10.1017/S0140525X02000134

Thomas, M. S. C., Knowland, V. C. P., & Karmiloff-Smith, A. (2011). What causes variability in the severity of developmental disorders? A neurocomputational account using the example of developmental regression in autism. In E. J. Davelaar (Ed.), *Connectionist models of neurocognition and emergent behavior: From theory to applications*. London, England: World Scientific.

Thomas, M. S. C., & McClelland, J. L. (2008). Connectionist models of cognition. In R. Sun (Ed.), *Cambridge handbook of computational cognitive modelling* (pp. 23–58). Cambridge, England: Cambridge University Press.

Vernes, S. C., Newbury, D. F., Abrahams, B. S., Winchester, L., Nicod, J., Groszer, M., . . . Fisher, S. E. (2008). A functional genetic link between distinct developmental language disorders. *New England Journal of Medicine*, *359*, 2337–2345. doi:10.1056/NEJMoa0802828

Wass, S. (2011). Distortions and disconnections: Disrupted brain connectivity in autism. *Brain and Cognition*, *75*, 18–28. doi:10.1016/j.bandc.2010.10.005

Werner, E., Dawson, G., Munson, J., & Osterling, J. (2005). Variation in early developmental course in autism and its relations with behavioural outcome at 3–4 years of age. *Journal of Autism and Developmental Disorders*, *35*, 337–350. doi:10.1007/s10803-005-3301-6

Williams, E. L., & Casanova, M. F. (2010). Autism and dyslexia: A spectrum of cognitive styles as defined by minicolumnar morphometry. *Medical Hypotheses*, *74*, 59–62. doi:10.1016/j.mehy.2009.08.003

Wilson, S., Djukic, A., Shinnar, S., Dharmani, C., & Rapin, I. (2003). Clinical characteristics of language regression in children. *Developmental Medicine and Child Neurology*, *45*, 508–514. doi:10.1111/j.14698749.2003.tb00950.x

Part IV

Taking the brain seriously

10 Neuroimaging of the developing brain

Taking "developing" seriously

Annette Karmiloff-Smith

Introduction

The seductive allure of brain images

For the scientist (and for the general public), there is something especially captivating about colored images of the human brain, as if at last we could get to see directly "inside the black box." But knowing that area X is activated ("lights up") tells us nothing, unless it adds a new explanation or new prediction beyond the behavioral measures. If developmental neuroimaging is to have predictive and clinical power, we should be able to reverse engineer and go from brain activation to a better than chance guess as to which cognitive function is being used. As a tool, brain imaging is no better than a pencil or a fishing trip, unless it is hypothesis-driven. If the key goal of cognitive neuroscience were to find "simple and direct connections between brain and behavior" [Raizada et al., 2010], then phrenology could raise its ugly head again! But of course, as these authors go on to point out, the key goal never turns out to be simple and direct. Indeed, is it ever the case that invoking the maturational coming online of a specific brain region explains developmental change? In fact, most regions in the infant brain are partially active from very early on; what develops is best captured at the level of the complexities of changing intra-and inter-regional networks [Johnson, 2001].

Hypothesis-driven imaging

What approaches really bring new insights from brain imaging? Work in the clinical field certainly has. One example is the discovery that co-activation of frontal and limbic regions is predictive of patients' response to antidepressant drugs, explaining why certain patients respond to drugs and others do not [Langenecker et al., 2007]. However, to my knowledge, there are no such studies in children of differential brain responses to drugs, such as the effects on the developing brain at different ages of the use of methylphenidate to treat ADHD. Such treatment/brain-response correlations can be extended to examining the usefulness of brain imaging at the cognitive level, for example, in understanding how/why intervention works or fails in different aged children [Posner and Rothbart, 2005]. Neural data can also be particularly relevant when considering identical behavioral scores across typically and atypically developing populations [see also, Luna et al., 2010, on the possibility that, even in the typically developing population, alternative circuitries may underlie equivalent behavior at different ages]. The demonstration that the brains of individuals with, say, Williams syndrome, reveal different neural processing in terms of localization and specialization of function from the brains of healthy controls when viewing faces [Karmiloff-Smith et al., 2004], despite equivalent behavioral scores on standardized face processing tasks, can yield new hypotheses about atypical brain development, leading to more informed intervention techniques as well as predictions about other aspects of the cognitive system that may have developed in a similarly deviant way [Karmiloff-Smith, 2009]. Radically differing γ-band activity in two syndromes both purported to focus on featural detail [Grice et al., 2001] suggests that the cognitive notion of "featural" needs reconceptualizing. In general, cross-syndrome comorbidities at the behavioral level may be differentiated at the neural level, and if they are not, then we may have to rethink traditional diagnostic categories [Shaw et al., 2010].

Interestingly, as the brain continues to mature in the healthy elderly—another developing group—language comprehension seems to be spared. It turns out that despite neuronal degeneration in the left cerebral areas active in younger controls during comprehension tasks, proficient comprehension in the ageing brain is sustained by compensatory bilateral frontotemporal and parietal activity, thereby offering a neural-level explanation for the behavioral level [Tyler et al., 2009]. Another example of the importance of examining the neural level comes from sensitivity to foreign language contrasts. It had long been thought that the capacity to discriminate non-native phonemes disappears towards the end of the first year of life. Indeed, although 6-month-old infants can distinguish non-native contrasts, this ability is absent behaviorally around 9–10 months when the infant comes to specialize in the phonemic repertoire of his/her native tongue. But neuroimaging of adults who show no behavioral signs of distinguishing the non-native contrasts reveals that their brains are in fact still registering the differences [Gaxiola-Rivera et al., 2000], highlighting the use of both the cognitive and neural levels of explanation and pointing to the potential for successful phonemic training even in the adult. And a developmental approach is critical to move the field away from simplistic notions like risk alleles, as Casey et al. (2010) make clear, because an allele that is a risk factor for one period of development or one type of environment may turn out to be a protective factor for others.

Methodological issues

Methodological issues are rife in the area of neuroimaging. Although findings seem clear as brain images are flashed on a screen, the data reduction issues behind the scenes are still far from resolved. One concerns selection bias. The problem of automatically mapping an adult Region of Interest (ROI) directly to the child brain is discussed in the articles by Luna et al. and by Poldrack (2010). But just as serious is the possibility that the criteria used in the first place to define the adult ROI are the same as those being tested for in the data from that region, meaning that any correlations may be biased [Rajeev et al., 2010; see also discussion in Konrad and Eickhoff, 2010]. In other words, is it the case that certain brain-behavior correlations actually only emerge when a set of specifically selected features is used? One recent solution to the ROI problem applied a single statistical test—linear regression—across the whole brain at once, without the need to carry out any pre-selection of voxels or features [Rajeev et al., 2010]. In other words, the study asked whether the degree to which there is separability of patterns on a whole-brain level between two conditions correlates with individual differences in a behavioral variable. Although ROI analyses may be useful if the targeted region is the right one, they do run the risk of selection bias. Rajeev and collaborators circumvented this risk by using a whole brain analysis and yet they successfully identified strong brain-behavior correlations for two distinct cognitive domains, despite having to deal with large numbers of uninformative voxels [Rajeev et al., 2010]. This method of analysis across the whole brain at once might be particularly useful when analyzing developmental data where brains change across time or for analyzing data from atypically developing brains where cerebral volumes/boundaries may differ substantially from the typical case.

Selection bias is not, of course, the only problem facing the field. Another revolves around the comparison of child and adult data if the two age groups are not performing at a similar level of accuracy and/or reaction time [see discussion in Church et al., 2010]. A further problem lies in the different limitations of each of the imaging methods themselves. Non-invasive neuroimaging techniques suitable for children come in two forms: they either detect direct changes in the electrophysiological activity in the brain, such as electroencephalography (EEG) and event related potentials (ERP), or they detect the resultant hemodynamic changes in cerebral blood flow, such as functional magnetic resonance imaging (fMRI) and functional near infrared spectroscopy (fNIRS). Direct measures capture the millisecond temporal details of brain activity, whereas indirect methods are far more accurate in terms of spatial location. In adults, but not in children because the method is invasive, transcranial magnetic stimulation (TMS) can directly target a hypothesized brain region and then be used to support causal rather than merely correlational arguments [Cohen-Kadosh et al., 2007; Mevorach et al., 2010; see also, discussion in Galván, 2010].

Curiously, when one speaks of "brain imaging," it is often taken for granted that this only refers to MRI or fMRI and, with a few exceptions, magnetic resonance imaging is the focus of most of the articles in this Special Issue. Yet, fMRI is just one among several functional imaging methods available to developmental neuroscientists, and by no means the most child-friendly one. For example, much less space was given in the articles here to the huge body of developmental neuroimaging research using ERPs, and no mention was made at all of the very promising optical imaging method, fNIRS, whose design has been rapidly progressing for use with infants over the past decade. Moreover, only the Poldrack article (2010) highlighted the importance of computational modeling for understanding the neurobiology of developmental change, yet such models are critical for testing hypotheses and generating new predictions [Elman et al., 1996].

Let's briefly look at some of the advantages and limitations of each of the imaging methods in turn, without of course claiming to be exhaustive, since many of the articles in this Special Issue already focus in detail on the methodological problems facing developmental neuroimaging. Of course, of concern to all methods is the fact that rapid brain growth as well as changes in head shape/size during early ontogeny must be taken account of in any analyses that span developmental time.

fMRI

Advantages

One of the major advantages of fMRI, be it for developmental or adult neuroimaging, is its very fine spatial resolution. Another is that MRI—specifically diffusion MRI (DTI)—allows the scientist to measure developmental changes in gray and white matter, as discussed in several articles in this Special Issue [Paus, 2010; Konrad and Eickhoff, 2010; Blakemore et al., 2010]. This is important because the two primary types of data available from DTI studies—water apparent diffusion coefficient and diffusion anisotropy measures—reveal significant developmental changes over time. Animal models demonstrate how DTI can discretely delineate the microstructure of white matter and gray matter in embryonic and early postnatal mouse brains [Zhang et al., 2006], highlighting the developmental potential of the approach.

Limitations

The complex issues concerning the possible effects of developmental differences in vascular physiology and of interpreting negative BOLD signal change are thoroughly addressed by Church et al. (2010). One practical limitation of fMRI for use with infants and children is that participants need to remain very still during fMRI data acquisition, without which movement artefacts render the data unusable. For this reason, when researchers opt for fMRI as their method of choice, they have either focused on very young infants who cannot yet move or they sedate them to prevent them from moving, or the focus has been solely on older children. In sedated participants, other than bright flashes of light that tell us little about visual cognition, the tendency has been to test auditory discriminations which the brain processes during sleep. Furthermore, because of the slow data acquisition (several seconds, compared to milliseconds in ERP and fNIRS), the fMRI signal cannot distinguish anticipatory processing from stimulus-generated activity. This can be a problem when assessing, for instance, the extent to which there is a developmental shift from data-driven to top–down neural processing. Moreover, when comparing changing brain processes across age or when comparing atypical brains to typically developing ones, the BOLD signal cannot distinguish between moderate activation of a greater number of neurons versus increased activation within the same neurons. Such differences could be relevant to human developmental change, with animal models providing illumination on this question [Bandettini and Ungerleider, 2001; Logothetis et al., 2001].

fNIRS

Advantages

One of the major advantages of fNIRS systems over, say, fMRI, is that they are inexpensive and portable. They can also tolerate a degree of movement, which is critical when testing awake infants sitting upright on their parent's lap. Also, fNIRS is even more suitable for infants than for older children and adults because the optical geometry of the infant head renders biological tissue more transparent to light in the near infrared part of the spectrum (particularly in those with no hair!). Moreover, fNIRS can acquire data at a rapid temporal rate [Huppert et al., 2006, 2008], overcoming some of the intrinsic limitations of fMRI mentioned above. fNIRS surpasses EEG in providing a better spatial resolution, thereby allowing more accurate localization of brain responses to specific cortical regions [for an excellent review of fNIRS over the past decade, see Lloyd-Fox et al., 2010]. fNIRS has been used to measure infant brain activity across a wide array of cognitive domains such as object processing [Wilcox et al., 2005], social communication [Grossmann et al., 2008], biological motion processing [Lloyd-Fox et al., 2009], action observation [Ahimada and Hiraki, 2006], and face processing [Blasi et al., 2007]. Another advantage is that fNIRS can distinguish between anticipatory and reactive neural processes.

Limitations

Although fNIRS produces better spatial resolution than EEG and better temporal resolution than fMRI, its temporal resolution is lower than EEG and its spatial resolution not as good as fMRI. Currently, fNIRS sits between the advantages and limitations of the two methods, but that also constitutes its major advantage. Unlike MRI, NIRS does not lend itself to the measurement of brain structure [Minagawa-Kawai et al., 2007, 2009], so debates continue as to how to locate the origin of the hemodynamic response from the scalp measurements, whether there is in fact an infant-specific pattern of hemodynamic response, and how precisely to interpret that response [Aslin and Mehler, 2005; Meek, 2002]. Finally, the headgear is still very heavy compared to the ultra-light HD-ERP net, although work on improving the fNIRS methodology is actively underway [Everdekk et al., 2005; Lloyd-Fox et al., 2010].

ERP

Advantages

ERP provides an excellent recording of the temporal processes of neural activity. Initially, it was limited by the small number of sources on the original caps for children, but with the advent of the Geodesic net enabling high density ERPs (HD-ERP), the infant scalp is now fitted with 128 channels, thereby becoming one of the methods of choice for infant and child brain imaging. As with fNIRS, the method circumvents any fear of scanners in children. Indeed, the child can sit upright, alone, or on the parent's lap. Unlike fMRI, HD-ERP can be used to distinguish predictive responses from data-driven responses showing, for instance, how 9-month-old infants exhibit sub-threshold motor activity, i.e., sensorimotor alpha band suppression, while they observe the actions of others, that matches directly the neural signal occurring during their own actions [Southgate et al., 2009]. This points to the existence of a form of mirror neurons in the infant brain.

Limitations

Although HD-ERP yields relatively good scalp maps, it obviously does not provide as good spatial location data as fMRI or fNIRS, so source reconstruction continues to pose a problem, particularly when the cognitive processes are complex and depend on large networks. Movement artefacts can also be more of an issue for ERP than fNIRS when acquiring child data.

The need for a multimethod converging approach

This very brief overview of the advantages and limitations of various direct and indirect methods of measuring brain activity makes it clear that no method alone will provide a full account of the developing brain. What is needed is simultaneous data acquisition using different methods which would lead to complementary, converging data about changes in the time course, the spatial location and connectivity of neural activity [Casey et al., this issue; see also Huppert et al., 2008; Steinbrink et al., 2006, for a multimodality approach with adults]. In infants, Grossmann and collaborators (2008) have used more than one method for the study of social perception of eye gaze, measuring fNIRS and EEG oscillatory signals in each of two different groups of infants. A small number of infants was tested with both systems, but this involved sequential rather than simultaneous multimodal acquisition of data, which must be a goal for future research.

Child neuroimaging versus developmental neuroimaging

I often start lectures with the provocative statement: Studying infants and children has little or nothing to do with development! This can hold for behavioral and genetic studies, and to a great extent also holds for brain imaging studies although, as mentioned, there are clear exceptions in the articles in this Special Issue [see also Casey and Durston, 2006, for discussion]. Neuroimaging of the developing brain involves a theoretical attitude of mind, a truly developmental framework, and a focus on progressive change [Karmiloff-Smith, 1992, 1998]. Comparing the adult brain with that of a single, specific age group of children is not a developmental study; at best it constitutes a pilot study for a truly developmental approach to gradual change over time. Say, for a given cognitive function, the child brain activates region or network X, and the adult brain region or network Y. This indeed demonstrates that child and adult brains process stimuli differently, but it tells us nothing about the developing brain, i.e., the mechanisms underlying the developmental trajectory that brought the brain from X to Y. Although there are now a few studies which have compared children at more than one age to adults [Galván et al., 2006; Minagawa-Kawai et al., 2009; van Duijvenvoorde et al., 2008; Velanova et al., 2009, and articles in this Special Issue], the vast majority of albeit interesting work on the infant and child brain tend to focus on a single age group like 9-month-old or 5-year-old, or on the comparison of one age group of children with adults. Rare are those who ask truly developmental questions about how neural networks gradually change over time. Moreover, as Poldrack (2010) points out, there remains a substantial gulf between the wealth of neurobiological knowledge about early infant brain development, on the one hand, and the changes being examined in most neuroimaging studies in children over 5 years of age, on the other.

Many developmental questions remain to be fully addressed. Do the boundaries between regions change developmentally? If they do, then it is questionable to generalize adult Regions of Interest to the child brain. For a given cognitive function, are the same intra- and inter-regional networks active? This is unlikely, given the lengthy time required for white matter tract development [Poldrack, 2010], together with significant differences in the ratio of gray to white matter in child and adult brains, as well as changes in plasticity over time [Huttenlocher, 2002; see discussion by Galván, 2010]. Is the only solution a (cost-intensive and labor-intensive) longitudinal study of the changing brain, as provided by the rich multisite, normative study of brain structure in children described in the article by Paus [2010; see also, Giedd et al., 1999]? Although longitudinal studies are not without problems [see discussion in Shaw et al., 2010], this is indeed one data-rich source for studying the developing brain over time, but by no means the only one. First, detailed developmental trajectories have been built cross-sectionally at the cognitive level [Karmiloff-Smith et al., 2004; Thomas et al., 2009] which can then be verified on much smaller groups longitudinally, and there is no reason why the cross-sectional trajectory approach cannot be applied to developmental neuroimaging. Second, training studies over short periods can be very informative in adults and children [see discussion in Galván, 2010]. A cleverly designed developmental study of cerebral change over a mere 2 days of training might tell us more about changes in adult and child brains across age than two single groups separated by many years of age but each measured only once. Adult number training studies in numerical problems and their neural consequences are already underway [Ansari, 2008], and should be extended more often to development over time. Developmental approaches also lead to bidirectional questions: Instead of automatically concluding that, say, reduced parietal volume is the cause of numerical impairments, one can ask whether atypical processing over developmental time in neurons in parietal or different cortical areas caused a progressive reduction in parietal volume. Only a developmental approach can answer such questions.

Examples of neural changes across development

Typical fine tuning of brain functional organization is an activity-dependent process [Kandel et al., 2000]. According to Huttenlocher [2002], plasticity changes over developmental time, with some mechanisms available throughout the lifetime (increase in synaptic strength, decrease in local inhibition, dendritric sprouting, formation of new synapses, formation of new neurons), whereas others are only available to the early developing brain (use of unspecified labile synapses including silent synapses, competition for synaptic sites, persistence of normally transient connections, myelination). Changes in plasticity turn out to be region specific, suggesting [Thomas, 2003] that there is no such general thing as "the brain's plasticity." Many structures (e.g., dendrites, axons, and synapses) initially undergo exuberant growth followed by a period of pruning in which the processing of environmental input gradually sculpts the resulting brain structure.

Neural processing tends initially to be diffuse across several regions in both hemispheres, but with developmental time and the continuous processing of inputs, brain activity becomes increasingly restricted to more specific networks [Brown et al., 2008; Durston et al., 2006 and the discussion by Poldrack, 2010, on the problem of the neurobiological plausibility of the gradual focalization hypothesis made on the basis of neuroimaging data]. If there is a gradual process of modularization over developmental time [Karmiloff-Smith, 1992], as opposed to the notion of built-in modules, then this is likely to improve processing efficiency. A recent study by Minagawa-Kawai and colleagues [2007] examined language-specific phonemic contrasts in infants from 3 months to 28 months and found differing age-specific onset of varying regions of the cortex. Another study suggests that comprehension of single words moves from bilateral processing between 13 and 17 months to left lateralized processing at 20 months [Mills et al., 1997]. Like vocabulary development, processing of human faces starts out with bilateral activity, with the brain displaying similar signatures for other stimuli like monkey faces [de Haan et al., 2002; Pascalis et al., 2001]. By the end of the first year, however, the brain becomes increasing fine-tuned for processing human faces, with other stimuli displaying different neural signatures, as well as increasing localization for human faces to specific networks in the right hemisphere [de Haan et al., 2002; Peelen et al., 2009]. We need to know more about how hemispheric differences influence developmental neural change. In adults, the RH seems to be involved in more parallel, coarse-grained, integrative processing, and the LH in more serial, fine-grained, predictive processing. How does this develop in children? Is information passage through corpus callosum always faster from RH to LH than from LH to RH, or does this alter over developmental time? Certainly, the thickness of the corpus callosum fibers changes developmentally over a lengthy period of time between infancy and adolescence [Keshavan et al., 2003]. Finally, short-range gray matter connectivity is greater in children, while white long-range connectivity develops considerably more slowly over time [Huttenlocher, 2002]. All of these and other developmental changes must be taken into account when analyzing neuroimaging data over time. And, as shown in several articles in this Special Issue [Luna et al., 2010, Blakemore et al., 2010; Shaw et al., 2010; see also, Crone et al., 2008], neural development doesn't end in childhood; puberty and adolescence witness many significant changes, which raises the important question of whether neural changes in learning and development are the same [Galván, 2010]. Moreover, rather than focusing on chronological age in studies of adolescents, onset of puberty might be a more sensitive way of understanding interactions between hormonal and gray matter development, gender differences, as well as the general structural reorganization of the adolescent brain [Blakemore et al., 2010].

Importance of resting state functional connectivity

In adult neuroscience, there has been renewed interest in resting state fMRI (R-fMRI), focusing on a default circuit comprising a large network of brain regions, associated with task-irrelevant mental processes: precuneus/posterior cingulate cortex, medial prefrontal cortex and medial, lateral, and inferior parietal cortex. Studies point to a high degree of functional connectivity during rest, i.e., inter-regional temporal synchrony [Raichle et al., 2001; see also discussions in Luna et al., 2010; Konrad and Eickhoff, 2010]. As self-organizing processes are a necessary part of the explanation of how the brain changes over developmental time, it is critical to understand whether and how the default mode network changes developmentally [Konrad and Eickhoff, 2010].

Spontaneous brain activity during sleep, for instance, plays a critical role in the consolidation of memory across the lifespan, involving redistribution of memory representations from temporary hippocampal storage to neocortical long-term storage sites. The dialog between neocortex and hippocampus generates sharp-wave ripples and is orchestrated by the <1 Hz EEG slow oscillation during slow wave sleep. Unlike adults whose sleep patterns involve cycles of slow wave sleep to REM sleep, young infants fall directly into REM sleep, with the proportion of slow wave sleep increasing only slowly over developmental time [Hill et al., 2007]. How this affects the neural processes involved in sleep-related consolidation of learning in children remains to be fully elucidated.

The importance of developmental changes in resting state brain activity will, I believe, become very prominent in the next few years. Many years ago [Karmiloff-Smith, 1992] I put forward a cognitive-level developmental hypothesis—the Representational Redescription Hypothesis—postulating that what is specifically human to human intelligence is a process by which task-specific representations stored in the brain become, via an internally generated process of representational redescription, domain-general knowledge to the brain. This internal self-organizing process, I argued, is generated by behavioral mastery, not by negative feedback, and allows knowledge relevant to one domain to become transportable to other domains without the need to process new external input. With the current advances in brain imaging, it should be possible to assess the hypothesis by detecting specific networks in cerebral resting state underlying representational redescription.

Futuristic? An idealized world for developmental brain imaging

Let us end on some speculations as to where the field might go. Clearly multiple converging methods on the same individuals will be paramount in providing increasingly detailed accounts of spatio-temporal neural network changes over developmental time. Subtle individual differences in brain development will, in my view, take centre stage, instead of being considered noise to be controlled for in large group studies [see discussion in Paus, 2010, on the emergence of population neuroscience as a field at the intersection of cognitive neuroscience, genetics, and epidemiology]. A combination of in-depth longitudinal case studies with cross-sectional brain trajectory approaches is critical, combined with a deeper understanding of acceleration and deceleration of developmental trajectories of brain development [Shaw et al., 2010]. More focus is required on differences in regional connectivity rather than identifying specific regions, and this may be particularly important when examining atypical development [Konrad and Eickhoff, 2010]. And, as neuroscience and genetics become increasingly sophisticated, we will need to examine how polymorphisms and their downstream effects at the genetic level [including the surprising amount of allele-specific methylation, Schalkwyk et al., 2010] might relate to subtle differences in brain structure or function, as well as elucidating more in-depth phenotypics and refining our approach to environmental influences [Paus, 2010]. Gene expression will need to be viewed as dynamic, rather than static, in different environmental and developmental contexts [Casey et al. and Paus, 2010]. And animal models must compare similar task demands at the cognitive level when examining the phenotypic effects of identical cross-species genes [Karmiloff-Smith, 2009].

The use of simple tasks, with children lying flat in a scanner, may no longer suffice. Studies will need to get out of the scanner and into the real world, using neuroimaging methods that allow the child to move naturally around the environment, thereby capturing every change in attention [see discussion in Paus, 2010]. After all, each time the child brain takes a step forward, the environment dynamically changes too. Perhaps in the not too distant future, we will witness the invention of a pushchair with two built-in imaging devices (one superior spatially, the other temporally), together with a portable eye tracker, to measure subtle changes in both brain activity and attention. And later, as the child becomes mobile, the neuroimaging devices and eye tracker could be inserted into a T-shirt or cap. This is not so far-fetched when one recalls just how recently neuroimaging technologies have been introduced into the lab. If we are really to understand progressive changes in the human brain, we have to take a multilevel dynamic approach to epigenetics, brain structure/function, network connectivity, cognition, behavior, and the environment, in which the notion "developing" really counts.

References

Annaz D, Karmiloff-Smith A (2005): Cross-syndrome, cross-domain comparisons of development trajectories. Curr Psychol Cogn 23:44–48.

Ansari D (2008): Effects of development and enculturation on number representation in the brain. Nat Rev Neurosci 9:278–291.

Aslin R, Mehler J (2005): Near-infrared spectroscopy for functional studies of brain activity in human infants: Promises, prospects and challenges. J Biomed Opt 10:1–3.

Bandettini PA, Ungerleider LG (2001): From neuron to BOLD: New connections. Nat Neurosci 4:864–867.

Blakemore SJ, Burnett S, Dahl RE (2010): The role of puberty in the developing adolescent brain. Hum Brain Mapp 31:926–933.

Blasi A, Fox S, Everdell N, Voelin A, Tucker L, Csibra G, Gibson A, Hebden JC, Johnson MH, Elwell CE (2007): Investigation of depth-dependent changes in cerebral hemodynamics during face perception in infants. Phys Med Biol 52:6849–6864.

Brown TT, Petersen SE, Schlaggar BL (2006): Does human functional brain organization shift from diffuse to focal with development? Dev Sci 9:9–11.

Casey BJ, Durston S (2006): From behavior to cognition to the brain and back: What have we learned from functional imaging studies of ADHD? Am J Psychiatry 163:957–960.

Casey BJ, Soliman F, Bath KG, Glatt CE (2010): Imaging genetics and development: challenges and promises. Hum Brain Mapp 31:838–851.

Church JA, Petersen SE, Schlaggar BL (2010): The "Task B problem" and other considerations in developmental functional neuroimaging. Hum Brain Mapp 31:852–862.

Cohen-Kadosh R, Cohen-Kadosh K, Schuhmann T, Kaas A, Goebel R, Henik A, Sack AT (2007): Virtual dyscalculia induced by parietal-lobe TMS impairs automatic magnitude processing. Curr Biol 17:689–693.

Crone EAM, Bullens L, Plas EAA, van der Kijkuit EJ, Zelazo PD (2008): Developmental changes and individual differences in risk and perspective taking in adolescence. Dev Psychopathol 20:1213–1229.

Csibra G, Henty J, Voelin A, Elwell C, Tucker L, Meek J, Johnson MH (2004): Near infrared spectroscopy reveals neural activation during face perception in infants and adults. J Pediatr Neurol 2:85–89.

Csibra G, Tucker L, Johnson MH (2001): Differential frontal cortex activation before anticipatory and reactive saccades in infants. Infancy 2:159–174.

Durston S, Davidson MC, Tottenham N, Galván A, Spicer J, Fosella JA, Casey BJ (2006): A shift from diffuse to focal cortical activity with development. Dev Sci 9:1–8.

Elman JL, Bates E, Johnson MH, Karmiloff-Smith A, Parisi D, Plunkett K (1996): Rethinking Innateness: A Connectionist Perspective on Development. Cambridge, MA: MIT Press.

Everdell NL, Gibson AP, Tullis IDC, Vaithianathan T, Hebden JC, Delpy DT (2005): A frequency multiplexed near-infrared topography system for imaging functional activation in the brain. Tev Sci Instrum 76:093705.

Galván A (2010): Neural plasticity of development and learning. Hum Brain Mapp 31: 879–890.

Galván A, Hare TA, Parra CE, Penn J, Voss H, Glover G, Casey BJ (2006): Earlier development of the accumbens relative to orbitofrontal cortex might underlie risk-taking behavior in adolescents. J Neurosci 26:6885–6892.

Giedd JN, Blumenthal J, Jeffries NO, Castellanos FX, Liu H, Zijdenbos A, Paus T, Evans AC, Rapoport JL (1999): Brain development during childhood and adolescence: A longitudinal MRI study. Nat Neurosci 2:861–863.

Grice S, Spratling MW, Karmiloff-Smith A, Halit H, Csibra G, de Haan M, Johnson MH (2001): Disordered visual processing and oscillatory brain activity in autism and Williams Syndrome. NeuroReport 12:2697–2700.

Grossmann T, Johnson MJ, Lloyd-Fox S, Blasi A, Deligianni F, Elwell C, Csibra G (2008): Early cortical specialization for face-to-face communication in human infants. Proc R Soc B 275: 2803–2811.

Hill CM, Hogan AM, Karmiloff-Smith A (2007): To sleep, perchance to enrich learning? Arch Dis Childhood 92:637–342.

Huppert TJ, Diamond SG, Boas DA (2008): Direct estimation of evoked hemoglobin changes by multimodality fusion imaging. J Biomed Opt 13:054031.

Huppert TJ, Hoge RD, Diamond SG, Franceschini MA, Boas DA (2006): A temporal comparison of BOLD, ASl and NIRS hemo-dynamic responses to motor stimuli in adult humans. Neuro-Image 29:368–382.

Huttenlocher PR (2002): Neural Plasticity: The Effects of the Environment on the Development of the Cerebral Cortex. Cambridge, MA: Harvard University Press.

Johnson MH (2001): Functional brain development in humans. Nat Rev Neurosci 2:475–483.

Kan KJ, Ploeger A, Raijmakers MEJ, Dolan CV, van der Maas HLJ (2009): Nonlinear epigenetic variance: review and simulations. Dev Sci 13:11–27.

Kandel ER, Jessell TM, Sanes JR (2000): Sensory experience and the fine tuning of synaptic connections. In: Kanel ER, Schwarz JH, Jessell TM, editors. Principles of Neural Science, 4th ed. New York: Elsevier.

Karmiloff-Smith A (1992): Beyond Modularity: A Developmental Perspective on Cognitive Science. Cambridge, MA: MIT Press/Bradford Books.

Karmiloff-Smith A (2009): Nativism vs neuroconstructivism: Rethinking developmental disorders. Special issue on the interplay of biology and environment. Dev Psychol 45:56–63.

Karmiloff-Smith A, Thomas M, Annaz D, Humphreys K, Ewing S, Brace N, van Duuren M, Pike G, Grice S, Campbell R (2004): Exploring the Williams syndrome face processing debate: The importance of building developmental trajectories. J Child Psychol Psychiatr 45:1258–1274.

Keshavan MS, Diwadkar DeBellis M, Dick E, Kotwal R, Rosenberg DR, Sweeney JA, Minshew N, Pettegrew JW (2002): Development of the corpus callosum in childhood, adolescence and early adulthood. Life Sci 70:1909–1922.

Kolb B, Gibb R (2001): Early brain injury, plasticity and behavior. In: Nelson CA, Luciana M, editors. Handbook of Developmental Cognitive Neuroscience. Cambridge, MA: MIT Press. pp 175–190.

Konrad K, Eickhoff SB (2010): Is the ADHD brain wired differently? A review on structural and functional connectivity in attention deficit hyperactivity disorder. Hum Brain Mapp 31:904–916.

Langenecker SA, Briceno EM, Hamid NM, Nielson KA (2007): Contributions of functional and volumetric MRI to understanding response control. Brain Res 1135:58–68.

Leppert IR, Almli CR, McKinstry RC, Mulkern RV, Perpaoli C, Rivkin MJ, Pike GB, The Brain Development Cooperative Group (2009): T2 relaxometry of normal pediatric brain development. J Magn Reson Imag 29:258–267.

Lloyd-Fox S, Blasi A, Elwell CE (2010): Illuminating the developing brain: The past, present and future of functional near infrared spectroscopy. Neurosci Biobehav Rev 34:269–284.

Lloyd-Fox S, Blasi A, Volein A, Everdell N, Elwell CE, Johnson MH (2009): Social perception in infancy: A near infrared spectroscopy study. Child Dev 80:986–999.

Logothetis NK, Pauls J, Augath M, Trinath T, Oeltermann A (2001): Neurphysiological investigation of the basis of the fMRI signal. Nature 412:150–157.

Luna B, Velanova K, Geier CF (2010): Methodological approaches in developmental neuroimaging studies. Hum Brain Mapp 31:863–871.

Meaney MJ, Fish EW, Shahrokh D, Bagot R, Caldji C, Bredy T, Szyf M (2004): Epigenetic programming of stress response through variations in maternal care. Acad Sci 1267–1180.

Meek J (2002): Basic principles of optical imaging and application to the study of infant development. Dev Sci 5:371–380.

Mevorach C, Hodsoll J, Allen H, Shalev L, Humphreys G (2010): Ignoring the Elephant in the Room: A Neural Circuit to Downregulate Salience. UK: University of Birmingham.

Mills DL, Coffy-Corins S, Neville H (1997): Language comprehension and cerebral specialization from 13 to 20 months. Dev Psychol 13:397–445.
Minagawa-Kawai Y, Mori K, Hebden JC, Dupoux E (2008): Optical imaging of infants' neurocognitive development. Dev Neurobiol 68:712–728.
Minagawa-Kawai Y, Mori K, Naoi N, Kojima S (2007): Neural attunement processes in infants during the acquisition of a language-specific phonemic contrast. J Neurosci 27:315–321.
Pascalis O, Demont E, de Haan M, Campbell R (2001): Recognition of faces of different species: A developmental study between 5 and 8 years of age. Infant Child Dev 10:39–45.
Paus T (2010): Population neuroscience: why and how. Hum Brain Mapp 31:891–903.
Peelen MV, Glaser B, Vuilleumier P, Eliez S (2009): Differential development of selectivity for faces and bodies in the fusiform gyrus. Dev Sci 12:16–25.
Poldrack RA (2010): Interpreting developmental changes in neuroimaging signals. Hum Brain Mapp 31:872–878.
Posner MI, Rothbart MK (2005): Influencing brain networks: Implications for education. Trends Cogn Sci 9:99–103.
Raizada RDS, Tsao FM, Lui HM, Holloway ID, Ansari D, Kuhl P (2010): Linking brain-wide multivoxel activation patterns to behavior: Examples from language and math. NeuroImage 51:462–471.
Rivera-Gaxiola M, Csibra G, Johnson MH, Karmiloff-Smith A (2000): Electrophysiological correlates of cross-linguistic speech perception in native English speakers. Behav Brain Res 111:13–23.
Schalkwyk LC, Meaburn EL, Smith R, Dempster EL, Jeffries AR, Davies MN, Plomin R, Mill J (2010): Allelic skewing of DNA methylation is widespread across the genome. Am J Hum Genet 86:196–212.
Shaw P, Gogtay N, Rapoport J (2010): Childhood psychiatric disorders as anomalies in neurodevelopmental trajectories. Hum Brain Mapp 31:917–925.
Southgate V, Johnson MH, Osborne T, Csibra G (2009): Predictive motor activation during action observation in human infants. Biol Lett 5:769–772.
Thomas MSC (2003): Review article: Limits on plasticity. J Cogn Dev 4:95–121.
Thomas MSC, Annaz D, Ansari D, Serif G, Jarrold C, Karmiloff- Smith A (2009): The use of developmental trajectories in studying developmental disorders. J Speech Lang Hear Res 52:336–358.
Tyler LK, Shafto MA, Randall B, Wright P, Marslen-Wilson WD, Stamatakis EA (2009): Preserving syntactic processing across the adult life span: The modulation of the fronto-temporal language system in the context of age-related atrophy. Cereb Cortex 20:352–364.
van Duijvenvoorde AC, Zanolie K, Rombouts SA, Raijmakers ME, Crone EA (2008): Evaluating the negative or valuing the positive? Neural mechanisms supporting feedback-based learning across development. J Neurosci 28:9495–9503.
Velonova K, Wheeler ME, Luna B (2009): The maturation of task set-related activation supports late developmental improvements in inhibitory control. J Neurosci 29:12558–12567.
Zhang J, Richards LJ, Miller MI, Yarowsky P, van Zijl P, Mori S (2006): Characterization of mouse brain and its development using diffusion tensor imaging and computational techniques. Conf Proc IEEE Eng Med Biol Soc 1:2252–2255.

Pulvermüller [illegible] [illegible] 2

[illegible] (2[illegible]) [illegible]

Raizada [illegible] [illegible] [illegible]

Part V

Taking the environment seriously

11 Genetic and environmental vulnerabilities in children with neurodevelopmental disorders

Annette Karmiloff-Smith, Dean D'Souza, Tessa M. Dekker, Jo Van Herwegen, Fei Xu, Maja Rodic, and Daniel Ansari

This paper examines some of the key differences between two interpretations of genetic and environmental vulnerabilities in children: one interpretation inspired by static adult neuropsychological models and the other interpretation inspired by dynamic developmental accounts. This paper presents a rather unusual blend of theoretical and empirical issues, a blend that we deem critical to make our case. In the first section, we contrast the ways in which the static and dynamic paradigms have addressed research on neurodevelopmental disorders and show why a developmental account is crucial to understanding the dynamics of change. The next two sections use concrete examples to illustrate a dynamic developmental approach to the cognitive and social domains. One section focuses on a cognitive domain—infant sensitivity to numerical displays—in two neurogenetic syndromes and illustrates how the adult and developmental paradigms yield very different interpretations of exactly the same data. The other section takes a similar approach by examining examples from the social domain—the effects of differences in parent–child interaction. Throughout the paper, we argue that the adult neuropsychological model should no longer be applied to genetic and environmental vulnerabilities that dynamically change over developmental time.

Static vs. dynamic approaches to neurodevelopmental disorders

Research on neurodevelopmental disorders has often been inspired by models of adult neuropsychological patients (1, 2), which is illustrated by the following quotation: "Williams syndrome can be explained in terms of selective deficits to an otherwise normal modular system" (ref. 2, p. 347). By contrast, we have consistently stressed the dynamic nature of neural and cognitive development over time:

> [B]rain volume, brain anatomy, brain chemistry, hemispheric asymmetry, and the temporal patterns of brain activity are all atypical in people with Williams syndrome. How could the resulting system be described as a normal brain with parts intact and parts impaired, as the popular view holds? Rather, the brains of infants with WS develop differently from the outset, with subtle, widespread repercussions.
>
> (ref. 3, p. 393)

We termed this latter approach neuroconstructivism (3–6), recognizing that the infant brain is not only less differentiated and less modular than the adult brain but that, early on, it is highly interconnected. Only through experience and pruning do brain circuits gradually become increasingly specialized and localized (i.e., relatively modularized) over the course of development (3, 7–9). Environmental factors play a key role in ontogenesis (10), affecting both gene expression and progressive neural specialization. In sum, the application of the static adult neuropsychological model to developmental disorders ignores the ontogenetic history of the organism, and the roots of development are often critical for understanding the dynamic trajectory that leads to the socio-cognitive end state (11).

With this distinction between static and dynamic paradigms to development in mind, we present cross-syndrome comparisons of infant cognitive data, which lend themselves to two very different interpretations. We then go on to extend similar reasoning to the social domain.

Two interpretations of infant sensitivity to number in neurodevelopmental disorders

Studies of adult neuropsychological patients have yielded a double dissociation between numerical abilities that affects different intraparietal circuits—one circuit for computing exact number and the other circuit for computing approximate numerical quantities (1, 12, 13). Research on typically developing (TD) infants reveals two similar systems that develop at different rates (14–18). Small exact number discrimination involves the computation of precise differences between one, two, three, or four items. Large approximate number discrimination is the ability to judge whether two quantities (e.g., 8 vs. 16 items) are different without being able to count them; this ability relies on magnitude judgments. Whether these two systems are innately specified or emerge as the product of gradual brain specialization remains a topic of considerable debate (19–21).

Here, we discuss findings (details in *SI Text*: http://www.pnas.org/content/pnas/suppl/2012/10/05/1121087109.DCSupplemental/pnas.201121087SI.pdf) from a study of large approximate number discrimination and small exact number discrimination in infants with Down syndrome (DS) and compare them with our previous work on infants with Williams syndrome (WS) (20, 21). We set the stage by first summarizing earlier findings from which we generated a prediction. Our initial cross-syndrome design had examined only small exact number discrimination in infants with WS and DS as well as two groups of TD controls matched on either chronological age or mental age. That study revealed that, like TD controls, infants with WS succeeded in discriminating changes in small exact number, whereas those infants with DS failed (21). We contrasted this finding with the serious numerical deficits that emerge in later WS development (22–24) as well as a cross-syndrome study showing that, although both syndromes are impaired relative to TD controls, older children/adults with DS significantly outstrip those individuals with WS on a battery of mathematical tasks (24). This finding would suggest that successful small exact number discrimination in infancy does not predict subsequent mathematical outcome.

At that juncture, data on large approximate number discrimination in TD infants were emerging. It turned out that TD infants can discriminate not only small numbers (one, two, and three) as early as 3 mo but subsequently, large approximate quantities; at 6 mo, they differentiate 8 dots from 16 dots (i.e., a ratio of 1:2), and by 9–10 mo, they distinguish 8 dots from 12 dots (i.e., a ratio of 2:3) (25, 26). Because infants with WS performed like TD controls on small number but had serious problems with subsequent mathematics, we hypothesized that their deficits might originate in early problems with large approximate quantity discrimination. With a new group of infants/toddlers with WS, we showed this hypothesis indeed to be the case (20). Just like the WS infant group in the earlier study, the new WS infants succeeded in discriminating small numbers. However, they showed significantly weaker discrimination of large approximate quantities (20), even with the easy 1:2 ratio and despite being significantly older than the age at which TD infants succeed.

A cross-syndrome comparison was, however, critical to a hypothesis (i.e., that large approximate number discrimination in infancy might be more predictive of subsequent mathematical abilities than small number discrimination). We, therefore, individually matched a new group of infants/toddlers (Table S1 in *SI Text*) with DS to our previous infants/toddlers with WS (20), and we tested them on the same two tasks measuring small (2 dots vs. 3 dots) and large (8 dots vs. 16 dots) number discrimination (Figs. S1 and S2 in *SI Text*). We predicted that infants/toddlers with DS would yield the opposite pattern as the infants/toddlers with WS.

Our results yielded a double dissociation between small exact number and large approximate number in infancy in the two neurogenetic syndromes. We replicated our previous findings that infants/toddlers with DS have serious difficulties discriminating small exact numbers, but this time, we used a different group of DS children of a similar age range, indicating that the current DS group is a representative sample. Most interesting was our demonstration that, unlike those children with WS (20), infants/toddlers with DS, who failed small number discrimination, succeeded in discriminating differences in large approximate quantities (*SI Text* and Fig. S3). We argue that the DS infant ability with large approximate quantities contributes to an explanation of why older children with DS subsequently go on to have better, albeit not normal, numerical abilities than their chronological age- or mental age-matched WS counterparts (24).

One might object that the DS findings can be explained by the fact that the small number task (2 dots vs. 3 dots) involved the harder 2:3 ratio, whereas the large number task (8 dots vs. 16 dots) used the easier 1:2 ratio. Two reasons discount such an explanation. First, the WS infancy data yield the opposite pattern, and therefore, one of the tasks cannot be intrinsically more difficult than the other. Second, the TD literature has clearly shown that small exact number discrimination is not subject to ratio constraints, whereas large approximate number discrimination is subject to such constraints (14, 17, 25, 26).

At first blush, our findings yield a double dissociation between two neurogenetic syndromes, typical of findings in the adult neuropsychological literature, that points to two separable numerical subsystems, which some might claim to be innately specified as either intact or impaired. Everything seems clear: for WS, one or more of the 28 genes deleted on one copy of chromosome 7q11.23 contributes to a domain-specific deficit in large approximate number discrimination, while leaving intact the small number system, and for DS, one or more of the extra genes on chromosome 21 contributes to a domain-specific deficit in small exact number discrimination, while sparing the large number system.

However, concepts like double dissociation, intact, and sparing are borrowed from the adult neuropsychological literature. Are they appropriate for developmental syndromes (3, 4, 27)? Do numerical systems start out prespecified in the infant brain, already dissociated into separate subsystems, or do these subsystems emerge over time through early cross-domain interactions as different brain circuits progressively specialized for different numerical functions (3, 4, 19)?

To address these questions, it is critical to examine which other aspects of development interact with infant sensitivity to numerical displays. In adopting this more dynamic developmental perspective (5–7, 28, 29), we related our DS numerical findings to earlier data on infant/toddler attention and saccadic eye movement planning in the two syndromes (30). The attention studies identified deficits in both syndromes—problems with attention shifting in WS and problems with sustained attention in DS. The eye movement research revealed that infants/toddlers with DS had similar patterns to TD infants (i.e., efficient saccadic eye movement planning), whereas those infants/toddlers with WS displayed severe deficits (30). We, thus, hypothesized that infants/toddlers with WS might be impaired with respect to their scanning of large numerical displays. To further explore this hypothesis, after the experiment, we used the Tobii Infrared 1750 Eye Tracker (31) and were able to subsequently collect data from some of the atypical infants while they were viewing numerical displays on the computer screen. Unfortunately, as can be the case when testing atypical infants, it was often difficult to calibrate their eye movements and thus, obtain sufficient data for statistical analysis. Nonetheless, an initial examination of scanning patterns of the few infants who did provide useful eye tracking data indicates that, like our studies of eye movement planning and attention (30), those children with DS tended to scan the overall array, whereas those children with WS tended to remain fixated on a few individual items (illustrations of WS and DS scanning patterns for large approximate number are in Fig. S4 in *SI Text*).

We, therefore, argue that the numerical deficits in WS may be rooted in basic level visuoattention problems that cascade over developmental time on other emerging cognitive level domains, such as number. For WS, a serious deficit in rapid saccade planning (30) causes problems in visually disengaging from individual objects in displays. This finding likely explains why WS infants/toddlers succeed at small exact number discrimination but have difficulty discriminating large approximate quantities. The opposite is true for infants with DS, because their problems lie in difficulties with sustained attention (32, 33), which makes it difficult for them to individuate objects in small displays. Thus, rather than identifying a double dissociation between the syndromes, a single basic level problem for each syndrome—attention shifting in WS and sustained attention in DS—contributes to the explanation of both the proficiencies and deficits in each syndrome concerning early sensitivities to differences in small and large numerical displays.

It is possible that an even more basic problem contributes to these differences, one which is again more domain-general and outside the domain of number. The work by Dakin et al. (34) reinterpreted numerosity processing in terms of the ratios between low and high spatial frequencies (LSF/HSF) in displays. Interestingly, individuals with WS have difficulty with LSF displays, and individuals with DS have problems with HSF displays (35, 36). Irrespective of whether the numerical problems are directly in the HSF and LSF demands on the visual system and/or related to differences in attention mechanisms, it is clear that the deficits and proficiencies of each syndrome (and perhaps, the different onset timing of small and large number discrimination in TD infants) do not entail an explanation solely in terms of domain-specific number abilities.

Clearly, these early cross-syndrome differences should not be interpreted in the adult neuropsychological terms of a double dissociation in numerical abilities, with small number impaired and large number spared in DS and vice versa in WS. Rather, the differences are likely to be traceable to basic level deficits or proficiencies in the visual and attention systems early in development, which have cascading effects on cognitive level outcomes over ontogenetic time.

Our studies highlight the need for syndrome-specific intervention. Importantly, training for number should not start out being domain-specific (i.e., focused on number per se). For WS, we suggest that training initially targets rapid visual saccade planning very early in the developmental trajectory, which could lead to an enhancement of their scanning abilities and encourage a focus on global quantities rather than only individual objects. For DS, by contrast, training in sustained attention might be more appropriate, leading to a focus on individual objects with better discrimination of small number displays. Our future research will coregister high-density event-related potentials (ERP) and eye tracking in older toddlers to ascertain whether such syndrome-specific training regimens impact on brain specialization over developmental time in these neurodevelopmental syndromes.

Our findings alert scientists to the limitations of some traditional developmental research focused on single age groups or single syndromes. They highlight the theoretical and applied importance of a neuroconstructivist approach [i.e., tracing cognitive level functions back to their basic level roots in infancy and then probing their ontogenetic progression (4, 6, 37), which elucidates how number abilities initially interact with other developing capacities, such as attention and visual scanning]. They also underline the critical role that cross-syndrome comparisons play in the planning of syndrome-specific intervention. Crucially, the cross-syndrome number study challenges the use of neuropsychological models of adult brain lesions for explanations of early proficiencies or deficits in neurodevelopmental syndromes.

Extending the neuroconstructivist approach to the social domain: need for in-depth studies of environments

This same neuroconstructivist, cross-syndrome approach can be extended to the social domain. Hitherto, experimental research into social impairments in, for example, autism spectrum disorders (ASDs), has often focused on older children and adults compared with TD controls (38, 39). However, the social deficits in ASD are likely to be rooted in early infancy (40, 41). We believe that a comparison between infants with WS and infants with ASD might constitute a fruitful avenue of research, despite the obvious syndromic differences. Genetically, the two syndromes are indeed different, with ASD likely to be caused by multiple genes of small effect and WS caused by a heterozygous deletion of some 28 contiguous genes on chromosome 7q11.23. Phenotypically, individuals with WS seem to have the opposite social profile of individuals with ASD (6, 38). Individuals with ASD are aloof and find looking at eyes and faces disconcerting, whereas individuals with WS are socially disinhibited and fascinated by eyes and faces. Individuals with ASD prefer to interact with objects, whereas individuals with WS actively seek engagement with people. Individuals with ASD fare better on spatial tasks compared with language and communication, whereas individuals with WS are more proficient at linguistic than spatial tasks. In sum, the two syndromes seem to present with very different sociocommunicative profiles in both childhood and adulthood (6, 38). However, if we assess their profiles during infant and toddler development, numerous cross-syndrome similarities emerge. Both syndromes have difficulty with rapid eye movement planning. Both have problems with attentional disengagement. Both display atypical eye gaze following and atypical referential pointing, and both are poor at triadic attention (6, 40, 41). From a neural perspective, both have atypical cortical maturation, corpus callosum abnormalities, impaired orbitofrontal cortex/amygdala connectivity, and dorsal and ventral stream vulnerabilities, with gray and white matter integrity being compromised in both (42). There are, of course, differences between the syndromes, particularly in later neuro- and sociocognitive outcomes, but tracing their increasingly diverging developmental outcomes back to their commonalities in infancy could reveal more subtle deficits than the more obvious comparison with TD controls. This is particularly true when start states are similar but sociocognitive end states are different.

A number of teams worldwide are carrying out longitudinal studies of infants within families in which an older sibling has already been diagnosed with ASD. The studies aim to uncover neural, cognitive, and behavioral markers of ASD not only in toddlerhood but in early infancy before the age at which the syndrome is normally diagnosed (40, 41). However, before a marker can be identified as autism-specific, cross-syndrome comparisons are crucial. Ongoing research in our laboratory is using the same protocol as the London British Autism Study of Infant Siblings (41)—behavioral experiments, eye tracking, resting state EEG, ERP, questionnaires, and standardized tests—with infants with other syndromes as well as infants from low socioeconomic status (SES) backgrounds. Our studies will be addressing the following questions. (*i*) Which processes are syndrome-specific, and which are syndrome-general? (*ii*) Which are modality-specific vs. -general? (*iii*) Are the neural and sociocognitive processes different, even when overt behavior is similar? (*iv*) Over time, is there compensation or compounding of effects? It will be critical to follow each syndrome's trajectory over developmental time at multiple levels of analysis, including changes in gene expression, neural circuit activation, and sociocognitive processes.

One question to emerge from cross-syndrome comparisons is why the positive effects of high SES are not greater in families with infants with genetic disorders. Unlike children from low SES environments (43–47), many children with neurogenetic syndromes are well-nourished, grow up in a caring environment, receive considerable cognitive stimulation, and do not suffer the physical and mental abuses that exist in some contexts of early social adversity. Therefore, why do such positive environments not compensate for genetic vulnerabilities? Is it just the severity of the genetic mutations that constrains environmental effects? Or is it possible that this finding is not only because of a genetically compromised computational system but also the fact that early environments differ in more subtle ways than is commonly realized? Having a neurodevelopmental disorder not only involves genetic mutations; it also modifies the environment in which the atypical infant develops. We hypothesize that the moment that a parent is informed that their child has a genetic disorder, the parent's behavior subtly changes. As a result, the baby's responses within the dyadic interaction will also be subtly modified.

A couple of examples serve to illustrate this hypothesis. The first example is from motor development. Observational data from families who visit our laboratory reveal that parents of infants/toddlers with genetic syndromes often find it difficult (compared with parents of TD infants) to allow their atypically developing offspring to freely mouth objects to explore their properties with the sensitive nerve endings in the mouth or crawl/walk uninhibited around the laboratory to fully discover their environment. We speculate that this reticence is because of a natural fear of accidents in vulnerable infants, but it nonetheless results in a less richly explored environment. The second example is from vocabulary learning (48). When TD toddlers start to name things, their parents allow them to overgeneralize. By contrast, in the case of toddlers with DS, for instance, parents veto overgeneralizations and correct immediately (48). We speculate that this finding is because they fear that their child with lower intelligence will never learn the right term if allowed to overgeneralize. However, initial overgeneralization in the TD child encourages category formation (e.g., by calling different animals cat, the child starts to create an implicit animal category), and categorization is known to be impaired in several neurodevelopmental disorders. We propose that such unconscious assumptions about what atypical children can and cannot learn may unwittingly lead parents to provide less variation in linguistic input and in general, a less varied environment to explore. These quite subtle environmental changes are likely to compound over time.

There is, therefore, a vital need for a more dynamic notion of environment (e.g., how having a neurodevelopmental disorder may subtly change the social, cognitive, linguistic, emotional, and physical environments in which the atypically developing child grows).

What about typical development? Are environments basically the same for those TD infants who suffer neither genetic nor environmental vulnerabilities? In fact, subtle individual differences in social interaction, even in the TD case, are ubiquitous and just as likely to become biologically embedded. Our study of the effects of differences in typical mother–infant interaction on the timing of infant cognitive milestones addressed this point (49). Healthy monolingual infants each underwent testing at 6- and 10-mo of age in several experimental tasks (i.e., processing of speech, human goal-directed actions, physical events, etc.) as well as videotaped recordings of mother/infant dyadic play with a structured set of toys. Our findings highlight the effects of differences in mother–infant interaction styles on the timing of the onset of cognitive milestones. At the group level, 6- and 10-mo-olds displayed all of the expected effects found in previous research. However, when we reanalyzed our data according to mother–child interaction ratings, the quality of dyadic interaction style—sensitive vs. controlling—turned out to subtly foster or delay development.

One might have expected that it would be dyads high on the sensitivity rating whose achievement of cognitive milestones would be advanced across all domains (i.e., that the positive effects of contingent mother–infant interaction would be domain-general). However, this expectation was not the case. For the domains of both physical event and speech processing, the infants from dyads with high sensitivity were, indeed, in advance of their peers (i.e., sensitive, contingent interaction fostered earlier specialization). By contrast, the opposite held for the processing of human goal-directed actions. In the latter case, it was the infants of the more controlling mothers who displayed earlier specialization.

Why are the infants of controlling mothers the ones who show earlier success in processing human goal-directed actions? Our analyses of the details of the dyadic play sessions revealed that controlling mothers tended to impose their own choice of toy on their infants and keep changing the toys, without showing sensitivity to the infant's current focus of attention. In this way, the more controlling mothers force their infants to frequently process the mother's goals rather than focusing on their own goals. By contrast, the sensitive mothers altered their own goals to follow their infants' focus of attention. These subtle variations in dyadic interaction style, we contend, place different processing demands on infants when interpreting human social interaction, helping to explain the differences in onset timing of the infants' understanding of human goal-oriented actions (49).

The reason why infants from sensitive dyads show earlier specialization in speech processing is in the fact that the dyadic play sessions showed that such mothers provide their offspring with a greater variety of appropriate level input. The more controlling mothers, by contrast, varied their speech less, without taking into account the progressively changing nature of their infants' vocalizations.

Much the same applied to physical event processing. The controlling mothers tended to interrupt their infants' exploration of objects and offer them a succession of new toys, whereas the sensitive mothers left their infants sufficient time to fully explore the properties of objects, which would, we believe, enhance their growing knowledge of physical objects.

If such subtle differences in early mother–infant interaction in TD infants growing up in nonadverse environments can have such effects on the timing of cognitive milestones (49), the developmental trajectories of those infants who grow up with genetic or environmental vulnerabilities are likely to be even more heavily influenced. Nothing is static in biology or psychology, and this finding holds equally for the environment.

Conclusions

Infant research has tended to raise static questions reminiscent of those questions asked of adult neuropsychological patients. Which modules are impaired, and which are intact? In which regions of the brain are they located? How are syndromes dissociated? By contrast, throughout this paper, we have advocated a more dynamic set of questions. How do phenotypic outcomes originate in infancy? How do neural circuits change over time? Which domains interact across their developmental trajectories? How can we use the cross-syndrome design to reveal more subtle differences than comparisons with TD controls? How do the multiple aspects of the dynamically changing environment affect development? Indeed, rather than the static approach of much of adult neuropsychology, scientists' basic question in studying genetic or environmental vulnerabilities should always be: is there a developmental explanation?

Acknowledgments

We thank the Down's Syndrome Association UK, Down Syndrome Education International, and the Williams Syndrome Foundation for their assistance with the recruitment of infants/toddlers as well as the families of the participants in the studies. The experimental studies reported here were supported by Medical Research Council Grant G0800554 (to A.K.-S.) as well as a studentship (to D.D.) funded by the Economic and Social Research Council (ESRC).

This paper results from the Arthur M. Sackler Colloquium of the National Academy of Sciences, "Biological Embedding of Early Social Adversity: From Fruit Flies to Kindergartners," held December 9–10, 2011, at the Arnold and Mabel Beckman Center of the National Academies of Sciences and Engineering in Irvine, CA. The complete program and audio files of most presentations are available on the NAS Web site at www.nasonline.org/biological-embedding.

Author contributions: A.K.-S., T.M.D., J.V.H., F.X., and D.A. designed research; D.D. and M.R. performed research; D.D. analyzed data; and A.K.-S. wrote the paper.

The authors declare no conflict of interest. This article is a PNAS Direct Submission.

This article contains supporting information online at http://www.pnas.org/content/pnas/suppl/2012/10/05/1121087109.DCSupplemental/pnas.201121087SI.pdf.

References

1 Butterworth B (2010) Foundational numerical capacities and the origins of dyscalculia. *Trends Cogn Sci* 14:534–541.
2 Clahsen H, Temple CM (2003) Words and rules in children with William's syndrome. *Language Competence Across Populations: Toward a Definition of Specific Language Impairment*, eds Levy Y, Schaeffer J (Erlbaum, Hillsdale, NJ), pp 323–352.
3 Karmiloff-Smith A (1998) Development itself is the key to understanding developmental disorders. *Trends Cogn Sci* 2:389–398.
4 Karmiloff-Smith A (2009) Nativism versus neuroconstructivism: Rethinking the study of developmental disorders. *Dev Psychol* 45:56–63.
5 Mareschal D, et al. (2007) *Neuroconstructivism: How the Brain Constructs Cognition* (Oxford Univ Press, Oxford).
6 Farran EK, Karmiloff-Smith A (2012) *Developmental Disabilities Across the Lifespan: A Neuroconstructivist Approach* (Oxford Univ Press, Oxford).
7 Johnson MH (2001) Functional brain development in humans. *Nat Rev Neurosci* 2: 475–483.
8 Huttenlocher PR, Dabholkar AS (1997) Regional differences in synaptogenesis in human cerebral cortex. *J Comp Neurol* 387:167–178.
9 Mills DL, Coffy-Corins S, Neville H (1997) Language comprehension and cerebral specialisation from 13–20 months. *Dev Psychol* 13:397–445.
10 Meaney MJ, Szyf M (2005) Environmental programming of stress responses through DNA methylation: Life at the interface between a dynamic environment and a fixed genome. *Dialogues Clin Neurosci* 7:103–123.
11 Thomas MSC, et al. (2009) Using developmental trajectories to understand developmental disorders. *J Speech Lang Hear Res* 52:336–358.
12 Dehaene S (1997) *The Number Sense: How the Mind Creates Mathematics* (Oxford Univ Press, Oxford).
13 Demeyere N, Lestou V, Humphreys GW (2010) Neuropsychological evidence for a dissociation in counting and subitizing. *Neurocase* 16:219–237.
14 Brannon EM (2006) The representation of numerical magnitude. *Curr Opin Neurobiol* 16:222–229.
15 Izard V, Dehaene-Lambertz G, Dehaene S (2008) Distinct cerebral pathways for object identity and number in human infants. *PLoS Biol* 6:e11.
16 Lipton JS, Spelke ES (2003) Origins of number sense. Large-number discrimination in human infants. *Psychol Sci* 14:396–401.
17 Xu F (2003) Numerosity discrimination in infants: Evidence for two systems of representations. *Cognition* 89:B15–B25.
18 Xu F, Spelke ES (2000) Large number discrimination in 6-month-old infants. *Cognition* 74:B1–B11.
19 Simon TJ (1997) Reconceptualizing the origins of number knowledge: A 'non-numerical' account. *Cogn Dev* 12:349–372.
20 Van Herwegen J, Ansari D, Xu F, Karmiloff-Smith A (2008) Small and large number processing in infants and toddlers with Williams syndrome. *Dev Sci* 11:637–643.

21 Paterson SJ, Brown JH, Gsödl MK, Johnson MH, Karmiloff-Smith A (1999) Cognitive modularity and genetic disorders. *Science* 286:2355–2358.
22 O'Hearn K, Luna B (2009) Mathematical skills in Williams syndrome: Insight into the importance of underlying representations. *Dev Disabil Res Rev* 15:11–20.
23 Ansari D, Donlan C, Karmiloff-Smith A (2007) Typical and atypical development of visual estimation abilities. *Cortex* 43:758–768.
24 Paterson SJ, Girelli L, Butterworth B, Karmiloff-Smith A (2006) Are numerical impairments syndrome specific? Evidence from Williams syndrome and Down's syndrome. *J Child Psychol Psychiatry* 47:190–204.
25 Brannon EM, Abbott S, Lutz DJ (2004) Number bias for the discrimination of large visual sets in infancy. *Cognition* 93:B59–B68.
26 Xu F, Arriaga RI (2007) Number discrimination in 10-month-old infants. *Br J Dev Psychol* 25:103–108.
27 Karmiloff-Smith A, Scerif G, Ansari D (2003) Double dissociations in developmental disorders? Theoretically misconceived, empirically dubious. *Cortex* 39:161–163.
28 Casey BJ, Giedd JN, Thomas KM (2000) Structural and functional brain development and its relation to cognitive development. *Biol Psychol* 54:241–257.
29 Gou Z, Choudhury N, Benasich AA (2011) Resting frontal gamma power at 16, 24 and 36 months predicts individual differences in language and cognition at 4 and 5 years. *Behav Brain Res* 220:263–270.
30 Brown JH, et al. (2003) Spatial representation and attention in toddlers with Williams syndrome and Down syndrome. *Neuropsychologia* 41:1037–1046.
31 Tobii (2003) *Tobii User Manual* (Tobii, Stockholm), 2nd Ed.
32 Krakow JB, Kopp CB (1982) Sustained attention in young Down syndrome children. *Topics Early Child Spec Educ* 2:32–42.
33 Casey BJ, Riddle M (2012) Typical and atypical development of attention. *Cognitive Neuroscience of Attention*, ed Posner MI (Guilford, New York), 2nd Ed., pp 345–356.
34 Dakin SC, Tibber M, Greenwood JA, Kingdom FA, Morgan MJ (2011) A common visual metric for approximate number and density. *Proc Natl Acad Sci USA* 108: 19552–19557.
35 Leonard HC, Annaz D, Karmiloff-Smith A, Johnson MH (2011) Developing spatial frequency biases for face recognition in autism and Williams syndrome. *J Autism Dev Disord* 41:968–973.
36 Annaz D, Karmiloff-Smith A, Johnson MH, Thomas MSC (2009) A cross-syndrome study of the development of holistic face recognition in children with autism, Down syndrome, and Williams syndrome. *J Exp Child Psychol* 102:456–486.
37 Choudhury N, Benasich AA (2011) Maturation of auditory evoked potentials from 6 to 48 months: Prediction to 3 and 4 year language and cognitive abilities. *Clin Neurophysiol* 122:320–338.
38 Frith U (2003) *Autism: Explaining the Enigma* (Blackwell, Oxford).
39 Barnard L, Muldoon K, Hasan R, O'Brien G, Stewart M (2008) Profiling executive dysfunction in adults with autism and comorbid learning disability. *Autism* 12: 125–141.
40 Charman T, et al. (1997) Infants with autism: An investigation of empathy, pretend play, joint attention, and imitation. *Dev Psychol* 33:781–789.
41 Elsabbagh M, et al. (2012) Infant neural sensitivity to dynamic eye gaze is associated with later emerging autism. *Curr Biol* 22:338–342.
42 Karmiloff-Smith A (2012) Brain: The neuroconstructivist approach. *Developmental Disabilities Across the Lifespan: A Neuroconstructivist Approach*, eds Farran EK, Karmiloff-Smith A (Oxford Univ Press, Oxford), pp 37–58.

43 Liston C, McEwen BS, Casey BJ (2009) Psychosocial stress reversibly disrupts prefrontal processing and attentional control. *Proc Natl Acad Sci USA* 106:912–917.

44 Isaacs EB, Edmonds CJ, Chong WK, Lucas A, Gadian DG (2003) Cortical anomalies associated with visuospatial processing deficits. *Ann Neurol* 53:768–773.

45 Isaacs EB, et al. (2010) Impact of breast milk on IQ, brain size and white matter development. *Pediatr Res* 67:357–362.

46 Tottenham N, et al. (2009) Prolonged institutional rearing is associated with atypically larger amygdala volume and difficulties in emotion regulation. *Dev Sci* 13:46–61.

47 Tottenham N, et al. (2011) Elevated amygdala response to faces following early deprivation. *Dev Sci* 14:190–204.

48 John AE, Mervis CB (2010) Comprehension of the communicative intent behind pointing and gazing gestures by young children with Williams syndrome or Down syndrome. *J Speech Lang Hear Res* 53:950–960.

49 Karmiloff-Smith A, et al. (2010) Constraints on the timing of infant cognitive change: Domain-specific or domain-general? *Eur J Dev Sci* 4:31–45.

Part VI

And, always, taking development seriously

12 Ontogeny, genetics, and evolution

A perspective from developmental cognitive neuroscience

Annette Karmiloff-Smith

During the 1980s and early 1990s, the study of genetic developmental disorders seemed to offer the promise of important theoretical outcomes: (a) the demonstration of pure dissociations between different cognitive functions; (b) the proof of the existence of innately specified modules in the human mind/brain; and (c) the direct mapping of mutated genes to specific impairments in higher level cognitive modules. The early enthusiasm was understandable. For example, although the genes involved in autism, dyslexia, and specific language impairment (SLI) remained to be identified, the fact that there is a genetic component of these developmental disorders was well documented by twin studies (e.g., Bishop 1997). When cognitive dissociations appeared to hold for each of these clinical groups, they were used to make sweeping claims about how the genome might prespecify the functional modularity of the human mind: a defective theory-of-mind module in autism (Leslie 1992; Baron-Cohen 1998), an impaired phonological module in dyslexia (Frith 1995), and a faulty grammatical module in certain forms of SLI (Gopnik and Crago 1991).

But it was particularly the neurodevelopmental disorder, Williams syndrome (WS), that attracted the attention of linguists, philosophers, psychologists, and neuroscientists, and led to very strong claims about cognitive dissociations, modularity, and direct genotype/phenotype mappings. Indeed, adults and older children with WS were found to present with impressively proficient language and face processing abilities, alongside impaired general cognitive abilities. To certain researchers, this suggested a dissociation between language and general cognition (Bellugi et al. 1994; Pinker 1994, 1999, 2001), and a dissociation between visuospatial cognition and face processing (Rossen et al. 1995; Tager-Flusberg et al. 2003). And, as more became known about the genetic basis of the syndrome, direct links were heralded between specific genes and the adult phenotypic outcome (Frangiskakis et al. 1996).

In my view, in their excitement of discovering a syndrome with such an uneven cognitive profile in the phenotypic end state, researchers lost sight of one fundamental explanatory factor in both typical and atypical populations: the actual process of *ontogenetic development*. Paradoxically, even when researchers of atypical development study children, they tend to fall back on the *adult* neuropsychological model of the mature brain, failing to take account of how the gradual process of development, from embryogenesis and infancy onward, contributes dynamically to the phenotypic outcome (Karmiloff-Smith 1992, 1998).

All theorists, whether entrenched nativists or empiricists, agree that human development must involve contributions from both genes and environment. However, first because we lack a testable theory of the precise way in which genes and environment interact, and second because of long-established philosophical views about what it is to be human, the debate remains as to whether it is *nature* or *nurture* that plays a greater role in constraining the developing infant brain. For some theorists, consistent regularities in the physical and social environments to which children are exposed play a critical role, whereas for others the environment merely acts as a trigger for the functioning of our biological endowment. For the latter position, data from adult neuropsychological patients and from studies of developmental disorders of genetic origin are often used to motivate strong claims about the evolution of the neonate brain in terms of innate cognitive modules, the contents of which are argued to be specified in our genetic makeup (Barkow et al. 1992; Pinker 1997).

This paper is divided into three parts: evolution, genetics, and ontogeny. Each section starts by examining nativist claims about innateness and modularity of function and subsequently evaluates them within a neuroconstructivist approach to human development.

The claimed modularity of mind

Insults to particular brain regions from accidents or stroke are alleged to have provided some of the most convincing evidence that the brain has modular structure (Rapp and Caramazza 2002). Agrammatic patients, for example, are claimed to present with severe impairments in the grammatical structures of their language, but otherwise normal vocabulary and cognition (Grodzinsky 2000). Other patients with different brain lesions seem to present with normal grammar but have serious word-finding difficulties (Miozzo 2003). Yet others may retain completely normal language but have extreme difficulties in recognizing faces, i.e., prosopagnosia (Farah et al. 1995). These and other such claims using the double dissociation logic have abounded in the literature from studies in adult neuropsychology (see discussion in Karmiloff-Smith, Scerif, and Ansari 2003).

Espousing similar theoretical aims as adult neuropsychology, many studies of children with genetic disorders have sought modular impairments and dissociations alongside normal scores in other domains claimed to be "intact/preserved/spared" (Leslie 1992; Smith and Tsimpli 1995; Temple 1997; Baron-Cohen 1998; Tager-Flusberg et al. 1998; see discussion in Karmiloff-Smith, Scerif, and Ansari 2003). Researchers have focused on a number of genetically based disorders to assert the existence of a juxtaposition of deficits and preservations in WS (Bellugi et al. 1994; Pinker 1994, 1999; Rossen et al. 1996; Clahsen and Almazan 1998; Tager-Flusberg et al. 1998, 2003), a neurodevelopmental disorder caused by the deletion of some 28 contiguous genes on one copy of chromosome 7 (Donnai and Karmiloff-Smith 2000). The impressive behavioral proficiency with language and face processing in WS was found to coexist with a mean IQ of 58 (Mervis et al. 2000), and seriously impaired spatial and numerical cognition (Bellugi et al. 1994).

Modularity claims have also been made with respect to SLI (Gopnik and Crago 1991; van der Lely 1997; Rice 2002) and developmental prosopagnosia (Kress and Daum 2003), i.e., that one aspect of the cognitive system is seriously impaired (grammar in the former case, face processing in the latter), with remaining cognitive functions claimed to have developed normally, as if there are no interactions across the brain.

These various developmental data and interpretations thereof, using the logic of adult neuropsychology, seem to suggest that the brain is strictly modular, with genetic disorders helping the scientist to discover that the content of modules is likely to be innately specified in our genetic makeup.

The modularity of mind: a neuroconstructivist critique

The arguments that pure cases of single deficits exist in children, as they may perhaps in adult neuropsychological patients (although this remains debatable), turn out to be difficult to sustain. For example, a metareview by Nunn et al. (2001) of so-called developmental prosopagnosia concluded that the face-processing deficit in young children *never* occurred in the absence of object processing deficits. This suggests that the relative independence of object/face processing, found in adults, *emerges* gradually as a function of ontogenetic development, but starts in young children with some *common* processing.

Similar arguments are now being marshaled with respect to SLI. This is, by definition, considered to involve a single impairment in language, with the rest of the cognitive system operating normally. However, in recent years disorders like SLI have been shown to stem from lower level deficits and to be accompanied by numerous other subtle impairments in the hitherto presumed "intact" nonlinguistic domains (Bishop 1997; Benasich and Spitz 1999; Chiat 2001; Botting 2005; Norbury et al. 2002). Moreover, even when performance IQ falls within the normal range, the IQ of the SLI individual is often significantly lower than that of his siblings (Botting 2005), pointing to a general impairment despite so-called normal scores. These data highlight the fact that, contrary to nativist views discussed earlier, developmental disorders rarely display a neat juxtaposition of intact and impaired modules.

In studies of WS, we challenged the intactness claims on several fronts (Karmiloff-Smith et al. 2005). First, although people with WS display proficient behavior for which scores fall in the normal range on some standardized face processing tasks like the Benton (Rossen et al. 1995) or the Rivermead (Udwin and Yule 1991), the means by which they achieve this success turn out to be different from controls. Whereas controls in our studies used configural processing, the WS group used featural or holistic processing of faces, just as they do for nonface spatial stimuli (Karmiloff-Smith et al. 2005; see also Karmiloff-Smith 1998 and Deruelle et al. 1999). Moreover, our brain imaging studies of WS face processing and spatial stimuli, using high-density event-related potentials, also reveal different brain processes from controls (Grice et al. 2001, 2003). It is not the case, then, that individuals with WS have an impaired spatial module and an intact facial module; both domains are impaired in similar ways, but space is more vulnerable to the deficit. People with WS fail to modularize their face processing over developmental time. So, a lack of modularization in developmental disorders may reveal *common initial processes* across domains, before each domain would normally have become increasingly segregated and modularized over time.

What about earlier claims regarding an intact language module in WS (Bellugi et al. 1994; Pinker 1994, 1999; Smith and Tsimpli 1995)? First, an abundance of empirical studies from numerous laboratories across the world now challenge these claims in respect of all aspects of WS language (e.g., the lexicon: Jarrold et al. 2000; Temple et al. 2002; morphosyntax: Karmiloff-Smith et al. 1997; Thomas et al. 2001; Volterra et al. 2001; Grant et al. 2002; phonology: Grant et al. 1997; pragmatics: Laws and Bishop 2004). Brain imaging of language processing again points to atypical processing in WS (Neville et al. 1994). Moreover, despite the superficially fluent language peppered with erudite-sounding words of adolescents and adults with WS, language onset in this clinical population is very late, often not until the fifth or sixth year (Singer Harris et al. 1997). Why is WS language so delayed? Is this due to a late-maturing module? Or is there a *developmental* explanation? In my view, the roots of the delay reside in the dynamic interactions of deficits in multiple earlier processes. For example, infants and toddlers with WS are extremely delayed in segmenting the speech stream (Nazzi et al. 2003). Second, unlike typical controls, toddlers and young children with WS rely more on perceptual cues than on linguistic labels when identifying new objects (Nazzi et al. 2005). Third, early categorization abilities in WS are impaired (Nazzi and Karmiloff-Smith 2002), and exhaustive sorting follows word onset rather than preceding it (Mervis and Bertrand 1997). Fourth, pointing is also atypical in WS toddlers. Whereas in typical development, referential pointing precedes the onset of language, in WS this order is usually reversed (Mervis and Bertrand 1997). Moreover, our recent studies revealed that WS toddlers do not use or follow eye gaze for referential communication and do not understand the referential function of pointing (Laing et al. 2002). Finally, the normal asymmetry between comprehension and production does not hold for WS (Paterson et al. 1999). In sum, multiple aspects of communication show an early, unusual pattern in WS, jointly contributing in very complex ways to the explanation of the late onset of their language.

However, an even earlier deficit outside the domain of language may offer a compelling explanation of some of these early deficits: atypical eye movement planning. In a study of saccadic planning in infants and toddlers with WS and DS compared to MA and CA controls, we found that although children with DS resembled controls (apart from being somewhat slower) the infants and toddlers with WS displayed a range of impairments (Brown et al. 2003). In other words, making eye movements to explore the environment, as well as to follow another's eye gaze or pointing gestures, is atypical in infants and toddlers with WS. Thus, early visuospatial deficits in the WS developmental trajectory *outside the domain of language* can have cascading developmental effects over time on several *emerging* higher level linguistic and cognitive domains. The fact that domains are highly interrelated early in brain development (Neville et al. 1994; Huttenlocher 2002) turns out to play a critical role in the formation of more general, albeit sometimes subtle, deficits in later development.

The claimed genetic underpinnings to cognitive-level modules

Because of our differences with other species, human language has been the domain most consistently claimed to be specified in our genes. Leading linguists and psycholinguists have consistently asserted that language is an innately specified endowment of our biology (Pinker 1994; Wexler 1996).

Much excitement for such claims was recently reinforced with the revelation of a specific genetic mutation in a family pedigree with speech and language deficits. The KE family was genotyped across several generations. It was found that affected family members had a point mutation on one copy of the *FOXP2* gene on chromosome 7 that encodes a protein of 715 amino acids belonging to the forkhead class of transcription factors. This point mutation was not, however, found in family members with normal language (Fisher et al. 1998; Lai et al. 2001). Although the geneticists remained cautious about the conclusions to be drawn from these cases, some linguists were quick to claim that a gene directly implicated in speech and language had been identified (Gopnik and Crago 1991), a seemingly exciting discovery which Pinker (2001) claimed to mark the "dawn of cognitive genetics."

Other work on variable gene mapping and animal models also seemed to hold the promise of direct mapping between genes and cognitive-level outcomes. Identifying patients with a small deletion within the WS critical region (WSCR), researchers have attempted to delineate the functions of certain genes. Families were discovered, some of whose members had a small deletion of two genes (*Elastin* and *Limkinase1*) within the WSCR. *Elastin* is a gene implicated in the building of connective tissue throughout the body, and likely to be linked to the supravalvular aortic stenoses suffered by people with WS and by these small deletion patients (Curran et al. 1993; Frangiskakis et al. 1996). *Limkinase1* (*LIMK1*) is a protein kinase gene, expressed in the developing brain (Proschel et al. 1995; Tassabehji et al. 1996). It turned out that family members with the *LIMK1* deletion displayed spatial deficits similar to people with WS, whereas family members without the deletion had no spatial problems (Frangiskakis et al. 1996). The Frangiskakis group concluded that the half dosage of *LIMK1* plays a vital role in contributing to the visuospatial constructive cognition deficits that occur in WS.

The fact that a mouse knockout model came to similar conclusions about the function of *LIMK1* seems to make such claims even more plausible. Meng et al. (2002) created a single knockout of *LIMK1* and demonstrated serious spatial learning problems in the mouse's behavior in the Morris water maze. Thus, both the mouse model and the small-deletion patient data seem to point to the same conclusion: deletion of the *LIMK1* gene is directly linked to an impaired visuospatial module in WS.

Genetic underpinnings to cognitive-level modules: a neuroconstructivist critique

Let us return to the KE pedigree in whom family members with the allelic mutation on *FOXP2* display speech and language deficits. It turns out that their problems are not specific to speech and language (Vargha-Khadem et al. 1998; Alcock et al. 2000). Family members with the mutation display impairments in multiple domains such as fine motor control, gait, orofacial movement, perception, and production of rhythm, all of which may subsequently impact on speech and language from infancy onward. The KE family's problems may be more overtly obvious in speech and language, but this does not mean that they were originally rooted only in speech and language modules, but rather in the learning of skilled coordination of rapid movement sequences and their timing.

What about the Meng and colleagues' mouse knockout model of *LIMK1*, one of the genes situated in the WSCR (Meng et al. 2002)? The spatial deficit found in the mouse's behavior in the Morris water maze seemed to replicate the spatial deficit found in individuals with WS who all also have a deletion of *LIMK1*. However, there are several problems. First, it is a single gene knockout, whereas WS involves the deletion of some 28 contiguous genes that may interact with one another. Second, *LIMK1* does not target a specific brain region like parietal cortex, responsible for spatial cognition, but is expressed widely across the brain early in embryonic development. Its protein products are thought to contribute to something far more general developmentally: dendritic spine growth and synaptic regulation across the whole brain.

Another seemingly clear example of direct links between genes and cognitive-level outcomes discussed earlier came from the variable deletion mapping of patients with small deletions in the WS critical region (Frangiskakis et al. 1996). However, several other patients with similar or even larger partial deletions in the WSCR, including *LIMK1*, failed to corroborate these conclusions (Tassabehji et al. 1999; Karmiloff-Smith, Grant, et al. 2003; Karmiloff-Smith, Scerif, and Ansari 2003; Gray et al. 2006). None displayed a spatial deficit. In my view, the claims of a direct link between spatial cognition and a specific gene, *LIMK1* (Frangiskakis et al. 1996), were premature and based on a false assumption, i.e., that specific genes will turn out to be linkable to specific cognitive-level outcomes. If *LIMK1* plays a role, then it is probably in low-level processes, interacting with other genes at the telemetric end of the typical WS deletion, ultimately to *result* over developmental time in the spatial cognition deficit.

The claimed evolutionary underpinnings of cognitive-level modules

With the discovery of the *FOXP2* mutation in some humans and its potential relationship to speech and language, researchers moved to genotyping our closest cousin, the ape. The *FOXP2* proteins of the chimpanzee, gorilla, and rhesus macaque are identical to one another. *FOXP2* is an extremely conserved gene across mammalian species, and has shown no changes in the chimp lineage since it separated from the human lineage some 4–6 million years ago. By contrast, it acquired two amino acid changes on the human lineage, one of which is likely to be functional, dated to some 200,000 years ago (Enard et al. 2002). Not surprisingly, this was an exciting discovery, since the timing of the protein changes on the human lineage coincide with estimates of when language started to emerge in our species (Hurford et al. 1998; Botha 2004; Newmeyer 2004). Put together with the data from the KE family, it is a small step to claim that the change in a single base pair in *FOXP2* altering protein synthesis must be a direct contributor to the evolution of human language. Likewise, a number of authors have made sweeping claims about the evolutionary underpinnings of cognitive-level modules (e.g., Barkow et al. 1992; Pinker 1997).

Evolutionary underpinnings of cognitive-level modules: a neuroconstructivist critique

First, it should be recalled that *FOXP2* is a transcription factor—its expression affects many other genes. Second, while the evidence from primate comparisons of *FOXP2* is at first blush exciting, more recent research on *FOXP2* expression in birds, which is very similar to *FOXP2* in humans, makes the original claims about the relation of *FOXP2* to language premature. Researchers compared songbirds that learn their vocalization (e.g., zebra finches, canaries, etc.) with songbirds that produce their vocalization without learning (Haesler et al. 2004). In the avian learners, *FOXP2* had greater expression in the equivalent of basal ganglia during phases of song *learning* than during song *production*. It is also mainly expressed in motor regions. The scientists concluded that *FOXP2* expression is associated with the learning of skilled coordination of rapid movement sequences and their timing, i.e., *FOXP2* expression was an important contributor to *vocal plasticity* (Haesler et al. 2004).

Evolution does not, then, seem to have opted for increasingly complex genes that specify the content of cognitive-level modules, but rather for allelic changes that contribute to increased plasticity for learning. I have repeatedly argued that one cannot simply take for granted homology of function or identical timing of genetic expression of the same gene across different species (Karmiloff-Smith et al. 2002). It has to be demonstrated empirically. Nonetheless, the fact that *FOXP2* in birds is not a gene that encodes a specific bird song, but rather facilitates the ability to learn, highlights the need for extreme caution in assuming that *FOXP2* is a gene contributing directly to language in humans.

Final thoughts

We have seen that simple, direct mappings between genes and cognitive-level modules are not sustainable. In fact, genes are more likely to contribute to much more general levels such as developmental timing, neuronal migration, neuronal type/size/density/orientation, myelination, lamination, ratio of gray matter to white matter, firing thresholds, neurotransmitter differences, and so forth, any or all of which may be atypical in developmental disorders. The neonate brain starts out highly connected, not with domain-specific higher level modular processing; this emerges gradually over developmental time (Karmiloff-Smith 1992).

In sum, genetic developmental disorders can inform theories of development, as long as ontogenetic processes are seen to play a vital, dynamic role and that they are considered against the backdrop of the plastic, activity-driven nature of normal cortical specialization, rather than as illustrations of a juxtaposition of "intact" versus "impaired" static modules. Developmental disorders point to altered constrains on neural plasticity in a *developing* organism, often affecting plasticity itself (Karmiloff-Smith 1998; Karmiloff-Smith and Thomas 2005). Although plasticity is seen by some as a response solely to injury (Wexler 1996), for others plasticity is the rule for development, normal or atypical, and not the exception (Cicchetti and Tucker 1994; Elman et al. 1996; Bates and Roe 2001; Johnson 2001; Huttenlocher 2002; Karmiloff-Smith and Thomas 2005). But plasticity is not, of course, unconstrained, and developmental disorders may turn out to be very informative about the constraints on plasticity. In sum, once one thinks from a truly *developmental* perspective, it is easy to imagine how even a tiny asynchrony or impairment early on in development can have a huge, cascading impact on the subsequent outcome.[1]

Acknowledgment

This paper was written with the support of a Fogarty/NIH grant (Grant No. R21TW06761-01).

Note

1 A longer but similar argument is developed in a chapter that appears in a volume edited by Y. Munakata and M. H. Johnson, *Attention and Performance XXI: Processes of Change in Brain and Cognitive Development* (Munakata and Johnson 2006).

References

Alcock KJ, Passingham RE, Watkins K, Vargha-Khadem F (2000) Pitch and timing abilities in inherited speech and language impairment. Brain and Language 75: 34–46.

Barkow JH, Cosmides L, Tooby J, eds (1992) The Adapted Mind: Evolutionary Psychology and the Generation of Culture. New York: Oxford University Press.

Baron-Cohen S (1998) Modularity in developmental cognitive neuropsychology: Evidence from autism and Gilles de la Tourette syndrome. In: Handbook of Mental Retardation and Development (Burack JA, Hodapp RM, Zigler E, eds), 334–348. Cambridge: Cambridge University Press.

Bates E, Roe K (2001) Language development in children with unilateral brain injury. In: Handbook of Developmental Cognitive Neuroscience (Nelson CA, Luciana M, eds), 281–307. Cambridge, MA: MIT Press.

Bellugi U, Wang P, Jernigan TL (1994) Williams syndrome: An unusual neuropsychological profile. In: Atypical Cognitive Deficits in Developmental Disorders: Implications for Brain Function (Broman S, Grafman J, eds), 23–56. Hillsdale, NJ: Erlbaum.

Benasich AA, Spitz RV (1999) Insights from infants: Temporal processing abilities and genetics contribute to language impairment. In: A Neurodevelopmental Approach to Specific Learning Disorders (Whitmore K, Hart H, Willems G, eds), 191–210. London: Mac Keith Press.

Bishop DVM (1997) Uncommon Understanding: Development and Disorders of Language Comprehension in Children. Hove: Psychology Press.

Botha R (2004) Windows with a view on language evolution. European Review 12: 235–243.

Botting N (2005) Non-verbal cognitive development and language impairment. Journal of Child Psychology and Psychiatry 46: 317–326.

Brown J, Johnson MH, Paterson S, Gilmore RO, Gsödl M, Longhi E, Karmiloff-Smith A (2003) Spatial representation and attention in toddlers with Williams syndrome and Down syndrome. Neuropsychologia 41: 1037–1046.

Chiat S (2001) Mapping theories of developmental language impairment: Premises, predictions and evidence. Language and Cognitive Processes 16: 113–142.

Ciccetti D, Tucker D. (1994) Development and self-regulatory structures of the mind. Development and Psychopathology 6: 533–549.

Clahsen H, Almazan M (1998) Syntax and morphology in Williams syndrome. Cognition 68: 167–198.

Curran ME, Atkinson DL, Ewart AK, Morris CA, Leppert MF, Keating MT (1993) The elastin gene is disrupted by a translocation associated with supravalvular aortic stenosis. Cell 73: 159–168.

Deruelle C, Mancini J, Livet MO, Cassé-Perrot C, de Schonen S (1999) Configural and local face processing in children with Williams syndrome. Brain and Cognition 41: 276–298.

Donnai D, Karmiloff-Smith A (2000) Williams syndrome: From genotype through to the cognitive phenotype. American Journal of Medical Genetics: Seminars in Medical Genetics 97: 164–171.

Elman JL, Bates EA, Johnson MH, Karmiloff-Smith A, Parisi D, Plunkett K (1996) Rethinking Innateness: A Connectionist Perspective on Development. Cambridge, MA: MIT Press.

Enard W, Przeworski M, Fisher S, Lai CSL, Wiebe V, Kitano T, Monaco AP, Pääbo S (2002) Molecular evolution of *FOXP2*, a gene involved in speech and language. Nature 418: 869–872.

Farah MJ, Levinson KL, Klein KL (1995) Face perception and within-category discrimination in prosopagnosia. Neuropsychologia 33: 661–674.

Fisher SE, Vargha-Khadem F, Watkins KE, Monaco AP, Pembrey ME (1998) Localisation of a gene implicated in a severe speech and language disorder. Nature Genetics 18: 168–170.

Frangiskakis JM, Ewart AK, Morris CA, Mervis CB, Bertrand J, Robinson BF, Klein BP, Ensing GJ, Everett LA, Green ED, Proschel C, Cutowski NJ, Noble M, Atkinson DL, Odelberg SJ, Keating MT (1996) *LIM-kinase1* hemizygosity implicated in impaired visuospatial constructive cognition. Cell 86: 59–69.

Frith U (1995) Dyslexia: Can we have a shared theoretical framework? Educational and Child Psychology 12: 6–17.

Gopnik M, Crago MB (1991) Familial aggregation of a developmental language disorder. Cognition 39: 1–30.

Grant J, Karmiloff-Smith A, Gathercole SA, Paterson S, Howlin P, Davies M, Udwin O (1997) Phonological short-term memory and its relationship to language in Williams syndrome. Cognitive Neuropsychiatry 2: 81–99.

Grant J, Valian V, Karmiloff-Smith A (2002) A study of relative clauses in Williams syndrome. Journal of Child Language 29: 403–416.

Gray V, Karmiloff-Smith A, Furnell E, Tassabehji M (2006) In-depth analysis of spatial cognition in williams syndrome: A critical assessment of the role of the *LIMK1* gene. Neuropsychologia 44: 679–685.

Grice SJ, de Haan M, Halit H, Johnson MH, Csibra G, Grant J, Karmiloff-Smith A (2003) ERP abnormalities of visual perception in Williams syndrome. NeuroReport 14: 1773–1777.

Grice S, Spratling MW, Karmiloff-Smith A, Halit H, Csibra G, de Haan M, Johnson MH (2001) Disordered visual processing and oscillatory brain activity in autism and Williams syndrome. NeuroReport 12: 2697–2700.

Grodzinsky Y (2000) The neurology of syntax: Language use without Broca's area. Behavioral and Brain Sciences 23: 1–71.

Haesler S, Wada K, Nshdejan A, Morrisey EE, Lints T, Jarvis ED, Scharff C (2004) FoxP2 expression in avian vocal learners and non-learners. Journal of Neuroscience 24: 3164–3175.

Hurford JR, Studdert-Kennedy M, Knight C, eds (1998) Approaches to the Evolution of Language. Cambridge: Cambridge University Press.

Huttenlocher PR (2002) Neural Plasticity: The Effects of Environment on the Development of the Cerebral Cortex. Cambridge, MA: Harvard University Press.

Jarrold C, Hartley SJ, Phillips C, Baddeley AD (2000) Word fluency in Williams syndrome: Evidence for unusual semantic organisation? Cognitive Neuropsychiatry 5: 293–319.

Johnson MH (2001) Functional brain development in humans. Nature Reviews Neuroscience 2: 475–483.

Karmiloff-Smith A (1992) Beyond Modularity: A Developmental Perspective on Cognitive Science. Cambridge, MA: MIT Press.

Karmiloff-Smith A (1998) Development itself is the key to understanding developmental disorders. Trends in Cognitive Sciences 2: 389–398.

Karmiloff-Smith A, Grant J, Berthoud I, Davies M, Howlin P, Udwin O (1997) Language and Williams syndrome: How intact is "intact"? Child Development 68: 246–262.

Karmiloff-Smith A, Grant J, Ewing S, Carette MJ, Metcalfe K, Donnai D, Read AP, Tassabehji M (2003) Using case study comparisons to explore genotype/phenotype correlations. Journal of American Medical Genetics 40: 136–140.

Karmiloff-Smith A, Scerif G, Ansari D (2003) Double dissociations in developmental disorders? Theoretically misconceived, empirically dubious. Cortex 39: 161–163.

Karmiloff-Smith A, Scerif G, Thomas MSC (2002) Different approaches to relating genotype to phenotype in developmental disorders. Developmental Psychobiology 40: 311–322.

Karmiloff-Smith A, Thomas M (2005) Can developmental disorders be used to bolster claims from evolutionary psychology? A neuroconstructivist approach. In: Biology and Knowledge Revisited: From Neurogenesis to Psychogenesis (Taylor Parker S, Langer J, Milbrath C, eds), 307–321. Mahwah, NJ: Erlbaum.

Karmiloff-Smith A, Thomas M, Annaz D, Humphreys K, Ewing S, Brace N, van Duuren M, Pike G, Grice S, Campbell R (2004) Exploring the Williams syndrome face processing debate: The importance of building developmental trajectories. Journal of Child Psychology and Psychiatry 45: 1258–1274.

Kress T, Daum I (2003) Developmental prosopagnosia: A review. Behavioral Neurology 14: 109–121.

Lai CSL, Fisher SE, Hurst JA, Vargha-Khadem F, Monaco A (2001) A forkhead-domain gene is mutated in a severe speech and language disorder. Nature 413: 519–523.

Laing E, Butterworth G, Ansari D, Gsödl M, Longhi E, Panagiotaki G, Paterson S, Karmiloff-Smith A (2002) Atypical development of language and social communication in toddlers with Williams syndrome. Developmental Science 5: 233–246.

Laws G, Bishop DVM (2004) Pragmatic language impairment and social deficits in Williams syndrome: A comparison with Down's syndrome and specific language impairment. International Journal of Language Communication Disorders 39: 45–64.

Leslie AM (1992) Pretence, autism, and the theory-of-mind-module. Current Directions in Psychological Science 1: 18–21.

Meng Y, Zhang Y, Tregoubov V, Janus C, Cruz L, Jackson M, Lu WY, MacDonald JF, Wang JY, Falls DL, Jia Z (2002) Abnormal spine morphology and enhanced LTP in LIMK-1 knockout mice. Neuron 35: 121–133.

Mervis CB, Robinson BF, Bertraud J, Morris CA, Klein-Tasman BP, Armstrong SC (2000) The Williams syndrome cognitive profile. Brain and Cognition 44: 604–628.

Mervis C, Bertrand J (1997) Developmental relations between cognition and language: Evidence from Williams syndrome. In: Research on Communication and Language Disorders: Contributions to Theories of Language Development (Adamson LB, Romski MA, eds), 75–106. New York: Brookes.

Miozzo M (2003) On the processing of regular and irregular forms of verbs and nouns: Evidence from neuropsychology. Cognition 87: 101–127.

Munakata Y, Johnson MH (2006) Processes of Change in Brain and Cognitive Development: Attention and Performance XXI. Oxford: Oxford University Press.

Nazzi T, Gopnik A, Karmiloff-Smith A (2005) Asynchrony in the cognitive and lexical development of young children with Williams syndrome. Journal of Child Language 32: 427–438.

Nazzi T, Karmiloff-Smith A (2002) Early categorization abilities in young children with Williams syndrome. NeuroReport 13: 1259–1262.

Nazzi T, Paterson S, Karmiloff-Smith A (2003) Early word segmentation by infants and toddlers with Williams syndrome. Infancy 4: 251–271.

Neville HJ, Mills DL, Bellugi U (1994) Effects of altered auditory sensitivity and age of language acquisition on the development of language–relevant neural systems: Preliminary studies of Williams syndrome. In: Atypical Cognitive Deficits in Developmental Disorders: Implications for Brain Function (Broman S, Grafman J, eds), 67–83. Hillsdale, NJ: Erlbaum.

Newmeyer FJ (2004) Cognitive and functional factors in the evolution of grammar. European Review 12: 245–264.

Norbury CF, Bishop DVM, Biscoe J (2002) Does impaired grammatical comprehension provide evidence for an innate grammar module? Applied Psycholinguistics 23: 247–268.

Nunn JA, Postma P, Pearson R (2001) Developmental prosopagnosia: Should it be taken at face value? Neurocase 7: 15–27.

Paterson SJ, Brown JH, Gsödl MK, Johnson MH, Karmiloff-Smith A (1999) Cognitive modularity and genetic disorders. Science 286: 2355–2358.

Pinker S (1994) The Language Instinct. London: Penguin.

Pinker S (1997) How the Mind Works. New York: Norton.

Pinker S (1999) Words and Rules. London: Weidenfeld and Nicolson.

Pinker S (2001) Talk of genetics and vice-versa. Nature 413: 465–466.

Proschel C, Blouin MJ, Gutowski NJ, Ludwig R, Noble M (1995) L1MK1 is predominantly expressed in neural tissue and phosphorylates serine, threonine and tyrosine residues in vitro. Oncogene 11: 1271–1281.

Rapp A, Caramazza A (2002) Selective difficulties with spoken nouns and written verbs: A single case study. Journal of Neurolinguistics 15: 373–402.

Rice ML (2002) A unified model of specific and general language delay: Grammatical tense as a clinical marker of unexpected variation. In: Language Competence Across Populations: Toward a Definition of Specific Language Impairment (Levy Y, Schaeffer J, eds), 63–95. Mahwah, NJ: Erlbaum.

Rossen ML, Jones W, Wang PP, Klima ES (1995) Face processing: Remarkable sparing in Williams syndrome. Genetic Counseling 6: 138–140.

Rossen M, Klima ES, Bellugi U, Bihrle A, Jones W (1996) Interaction between language and cognition: Evidence from Williams syndrome. In: Language Learning and Behaviour (Beitchman JH, Cohen N, Konstantareas M, Tannock R, eds), 367–392. New York: Cambridge University Press.

Singer Harris NG, Bellugi U, Bates E, Jones W, Rossen M (1997) Contrasting profiles of language development in children with Williams and Down syndromes. Developmental Neuropsychology 13: 345–370.

Smith N, Tsimpli IM (1995) The Mind of a Savant: Language, Learning and Modularity. Oxford: Blackwell.

Tager-Flusberg H, Boshart J, Baron-Cohen S (1998) Reading the windows to the soul: Evidence of domain-specific sparing in Williams syndrome. Journal of Cognitive Neuroscience 10: 631–639.

Tager-Flusberg H, Plesa-Skwerer D, Faja S, Joseph RM (2003) People with Williams syndrome process faces holistically. Cognition 89: 11–24.

Tassabehji M, Metcalfe K, Fergusson WD, Carette MJ, Dore JK, Donnai D, Read AP, Proschel C, Gutowski NJ, Mao X, Sheer D (1996) LIM-kinase deleted in Williams syndrome. Nature Genetics 13: 272–273.

Tassabehji M, Metcalfe K, Karmiloff-Smith A, Carette MJ, Grant J, Dennis N, Reardon W, Splitt M, Read AP, Donnai D (1999) Williams syndrome: Use of chromosomal microdeletions as a tool to dissect cognitive and physical phenotypes. American Journal of Human Genetics 63: 118–125.

Temple C (1997) Developmental Cognitive Neuropsychology. Hove: Psychology Press.

Temple C, Almazan M, Sherwood S (2002) Lexical skills in Williams syndrome: A cognitive neuropsychological analysis. Journal of Neurolinguistics 15: 463–495.

Thomas MSC, Grant J, Gsödl M, Laing E, Barham Z, Lakusta L, Tyler LK, Grice S, Paterson S, Karmiloff-Smith A (2001) Past tense formation in Williams syndrome. Language and Cognitive Processes 16: 143–176.

Udwin O, Yule W (1991) A cognitive and behavioural phenotype in Williams syndrome. Journal of Clinical and Experimental Neuropsychology 13: 232–244.

van der Lely HKJ (1997) Language and cognitive development in a grammatical SLI boy: Modularity and innateness. Journal of Neurolinguistics 10: 75–107.

Vargha-Khadem F, Watkins KE, Price CJ, Ashburner J, Alcock K, Gadian DG, Passingham R (1998) Neural basis of an inherited speech and language disorder. Proceedings of the National Academy of Sciences USA 95: 12695–12700.

Volterra V, Capirci O, Caselli MC (2001) What atypical populations can reveal about language development: The contrast between deafness and Williams syndrome. Language and Cognitive Processes 16: 219–239.

Wexler K (1996) The development of inflection in a biologically based theory of language acquisition. In: Toward a Genetics of Language (Rice ML, ed), 113–144. Mahwah, NJ: Erlbaum.

13 Nativism versus neuroconstructivism

Rethinking the study of developmental disorders

Annette Karmiloff-Smith

In this article, it is argued that one of the hitherto dominant positions in the fields of psychology, linguistics, neuroscience, and philosophy concerning the way in which genetic disorders inform the scientist about the innate specification of dissociated modules in the human brain should be replaced by a dynamic, neuroconstructivist approach in which genes, brain, cognition, and environment interact multidirectionally. The following quotations illustrate with respect to autism these two very different approaches (tagged as [a] nativist and [b] neuroconstructivist):

> [a] Autism involves a damaged theory-of-mind module (Leslie, 1992, p. 21).
>
> [a] Results implicate the orbito-frontal cortex as the basis of this ability (p. 640) . . . specifically damaged in autism (pp. 642–643; Baron-Cohen et al., 1994).
>
> [b] Autism affects the interconnectivity among and within various cognitive systems. . . . In autism, functional brain development goes awry such that there is increased intra-regional specialization and less inter-regional interaction (Carpenter et al., 2001, p. 373).
>
> [b] . . . the crucial role of unbalanced excitatory-inhibitory networks . . . complex pathogenetic pathways . . . leading to Autism Spectrum Disorder through altered neuronal morphology, synaptogenesis and cell migration (Persico & Bourgeron, 2006, p. 349).

Similar fundamental differences in approach exist with respect to another disorder, Williams syndrome (WS), as the following quotations bear witness:

> [a] Overall, the genetic double dissociation is striking. . . . The genes of one group of children [specific language impairment] impair their grammar while sparing their intelligence; the genes of another group of children [WS] impair their intelligence while sparing their grammar (Pinker, 1999, p. 262).
>
> [a] For instance, children with WS have a barely measurable general intelligence and require constant parental care, yet they have an exquisite mastery of syntax and vocabulary. They are, however, unable to understand even

the most immediate implications of their admirably constructed sentences (Piattelli-Palmarini, 2001, p. 887).

[b] We argue that rather than being the paradigm case for the independence of language from cognition, WS provides strong evidence of the interdependence of many aspects of language and cognition (Mervis & Becerra, 2007, p. 3).

[b] In sum, brain volume, brain anatomy, brain chemistry, hemispheric asymmetry, and the temporal patterns of brain activity are all atypical in people with WS. How could the resulting system be described as a normal brain with parts intact and parts impaired, as the popular view holds? Rather, the brains of infants with WS develop differently from the outset, which has subtle, widespread repercussions (Karmiloff-Smith, 1998, p. 393).

Where do arguments for innate modularity stem from? There are at least four sources. First, they draw on cases from adult neuropsychology where some patients whose brains had previously developed in a typical way subsequently suffer a brain trauma and end up with a pattern of relatively dissociated impairments (e.g., cases of agrammatism, prospagnosia, or agnosia). The second source can be found in one version of evolutionary psychology, which maintains that the human brain has evolved into the equivalent of a Swiss army knife in which each innately specified module is exquisitely adapted for each specific, independent function (Barkow, Cosmides, & Tooby, 1992; Duchaine, Cosmides, & Tooby, 2001). (The analogy ignores the fact that most users of the Swiss army knife actually employ for all purposes only a few of the numerous special-purpose tools.) Third, surprisingly early competences discovered in young infants have been hailed also as a demonstration of innately specified, core knowledge/core principles (e.g., Gelman & Butterworth, 2005; Pinker, 1999; Spelke & Kinzler, 2007). Fourth, genetic disorders, that present with uneven cognitive profiles displaying a juxtaposition of scores "in the normal range" in one or more domains alongside serious deficiencies in others are claimed to illustrate the dissociation of general intelligence from specific domains like grammar, number, face processing, and the like, as many of the above [a] quotations illustrate. So, why do these data and arguments turn out to be less compelling than they at first blush seem?

Do significantly better scores in one domain necessarily indicate an intact/preserved module?

There is a worrying tendency in the developmental disorders literature (as well as in adult neuropsychology) to slip from relative comparisons to absolute ones. So, for instance, a clinical group may score significantly better in Domain A than in Domain B. This is then interpreted as Domain A being intact/preserved and Domain B being impaired (e.g., Tager-Flusberg, Boshart, & Baron-Cohen, 1998). But camouflaged beneath such interpretations is the fact that the scores in both domains may actually be well below those of chronological-age-matched controls. In other words, both domains are impaired; it is simply that, because of its processing demands, one domain is more impaired than the other, not that one is impaired and the other intact, or even, as many authors write *relatively intact*—a theoretically loaded expression with which users want to have their modularity cake and eat it. It is thus critical when reading arguments in favor of innately specified modularity to ensure that the reporting of findings has not slipped from relative comparisons to absolute ones. But, what if scores in proficient domains are actually in the normal range?

What do scores in the normal range tell researchers?

The study of genetic disorders has indeed identified syndromes in which certain domains of relative proficiency coexist with others of more serious impairment. This frequently leads to a research strategy in which the domains of proficiency are merely assessed by standardized tests, with little further exploration once scores fall in the normal range. Subsequently all the research effort is concentrated on the domain(s) of serious deficit. But, ascertaining that scores fall in the normal range can ignore several crucial factors that raise a number of challenging questions: (a) Are the cognitive processes underlying the proficient overt behavior the same as those used by typical controls? (b) Are the brain networks underlying the proficient behavior the same as those used by typical controls? (c) Given the potential of siblings within the same family, are the scores of the atypical sibling closer to the level expected for the family, even though they are within the normal range as well as being significantly higher than the average for the disorder? (d) Did the individual display impairment earlier in development, which has been compensated for subsequently via an atypical trajectory? (e) Is the standardized test sensitive enough to identify subtle impairments that may remain after compensation? And, in general, has the actual trajectory of development been taken into account?

The first two questions can be addressed by work by my colleagues and me on the genetic disorder, WS (see Donnai & Karmiloff-Smith, 2000, and Meyer-Lindenberg et al., 2005, for details of the WS genotype and phenotype). Research on face processing is a relevant example. Individuals with WS score in the normal range on the Benton Test of Face Recognition (Bellugi, Wang, & Jernigan, 1994) as well as on the Rivermead Test of Face Memory (Udwin & Yule, 1991). These findings have been replicated by several labs worldwide (Annaz, Karmiloff-Smith, & Thomas, 2008; Bellugi et al., 1994; Grice et al., 2003; Karmiloff-Smith et al., 2004; Rossen, Jones, Wang, & Klima, 1996; Udwin & Yule, 1991). So, the behavioral facts are not challenged. However, the cognitive and brain processes underlying this proficient behavior are hotly debated. For some researchers, face processing in WS is claimed to be no different from controls without learning difficulties (e.g., Rossen et al., 1996; Tager-Flusberg, Pless-Skewer, Faja, & Joseph, 2003). For others, face processing in WS differs from controls at both the cognitive and brain levels (Deruelle, Mancini, Livet, Cassé-Perrot, & de Schonen, 1999; Grice et al., 2003; Karmiloff-Smith et al., 2004; Mills et al., 2000; Neville, Mills, & Bellugi, 1994). In fact, research by my colleagues and me on electrophysiological studies of face processing in the WS brain have shown that even by adulthood, individuals with WS fail to display the gradual localization and specialization of function (Grice et al., 2003; Karmiloff-Smith et al., 2004) that is the progressive brain signature of normal development (Cohen-Kadosh & Johnson, 2007; de Haan, Humphreys, & Johnson, 2002; Johnson, 2001). So, scores in the normal range do not necessarily entail normal developmental trajectories.

With respect to question (c), in-depth studies are urgently needed of individual differences in the environment and genetic potential within the families of individuals with a disorder of known genetic origin. Take the following hypothetical example. If all of the siblings in a family are particularly talented and eloquent language is continually used in the family environment, with siblings' verbal IQs being around 140–160, and if the atypical sibling has a verbal IQ of 89 and thus falls in the normal range, is that individual more impaired than one whose verbal IQ is also 89 but whose family verbal IQ average is 98? Some of my participants with WS, for instance, reach the upper end of the normal range on vocabulary tests, whereas others are more delayed. However, responses to a preliminary questionnaire indicate that in these more high-functioning cases other family members are often well above the normal range, suggesting a probable impairment in those individuals with WS despite their normal scores. Moreover, studies of other disorders (e.g., specific language impairment [SLI]) already speak to the importance of the environmental and genetic factors. Meta-analyses of research on SLI reveals that although individuals may score in the normal range for nonverbal intelligence, they are sometimes as much as two standard deviations below their potential compared to their siblings, with their levels fluctuating considerably over developmental time (Botting, 2004; Chiat, 2001; Conti-Ramsden & Botting, 1999). This suggests that although language is indeed more seriously impaired in SLI, nonverbal intelligence may also be impaired, albeit to a lesser degree. This raises the possibility of early, more general, low-level processing deficits that affect several domains but to differing degrees and at different developmental times (Benasich & Spitz, 1999; Karmiloff-Smith, 1998). Even if this turns out to be an erroneous assumption for SLI, such a possibility must always be explored when uneven profiles present themselves, rather than using an uneven profile automatically to assume the existence in the brain of independently functioning, domain-specific modules.

Question (d) underlines the crucial role of developmental time in developmental disorders (Karmiloff-Smith, 1992, 1998, 2007). Paradoxically, numerous studies of development (typical or atypical) are not developmental at all, because studying children by no means guarantees a developmental approach (Karmiloff-Smith, 1992, 1998). And one can study adults developmentally (Cornish, 2008). The truly developmental, neuroconstructivist perspective embraces a developmental way of thinking, irrespective of the age of the population studied; even studies of infants can be nondevelopmental. In my view, to understand developmental outcomes, it is vital to identify full developmental trajectories, to assess how progressive change occurs from infancy onwards, and how parts of the developing system may interact with other parts differently at different times across ontogenesis. A process that is vital, say, at Time 2 may no longer play a role at Time 5. Yet its delay at Time 2 may have been crucial to a healthy developmental trajectory and outcome. Indeed, developmental timing is among the most important of factors that need to be taken into account when endeavoring to understand human development, particularly in the atypical case. Whatever the case, in a developmental disorder when scores in the normal range are found in some domains, it is vital to probe the cognitive and brain processes that underlie such efficient behavior and not merely concentrate on domains of deficit. Sometimes the discovery of a different trajectory in a proficient domain (e.g., a featural strategy for face processing) can provide clues to the mechanisms that have gone awry in an impaired domain (e.g., impairments in numerical magnitude comparisons; van Herwegen, Ansari, Xu, & Karmiloff-Smith, 2008).

Finally, Question (e) stresses how vital it is to carry out in-depth task analyses of standardized tests before concluding that participants' scores that fall in the normal range are the same as those of controls without learning difficulties. Can the test in question really detect subtle impairments? Often the granularity of the test is rather coarse and at best provides the researcher with a ballpark idea of how well the individual might be performing compared to the general levels of typical controls. If compensation has taken place over developmental time, it is unlikely that any remaining subtle deficits will be detected. Moreover, standardized tests rarely differentiate between overt behavior and underlying cognitive or brain processes. Hypothesis-driven neurocognitive experiments must be devised to address such questions.

What is wrong with mental-age matching?

Of course, if the researcher is of a nativist persuasion, then paradoxically she or he should not need to match on mental age at all, because this implies that general intelligence does play a role in specific domains and that this role must be neutralized by the matching procedure.

Cross-syndrome comparisons at the behavioral, cognitive, and brain levels can involve very large numbers of mental-age-matched controls, where decisions as to the measures on which to carry out the matching can favor one syndrome and disadvantage another because of their differing, uneven phenotypic profiles. For instance, if Syndrome A shows greater strength in language and Syndrome B greater strength in spatial cognition, then matching on either verbal or nonverbal scores could radically change the results and conclusions drawn therefrom. For this reason, it is vital to develop new approaches in which full, task-specific developmental trajectories are first built of the typical developmental profile (Annaz et al., 2008; Ansari, Donlan, & Karmiloff-Smith, 2007; Ansari et al., 2003; Ansari & Karmiloff-Smith, 2002; Cornish, Scerif, & Karmiloff-Smith, 2007; Karmiloff-Smith, 1998; Karmiloff-Smith et al., 2004; Scerif, Cornish, Wilding, Driver, & Karmiloff-Smith, 2004; see particularly, Thomas et al., 2009). A major advantage of the trajectory approach is that it is theory neutral compared with all forms of mental-age or chronological-age matching. Once a typical, task-specific trajectory is established, each of the atypical participants can be plotted on it and, via regression analyses, it is then possible to assess whether they display deviance or delay, or both, for that task. One can then carry out comparisons across tasks, across domains, and/or across syndromes (for full details, see Thomas et al., 2009). The trajectory method also makes it possible to differentiate between different forms of delay even when the amount of delay is the same across domains within syndromes and/or across syndromes (Annaz et al., 2008; Thomas et al., 2009). To build a full developmental trajectory, it is of course important to devise processing tasks that can be used with very young children (infants and toddlers) through to older children, adolescents, and adults or, at the very least, tasks that yield clear developmental changes across a fairly wide age range, avoiding floor and ceiling effects. The developmental trajectory approach makes it possible to carry out cross-syndrome comparisons more directly than has been the case in the past and to do so at multiple levels of analysis (Johnson, Halit, Grice, & Karmiloff-Smith, 2002; Karmiloff-Smith, 1998, 2006; Karmiloff-Smith, Scerif, & Thomas, 2002; Karmiloff-Smith, Scerif, & Ansari, 2003; Thomas et al., 2009).

Why is the notion of an intact/preserved module unlikely?

The very notion of intactness/preservation has a static flavor and implies genetic determination, as if states in the brain were hard wired, unchanging, and unaffected by developmental or environmental factors. A different, neuroconstructivist view is to consider the brain as a self-structuring, dynamically changing organ over developmental time as a function of multiple interactions at multiple levels, including gene expression (e.g., Casey, 2002; Johnson, 2001). Research on birds and mammals eloquently illustrates this point. Extensive evidence from studies of the neural and epigenetic consequences of song listening and song production in passerine birds (Bolhuis, Zijlstra, den Boer-Visser, & van der Zee, 2000) shows how gene expression changes over developmental time and may be significantly more important during learning than during final production. Rather than something fixed and predetermined, gene expression in the birds turned out to be a function of how many elements the bird copied from its tutor. A second example comes from early mammalian development and also underlines the potential role of the environment in shaping patterns of gene expression (Kaffman & Meaney, 2007). These authors have studied brain development in rodent pups and have elegantly traced how differences in maternal behavior influence patterns of gene expression, which have lifelong effects on behavior. They showed that rather than thinking of gene expression as preprogrammed, differences in the amount of postnatal pup grooming and stroking change the chemistry of the DNA of certain genes involved in the body's responses to stress. These kinds of dynamic environment/gene relations may well be pervasive in mammalian brain development, including that of humans. In general, epigenesis is not deterministic under tight genetic control. Rather, as Gotlieb (2007) stressed, epigenesis is probabilistic and only under very broad genetic control.

Furthermore, what researchers now know about the dynamics of typical brain development points to major structural and functional changes across development that run counter to any arguments in favor of preserved versus impaired modules. First, the cortex starts out highly interconnected in the very young infant (Huttenlocher & Dabholkar, 1997; Huttenlocher & de Courten, 1987), and it is only very gradually over time that localization and specialization of brain function occur (Johnson, 2001). Second, the ratio of white matter to gray matter changes from infancy to later development (Giedd et al., 1999). Third, the thickness of fibre bundles in the corpus callosum between the two hemispheres is different in infancy compared to later development (Giedd et al., 1996). Fourth, studies of the electrophysiology of the brain in processing, say, faces or language reveal widespread activity across several regions of cortex in both hemispheres. It is only over developmental time that the electrophysiological activity becomes progressively fine tuned to predominantly one hemisphere (right hemisphere for faces; left hemisphere for grammar; de Haan et al., 2002; Johnson, 2001; Mills et al., 2000; Neville et al., 1994). These developmental examples clearly indicate that the brain is not a static entity. Indeed, cortical networks are not genetically predetermined or built in to be preserved or impaired in genetic disorders. Rather, they are the emergent outcome of progressively changing processes, which dynamically interact with one another and with environmental input over developmental time, ultimately to give rise to the structured adult brain. But this is not to imply that the neonate brain is a blank slate with no structure, as empiricists would claim. Nor does it imply that any part of the brain can process any and all inputs. On the contrary, neuroconstructivism maintains that the neonate cortex has some regional differentiation in terms of types of neuron, density of neurons, firing thresholds, and so forth. These differences are not domain specific aimed at the sole processing of proprietary inputs nor do they amount to domain-general constraints. Rather, they are domain relevant (i.e., different parts of the brain have small structural differences, which turn out to be more appropriate/relevant to certain kinds of processing over others). But initially, brain activity is widespread for processing all types of input and competition between regions gradually settles which domain-relevant circuits become domain specific over time. Emergent specialization of function (e.g., for faces) might well be viewed as the fine tuning of initially domain-relevant but coarsely coded systems (e.g., for visual patterns), but this is for visual patterns in general, not for faces in particular. The face specialization emerges from the interaction between the environment (huge numbers of face stimuli over time) and the initial visual processing constraints, not from a prespecified, dedicated face-processing module, as some would argue (e.g., Duchaine & Nakayama, 2006).

An eloquent illustration of how emergent specialization can occur comes from a computational model of the dorsal and ventral streams. A small difference in activation levels (equivalent to a difference in neuronal firing thresholds) between two streams sufficed, after competing to process identical inputs, to result in one stream ending up processing where objects were, and the other stream processing the features of objects. In other words, the *where* and *what* pathways were not built in with one only processing spatial information and the other only processing object featural information (O'Reilly & McClelland, 1992). Although both streams initially processed all inputs, an initial, tiny difference in the speed of activation levels was sufficient, then, to progressively give rise to gradual specialization of the where/what pathways. Without this domain-relevant difference in firing thresholds, both streams would have continued to process all inputs in a domain-general way. Moreover, one can then see how a small deficit in, say, the dorsal stream could not only impair spatial processing but could also interfere with the processing of low-spatial frequencies, which could in turn have a cascading subsequent effect on global and configural processing.

Cascading developmental effects of small perturbations are particularly relevant to researchers' understanding of human disorders. While there is still much to be learned about the details of the relations between gene expression and phenotypic outcomes, researchers' current knowledge does allow us to begin to make educated guesses, particularly where the genotype and phenotype have been studied in some depth. In WS, for instance, the genetic mutations are present from conception (due to a misalignment on one copy of Chromosome 7 during meiosis). A half-dosage of the protein that would normally have been expressed in the brain will be missing throughout cortical regions, so the effects of the deletion are likely to be widespread, not specific to a single region of cortex nor to a single purported module. But their deficient expression will affect different regions to greater or lesser degrees, depending on how vital their expression is to the most relevant processing in that region. In fact, developmental disorders will in my view only be explicable at very different levels from higher cognitive modules; rather, they will turn out to be explained in terms of perturbation in far more basic processes very early in development, such as a lack of sufficient pruning, or of overexuberant pruning, of differences in synaptogenesis, in the density or type of neurons, in differing firing thresholds, in poor signal-to-noise ratios in neuronal processing, or generally in terms of atypical timing across developing systems. Rather than invoking a start state of innately specified modules handed down by evolution, the neuroconstructivist approach argues for increased plasticity for learning (Finlay, 2007), that is, for a limited number of domain-relevant biases, which become domain specific over developmental time via their competitive interaction with each other when attempting to process environmental input (Elman et al., 1996). In other words, neuroconstructivism maintains that if the adult brain contains modules, then these emerge developmentally during the ontogenetic process of gradual modularization (Karmiloff-Smith, 1992, 1998). In this sense, domain-specific outcomes may not even be possible without the gradual process of development over time.

Do developmental disorders point to associations more than to dissociations?

The search for dissociations, and particularly for double dissociations, has been a primary goal of much of the work in adult neuropsychology and of many studies of genetic disorders in children. By contrast, it has been argued that to understand the nonstatic atypical processes of human development, the quest for double dissociations is both theoretically misconceived and empirically dubious (Karmiloff-Smith et al., 2003). In fact, developmental disorders often turn out to pinpoint associations across domains rather than dissociations (Bishop, 2002). In the case of WS, for instance, a featural processing bias has been documented across several different domains, such as face processing, spatial processing, auditory processing, and numerical processing (Bellugi et al., 1994; Elsabbagh, 2005; Karmiloff-Smith et al., 2004; Paterson, Brown, Gsodl, Johnson, & Karmiloff-Smith, 1999; van Herwegen et al., 2008). This featural bias points to early, common processing problems across several domains before, in the typically developing individual, they would have become naturally segregated and specialized over developmental time.

Where does this featural bias in WS originate? A study of gamma-band oscillatory activity in frontal cortex in the brain's reaction to viewing upright and inverted faces yielded unusual patterns in participants with WS and in those with autism (Grice et al., 2001), both of whom have been claimed to process featurally and to have difficulties in integrating/binding features into a configural whole. However, although gamma-band bursts were atypical in both clinical groups, the gamma-band patterns in the brains of individuals with WS and autism differed radically, suggesting that researchers need to rethink the notion of featural processing at the cognitive level. In the case of WS, our studies of infants suggest that featural processing may originate in sticky fixation and in the inability to plan rapid saccadic eye movements (Brown et al., 2003), which could result in difficulties in rapid configural processing. Interestingly, infants with Down syndrome do not have problems planning saccadic eye movements (Brown et al., 2003) and they do not suffer from a featural processing bias later in development. The cause of the featural bias in autism is likely to be different from that of WS, given the significant differences in gamma-band activity. In general, researchers need to recall that similar behavioral outcomes may stem from very different cognitive/brain causes (see, also, comparisons in the social domain between autism and WS in Tsirempolou, Lawrence, Lee, Ewing, & Karmiloff-Smith, 2006).

Is the environment the same for typically and atypically developing individuals?

A frequent question asked by nativists and behavioral geneticists is whether specific aspects of human cognition are due to nature or nurture. But from the neuroconstructivist point of view, this is clearly a false dichotomy. Genes, brain, and environment play a dynamic, multidirectional role in shaping, not merely triggering, developmental outcomes. However, a question that is rarely addressed in the developmental neuroscience literature is whether the environment is the same for individuals developing typically and those developing atypically. In other words, does having a developmental disorder not only involve genetic mutations but also subtly change the environment in which the atypical infant/child develops?

A couple of examples serve to make a strong case for hypothesizing that the environment does indeed change with respect to atypically developing infants, probably continuing to do so throughout development. The first example is from motor development. Informal observations of families who visit our lab reveal that parents of infants and toddlers with genetic syndromes find it difficult (compared to parents of typically developing children) to allow their atypically developing offspring to mouth objects freely and to crawl/walk uninhibited in order to fully explore their environment. This reticence is probably because of greater fear of potential danger and accidents, but it results in a less richly explored environment. The second example comes from the learning of vocabulary. In the typical case, parents allow young children to overgeneralize in the early stages of language acquisition when they start to name things (e.g., when the toddler says "cat" when it is actually a dog, the parent often lets it go because both are small animals and they know their child will learn the correct term in the long run). By contrast, in the case of parents of toddlers with, for instance, Down syndrome, parents tend to rapidly veto any overgeneralization (C. Mervis, personal communication, July 10, 1999), probably because they fear that the child with lower intelligence will never learn the correct term if allowed to overgeneralize. However, initial overgeneralization in the healthy child may actually encourage category formation, known to be subsequently impaired in the atypical case. Such unconscious assumptions about atypical development may lead parents to provide less variation in linguistic input, shorter sentences, and in general a less richly varied environment. These quite subtle changes in the child's environment are likely to compound over time, such that the environment of the atypically developing child may increasingly differ from that of the typically developing child. There is, therefore, a vital need for scientific studies of how having a developmental disorder subtly changes the social, cognitive, linguistic, and physical environment in which the atypically developing child grows, which has important implications for intervention.

Implications of a neuroconstructivist approach

Recent changes in position of hitherto staunch nativist theorists might be seen as bringing them closer to the neuroconstructivist framework. For example, Baron-Cohen (1998) argued for a "minimalist innate modularity theory" (p. 184), suggesting that the theory-of-mind module might emerge from lower-level systems for detecting eye gaze, intentionality, and shared attention. Likewise, van der Lely (2005) has indicated that her initial syntactic hypothesis has now been replaced by the computational grammatical complexity hypothesis, arguing now that both syntax and phonology rely on a common computational property operating over linguistic representations, which is claimed to be atypical in grammatical SLI. However, like Baron-Cohen's thinking, this remains a very domain-specific hypothesis (complex computations confined to operating solely on linguistic representations) and does not consider possible interactions with nonlinguistic parts of the developing system over developmental time. In other words, these hypotheses do not pertain to domain-relevant processes but do pertain to domain-specific computations over proprietary inputs. Indeed, the theorizing is based on the claim that the grammatical neurocircuitry underlying language is a developmentally unique higher cognitive system in the functional architecture of the brain, which can be selectively impaired (Fonteneau & van der Lely, 2007).

Nonetheless, the notion of impaired versus intact brain systems in uneven cognitive profiles might be considered useful for clinical practice, even if theoretically it underplays the role of development. If a patient has scores in the normal range in a specific domain, surely there is no need to consider remediation in that domain? The nativist would agree, but the neuroconstructivist would not rule out training in a proficient domain. For instance, take a patient who presents with a serious deficit in, say, number and scores in the normal range in face processing, seemingly very different domains. It would be tempting in such a case to tailor remediation solely to the domain of number. But that misses the very point of the neuroconstructivist framework. Once one explores multiple, low-level interacting processes that underpin face processing early on in development, this leads to a more dynamic view of remediation. In adulthood, the proficient behavior of individuals with WS on face processing tasks is due to a focus on features. Now, if an infant cannot plan saccades and therefore has sticky fixation (as is the case for those with WS, e.g.), then they are more likely to fixate on features than rapidly process the configuration of a face. So, despite the proficient behavioral outcome, face processing in WS is based on different cognitive and brain processes compared to controls (Grice et al., 2001, 2003; Mills et al., 2000). Thus, remediation is necessary in a domain where the outcome gives rise to scores in the normal range. Moreover, early on in development domains are not isolated from one another in their developmental trajectories. Number, too, is influenced by deficits in visual scanning and planning of saccades. Infants with WS fail to scan numerical displays as fully as required in order to discriminate changes in number (van Herwegen et al., 2008). So remediation for number and for face processing might start out by stimulating saccadic movements, and not with number or face processing training at all. Furthermore, take the case of a patient with spatial and numerical deficits, and a parietal cortex that is small compared to healthy controls. The tempting conclusion might be that the atypical size of the parietal region causes the deficits in numerical outcome. But there are two caveats to such a conclusion. First, data about brain regions is usually from adult brains. This tells researchers nothing about possible proportional changes over developmental time. Second, the opposite direction of causality is also possible. From inadequate processing of inputs relevant to parietal cortex, this region may develop less connectivity over time and end up smaller. Only a truly developmental, neuroconstructivist approach could settle such differing interpretations.

Concluding thoughts

Neuroconstructivism does not rule out domain specificity; it argues that it cannot be taken for granted and must always be questioned. Unlike the nativist perspective, neuroconstructivism offers a truly developmental approach that focuses on change and emergent outcomes. And, every aspect of development turns out to be dynamic and interactive. Genes do not act in isolation in a predetermined way. Even the FOXP2 gene, about which there was much excitement regarding its role in human language, must be thought of in terms of the downstream gene targets to which FOXP2 binds. The profiles of those downstream genes suggest roles in a wide range of general, not domain-specific, functions including morphogenesis, neurite growth, axon guidance, synaptic plasticity, and neurotransmission (Teramitsu & White, 2007). This is a very different level from theorizing at the level of cognitive modules and points to the multilevel complexities of understanding human development in any domain.

For many decades, the notion of plasticity tended to be reserved for the human system's response to damage. By contrast, it has become abundantly clear that development—whether typical or atypical, whether human or nonhuman—is fundamentally characterized by plasticity for learning, with the infant brain dynamically structuring itself over the course of ontogeny. While some macrostructures like the overall six-layer structure of cortex may well be under general genetic constraints, much of the microcircuitry of cortex turns out to be the result of complex multilevel interactions over time. Human intelligence is not a state (i.e., not a collection of static, built-in modules handed down by evolution and that can be intact or impaired). Rather, human intelligence is a process (i.e., the emergent property of dynamic multidirectional interactions between genes, brain, cognition, behavior, and environment).

References

Annaz, D., Karmiloff-Smith, A., & Thomas, M. C. (2008). The importance of tracing developmental trajectories for clinical child neuropsychology. In J. Reed & J. Warner Rogers (Eds.), *Child neuropsychology: Concepts, theory and practice*. Oxford, England: Blackwell.

Ansari, D., Donlan, C., & Karmiloff-Smith, A. (2007). Typical and atypical development of visual estimation abilities. *Cortex*, *43*, 758–768.

Ansari, D., Donlan, C., Thomas, M., Ewing, S., Peen, T., & Karmiloff- Smith, A. (2003). What makes counting count? Verbal and visuo-spatial contributions to typical and atypical number development. *Journal of Experimental Child Psychology*, *85*, 50–62.

Ansari, D., & Karmiloff-Smith, A. (2002). Atypical trajectories of number development. *Trends in the Cognitive Sciences*, *6*, 511–516.

Barkow, J. H., Cosmides, L., & Tooby, J. (Eds.). (1992). *The adapted mind: Evolutionary psychology and the generation of culture*. New York: Oxford University Press.

Baron-Cohen, S. (1998). Does the study of autism justify minimalist innate modularity? *Learning and Individual Differences*, *10*, 179–191.

Baron-Cohen, S., Ring, H., Moriarty, J., Schmitz, P., Costa, D., & Ell, P. (1994). Recognition of mental state terms: Clinical findings in children with autism and a functional neuroimaging study of normal adults. *British Journal of Psychiatry*, *165*, 640–649.

Bellugi, U., Wang, P., & Jernigan, T. L. (1994). Williams syndrome: An unusual neuropsychological profile. In S. Broman & J. Grafman (Eds.), *Atypical cognitive deficits in developmental disorders: Implications for brain function* (pp. 23–56). Hillsdale, NJ: Erlbaum.

Benasich, A. A., & Spitz, R. V. (1999). Insights from infants: Temporal processing abilities and genetics contribute to language impairment. In K. Whitmore, H. Hart, & G. Willems (Eds.), *A neurodevelopmental approach to specific learning disorders* (pp. 191–210). London: Mac Keith Press.

Bishop, D. V. M. (2002). Motor immaturity and specific speech and language impairment: Evidence for a common genetic basis. *American Journal of Medical Genetics: Neuropsychiatric Genetics, 114*, 56–63.

Bolhuis, J. J., Zijlstra, G. G. O., den Boer-Visser, A. M., & van der Zee, E. A. (2000). Localized neuronal activation in the zebra finch brain is related to the strength of song learning. *Proceedings of the National Academy of Sciences, USA, 97*, 2282–2285.

Botting, N. (2004). Non-verbal cognitive development and language impairment. *Journal of Child Psychology and Psychiatry, 46*, 317–326.

Brown, J., Johnson, M. H., Paterson, S., Gilmore, R., Gsödl, M., Longhi, E., & Karmiloff-Smith, A. (2003). Spatial representation and attention in toddlers with Williams syndrome and Down syndrome. *Neuropsychologia, 41*, 1037–1046.

Carpenter, P. A., Just, M. A., Keller, T. A., Cherkassky, V., Roth, J. K., & Minshew, N. J. (2001). Dynamic cortical systems subserving cognition: fMRI studies with typical and atypical individuals. In J. L. McClelland & R. S. Siegler (Eds.), *Mechanisms of cognitive development: Behavioral and neural perspectives* (pp. 353–383). Mahwah, NJ: Erlbaum.

Casey, B. J. (2002, May 24). Windows into the human brain. *Science, 296*, 1409–1410.

Chiat, S. (2001). Mapping theories of developmental language impairment: Premises, predictions and evidence. *Language & Cognitive Processes, 16*, 113–142.

Cohen-Kadosh, K., & Johnson, M. H. (2007). Developing a cortex specialized for face perception. *Trends in Cognitive Sciences, 11*, 367–369.

Conti-Ramsden, G., & Botting, N. (1999). Classification of children with specific language impairment: Longitudinal considerations. *Journal of Speech, Language, & Hearing Research, 42*, 1195–1204.

Cornish, K. (2008, October). *Relatives of children with Fragile X syndrome: Merely carriers or subtle cognitive impairments over time? Colloquium presented to Birkbeck Centre for Brain & Cognitive Development*, London.

Cornish, K., Scerif, G., & Karmiloff-Smith, A. (2007). Tracing syndrome-specific trajectories of attention across the lifespan. *Cortex, 43*, 672–685.

de Haan, M., Humphreys, K., & Johnson, M. H. (2002). Developing a brain specialized for face perception: A converging methods approach. *Developmental Psychobiology, 40*, 200–212.

Deruelle, C., Mancini, J., Livet, M. O., Cassé-Perrot, C., & de Schonen, S. (1999). Configural and local processing of faces in children with Williams syndrome. *Brain and Cognition, 41*, 276–298.

Donnai, D., & Karmiloff-Smith, A. (2000). Williams syndrome: From genotype through to the cognitive phenotype. *American Journal of Medical Genetics, 97*, 164–171.

Duchaine, B., Cosmides, L., & Tooby, J. (2001). Evolutionary psychology and the brain. *Current Opinion in Neurobiology, 11*, 225–230.

Duchaine, B., & Nakayama, K. (2006). Developmental prosopagnosia: A window to content-specific face processing. *Current Opinion in Neurobiology, 16*, 166–173.

Elman, J. L., Bates, E., Johnson, M. H., Karmiloff-Smith, A., Parisi, D., & Plunkett, K. (1996). *Rethinking innateness: A connectionist perspective on development*. Cambridge, MA: MIT Press.

Elsabbagh, M. (2005). Domain-relevant mechanisms of developmental change: Typical and atypical pathways of perceptual organization. Un-published doctoral dissertation, University of Quebec, Quebec, Montreal, Canada.

Finlay, B. L. (2007). E pluribus unum: Too many unique human capacities and too many theories. In S. Gangestad & J. Simpson (Eds.), *The evolution of mind: Fundamental questions and controversies* (pp. 294–304). New York: Guilford Press.

Fonteneau, C., & van der Lely, H. J. K. (2007). Electrical brain responses in language-impaired children reveal grammar-specific deficits. *Public Library of Science ONE 3*(3), e1832.do. doi: 10.1371/journal.pone.0001832

Gelman, R., & Butterworth, B. (2005). What is the relationship between number and language? *Trends in Cognitive Science*, *9*, 6–10.

Giedd, J., Blumenthal, J., Jeffries, N., Castellanos, F., Liu, H., Zijdenbos, A., et al. (1999). Brain development during childhood and adolescence: A longitudinal MRI study. *Nature Neuroscience*, *2*, 861–863.

Giedd, J., Rumsey, J., Castellanos, F., Rajapakse, J., Kaysen, D., Vaituzis, A., et al. (1996). A quantitative MRI study of the corpus callosum in children and adolescents. *Developmental Brain Research*, *91*, 274–280.

Gotlieb, G. (2007). Probabilistic epigenesis. *Developmental Science*, *10*, 1–11.

Grice, S., Spratling, M. W., Karmiloff-Smith, A., Halit, H., Csibra, G., de Haan, M., & Johnson, M. H. (2001). Disordered visual processing and oscillatory brain activity in autism and Williams syndrome. *NeuroReport*, *12*, 2697–2700.

Grice, S. J., de Haan, M., Halit, H., Johnson, M. H., Csibra, G., Grant, J., & Karmiloff-Smith, A. (2003). ERP abnormalities of visual perception in Williams syndrome. *NeuroReport*, *14*, 1773–1777.

Huttenlocher, P. R., & Dabholkar, A. S. (1997). Regional differences in synaptogenesis in human cerebral cortex. *Journal of Comparative Neurology*, *387*, 167–178.

Huttenlocher, P. R., & de Courten, C. (1987). The development of synapses in striate cortex of man. *Human Neurobiology*, *6*, 1–9.

Johnson, M. H. (2001). Functional brain development in humans. *Nature Reviews Neuroscience*, *2*, 475–483.

Johnson, M. H., Halit, H., Grice, S. J., & Karmiloff-Smith, A. (2002). Neuroimaging and developmental disorders: A perspective from multiple levels of analysis. *Development and Psychopathology*, *14*, 521–536.

Kaffman, A., & Meaney, M. J. (2007). Neurodevelopmental sequelae of postnatal maternal care in rodents: Clinical and research implications of molecular insights. *Journal of Child Psychology and Psychiatry*, *48*(3–4), 224–244.

Karmiloff-Smith, A. (1992). *Beyond modularity: A developmental approach to cognitive science*. Cambridge, MA: MIT Press.

Karmiloff-Smith, A. (1998). Development itself is the key to understanding developmental disorders. *Trends in Cognitive Sciences*, *2*, 389–398.

Karmiloff-Smith, A. (2006). The tortuous route from genes to behaviour: A neuroconstructivist approach. *Cognitive, Affective and Behavioural Neuroscience*, *6*, 9–17.

Karmiloff-Smith, A. (2007). Atypical epigenesis. *Developmental Science*, *10*, 84–88.

Karmiloff-Smith, A., Scerif, G., & Ansari, D. (2003). Double dissociations in developmental disorders? Theoretically misconceived, empirically dubious. *Cortex*, *39*, 161–163.

Karmiloff-Smith, A., Scerif, G., & Thomas, M. S. C. (2002). Different approaches to relating genotype to phenotype in developmental disorders. *Developmental Psychobiology*, *40*, 311–322.

Karmiloff-Smith, A., Thomas, M., Annaz, D., Humphreys, K., Ewing, S., Brace, N., et al. (2004). Exploring the Williams Syndrome face processing debate: The importance of building developmental trajectories. *Journal of Child Psychology and Psychiatry, 45*, 1258–1274.

Leslie, A. M. (1992). Pretence, autism, and the theory-of-mind-module. *Current Directions in Psychological Science, 1*, 18–21.

Mervis, C. B., & Becerra, A. M. (2007). Language and communicative development in Williams syndrome. *Mental Retardation and Developmental Disabilities Research Reviews, 13*, 3–15.

Meyer-Lindenberg, A., Mervis, C. B., Sarpal, D., Koch, P., Steele, S., Kohn, P., et al. (2005). Functional, structural and metabolic abnormalities of the hippocampal formation in Williams syndrome. *Journal of Clinical Investigation, 115*, 1888–1895.

Mills, D. L., Alvarez, T. D., St. George, M., Appelbaum, L. G., Bellugi, U., & Neville, H. (2000). Electrophysiological studies of face processing in Williams syndrome. *Journal of Cognitive Neuroscience, 12*, 47–64.

Neville, H. J., Mills, D. L., & Bellugi, U. (1994). Effects of altered auditory sensitivity and age of language acquisition on the development of lang\uage-relevant neural systems: Preliminary studies of Williams syndrome. In S. Broman & J. Grafman (Eds.), *Atypical cognitive deficits in developmental disorders: Implications for brain function* (pp. 67–83). Hillsdale, NJ: Erlbaum.

O'Reilly, R. C., & McClelland, J. L. (1992). *The self-organization of spatially invariant representations*. (Tech. Rep. No. PDP.CNS.92.5). Pittsburgh, PA: Carnegie Mellon University.

Paterson, S. J., Brown, J. H., Gsodl, M. K., Johnson, M. H., & Karmiloff- Smith, A. (1999, December 17). Cognitive modularity and genetic disorders. *Science, 286*, 2355–2358.

Persico, A. M., & Bourgeron, T. (2006). Searching for ways out of the autism maze: Genetic, epigenetic and environmental clues. *Trends in Neuroscience, 29*, 349–358.

Piattelli-Palmarini, M. (2001, June 21). Speaking of learning. *Nature, 411*, 887–888.

Pinker, S. (1999). *Words and rules*. London: Weidenfeld & Nicolson.

Rossen, M. L., Jones, W., Wang, P. P., & Klima, E. S. (1996). Face processing: Remarkable sparing in Williams syndrome. *Genetic Counseling, 6*, 138–140.

Scerif, G., Cornish, K., Wilding, J., Driver, J., & Karmiloff-Smith, A. (2004). Visual selective attention in typically developing toddlers and toddlers with fragile X and Williams syndrome. *Developmental Science, 7*, 116–130.

Spelke, E. S., & Kinzler, K. D. (2007). Core knowledge. *Developmental Science, 10*, 89–96.

Tager-Flusberg, H., Boshart, J., & Baron-Cohen, S. (1998). Reading the windows to the soul: Evidence of domain-specific sparing in Williams syndrome. *Journal of Cognitive Neuroscience, 10*, 631–639.

Tager-Flusberg, H., Pless-Skewer, D., Faja, S., & Joseph, R. M. (2003). People with Williams syndrome process faces holistically. *Cognition, 89*, 11–24.

Teramitsu, I., & White, S. A. (2007). Motor Learning: The FoxP2 puzzle piece. *Current Biology, 18*, R335–R337.

Thomas, M. S. C., Annaz, D., Ansari, D., Scerif, G., Jarrold, C., & Karmiloff-Smith, A. (2009) Using developmental trajectories to understand developmental disorders. *Journal of Speech, Language, and Hearing Research*, 52, 336–358.

Tsirempolou, E., Lawrence, K., Lee, K., Ewing, S., & Karmiloff-Smith, A. (2006). Understanding the social meaning of the eyes: Is Williams syndrome so different from autism? *World Journal of Pediatrics, 2*, 288–296.

Udwin, O., & Yule, W. (1991). A cognitive and behavioural phenotype in Williams syndrome. *Journal of Clinical Experimental Neuropsychology*, *13*, 232–244.

van der Lely, H. K. J. (2005). Domain-specific cognitive systems: Insight from grammatical specific language impairment. *Trends in Cognitive Sciences*, *9*, 53–59.

Van Herwegen, J., Ansari, D., Xu, F., & Karmiloff-Smith, A. (2008). Small and large number processing in infants and toddlers with Williams syndrome. *Developmental Science*, *11*, 637–643.

14 An alternative to domain-general or domain-specific frameworks for theorizing about human evolution and ontogenesis

Annette Karmiloff-Smith

1. Domain-specific vs domain-general frameworks

The Nature *or* Nurture debate is obviously not new. It already raged in the 4th and 5th centuries BC amongst the ancient Greeks. The modern version is often, although not always, couched in terms of domain-specific versus domain-general accounts of human cognition, in which some theorists argue that the infant brain comes equipped with primitive conceptual representations or domain-specific core knowledge or domain-specific learning algorithms (Baillargeon & Carey, 2012; Carey, 2011; Spelke & Kinzler, 2007; van der Lely, 2005; van der Lely & Pinker, 2014), while others invoke more domain-general learning mechanisms without the need for representational content (Elman et al., 1996; Kirkham, Slemmer & Johnson, 2002; Lany & Saffran, 2013). Yet, despite the fact that most scientists now fully recognise that evolution and ontogenetic development must derive from very complex interactions of Nature *and* Nurture, the dichotomy continues in the 21st century to influence arguments about the structure of the human mind/brain (Pinker, 2002), how it evolved (Cosmides, Barrett & Tooby, 2010), and how to interpret data such as category-specific or domain-specific deficits in children and adults (Aguillo, Rampyura & Butterworth, 2010; Clahsen & Temple, 2003; Cohen Kadosh, Bahrami, Walsh, Butterworth, Popescu, & Price, 2011). Is the infant brain an undifferentiated tabula rasa on which experience imprints itself via (innate) general learning mechanisms, or does the infant brain come with innate, specialized knowledge upon which further domain-specific learning takes place? Caution is required, however, because opting for the innately-specified perspective can, as Bates and colleagues (Bates et al., 1998; Karmiloff-Smith et al., 1998) pointed out, lead to conflating innateness with: (a) *domain specificity* (outcome X is so singular that it must be innate), (b) *species specificity* (humans are the only species who do X, so X must be specified in the human genome), (c) *localization* (outcome X is mediated by a particular brain region, so X must be innate), and (d) *learnability* (we cannot establish how X could be learned, so X must be innate).

The existence of brain-damaged adult patients presenting with uneven neuropsychological profiles and very specific deficits led many researchers to divide the mind/brain into separate modules for number, face processing, space, semantics, syntax, and so forth, each cognitive domain being processed within a specialized region of the brain, characterized as either intact or impaired. This view is of course not one endorsed by all neuropsychologists. However, modular, domain-specific explanations have not been confined to neuropsychological patients. The concept has also been generalized to studies of typically developing infants/children by researchers of a nativist persuasion (e.g., Baillargeon & Carey, 2012; Carey, 2011; Hyde & Spelke, 2011; Lee & Spelke, 2010; Spelke & Kinzler, 2007; Xu, Spelke & Goddard, 2005). Rather than being accounted for by plasticity and an early capacity for learning, competences detected within the first months of life have often been explained in terms of built-in core knowledge/conceptual representational primitives, i.e., infants are born with innately-specified modules or sub-modules for processing specific types of input from each domain: number processing modules (Dehaene, 1997; Butterworth, 1999; Gelman & Gallistel, 1986), face-processing modules (Duchaine 2000; Duchaine & Nakayama, 2005, 2006; Duchaine, Yovel, Butterworth, & Nakayama, 2006), grammatical sub-modules (van der Lely & Pinker, 2014), spatial cognition sub-modules (Landau, Hoffman & Kurz, 2005), and modules containing core knowledge of the constraints governing the physical world (Spelke & Kinzler, 2007). Within this framework, learning was initially relegated to a very secondary role (Piattelli-Palmarini, 2001). However, as the importance of learning has increasingly come to the fore, researchers of this persuasion have invoked conceptual reorganization or the role of language in extending domain-specific core knowledge of infant sensitivities to different cognitive domains into more abstract, adult-like knowledge (Baillargeon & Carey, 2012; Spelke & Kinzler, 2009).

Furthermore, one brand of so-called evolutionary psychology (Duchaine, Cosmides & Tooby 2001; Cosmides, Barrett & Tooby, 2010; Hauser & Spelke, 2004) makes similar domain-specific claims, arguing that the relationship between our ancestral past and the human brain today can be understood in terms of innately-specified, cognitive-level modules passed on through Evolution (see discussion in Bolhuis et al., 2011), e.g., a cheater detection module, a grammar module, a face-processing module, a number module, and so forth, each coded for by specific sets of genes. Under this view, the brain is conceptualized in terms of the metaphor of a Swiss army knife, each tool (cognitive domain or sub-domain) being exquisitely fashioned and dedicated solely to carrying out a set of very circumscribed tasks, passed on by evolution from our hunter-gatherer ancestors.

Some researchers studying neurodevelopmental disorders in children have also proposed a strictly modular explanation. Among the first to take this position were Baron-Cohen, Leslie, Frith and colleagues who claimed that autism could be accounted for by the lack of or damage to a theory-of-mind module (Baron-Cohen et al., 1985; Leslie, 1992), due to the mutation of a specific gene or set of genes which interfered with the development of a specific brain region, the orbito-frontal cortex (Baron-Cohen et al. 1999). This region was dedicated, it was argued, to computations dealing with the attribution of intentional states to others, an ability that is compromised in autism. Rapidly the explanatory framework of damaged versus intact modules or sub-modules was generalized to a vast number of other neurodevelopmental disorders (Temple, 1997; Butterworth, 2008;

Clahsen & Temple, 2003; Duchaine, Nieminen-von Wendt, New, & Kulomaki, 2003; Molko et al., 2003; Rice, 1999; Shalev, Manor & Gross-Tsur, 2005), particularly those which present with uneven cognitive profiles, such as dyslexia (Castle & Coltheart, 1993), Specific Language Impairment (Gopnik, 1990; van der Lely, 2005; van der Lely & Pinker, 2014), Williams syndrome (Clahsen & Temple, 2003), developmental dyscalculia (Butterworth, 1999; Temple, 1997), and developmental prosopagnosia (Duchaine 2000).

In summary, early competences identified in typically developing infants, deficits found in brain-damaged adults or in children with genetic disorders, as well as arguments from evolutionary psychology, all seemed to corroborate the claim that the domain-general framework could not explain early competences nor atypical uneven cognitive profiles and that, instead, the human mind/brain had to be conceived of as being composed of highly specialized input/output systems, at both the perceptual and cognitive levels. So, why not indeed endorse this domain-specific framework? It would seem to account well for those typically developing children who show strong proficiency in, say, numeracy and relative weakness in literacy, or vice versa. At first blush, it also seems to be the appropriate explanation for adult neuropsychological patients presenting with domain-specific or category-specific deficits. Likewise for atypically developing children: the domain-specific framework would seem to offer a plausible explanation for the existence of children with autism who may present with high abilities in, say, mathematics but are incapable of dealing with the simplest of aspects of social interaction, or those with Williams syndrome who speak fluently but cannot do simple additions. How could a domain-general view explain such specificities? Indeed, the existence of such uneven cognitive profiles is well established. So, is the only alternative to the domain-general approach that of opting for innate, domain specificity as the most appropriate explanatory framework for understanding the roots of human cognition? Not necessarily, because the domain-specific framework is itself questionable. Crucially, it ignores the developmental history of the organism.

2. Neuroconstructivism and the *domain-relevant* framework

So, are there only two alternatives – domain-specific/domain-general – for theorizing about human evolution and ontogenesis? I argue that there is a third alternative: a *domain-relevant* framework – one which would likely be endorsed by several theorists working within a more domain-general framework. A domain-relevant approach to understanding specialization in adult brains argues that the brain starts out with a number of basic-level biases, each of which is somewhat more relevant to the processing of certain kinds of input over others, but which only ***become*** domain-specific over developmental time. This occurs, it is argued, through a process of neuronal competition and gradual specialization, location and modularization of function – a neuroconstructivist approach (Elman et al., 1996; Karmiloff-Smith, 1992, 1998; Marescal et al., 2007; Westerman et al., 2007, 2010).

Neuroconstructivism does not believe that the infant brain is an undifferentiated tabula rasa upon which experience simply imprints itself. Nor does it rule out domain-specificity; it argues that, when one discovers specialized functions in the adult brain, it cannot be taken for granted that the same automatically holds for the start state of the infant mind/brain (Karmiloff-Smith, 1998, 2013; Paterson et al., 1999). Rather, neuroconstructivism maintains that domain-specificity, i.e., functional specialization, is the emergent outcome of developmental processes rather than the start state.

It is within the neuroconstructivist account of development (Karmiloff-Smith, 1992, 1998; Elman et al., 1996; Johnson, 2001; Mareschal et al., 2007; Stiles, 2009; Thomas, Knowland & Karmiloff-Smith, 2011; Westerman, Karmiloff-Smith & Thomas, 2010) that domain-relevant approaches have been put forward, particularly with respect to neurodevelopmental disorders. These latter are deemed to be explicable at a very different level from the intact/impaired domain-specific cognitive modules often invoked. Rather, atypical phenotypic outcomes are argued to be rooted in perturbations in far more basic processes early in development, such as a lack of/over-exuberant pruning, or differences in synaptogenesis, dendritic growth, in the density/type of neurons, in firing thresholds, in poor signal to noise ratios, or generally in terms of atypical timing across developing systems. In other words, from a neuroconstructivist viewpoint, adult brain specialization *emerges developmentally* (Casey, Giedd & Thomas, 2000; Elman et al., 1996; Johnson, 2001; Karmiloff-Smith, 1992, 1998). In this sense, I would argue that domain-specific outcomes may actually be impossible in the absence of a gradual process of development over time.

But why shouldn't the scientist consider the infant brain as starting out highly specialized with built-in conceptual knowledge, as some leading theorists maintain (Carey, 2011; Spelke & Kizler, 2007)? This is because multiple facets of early human development point instead to a flexible, plastic, self-structuring system, open to extensive environmental influences at the level of gene expression, brain, cognition, and behaviour. Indeed, developmental change is the rule at every level, not the exception. Four examples serve to illustrate this: (1) cortical areas are initially much more highly interconnected in the infant brain than in the adult brain (Huttenlocher & de Courten, 1987; Huttenlocher & Dabholkar, 1997; Stiles, 2009), and it is only progressively over time, with the strengthening of some connections and the pruning of others, that localization and specialization of brain function occur (Johnson, 2001); (2) the ratio of white matter to gray matter is not static; it changes over developmental time (Giedd et al., 1999); (3) the thickness of fibre bundles in the corpus callosum between the two hemispheres is different in infancy compared to later brain development (Giedd et al., 1996); and, (4) studies of neural processing of faces or language, for instance, reveal that early on in development neural activity is widespread in several cortical regions across both hemispheres. It is only later in development that neural activity becomes progressively fine-tuned more predominantly to one hemisphere (RH for face identification; LH for grammar production and phonemic processing) (Cohen-Kadosh, Henson, Cohen Kadosh, Johnson, & Dick, 2009; de Haan, Humphreys & Johnson, 2002; Johnson, 2001; Krishnan, Leech, Mercure, Lloyd-Fox, & Dick, 2014; Mills, Coffy-Corins & Nevelle, 1997; Minagawa-Kawai et al., 2004, 2007;

Mills, & Bellugi, 1994; Stiles, 2012). Indeed, as Stiles stresses (Stiles, 2012) decades of cross-sectional and longitudinal studies of children with peri-natal focal lesions (reviewed in Bates & Roe, 2001; Stiles, 2012) have shown over developmental time only very transient relationships between specific lesion sites and language deficits. Furthermore, such relationships turn out to be very different from those present in adult aphasic patients. As Stiles points out, it turns out that there is no evidence of long-lasting language delays associated with left versus hemisphere perinatal focal brain injury (Stiles, 2012).

These four developmental examples clearly indicate that the microstructure of the brain is neither pre-specified nor static. Indeed, cortical networks are not genetically determined, to be spared or impaired in genetic disorders. Rather, they are the emergent outcome of progressively changing neural function and structure (Casey, Tottenham, Liston, & Durston, 2005; Durston et al., 2006; Paterson, Heim, Friedman, Choudhury, & Benasich, 2006), which dynamically interact with one another and with environmental input, ultimately giving rise to the structured adult brain. Emergent specialization of function is viewed by neuroconstructivists as the fine-tuning of initially diffuse, domain-relevant, but coarsely coded systems, which become increasingly domain-specific over developmental time.

3. Changing views on modularity

Of course, neuroconstructivism is not alone in taking a far more dynamic approach to developmental change and to adult patient data. For development, this has been particularly true of those espousing dynamical systems accounts (e.g., Smith & Thelen, 2003), although they tend to rule out any notion of representation. For healthy ageing in adults, similar arguments have emerged about the dynamic and changing nature of neural processes with respect to grammatical processing (Tyler et al., 2010). Modules are now considered far less encapsulated, allowing them to operate both in a relatively independent way in some circumstances, but modifiable by other processes in other circumstances (e.g., Dehaene & Cohen, 2007). However, while it is unlikely that theorists such as Spelke or Pinker would take a strictly Fodorian view of modules (Fodor, 1983), their current theorizing nonetheless continues to invoke innate specification of highly specialized systems (Spelke & Kinzler, 2007; van der Lely & Pinker, 2014), a very different approach from that of neuroconstructivists.

Dehaene and collaborators' recent work (Dehaene & Cohen, 2007; Dehaene, Charles, King, & Marti, 2014; see, also, Anderson, 2010) has several features in common with the domain-relevant approach. The neuronal recycling hypothesis argues that cultural inventions like reading and writing, which are too recent to be genetically determined, invade evolutionarily older cortical circuits, initially devoted to different but similar functions, thereby inheriting many of the structural constraints of the original circuits (Dehaene, 2009). The notion that these new functions seek out a "neuronal niche", i.e., a cortical area in the brain *relevant* to the processing required, is clearly along the same lines as the domain-relevant approach outlined above (Karmiloff-Smith, 1998). Dehaene argues that these novel cultural functions must identify a cortical area whose prior function is similar but also sufficiently plastic to accommodate its processing demands. A domain-general account could not accommodate these ideas because the neuronal niche must already be domain-relevant to the invading process. It also would not be accommodated by a strictly domain-specific modular approach, because the "invasion" requires plasticity and flexibility.

Dehaene and collaborators also address the perennial problem of conscious access to knowledge, offering an impressive mathematical and neural model (Dehaene et al., 2014). Here again, they argue for plasticity and neural cross-talk, relaxing the encapsulated nature of modules in favour of flexible routing and global sharing across brain regions, i.e. the flexible sharing of information throughout cortex. As the authors state: "While non-conscious stimuli are processed in parallel by specialized cortical processors, conscious perception would be needed in order to flexibly route a selected stimulus through a series of non-routine information processing stages". Global information sharing would therefore depend on a set of interconnected high-level cortical regions forming what Dehaene calls a "global workspace", i.e., a distributed network of cortical areas tightly interconnected by long-distance axons, which sends information back to specialized processors.

Dehaene's theory mainly targets the explanation of data from the adult brain. But what about developmental issues, the focus of this paper? Some time ago I proposed the Representational Redescription Hypothesis, arguing that two parallel processes underlie human cognitive development (Karmiloff-Smith, 1992). Based on the notion of domain relevance, the first concerned how the child brain becomes increasingly specialized/automatized in processing of different kinds of stimuli. Instead of modules, I argued for a gradual process of relative modularization over developmental time, i.e., functional specificity was viewed as the outcome of this process. However, to allow for conscious access to the same knowledge, I argued for a second, parallel process: representational redescription, i.e., representations embedded *in* brain processing that are implicit to the organism are redescribed, and thereby become knowledge *to* the brain, with the redescriptions from one domain becoming transportable to other domains (see details and supporting developmental data in Karmiloff-Smith, 1992). I would now argue that this process is likely to occur via brain activity during sleep. In summary, each of the two parallel processes plays a different role in development: the first increases automaticity, the second makes redescribed representations available to conscious access without interfering with the automaticity of rapid processing.

4. Genetics within the neuroconstructivist framework

The human genome contains a large number of transcription factors, whose function it is to turn on and off the functions of other genes. Given the complexity of a fully-formed brain (over 100 billion neurons, each connected to up to 10,000 others), and the dearth of genetic material available to make a brain (some 30,000 genes, at most), DNA clearly does not/cannot provide a total blueprint for the microstructure of the brain. Rather, it provides a sufficient outline to kick-start development with, for instance, higher than necessary connectivity levels within and between cortical regions (Huttenlocher & Dabholkar, 1997). Generally, the newborn cortex does not display strict localization or specialization of function (Goldman-Rakic, 1987); rather, these *emerge* as an activity-dependent function of interactions at the cellular, neural, cortical, and environmental levels (Johnson, 2001, 2004; Karmiloff-Smith, 1998; Kuhl, 2004; Majdan & Shatz, 2006; Mareschal et al., 2007; Meaney & Szyf, 2005; Stiles, 2007). Near and distant brain regions not only become progressively *co-active* but also gradually functionally *cooperative*, leading to a dense brain network with functionally connected, multiple brain regions (Bhattacharya & Petsche, 2005). The shift from distributed to more localized processing is a developmental process that unfolds over many months or even years, well into adolescence (Crone & Elzinga, 2014), with other processes revealing a pattern of local to global change (Brown, Petersen & Schlaggar, 2006), i.e., various forms of neural change are the rule across developmental time. Thus, the adult's relatively specialised cognitive architecture can be thought of in terms of gradual emergence over time, but the starting point is neither predetermined nor fixed (Karmiloff-Smith, 1997, 1998, 2007).

Indeed, to date there is little if any evidence to suggest tight functional specificity of gene expression in the brain, i.e., that genes which are expressed in the brain target from the very start discrete cognitive-level cortical circuits. Rather, gene expression in the brain changes from initial widespread, diffuse, large-scale gradients across cortex (Kingsbury & Finlay, 2001), only later progressively restricting expression to more specialized cognitive-level circuits, although genetic control of primary areas seems to occur very early in development (Bishop, Goudreau & O'Leary, 2000). Thus, genetic mutations contributing to developmental disorders in infants are likely to affect widespread systems within the brain, some more seriously/more subtly than others, depending on their domain relevance (Karmiloff-Smith, 1998). This does not preclude that the outcome of the dynamic developmental processes could result in some areas being more impaired than others, due to the processing demands of certain types of input to those areas as well as to differences in synaptogenesis across various cerebral regions (Huttenlocher & Dabholkar, 1997).

It is important to recall that gene expression in the brain (when a gene is expressed during day/night or across development, how much protein product is expressed, and in which brain region[s] it is expressed) is not strictly predetermined, but also a function of environmental experience over developmental time. Studies of rodents illustrate this point, highlighting the potential role of the environment in shaping patterns of gene expression (Kaffman & Meaney, 2007). The researchers tracked brain development in rodent pups and showed that differences in the amount of maternal postnatal pup grooming/stroking actually changed the amount and location of the expression of genes involved in the brain's responses to stress, which had lifelong effects on the animal's behaviour. Such dynamic environment-gene interactions are likely to be pervasive in mammalian brain development, including that of humans. In general, epigenesis is not deterministic under tight genetic control. Rather, epigenesis is probabilistic and only under broad genetic control (Gotlieb, 2007). So, if the architecture of the adult brain is highly specialized, this is likely to be the end-product of very complex gene-brain-cognition-behaviour-environment dynamics (Scerif & Karmiloff-Smith, 2001), which give rise over developmental time to relatively domain-specific outcomes and, in the case of semantics, to category-specific specializations. And this flexible, dynamic framework makes evolutionary sense.

5. Evolution and the neuroconstructivist framework

In their excellent review of comparative neuroscience, Quartz and Sejnowski (1997) remark on how the degree of genetic pre-specification varies in non-random ways across species. They argue that it is highest in animals most distant from humans, and lowest in our closest relatives. Recall that many other species have complex special-purpose responses to the environment, e.g., the spider's web, that human infants do not possess. Yet humans develop an exceedingly rich, flexible cognitive system over time. Thus, rather than endow humans with maximal pre-specified core knowledge (hyperspecialization), it seems that evolution leans instead toward increasing plasticity for learning. So, instead of being hyperspecialized, human infants are more likely born with a collection of reflexes together with some domain-general learning algorithms (for attention, discrimination, novelty detection, memory, etc.), but also some domain-relevant biases that provide not only a starting point but also an initial trajectory vector in cognitive space, one that will be affected not only by experience but also by interactions within and between levels of causal change (cellular, neural, body, environment; see Marescal et al., 2007; Westerman et al., 2007, 2010). It is also worth recalling that, unlike other species, humans remain totally dependent upon their social environment during a lengthy period of early development, allowing the social environment to impact significantly upon brain development.

So, instead of invoking a start state of innate, domain-specific modules handed down by evolution, the neuroconstructivist framework would argue that evolution may be driven predominantly by increased plasticity for learning (Finlay, 2007; Karmiloff-Smith, 2010, 2012; Karmiloff-Smith & Thomas, 2004), rather than increased genetic complexity, i.e., for a limited number of domain-relevant biases, which *become* domain-specific over developmental time via their competitive interaction with each other when attempting to process different kinds of environmental stimuli (Johnson, 2001; Karmiloff-Smith, 1998). In this sense, evolution can be considered a trade-off between hyperspecialization but a lack of flexibility, on the one hand and, on the other hand, maximum (but not unbounded) plasticity with some domain-relevant constraints (Karmiloff-Smith, 1992, 2009; Quartz & Sejnowski, 1997).

6. Why has the domain-specific view remained so attractive?

Why, then, does the domain-specific framework continue to be so attractive to many of those studying typical and atypical development in children? This may reside in the fact that the explanatory framework is static, thereby leading to simpler types of research strategy focused on a specific domain. Moreover, if the researcher considers the normal brain to be composed of pre-specified modules and the atypical brain to be a juxtaposition of intact and impaired modules, then the brain can theoretically be represented by a number of independently functioning modules, suggesting that impairments in one module will have no developmental effects on other specialized functions. This gives rise to a focus on the impaired domains and a mere cursory investigation of the "intact" ones. Interestingly, once such a strategy forms the basis of research on children with genetic disorders, *relative* differences (domain X is more impaired than domain Y) slip into *absolute* statements: X is impaired, domain Y intact (Clahsen & Temple, 2003; Landau, Hoffman & Kurz, 2005; Piattelli-Palmarini, 2001; Pinker, 1994, 1999, 2002), whereas in fact *both* are impaired, albeit to different degrees, when compared with the levels of healthy controls.

A very different approach is taken if the researcher considers the initial state of the neonate cortex to be composed of many interconnected, interacting parts. The neuroconstructivist framework would consider a genetic mutation to be initially expressed quite widely throughout many brain regions and to affect many emerging cognitive domains, but to different degrees. What may seem like a domain-specific (or category-specific) impairment in the adult phenotypic outcome may simply be due to the fact that the neuronal and biochemical properties of one brain region are more affected by the mutation than other regions but, crucially, that these other regions may also be affected albeit to a less obvious degree. This means that the neuroconstrucivist researcher will not only focus on areas of serious deficit, but pay as much attention to domains where the child displays proficient performance, even those in which the child's scores fall in the "normal range". This often leads to the identification of unusual cognitive and neural processes that underlie "normal" behavioural scores (Karmiloff-Smith et al., 2004). Furthermore, the neuroconstructivist researcher will systematically try to trace cognitive-level deficits back to their basic-level origins in infancy (Karmiloff-Smith, 1998; Karmiloff-Smith et al., 2012).

A lack of specialization and localization of function, also referred to as a lack of progressive modularization (Karmiloff-Smith, 1992; D'Souza & Karmiloff-Smith, 2011), leads to the speculation that the brains of individuals with developmental disorders may remain more highly interconnected than the brains of healthy controls which undergo progressive pruning over the course of development. The resulting atypical (under-pruned) brain would then be overly active across multiple brain regions resulting, for instance, in problems with multitasking (Mackinlay et al., 2006). This certainly holds for individuals with fragile X syndrome, whose brains have been shown to have abnormally high synaptic densities through to adulthood (Comery et al., 1997; Huttenlocher & Dabholkar, 1997). But the converse is also possible. In some developmental disorders, the brain may commit too rapidly to specialization and localization of function (Oliver et al., 2000; Thomas, Knowland & Karmiloff-Smith, 2011), resulting in less flexibility for processing novel stimuli. Such considerations, in which the time course of ontogenetic change plays a pivotal role, lead us far from the metaphor of static intact and impaired modules.

A crucial error is to conflate the specialized, mature brains of adults, which have developed normally prior to damage in later life, with those of infants and children, which are still in the process of developing (Casey, Giedd & Thomas, 2000; Karmiloff-Smith, Scerif & Ansari, 2003; Karmiloff-Smith, 2010, 2012). Rather, we need to think in terms of a gradual process of recruitment of particular pathways and structures for specific functions (Elman et al., 1996), such that brain pathways that were previously partially activated in a wide range of contexts increasingly confine their activation to a narrower range of inputs and situations (Johnson, Halit, Grice, & Karmiloff-Smith, 2002). Importantly, to fully comprehend typical and atypical developmental pathways, the process of ontogenetic change must always constitute a fundamental part of the explanation of human cognition. The brain is not static; it undergoes extensive developmental changes over ontogenesis (Casey et al., 2005; Durston, 2006; Giedd et al., 1999; Johnson, 2001).

Finally, it remains an open question as to whether even the mature adult brain is as strictly modular as some theorists would claim, particularly with respect to the cognitive level, since changing interactivity of dynamic cerebral networks seems to be the case throughout life. This is nicely illustrated by neural studies of healthy ageing adults whose behavioural scores on, say, syntactic comprehension tasks are identical to those of younger adults but whose ageing brains approach the language task bilaterally compared to the predominantly left-hemisphere specialization of the younger adults (Tyler et al., 2010; see, also, Dehaene, 2009).

7. Concluding thoughts

So, theorists have several options to explain the start state of the human brain and its subsequent development, amongst which the four frameworks discussed in this paper: (1) the domain-general framework of an initially undifferentiated brain which gains its structure solely from interacting with the environment; (2) the core knowledge or conceptual representations framework where the brain starts out with very domain-specific knowledge upon which more abstract knowledge is built through, inter alia, language or conceptual reorganization; (3) the neuronal recycling, plasticity/flexibility framework, built on domain-specific starting states, but open subsequently to substantial cross-domain interactions; or, (4) the neuroconstructivist framework, together with a process of representational redescription, which invokes domain-relevant – not domain-specific – biases to kick-start development, as well as initial neuronal competition and gradual emergent functional specialization.

Although plasticity is seen by some as a response solely to injury, for many neuroscientists nowadays, plasticity is the rule for development, normal or atypical (Bates & Roe, 2001; Bolhuis et al., 2011; Cicchetti & Tucker, 1994; Dehaene et al., 2014; Sur, Pallas & Roe, 1990; Webster, Bachevalier & Ungerleider, 1995). But plasticity is not, of course, unconstrained. As Hensch and collaborators (Bavelier et al., 2010; Hensch, 2005) have elegantly demonstrated in a series of molecular studies on the excitatory-inhibitory balance across brain regions and systems that place constraints on plasticity, it would make no sense in evolutionary terms to have unbounded plasticity. A developing organism needs to be both constrained and flexible (Karmiloff-Smith, 1992, 1994), and achieving that dynamic balance is what ontogenetic development is all about.

Acknowledgements

The writing of this article was partially funded by a Wellcome Trust Strategic Award (Grant Number: 098330/Z/12/Z) conferred upon The London Down Syndrome (LonDownS) Consortium. I would like to thank Dr. Fred Dick, Dr. Dean D'Souza, and an anonymous reviewer for their helpful comments on the first draft.

References

Agrillo C, Ranpura A, Butterworth B. Time and numerosity estimation are independent: Behavioral evidence for two different systems using a conflict paradigm. Cog Neurosci. 2010; 1(2):96–101.

Anderson ML. Neural reuse: A fundamental organizational principle of the brain. Behav Brain Sci. 2010; 33:245–313. [PubMed: 20964882]

Baillargeon R, Carey S. Core cognition and beyond: The acquisition of physical and numerical knowledge. In: Pauen, S, editor. Early Childhood Development and Later Outcome. Cambridge University Press; Cambridge, England: 2012. p. 33–65.

Baron-Cohen S, Leslie AM, Frith U. Does the autistic child have a "theory of mind"? Cognition. 1985; 21(1):37–46. [PubMed: 2934210]

Baron-Cohen S, Ring HA, Wheelwright S, Bullmore ET, Brammer MJ, Simmons A, Williams SC. Social intelligence in the normal and autistic brain: An fMRI study. Eur J Neurosci. 1999; 11(6):1891–1898. [PubMed: 10336657]

Bates E, Elman J, Johnson MH, Karmiloff-Smith A, Parisi D, Plunkett, K. Innateness and emergentism. In: Bechtel W, Graham G, editors. A Companion to Cognitive Science. Basil Blackwell; Oxford: 1998. p. 590–601.

Bates E, Roe K. Language development in children with unilateral brain injury. In: Nelson CA, Luciana M, editors. Handbook of Developmental Cognitive Neuroscience. MIT Press; Cambridge, MA: 2001. p. 281–307.

Bavelier D, Levi DM, Li RW, Dan Y, Hensch TK. Removing brakes on adult plasticity: From molecular to behavioural interventions. J Neurosci. 2010; 30(45):14964–14971. [PubMed: 21068299]

Bhattacharya J, Petsche H. Drawing on mind's canvas: Differences in cortical integration patterns between artists and non-artists. Hum Brain Mapping. 2005; 26:1–14.

Bishop KM, Goudreau G, O'Leary DDM. Emx2 and Pax6 regulate area identity in the mammalian neocortex. Science. 2000; 288:344–349. [PubMed: 10764649]

Bolhuis JJ, Brown GR, Richardson RC, Laland KN. Darwin in mind: New opportunities for evolutionary psychology. PLoS Biology. 2011; 9(7):1–8.

Brown TT, Petersen SE, Schlaggar BL. Does human functional brain organization shift from different to focal with development? Dev Sci. 2006; 9(3):9–10. [PubMed: 16445388]

Butterworth B. The Mathematical Brain. Macmillan; London: 1999.

Butterworth B. State-of-science review: Dyscalculia. In: Goswami UC, editor. Foresight Mental Capital and Mental Wellbeing. Office of Science and Innovation; London: 2008.
Casey BJ, Giedd JN, Thomas KM. Structural and functional brain development and its relation to cognitive development. Biol Psychol. 2000; 54:241–257. [PubMed: 11035225]
Casey BJ, Tottenham N, Liston C, Durston S. Imaging the developing brain: What have we learned about cognitive development? Trends Cog Sci. 2005; 9(3):104–110.
Castle A, Coltheart M. Varieties of developmental dyslexia. Cognition. 1993; 47(2):149–180. [PubMed: 8324999]
Cicchetti D, Tucker D. Development and self-regulatory structures of the mind. Dev Psychopath. 1994; 6:533–549.
Clahsen H, Temple C. Words and rules in children with Williams syndrome. In: Levy Y, Schaeffer J, editors. Language Competence across Populations. Erlbaum; Mahwah, NJ: 2003. p. 323–352.
Cohen Kadosh R, Bahrami B, Walsh V, Butterworth B, Popescu T, Price CJ. Specialization in the human brain: The case of numbers. Front Hum Neurosci. 2011; 5:62. doi:10.3389/fnhum.2011.00062. [PubMed: 21808615]
Cohen Kadosh K, Henson RNA, Cohen Kadosh R, Johnson MH, Dick F. Task-dependent activation of face-sensitive cortex: An fMRI adaptation study. J Cog Neurosci. 2009; 22(5):903–917.
Comery TA, Harris JB, Willems PJ, Oostra BA, Irwin SA, Weiler IJ, Greenough WT. Abnormal dendritic spines in fragile X knockout mice: Maturation and pruning deficits. Proc Natl Acad Sci. 1997; 94:5401–5404. [PubMed: 9144249]
Cosmides L, Barrett HC, Tooby J. Adaptative specializations, social exchange, and the evolution of human intelligence. Proc Natl Acad Sci. 2010; 107:9007–9014. [PubMed: 20445099]
Crone EA, Elzinga B. Changing brains: How longitudinal fMRI studies can inform us about cognitive and social-affective growth trajectories. WIREs Cogn Sci. 2014; 6:53–63.
De Haan M, Humphreys K, Johnson MH. Developing a brain specialized for face processing: A converging methods approach. Dev Psychobiology. 2002; 40:200–212.
Dehaene S. The Number Sense: How the Mind Creates Mathematics. Oxford University Press; Oxford: 1997.
Dehaene S. Reading in the Brain: The Science and Evolution of a Human Invention. Penguin Group; New York, NY: 2009.
Dehaene S, Cohen L. Cultural recycling of cortical maps. Neuron. 2007; 56(2):384–398. [PubMed: 17964253]
Dehaene S, Charles L, King JR, Marti S. Toward a computational theory of conscious processing. Curr Op Neurobio. 2014; 25:76–84.
D'Souza D, Karmiloff-Smith A. When modularization fails to occur: A developmental perspective. Cog Neuropsych. 2011; 28(3–4):276–287.
Duchaine B. Developmental propagnosia with normal configural processing. NeuroReport. 2000; 11(1):79–83. [PubMed: 10683834]
Duchaine B, Cosmides L, Tooby J. Evolutionary psychology and the brain. Curr Op Neurobio. 2001; 11:225–230.
Duchaine B, Nakayama K. Dissociations of face and object recognition in developmental prosopagnosia. J Cog Neurosci. 2005; 17:249–261.
Duchaine B, Nakayama K. Developmental prosopagnosia: A window to content-specific face processing. Cur Op Neurobio. 2006; 16(2):166–173.
Duchaine B, Nieminen-von Wendt T, New J, Kulomaki T. Dissociations of visual recognition in a developmental agnosic: Evidence for separate developmental processes. Neurocase. 2003; 9:380–389. [PubMed: 14972753]

Duchaine B, Yovel G, Butterworth E, Nakayama K. Prosopagnosia as an impairment to face-specific mechanisms: Elimination of the alternative explanations in a developmental case. Cognitive Neuropsychology. 2006; 23:714–747. [PubMed: 21049351]

Durston S, Davidson MC, Tottenham N, Galván A, Spicer J, Fosella JA, Casey BJ. A shift from diffuse to focal cortical activity with development. Dev Sci. 2006; 9(1):1–8. [PubMed: 16445387]

Elman JL, Bates E, Johnson MH, Karmiloff-Smith A, Parisi D, Plunkett K. Rethinking Innateness: A Connectionist Perspective on Development. MIT Press; Cambridge, MA: 1996.

Finlay BL. E pluribus unum: Too many unique human capacities and too many theories. In: Gangestad S, Simpson J, editors. The Evolution of Mind: Fundamental Questions and Controversies. Guilford Press; New York: 2007. p. 294–304.

Fodor J. Modularity of Mind. MIT Press; Cambridge, MA: 1983.

Gelman R, Gallistel R. The Child's Understanding of Number. Harvard University Press; Cambridge, MA: 1986.

Giedd J, Blumenthal J, Jeffries N, Castellanos F, Liu H, Zijdenbos A, et al. Brain development during childhood and adolescence: A longitudinal MRI study. Nat Neurosci. 1999; 2:861–863. [PubMed: 10491603]

Giedd J, Rumsey J, Castellanos F, Rajapakse J, Kaysen D, Vaituzis A, et al. A quantitative MRI study of the corpus callosum in children and adolescents. Dev Brain Res. 1996; 91:274–280. [PubMed: 8852379]

Goldman-Rakic, PS. Circuitry of the pre-frontal cortex and the regulation of behavior by representational knowledge. In: Plum F, Mountcastle V, editors. Handbook of Physiology. Vol. 5. American Physiological Society; Bethesda, MD: 1987. p. 373–417.

Gopnik M. Genetic basis of grammar defect. Nature. 1990; 347(6288):26. [PubMed: 2395458]

Gotlieb G. Probabilistic epigenesis. Dev Sci. 2007; 10:1–11. [PubMed: 17181692]

Hauser MD, Spelke ES. Evolutionary and developmental foundations of human knowledge: A case study of mathematics. In: Gazzaniga M, editor. The Cognitive Neurosciences. Vol. 3. MIT Press; Cambridge: 2004. p. 853–864.

Hensch TK. Critical period plasticity in local cortical circuits. Nat. Rev. Neurosci. 2005; 6:877–888. [PubMed: 16261181]

Huttenlocher PR, de Courten C. The development of synapses in striate cortex of man. Hum Neurobio. 1987; 6:1–9.

Huttenlocher PR, Dabholkar AS. Regional differences in synaptogenesis in human cerebral cortex. J Comp Neurol. 1997; 387:167–178. [PubMed: 9336221]

Hyde DC, Spelke ES. Neural signatures of number processing in human infants: Evidence for two core systems underlying numerical cognition. Dev Sci. 2011; 14(2):360–371. [PubMed: 21399717]

Johnson MH. Functional brain development in humans. Nat Rev Neurosci. 2001; 2:475–483. [PubMed: 11433372]

Johnson MH. Plasticity and functional brain development: The case of face processing. In: Kanwisher N, Duncan J, editors. Attention & Performance XX: Functional Neuroimaging of Visual Cognition. Oxford University Press; Oxford: 2004. p. 257–263.

Johnson MH, Halit H, Grice S, Karmiloff-Smith A. Neuroimaging of typical and atypical development: A perspective from multiple levels of analysis. Dev Psychopath. 2002; 14:521–536.

Kaffman A, Meaney MJ. Neurodevelopmental sequelae of postnatal maternal care in rodents: Clinical and research implications of molecular insights. J Child Psychol. Psychiatry. 2007; 48:224–244. [PubMed: 17355397]

Karmiloff-Smith A. Beyond Modularity: A Developmental Perspective on Cognitive Science. MIT Press/Bradford Books; Cambridge, MA: 1992.

Karmiloff-Smith A. Transforming a partially structured brain into a creative mind. Behav Brain Sci. 1994; 17(4):732–745.

Karmiloff-Smith A. Promissory notes, genetic clocks or epigenetic outcomes? Behav Brain Sci. 1997; 20:359–377.

Karmiloff-Smith A. Development itself is the key to understanding developmental disorders. Trends Cog Sci. 1998; 2(10):389–398.

Karmiloff-Smith A. Atypical epigenesis. Dev Sci. 2007; 10(1):84–88. [PubMed: 17181704]

Karmiloff-Smith A. Nativism versus neuroconstructivism: Rethinking the study of developmental disorders: Interplay of biology and environment. Dev Psych. 2009; 45(1):56–63.

Karmiloff-Smith A. Neuroimaging of the developing brain: Taking "develop*ing*" seriously. Hum Brain Map. 2010; 31(6):934–941.

Karmiloff-Smith A. Brain: The neuroconstructivist approach. In: Farran EK, Karmiloff-Smith A, editors. Neurodevelopmental Disorders across the Lifespan: A Neuroconstructivist Approach. Oxford University Press; Oxford: 2012. p. 37–58.

Karmiloff-Smith A. Challenging the use of adult neuropsychological models for explaining neurodevelopmental disorders: Developed versus developing brains. Quart J Exp Psych. 2013; 66:1–14.

Karmiloff-Smith A, D'Souza D, Dekker TM, Van Herwegen J, Xu F, Rodic M, Ansari D. Genetic and environmental vulnerabilities in children with neurodevelopmental disorders. Proc Natl Acad Sci. 2012; 109(2):17261–17265. [PubMed: 23045661]

Karmiloff-Smith A, Plunkett K, Johnson M, Elman JL, Bates E. What does it mean to claim that something is "innate"? Mind Lang. 1998; 13(4):588–597.

Karmiloff-Smith A, Scerif G, Ansari D. Double dissociations in developmental disorders? Theoretically misconceived, empirically dubious. Cortex. 2003; 39:161–163. [PubMed: 12627769]

Karmiloff-Smith A, Thomas MSC. Can developmental disorders be used to bolster claims from Evolutionary Psychology? A neuroconstructivist approach. In: Langer J, Taylor Parker S, Milbrath C, editors. Biology and Knowledge Revisited: From Neurogenesis to Psychogenesis. 2004. p. 307–322.

Karmiloff-Smith A, Thomas MSC, Annaz D, Humphreys K, Ewing S, Brace N, van Duuren M, Pike G, Grice S, Campbell R. Exploring the Williams Syndrome Face Processing Debate: The importance of building developmental trajectories. J Child Psych Psychiatry. 2004; 45(7):1258–1274.

Kingsbury MA, Finlay LF. The cortex in multidimensional space: Where do cortical areas come from? Developmental Science. 2001; 4(2):125–142.

Kirkham NZ, Slemmer JA, Johnson SP. Visual statistic learning in infancy: Evidence for a domain-general learning mechanism. Cognition. 2002; 83:B35–B42. [PubMed: 11869728]

Krishnan S, Leech R, Mercure E, Lloyd-Fox SO, Dick F. Convergent and divergent fMRI responses in children and adults to increasing language production demands. Cereb Cortex. 2014 Epub ahead of print.

Kuhl P. Early language acquisition: Cracking the speech code. Nat Rev Neurosci. 2004; 5:831–843. [PubMed: 15496861]

Landau B, Hoffman JE, Kurz N. Object definitions with severe spatial deficits in Williams syndrome: sparing and breakdown. Cognition. 2005; 100:483–510. [PubMed: 16185678]

Lany J, Saffran JR. Statistical learning mechanisms in infancy. In: Rubenstein JLR, Rakic P, editors. Comprehensive Developmental Neuroscience: Neural Circuit Development and Function in the Brain. Vol. 3. Elsevier; Amsterdam: 2013. p. 231–248.

Lee SA, Spelke ES. A modular geometric mechanism for reorientation in children. Cognitive Psychology. 2010; 61(2):152–176. [PubMed: 20570252]

Leslie AM. Pretence, autism, and the theory-of-mind-module. Cur Dir Psych Sci. 1992; 1:18–21.

Mackinlay R, Charman T, Karmiloff-Smith A. High functioning children with autism spectrum disorder: A novel test of multitasking. Brain Cog. 2006; 61(1):14–24.

Majdan M, Schatz CJ. Effects of visual experience on activity-dependent gene regulation in cortex. Nat Neurosci. 2006; 9:650–659. [PubMed: 16582906]

Mareschal D, Johnson MH, Sirios S, Spratling M, Thomas MSC, Westermann G. Neuroconstructivism: Vol. I. How the Brain Constructs Cognition. Oxford University Press; Oxford, England: 2007.

Meaney MJ, Szyf M. Maternal care as a model for experience-dependent chromatin plasticity? Trends Neurosci. 2005; 28:456–463. [PubMed: 16054244]

Minagawa-Kawai Y, Mori K, Naoi N, Kojima S. Neural attunement processes in infants during the acquisition of language-specific phonemic contrasts. J Neurosci. 2007; 3:315–321. [PubMed: 17215392]

Mills DL, Coffy-Corins S, Neville H. Language comprehension and cerebral specialisation from 13–20 months. Dev Psych. 1997; 13:397–445.

Molko N, Cachia A, Rivière D, Mangin J-F, Bruandet M, Le Bihan D, Cohen L, Dehaene S. Functional and structural alterations of the intraparietal sulcus in a developmental dyscalculia of genetic origin. Neuron. 2003; 40:847–858. [PubMed: 14622587]

Neville H, Mills D, Bellugi U. Effects of altered auditory sensitivity and age of language acquisition on the development of language-relevant neural systems: Preliminary studies of William syndrome. In: Broman S, Grafman J, editors. Atypical Cognitive Deficits in Developmental Disorders: Implications for Brain Function. Erlbaum; Hillsdale, NJ: 1994. p. 67–83.

Oliver A, Johnson MH, Karmiloff-Smith A, Pennington B. Deviations in the emergence of representations: A neuroconstructivist framework for analysing developmental disorders. Dev Sci. 2000; 3:1–23.

Paterson SJ, Brown JH, Gsödl MK, Johnson MH, Karmiloff-Smith A. Cognitive modularity and genetic disorders. Science. 1999; 286:2355–2358. [PubMed: 10600749]

Paterson SJ, Heim S, Friedman JT, Choudhury N, Benasich AA. Development of structure and function in the infant brain: Implications for cognition, language and social behaviour. Neurosci Biobehav Rev. 2006; 30:1087–1105. [PubMed: 16890291]

Piattelli-Palmarini M. Speaking of learning: How do we acquire our marvellous facility for expressing ourselves in words? Nature. 2001; 411:887–888.

Pinker, S. The Language Instinct: How the Mind Creates Language. W. Morrow; New York: 1994.

Pinker, S. Words and Rules: The Ingredients of Language. Basic Books; New York: 1999.

Pinker, S. The Blank Slate: The Modern Denial of Human Nature. Penguin Group; New York, NY: 2002.

Quartz S, Sejnowski T. The neural basis of cognitive development: A constructivist manifesto. Behav Brain Sci. 1997; 20:537–596. [PubMed: 10097006]

Rice, M. Specific grammatical limitations in children with Specific Language Impairment. In: Tager-Flusberg H, editor. Neurodevelopmental Disorders. MIT Press; Cambridge, MA: 1999. p. 331–360.

Scerif G, Karmiloff-Smith A. Genes and environment: What does interaction really mean? Trends Gen. 2001; 17:418–419.

Shalev RS, Manor O, Gross-Tsur V. Developmental dyscalculia: A prospective six-year follow-up. Dev Med Child Neurol. 2005; 2:121–125. [PubMed: 15707235]

Smith LB, Thelen E. Development as a dynamic system. Trends Cog Sci. 7(8):343–348. 23003.

Spelke ES, Kinzler KD. Core knowledge. Dev Sci. 2007; 10:89–96. [PubMed: 17181705]

Spelke ES, Kinzler KD. Innateness, learning and rationality. Child Dev Pers. 2009; 3:96–98.

Stiles J. The Fundamentals of Brain Development. Harvard University Press; Cambridge, MA: 2009.

Stiles J. Neural Plasticity and Cognitive Development: Insights from Children with Perinatal Brain Injury. Oxford University Press; Oxford UK: 2012.

Sur M, Pallas SL, Roe AW. Crossmodal plasticity in cortical development: Differentiation and specification of sensory neocortex. TINS. 1990; 13:227–233. [PubMed: 1694329]

Temple CM. Cognitive neuropsychology and its application to children. J Child Psychol Psychiatry. 1997; 38:27–52. [PubMed: 9232457]

Thomas MSC, Knowland VC, Karmiloff-Smith A. Mechanisms of developmental regression in autism and the broader phenotype: A neural network modeling approach. Psych Rev. 2011; 118(4):637–654.

Tyler LK, Shafto MA, Randall B, Wright P, Marslen-Wilson WD, Stamatakis EA. Preserving syntactic processing across the adult life span: The modulation of the fronto-temporal language system in the context of age-related atrophy. Cereb Cortex. 2010; 20(2):352–364. [PubMed: 19505991]

van der Lely HKJ. Domain-specific cognitive systems: Insight from grammatical specific language impairment. Trends Cog Sci. 2005; 9:53–59.

van der Lely JKJ, Pinker S. The biological basis of language: Insights from developmental grammatical impairments. Trends Cog Sci. 2014; 18(11):586–595.

Webster MJ, Bachevalier J, Ungerleider LG. Development and plasticity of visual memory circuits. In: Julesz B, Kovacs I, editors. Maturational Windows and Adult Cortical Plasticity in Human Development: Is There Reason for an Optimistic View? Addison-Wesley; Reading, MA: 1995.

Westerman G, Marescal D, Johnson MH, Sirois S, Spratling MW, Thomas MSC. Neuroconstructivism. Dev Sci. 2007; 10(1):75–83. [PubMed: 17181703]

Westermann G, Thomas MSC, Karmiloff-Smith A. Neuroconstructivism. In: Goswami U, editor. Handbook of Childhood Development. Wiley-Blackwell; Oxford: 2010. p. 723–748.

Xu F, Spelke ES, Goddard S. Number sense in human infants. Dev Sci. 2005; 8(1):88–101. [PubMed: 15647069]

Index

accommodation 69, 72
adaptive resonance theory 196
adults: adult neuropsychological model 99–100, 107, 118–119, 124, 132–133, 247–258, 262, 263, 274, 298; brain damaged adults 71, 102, 118–119, 251, 289–290, 291, 293; brain imaging studies 232–233, 236–237; brain-damaged adults and domain specificity 71; focus on adult endstates 11, 12, 13; psychological research with 65–66; static adult neuropsychological model 99–100
Alegria, J. 57
Almazan, M. 119–120, 121, 176, 262
Alzheimer's disease 1
amyloid precursor protein (APP) 1
analogies: cognitive vs. perceptual understandings of 78–79; explicit theory change 75
ANCOVA analysis 144, 149, 150
animal modelling 14, 169–172, 240, 265, 266, 278
Ansari, D. 8
architectures, neural 84–85, 87, 88, 114, 119, 122, 174, 199, 200, 295
artificial intelligence 8, 10, 41
artificial neural networks (ANNs) 9, 197
Asperger syndrome 112
assimilation 69, 72
association, laws of 69
associator networks 196, 197
asynchronous development 5–6, 268 *see also* developmental timing
auditory processing 112–113, 176
autism: and brain plasticity 194–195; central coherence 195; and computational modelling 196–198; connectivity of brain regions 194–195, 196, 197, 205–206, 209, 210–211, 219, 221–222; deprivation and quasi-autism 196, 212, 217; developmental regression 192–222; domain specificity 220, 221–222; and domain-specificity of cognitive systems 70–71, 112; and the environment 207, 212, 221, 252–255; face processing 252; featural processing 281; genotype-phenotype relations 15–16, 192–228, 261; intentional state attribution 290; language 192, 193, 195, 252; nativism vs. neuroconstructivism 273
automaticity 43, 50, 54, 58, 75–76, 294

Baird, G. 221
balance scale computer modelling task 85
Baron-Cohen, S. 118, 261, 273, 274, 282, 290
Bayley, D. B. 173
Bayley Infant Scales II 126
behavioural mastery: brain imaging studies 239; and children's drawing 54, 56; and connectionism 85–86; phonological awareness 57; proceduralization 75–76; and representational change 57, 58; and representational redescription (RR) 10, 41–42, 43, 44, 76–81, 85–86, 89
behavioural regression 192–228
behaviourism 69
belief systems 67
Bellugi, U. 56, 118, 122, 125, 127, 133, 134, 156, 175, 261, 262, 263, 275, 281
Benton Facial Recognition Test 123, 134, 135, 137, 142, 143–144, 145–146, 147, 148, 149, 150, 151, 152, 153, 154, 156–157, 184, 187, 263, 275
Benton Line Orientation Task 185
Bertrand, J. 120, 126, 134, 264

Beversdorf, D. Q. 196
Beyond Modularity (Karmiloff-Smith, 1992) 2, 4, 8–11, 12, 64–94
bird song 267
Bishop, D. V. M. 195, 216, 261, 263, 281
balance beam experiment 3, 24–26, 85
Borovsky, A. 2
Bourgeron, T. 273
Brace, N. A. 142, 143
brain activation studies 9, 68, 104–105, 172–173, 176, 200, 231, 234, 279–280, 298
brain anatomy: Fragile X 168–169; Williams syndrome 127
brain damaged adults 71, 102, 118–119, 251, 289–290, 291, 293
brain imaging studies 14, 16, 113, 124, 194, 231–243, 263–264, 275–276
brain plasticity: and autism 194–195; domain relevance 292, 294, 296; early brain development 68, 72; and evolution 267, 268; experience-dependent synaptic plasticity 168, 169, 173; Fragile X 168–169, 173; nativism vs. neuroconstructivism 280, 284; neural changes across development 238–239; in non-human species 68–69
brain size differences 195–196, 210, 211, 217
British Ability Scales 125, 137, 142, 183–184, 187, 188 *see also* Pattern Construction subtest of the British Abilities Scale
British Picture Vocabulary Scale (BPVS) 125, 142, 145–146, 147, 149, 154, 187
Broadbent, H. 15
Bronckart, J.-P. 5
Brown, J. 108, 124, 127, 128, 264, 281
Bruner, J. S. 35, 53
Bryant, J. 57
Bryson, S. E. 221
Butterworth, B. 163–164, 274, 289, 290, 291

Carpenter, P. A. 273
cascades of effects 114, 250, 280
case study methods 15, 182–191, 240
causal modelling 114
ceiling effects 112, 119, 121, 136, 142, 148, 187, 278
Cellérier, Guy 23
central processing 57, 67, 72
chaining strategies 58
childhood disintegrative disorder (CDD) 193, 213
children's drawing 7, 40–63
Children's Nonword Repetition task 121
chimpanzees 65, 73, 81, 89, 266–267
Chomsky, N. 50, 71, 72, 75, 97, 119
chronological age (CA) matching: neural changes across development 239; problems with 277–278; static vs. dynamic approaches 248; in William syndrome research 120, 121, 123, 125–126, 128, 134, 135, 136, 142, 143, 148, 149, 151, 152, 153, 155
Churchill, J. D. 168, 170
Clahsen, H. 119–120, 121, 176, 262, 289, 291, 297
Clark, A. C. 83, 88
co-activity 295
cognitive discovery processes 34
cognitive flexibility 8, 10, 50–54, 58, 65, 79, 88, 101, 294, 296
cognitive genetic profiling 182–191
Cohen, I. L. 196
compensatory processing 99, 100, 232, 253, 275, 277
competition 81, 89
componential (feature-by-feature) processing 107, 123, 127, 133, 134–141, 147–154, 232, 263, 283
computational deficits 71
computational modelling 8, 14–16, 82–84, 85, 102, 196–198, 219–220
computational symbolism 6, 8
computer simulations 82–84
configural (holistic) processing 107, 123, 127, 133, 134–141, 147–154, 157, 263
confounding errors 53
connectionist models 7–9, 11, 15–16, 82, 83–89, 174
connectivity of brain regions: autism 194–195, 196, 197, 205–206, 209, 210–211, 219, 221–222; brain imaging studies 238, 240; cooperative brain regions 295; domain relevance 292, 295; and gene expression 114
conscious access 5, 6, 18, 58, 65, 74, 77, 79–80, 294
constraints: attention biases 68; atypical computational constraints 176; initial computational constraints 174; linguistic 86, 121; and the nativist thesis 67; procedural constraints 50; and representational change 40–63;

representational redescription (RR) 78, 80; sequential constraints 50, 52–54, 56, 57–58; on strategies 58; typical development 98
constructivism: complementarity with nativism 64–65, 69, 71–74; Fodor vs. Piaget 72; nativism vs. neuroconstructivism 273–288
Content, A. 57
co-occurring impairments 113
cooperative brain regions 295
counterexamples 30–31, 35, 36, 81
counterfactuals 79
Courchesne, E. 195, 210, 218–219
Cox, M. V. 55
Crabbe, J. C. 171–172
creativity: cognitive discovery processes 34; and cognitive science 69, 90; creative simplification 36; and domain-specificity of cognitive systems 71; problem-solving skills 78; and representational flexibility 41, 52, 64, 71, 76, 89, 90
Cromer, R. F. 56, 58
cross-domain interactions 13, 18, 57, 71, 77, 78, 90, 250, 298
cross-sectional data 13, 14, 25, 137, 142, 143, 151, 153, 195, 237, 240, 293
cross-system codes 79–80
Crowley, K. 80
culture 10, 75 *see also* environment
cytoarchitectural regions 114

Dakin, S. C. 251
Dasser, V. 54
data-driven learning 77
de Haan, M. 108, 127
deaf people 72, 101
deep neural networks 10
Dehaene, S. 18, 190, 293–294, 298
dementia 1
dendritic spine morphology 114, 168, 170, 266, 292
Dennett, D. C. 88
denotation 54
Deruelle, C. 123, 127, 133, 134, 135, 136, 137, 156, 175, 263, 275
developmental delay 192, 264, 278
developmental disorders: continuum model of 100; development itself as key to understanding 97–117; genetics/environment debate 247–258; nativism vs. neuroconstructivism 273–288; and the neuroconstructivist approach 99–111; neuroimaging 231–243; quantitative genetics 166–167 *see also specific developmental disorders*
developmental failure 212–213, 215–216, 217
developmental neuropsychology 70
developmental profiles 17
developmental regression 15–16, 192–222
developmental timing 112–113, 114, 207–208, 212, 217, 264, 276–277, 292
developmental trajectories 132–160, 176, 192, 220, 275–278
difference detection tests 147–154
diffusion tensor imaging 194
discovery 34–36
dissociations 99–100, 102, 113, 118, 124, 261, 280–281
domain impairment 110, 274–275, 277, 292, 297
domain relevance 12, 14–15, 18, 264–265, 279, 280, 291–293, 294, 296
domain specificity: atypical development 98, 102, 112–113; autism 220, 221–222; compared to domain-general 98–99; and computational modelling 220; and connectionism 84; developmental perspective on cognitive science 64–65, 67, 68, 70–71, 72–74; vs. domain relevance 289–293, 296–298; genes and cognition 164–165; inhibition 98; nativism vs. neuroconstructivism 279, 280, 283–284
domain-general processes 69, 77, 81–82, 84, 98, 279, 289–291, 294
double dissociations 99, 102, 119, 248, 249–250, 251, 262, 273, 280–281
Down syndrome: environment 17, 282; featural processing 281; heritability 166–167; language 1, 108, 125–126, 264; as model to study Alzheimer's 13; motor development 253; number processing 248–251; specialization of function 101; sustained attention 250–251; and William syndrome 124–126
drawing, children's 7, 40–63
Dugas, René 36
dyslexia 112, 261

efficiency 50
electroencephalography (EEG) 233, 235
electrophysiology 14, 16, 124, 175, 233, 275, 279

Elman, J. L. 11, 73, 83, 84, 86, 174, 196, 233, 268, 280, 289, 291, 292, 298
embedded knowledge 57
embryogenesis 100
empiricism 72, 97, 111, 279
encapsulation, cognitive 41, 67, 68, 75, 294
endogenously-driven change 54–55, 77
environment: and autism 207, 212, 221, 252–255; brain imaging studies 17, 240; and brain plasticity 72; causal role in ultimate cognitive structures 164; deprivation and quasi-autism 196, 212, 217; and the development of predispositions 75; domain-specific predispositions 64–65, 68; Down sydrome 17, 282; and genetics 166, 247–258, 262, 276, 278, 281–282, 289–299; and modularity 73; and neuroconstructivism 13; and ontogenesis 248; progressive selection of genes 98; and RR (representational redescription) 10; as skeletal outline 75; as trigger 68, 71, 72–73, 75, 77, 90–91, 97, 107, 110, 114, 262, 281; typically and atypically developing individuals 281–282; Williams syndrome 17, 276
epigenetics: brain imaging studies 240; and constructivism 72; and the development of predispositions 75; and domain-specificity of cognitive systems 71, 73; nativist vs. constructivist approaches 64; nativist vs. empiricist approaches 98; and the neocortex 113–114; predetermined vs. probabilistic 97; probabilistic 278, 295–296
equilibration 69, 72
ethology 90
event-related potentials (ERP) 124, 176, 233, 235–236, 251
evolutionary processes 41, 74–75, 98, 99, 112, 113, 266–267, 290–293, 296–298
evolutionary psychology 98, 274, 290–291
exhaustive category sorting 120, 264
exogenously-driven change 10, 54, 55
experience-dependent synaptic plasticity 168, 169, 173
explicitation 76
eye movement planning 128, 250, 252, 264, 281, 283
eye trackers 240, 250, 251, 252

face processing: autism 252; brain imaging studies 238; configural vs. featural processing experiment 138–141; developmental prosopagnosia 263; hemisphere specialization 279; identity recognition and difference detection 139–141; neural connectivity 292; recognition in a story-supported task experiment 141–147; Williams syndrome 13–14, 104–105, 107, 118, 122–128, 132–160, 175, 232, 252, 261, 263–264, 275, 281, 283
failure to progress 212–213, 215–216, 217
false beliefs 79
false theory construction 36
fast-mapping ability 120
feature-by-feature (componential) processing 107, 123, 127, 133, 134–141, 147–154, 232, 263, 283
feedback loops 80, 99, 102
feedforward networks 102
firing thresholds 101, 102, 113, 268, 279, 280, 292
flatliners 215
floor effects 122, 123, 136, 278
FMR1 gene 14–15, 168–169, 170, 172–173
fMRI (functional magnetic resonance imaging) 194, 233, 234, 239
fNIRS (functional near infrared spectroscopy) 233, 235
Fodor, J. A. 6, 8–9, 10, 12, 67, 68, 69, 72, 90, 293
formal models 9, 15–16
formula-driven change 54–55
FOXP2 gene 265, 266–267, 284
Fragile X syndrome 167–177, 218
Frangiskakis, J. M. 261, 265, 266
Freeman, N. H. 40, 42, 54–55, 58
Frith, C. D. 195
Frith, U. 70, 114, 261, 290

gamma band frequencies analysis 175
Garcia, R. 26
Gelman, R. 70, 274
gene deletions 13, 15, 104, 171, 175, 182, 185–187, 189, 266
general conceptual competence 30–31, 32
generalization processes 127
genetics: and autism 112; and brain anatomy 295; brain imaging studies 240; and cognition 163–181; cognitive genetic profiling 182–191; and computational modelling 14–16, 163–181, 182–191, 192–228; and developmental timing 112–113; and environment 166, 247–258, 262, 276, 278, 281–282, 289–299; genetic

pre-specification 296; nativism vs. neuroconstructivism 273–288; and the neocortex 113–114; and the neuroconstructivist approach 99–111, 294–296; ontogeny, genetics and evolution 261–272; Williams syndrome 103–104, 261, 265, 266, 275, 280
genotype-phenotype relations 14–16, 163–181, 182–191, 192–232, 261–262, 280
Gilliéron, C. 58
global processing 123, 294 *see also* configural (holistic) processing
goal-orientation 23, 35, 54, 85, 254
Goodnow, J. J. 55–56
Gotlieb, G. 278, 296
Grant, J. 121, 264
Greenfield, P. M. 53, 56, 58, 73
Greenough, W. T. 68, 73, 168
Grice, S. 108, 124, 127, 156, 175, 232, 264, 275, 276, 281, 283
Grossberg, S. 196, 220
Grossmann, T. 235, 236
Gruber, H. I. 34
Gsödl, M. 108
Gustafsson, L. 196

haploinsufficiency 171, 182, 186–187
Hebbian learning 84
hemisphere specialization 14, 105, 127, 132, 238, 279, 292
heritability 165–166, 218–219
Hermelin, B. 56, 57, 71, 76
Hinton, G. E. 53
holistic (configural) processing 107, 123, 127, 133, 134–141, 147–154, 157, 263
Huttenlocher, P. R. 53, 56, 194, 221, 237, 238, 265, 268, 279, 292, 295, 297
Huxley, T. E. 48
hybrid models of representational formats 88
hypotheses: central processing of 67; versus theories-of-action 35–36

illiteracy 57
imageability effects 121
inconsistency across attempts 54
incremental learning 84
infants *see* neonates and infants
inferential processes 81
information constructors vs. information storers 69
Inhelder, B. 2–3, 23, 26, 27, 35, 37, 40, 41, 58
inhibition 98, 196
input vs. output systems 73, 80
interdisciplinarity 2
interdomain relationships *see* cross-domain interactions
inter-representational flexibility 42, 52
interruption, principle of 58
intervention, implications for 221–222, 231–232, 251, 282, 283
intradomain relationships 77, 78, 90
inversion effects 123, 134, 136, 137, 138–147, 154–155
IQ scores: Fragile X 172; and language acquisition 175–176; low IQ children 56; Specific Language Impairment 263; Williams syndrome 108, 119, 133, 187, 189
Irwin, S. A. 170

Johnson, M. H. 68, 73, 75, 108, 124, 127, 132, 175, 193, 194, 231, 268, 276, 278, 279, 281, 292, 295, 296, 298
Johnston, T. D. 9
judgement preference tasks 147–154

Kaufmann, W. E. 172, 173
kinaesthetically encoded representations 80
Klahr, D. 75, 81, 82, 83
Klein, B. P. 118, 120, 122, 125
knockout models 169–172, 265, 266
Knowland, V. C. P. 16
knowledge: active construction of 72; and central processing 67; conscious access 5, 6, 18, 58, 65, 74, 77, 79–80, 294; embedded knowledge 57; explicit theory change 75; how new knowledge gets into the mind 74–76; implicit into explicit 75–76, 79; innate knowledge 41; knowledge acquisition 41; multiple redescriptions of knowledge 88; nativism 98; playing with 89; process of representational redescription 76–81
Koslowski, B. 35

Laing, E. 121, 122, 126, 134, 264
language: analogies with acquisition of physical knowledge 4, 36–37; autism 192, 193, 195, 252; brain imaging studies 238; brain lesions 262; computational grammar complexity hypothesis 282; and connectionism 86; delayed development 126, 195; domain specificity 290; and domain-specificity of cognitive systems 73–74, 84, 112; Down sydrome 1, 108, 125–126, 264; in elderly people 232; and environment

253–255; evolutionary processes 266–267; Fragile X 167; genetics 13, 265, 266; hemisphere specialization 279; innateness 8, 119, 265; language deficit disorders 112–113; linguistic vs. nonlinguistically encoded representations 80; naming spurt 120; nativist vs. empiricist approaches 97; neural connectivity 292; nonlinguistic precursors to 126–127; non-native contrasts 232; principle of interruption 58; representational redescription (RR) 5, 40, 56–57, 89–90; sequential constraints 54; theories-in-language 36–37; Williams syndrome 104–105, 107–108, 118, 119–122, 125–127, 133, 175–176, 185, 189, 252, 261, 262, 264, 265
language of thought 67–68
learning algorithms 84, 174, 220, 296
learning capacity 98, 197, 200
Leslie, A. M. 50, 81, 118, 261, 262, 273, 290
Lewis, J. D. 196
localization of function 14, 16, 132, 175, 232, 235, 238, 248, 276, 279, 289, 295, 297
London British Autism Study of Infant Siblings 252
longitudinal studies 108, 194, 237, 240, 252–253

magnetic resonance spectroscopy 104
Mandler, J. M. 78, 81
Marcus, G. F. 14
Marler, P. 64, 73, 90
mastery, behavioural *see* behavioural mastery
match-to-sample design 123
maturational change 84
Max Planck Institute 4, 5
McClelland, J. L. 82, 83, 85, 88, 196, 220
mechanism, notions of 6
memory 67, 122, 239
Meng, Y. 265, 266
Menon, V. 172, 173
mental age (MA) matching: problems with 277–278; Williams syndrome 107–108, 119, 122, 123, 125–126, 128, 134, 136–137, 155, 248
mental imagery 53–54, 81
Mervis, C. B. 120, 122, 123, 125, 126, 127, 134, 263, 264, 274, 282
metacognition 8, 65, 79–80, 89
metalinguistic awareness 5, 6
metarepresentation 112
micro-development 3
microdomains 70, 77, 80
microgenetic approach 2
Mills, D. L. 124, 127, 133, 175, 176, 238, 275, 279, 283, 292, 293
Minagawa-Kawai, Y. 235, 237, 238
Modular Continuity Hypothesis 124, 126
modularity: and atypical development 98, 99, 100–101; in *Beyond Modularity* 67–68; brain imaging studies 238; domain relevance 290; Down sydrome 126; evolutionary processes 267; and face processing 132; genes and cognition 165, 265; and genetics 261, 262–263; implications of neuroconstructivist theory 282–283; innate modularity 6, 8, 11–12, 13, 72–73; intact/preserved vs. impaired modules 12, 16, 71, 79, 98–100, 103, 105, 112, 118–119, 155, 250, 263–264, 274, 278–280; modules vs. domains 70, 85; and nativism 72, 124, 273–274; and neuroconstructivism 263–265, 266, 273–274, 293–294; and selective deficits in adults 11–12; and the study of developmental disorders 274–275; in syntax acquisition 56; Williams syndrome 107, 118, 121–122, 123–128, 133, 134, 175, 247, 262, 263–264
modularization processes: in *Beyond Modularity* 9, 72, 74–75, 76, 85; brain imaging studies 238; emergent modularization 14; face processing 132; gradual modularization 68–69; neuroconstructivism 264, 280, 291–293; as product of development 68; progressive modularization 74–75; Williams syndrome 123, 124
molecular genetics 14, 167–169, 185–190
Mondloch, C. J. 133, 138, 139
Morais, J. 57
morphology 37, 54, 56, 119–122, 176
Morton, J. 73, 83, 114, 132
mosaicism 189
motor development 253, 282
mouse studies 169–172, 265, 266
multi-disciplinary research 13
multimodal approaches 236, 240
multiple encodings 80
musical skill acquisition 57–58, 75–76

naming spurt 126
nativism: and atypical development 13, 110, 124; in *Beyond Modularity* 9, 67, 68, 69, 71, 262–263; complementarity with constructivism 64–66, 69,

71–74; and developmental disorders 101; genetics/ environment debate 97–98; innate modularity 290; Modular Continuity Hypothesis 124; vs. neuroconstructivism 18, 273–288; and representational redescription (RR) 50; universal grammar 98; Williams syndrome 119
Navon tasks 157
Nazzi, T. 122, 127, 264
negative feedback 80
Nelson, K. E. 55, 83
neocortex 98, 113–114
neonates and infants: autism 195, 221, 252–255; brain imaging studies 231, 236–237; brain plasticity 292; brain structure 279; developmental disorder studies 113, 114; domain specificity 71, 85, 297; domain-general versus nativist approaches 69; inferential processes 81; modularity of the mind/brain 67–68; neonates as "knowledge-empty"/ tabula rasa 69, 84, 289, 291; number processing 248–258; prototype effects 127; representational redescription (RR) 50, 64–66; sensorimotor infants 50, 64, 69, 72, 81; Williams syndrome 122, 124–128
networks: autism 211; connectionism 84–85, 86–88; deep neural networks 10; dynamic nature of 293; and genetic disorders 279; implications for developmental disorders 102; limitations of modelling 220; neural changes across development 238; quantitative genetics 168; Williams syndrome 176
neural codes 196
neural information processing principles 174
neuroimaging 16, 231–243
neuronal recycling hypothesis 18, 293–294
neuropsychology 70–71
Neville, H. J. 68, 72, 176, 264, 265, 275, 279
nodes 87, 88
nonlinearity 86, 204, 217
non-specific predispositions 75
normal ranges, scores in 275–277, 283, 297
notational competence 40
number processing 13, 17, 118, 122, 125, 126, 164, 248–251, 263, 283
Nunn, J. A. 263
observation methods 15, 27, 134
O'Connor, N. 56, 57, 71, 76
ontogenesis 68, 98, 114, 261–272, 280
overgeneralization 36, 37, 253, 282
Oyama, S. 71, 73

parallel distributed processing 88
part-whole tasks 135, 136
Paterson, S. 13, 108, 122, 124, 125–126, 175, 176, 264, 281, 292, 293
Pattern Construction subtest of the British Abilities Scale 138, 143–144, 145–146, 147, 148, 149, 151, 152, 153, 154, 156–157, 187
Peabody Picture Vocabulary test 138, 184, 187
Pemberton, E. F. 40, 55
perceptual vs. cognitive understandings 78–79
Persico, A. M. 273
phase vs. stage models of development 70
Phillips, W. A. 55
phonology 57, 121, 126, 176, 232
phylogenesis 98
Piaget, Jean 2, 3, 4–5, 6, 8–9, 10, 12, 15, 23, 26, 35, 36, 58, 64, 65, 69, 71–72, 81–82, 83
Pickles, A. 192, 193, 197, 208, 209, 212, 216
Pinker, S. 13, 14, 118, 119, 122, 163, 164, 165, 261, 262, 265, 273, 293
plasticity *see* brain plasticity
play 79, 81, 89
Plomin, R. 166
Plunkett, K. 11, 82, 83, 84
pointing (infant development) 126, 264
population modelling 197–198, 205, 216
preferential looking paradigms 125–126
prefrontal brain damage 71
prefrontal cortex and domain-general processes 81
Premack, D. 53, 54, 73, 81, 89
pre-specialization 113
prespecified functionality 113–114
prespecified representations 102
pretend play 79, 81
problem-solving skills 8, 13, 40, 42, 65, 71, 74, 76, 78, 107, 118, 119, 133, 175
procedural constraints 50
proceduralization 75–76
process-oriented research tasks 23
progressive explicitation 55, 66, 74–91
progressive modularization 74–75
progressive ontogenic change 99
progressive selection of genes 98

proprietary inputs, infant attention on 65, 72, 85
proprioception 3, 27, 30, 31, 32, 33, 35
prosopagnosia 132–133, 263
protective factors 16, 206, 207, 216, 217, 219, 232
prototype effects 127, 128

quantitative genetics 14, 165–167
Quartz, S. R. 9, 296

Rae, C. 127
Raizada, R. D. S. 231
real-time processing vs. developmental progression 66
recurrent phase changes 70
Redcay, E. 195, 210
redundancy 74, 80, 171
regression analysis 120, 207, 209, 233, 278
reiterative developmental phases 80
relative vs. absolute strengths 120, 122, 276, 297
repairs, on-the-spot 54, 74
representational adjunction 55
representational change: and children's drawing 40–63; implicit into explicit 86–89; over time 66, 74
representational deficits 71
representational redescription (RR): and behavioural mastery 10, 41–42, 43, 44, 76–81, 85–86, 89; in *Beyond Modularity* 5–9, 65, 74–91; and brain imaging 17, 239; children's drawing study 40–63; and connectionism 83–89; domain relevance 18; genetics 294–295; in non-human species 89, 90; particular to human cognition 75, 89; process of 76–81; progressive change over time 66; U-shaped developmental profiles 12
representational status of infant knowledge 73
resting state fMRI (R-fMRI) 239
Rethinking Innateness (Elman et al., 1996) 11–12
Rett syndrome 218
Richler, J. 193
risk factors vs. causes 209–210, 211, 216–217, 219
Rivermead Behavioural Memory Test 123, 134, 263, 275
Rochat, P. 6
rodent studies 68, 169–172, 265, 266, 278, 295
Rogers, S. J. 194, 217, 221
Rossen, M. 119, 122, 136, 163, 175, 261, 262, 263, 275
Rutkowska, J. C. 41
Rutter, M. 166, 196, 212, 217

saccade planning 128, 250, 252, 264, 281, 283
savants 56–57, 71
schematic stimuli processing 147–154
second-order configural processing 156–157
second-order relational information 133, 135, 136, 154
segmentation (speech) 87, 127, 264
Seidman, D. 196, 220
Sejnowski, T. J. 9, 296
selection bias 232–233
selective preservation of capacities 122–123
Selfe, L. 56
self-organizing systems 72, 196, 239
self-repair 5, 6
semantics 120–121, 126, 176, 296
sensitive periods 194
sensorimotor infants 50, 64, 69, 72, 81
sequential constraints 50, 52–54, 56, 57–58
sequential manipulation of discrete symbols 88
seriation and hierarchical constructions 58
Shultz, T. 9, 84, 85, 197, 220
siblings 219, 221, 252, 263, 275, 276
Siegler, R. S. 80
Simmons, D. R. 196
Sinha, C. 82, 83, 84
Skinner, B. F. 69
sleep 239, 294
Slobin, D. I. 54
Sloman, A. 10–11
social stimuli processing 112
socio-affective behaviours 104
somatic cell hybrids 183, 185, 186
spatial cognition 29, 122, 125, 128, 157, 173 *see also* visuospatial cognition
spatially encoded representations 80
specialization of function 16, 101, 102, 124, 132, 147, 276, 279, 291–293, 295, 297
Specific Language Impairment (SLI): compared to Williams syndrome 13, 122; developmental regression 192, 195, 209, 217; developmental timing 112–113; and domain-specificity of cognitive systems 112; environment 276; genetics 261, 276; innate mechanisms 119; modularity 263
Spelke, E. S. 50, 66, 70, 72, 274, 289, 290, 292, 293
spontaneous procedures 3, 23, 24, 28, 37, 43, 48, 50, 57, 74, 77, 86–87, 239

stable states 80, 87
stage theories 83
standardized tests, limitations of 275–277
stepwise logistic progression 205
stereotyped change 54
Stiles, J. 194, 292, 293
story-supported tasks 141–147, 154–155
structure-dependent predictions 86
sub-routines 52, 53, 58
success-based view of cognitive change 80, 89
Superlab 2.0 142
surface structures 58
synaptic pruning 193, 194, 195, 197–198, 248, 280, 292, 297
synaptic regulation 266
synaptogenesis 114
syntax: behavioural mastery 86–87; and connectionism 86; domain specificity 112–113; and domain-specificity of cognitive systems 73–74; environment 282; and representational change 56; syntactic pruning 201–222; universal grammar 98, 163; Williams syndrome 107–108, 119–122, 176

Tager-Flusberg, H. 135, 136, 137, 156, 261, 275
task mastery 3–4, 6
task-specificity 155–156, 278
theories-in-action 23–37
theories-in-language 36
theory-of-mind 70, 81, 98, 112, 261, 282, 290
Thomas, M. S. C. 14, 16, 120, 136, 144, 174, 176, 197, 198, 200
thought experiments 75
Tomasello, M. 6, 70
trajectory analysis methods 14, 124, 128, 144, 155, 201, 237, 240, 253, 264, 275, 276, 277, 278
transcranial magnetic stimulation (TMS) 233
transcription factors 294–295
transgenic animals 169–172
Turner's syndrome 112
twin studies 166, 261

unified systems 36, 37
universal grammar 98, 163
U-shaped developmental profiles 4, 12, 77

van der Lely, H. K. J. 120, 263, 282, 293
Van Sommers, P. 40, 54
verbal report 79–80
Vinh Bang 26
vision 101–102
visual array segmentation 66
visuospatial cognition: autism 221; Down sydrome 250–251; in infants 132; second-order configural processing 157; Williams syndrome 15, 118, 119, 128, 137, 142, 147, 157, 250–251, 261, 264
vocabulary 107–108, 119, 121, 125–126, 193
Volterra, V. 118, 122, 264

Wang, P. P. 118, 119, 123, 133, 136, 175, 275
Wechsler Adult Intelligence Scale 187
Weir, R. H. 36–37
Williams syndrome: brain biochemistry 104, 127; brain imaging studies 232; clinical characteristics of the phenotype 106; cognitive-behavioural phenotype 107; and domain-specificity of cognitive systems 12, 70–71, 281; and Down syndrome 124–126; early development 124–128; early studies 118–119; environment 17, 276; face processing 13–14, 104–105, 107, 118, 122–128, 132–160, 175, 232, 252, 261, 263–264, 275, 281, 283; genetics 15, 103–104, 261, 265, 266, 275, 280; genotype-phenotype relations 174–176, 182–191; heritability 166–167; IQ scores 108, 119, 133, 187, 189; language 13–14, 104–105, 107–108, 118, 119–122, 125–127, 133, 175–176, 185, 189, 252, 261, 262, 264, 265; modularity 107, 118, 121–122, 123–128, 133, 134, 175, 247, 262, 263–264; nativism vs. neuroconstructivism 273; number processing 118, 122, 125, 126, 248–251; social impairments 252–255; static vs. dynamic approaches 247–248
Wilson, B. 123
wireless technology 17
word order 54, 73

Yin, R. K. 154

For Product Safety Concerns and Information please contact our EU representative GPSR@taylorandfrancis.com Taylor & Francis Verlag GmbH, Kaufingerstraße 24, 80331 München, Germany